THE ULTIMATE BASEBALL BOOK

Edited by

Daniel Okrent
and
Harris Lewine

With Historical Text By David Nemec

Houghton Mifflin Company / A Hilltown Book

Boston

This book was prepared for publication by Eisenberg, McCall & Okrent, Inc.,
New York City.

Grateful acknowledgement is made to the following for permission to reprint
previously published material:
Little, Brown and Co., for an excerpt from *Versus* by Ogden Nash, copyright 1949
by Ogden Nash.
Candida Donadio & Associates, Inc., for lines from "Swede is a Hard Guy,"
reprinted from *The Last Carousel* © 1973 by Nelson Algren.

Library of Congress Cataloging in Publication Data
Main entry under title:
The Ultimate baseball book.

Includes index.
1. Baseball — United States — History — Addresses,
essays, lectures. 2. Baseball players — United States
— Biography — Addresses, essays, lectures. I. Okrent,
Daniel. II. Lewine, Harris, III. Nemec, David.
GV863.A1U47   796.357'09   79-15132
Paper ISBN 0-395-36145-1

Printed in the United States of America

M   14   13   12   11   10   9   8   7

Houghton Mifflin Company paperback 1988

Art Direction: Harris Lewine
Design: Robert Aulicino

The text of this book was set on the Linotype in a typeface called Scotch. A
cutting of such a face was undertaken and recorded by Messrs. Miller and
Richard, of Edinburgh, in 1808. The original Linotype version of Scotch was cut
in 1902 by Theodore L. DeVinne. The essential characteristics of Scotch are
sturdy capitals, full-rounded lower-case letters, the graceful fillet of the serifs,
and a general effect of crispness through sharply contrasting "thicks and thins."

PLAY-BY-PLAY

ANTHEM

Catfish, Mudcat, Ducky, Coot.
The Babe, The Barber, The Blade, The Brat.
Windy, Dummy, Gabby, Hoot.
Big Train, Big Six, Big Ed, Fat.

Greasy, Sandy, Muddy, Rocky.
Bunions, Twinkletoes, Footsie. The Hat.
Fuzzy, Dizzy, Buddy, Cocky.
The Bull, The Stork, The Weasel, The Cat.
    Schoolboy, Sheriff,
    Rajah, Duke,
    General, Major,
    Spaceman, Spook.

The Georgia Peach, The Fordham Flash,
The Flying Dutchman. Cot.
The People's Cherce, The Blazer. Crash.
The Staten Island Scot.
    Skeeter, Scooter,
    Pepper, Duster,
    Ebba, Bama, Boomer, Buster.

The Little Professor, The Iron Horse. Cap.
Iron Man, Iron Mike, Iron Hands. Hutch.
Jap, The Mad Russian, Irish, Swede. Nap.
Germany, Frenchy, Big Serb, Dutch,
    Turk. Tuck, Tug, Twig.
    Spider, Birdie, Rabbit, Pig.

Fat Jack, Black Jack, Zeke, Zack. Bloop.
Peanuts, Candy, Chewing Gum, Pop.
Chicken, Cracker, Hot Potato, Soup.
    Ding, Bingo.
    Hippity-Hopp.

Three-Finger, No-Neck, The Knuck, The Lip.
Casey, Gavvy, Pumpsie, Zim.
Flit, Bad Henry. Fat Freddie, Flip.
Jolly Cholly, Sunny Jim.
    Shag, Schnozz,
    King Kong, Klu.
    Boog, Buzz,
    Boots, Bump, Boo.

King Carl, The Count. The Rope, The Whip.
Wee Willie, Wild Bill, Gloomy Gus. Cy.
Bobo, Bombo, Bozo. Skip.
Coco, Kiki, Yo-yo. Pie.
    Dinty, Dooley,
    Stuffy, Snuffy,
    Stubby, Dazzy,
    Daffy, Duffy.

Baby Doll, Angel Sleeves, Pep, Sliding Billy,
Buttercup, Bollicky, Boileryard, Juice.

Colby Jack, Dauntless Dave, Cheese,
  Gentle Willie,
Trolley Line, Wagon Tongue, Rough,
  What's the Use.

    Ee-yah,
    Poosh 'Em Up,
    Skoonj, Slats, Ski.
    Ding Dong,
    Ding-a-Ling,
    Dim Dom, Dee.

Famous Amos. Rosy, Rusty.
Handsome Ransom. Home Run, Huck.
Rapid Robert. Cactus, Dusty.
Rowdy Richard. Hot Rod, Truck.
    Jo-Jo, Jumping Joe,
    Little Looie,
    Muggsy, Moe.

Old Folks, Old Pard, Oom Paul. Yaz.
Cowboy, Indian Bob, Chief, Ozark Ike.
Rawhide, Reindeer Bill. Motormouth. Maz.
Pistol Pete, Jungle Jim, Wahoo Sam. Spike.
    The Mad Hungarian.
    Mickey, Minnie.
    Kitten, Bunny.
    Big Dan, Moose.
    Jumbo, Pee Wee; Chubby, Skinny.
    Little Poison.
        Crow, Hawk, Goose.

Marvelous Marv.
    Oisk, Oats, Tookie.
Vinegar Bend.
    Suds, Hooks, Hug.
Hammerin' Hank.
    Cooch, Cod, Cookie.
Harry the Horse.
    Speed, Stretch, Slug.

The Splendid Splinter. Pruschka. Sparky.
Chico, Choo Choo, Cha-Cha, Chub.
Dr. Strangeglove. Deacon. Arky.
Abba Dabba. Supersub.

Bubbles, Dimples, Cuddles, Pinky.
Poison Ivy, Vulture, Stinky.
    Jigger, Jabbo
    Jolting Joe
    Blue Moon
    Boom Boom
    Bubba
    Bo

        —William (Sugar) Wallace

INTRODUCTION

I T IS CERTAINLY presumptuous to publish a book with a title so grand as this one's. One baseball historian, told of the editors' intentions, felt the title could not be accurate, no matter how well-assembled the book might be: baseball's very appeal, he said, is that it has no ultimates, that it is dependent upon, and draws its great beauty from, fine shadings and subtleties. Of course, the word "ultimate" in the title does not qualify the word "baseball"; rather, it means to define the book, or at least the editors' view of it.

Likewise, the nine essays that comprise one of the three distinct elements of the book (the other elements are the historical text and the illustrations), do not deal with ultimates. Admittedly, several of the subjects are among the game's olympian figures, but their inclusion here does not imply that they are the best that ever were. Rather, we chose to find nine baseball paradigms, spread over the game's history, and nine excellent writers to characterize, portray, honor or deflate them, according to each writer's particular view.

The nature of the writers who are included was, we felt, at least as important as the subjects they chose to write about. The choice of nine essayists who happen to possess both felicity of style and an eye to the nuance of the game was not easy. With the technical exception of William S. Wallace's poem, this book's "Anthem," which appeared in different form in the *New York Times*, all the writing here is original, commissioned especially for the present volume. An exception was made for Wallace's poem not just on the basis of a technical loophole: it is included because there has never been anything like it in baseball literature.

If a literary aspect is baseball's marrow—and it is—then its historical context is its blood. Names, facts, statistics make up the stream in which baseball's history is nourished; David Nemec's historical text serves to present these in an interpretive form.

The illustrative element of the book was prepared in recognition of the fact that baseball is an endeavor that celebrates the individual and his image. Alone among the team sports, it isolates one person at a time. Thus are these men burned into memory, each blessed with a distinct image and personality. More than 15,000 photographs were examined, and the painful task of eliminating nearly 20 for every one included fell to Harris Lewine, than whom there could be no better art director. Together, the pictures included are meant to be representative; they were chosen because of graphic interest, historical interest or because of an appeal not readily definable. Joe Vosmik, say, may not be as important in baseball's history as one or another of the Hall of Fame members not pictured here—but I could readily argue why he's as interesting, and no one could doubt that he is representative. When he stood in the batter's box, he was every bit as individual, as memorable, as the greatest star. Vosmik, and so many like him, make up baseball's immutable context.

A word should be devoted to the publishing history of baseball books. Anton Grobani's *Guide to Baseball Literature* lists well over 2,000 books dating back to 1838. For the most part, these are pallid, inconsequential works. But among them are books undertaken seriously by men of talent, and the editors drew extensively upon many of them in our research. Included among these are the works of Lee Allen, Maury Allen, Roger Angell, Eliot Asinof, Warren Brown, Henry Berry, John Carmichael, Robert Creamer, Alison Danzig, Joseph Durso, Peter Golenbock, Frank Graham, Tommy Holmes, Donald Honig, Fred Lieb, Bill James, Tom Meany, Robert Peterson, John Pardon and his colleagues in the Society for American Baseball Research, Joseph Reichler, Robert Riger, Lawrence Ritter, Harold Seymour, Al Silverman, Marshall Smelser, Robert Smith, J. Roy Stockton, David Voigt and Douglass Wallop. Most especially, though, we bear a debt to Charles Einstein. If we have accomplished with original material, plus extensive illustrations, what Einstein accomplished in the three superb anthologies that comprise the *Fireside Book of Baseball* series, then we will be satisfied indeed. The Fireside Books may be baseball literature's greatest monument; that they are today out of print is baseball publishing's greatest shame. Still in print, and now in its fourth edition, is *The Baseball Encyclopedia*, initially published by Macmillan in 1969. It has been used as the court of final authority for statistical matter included in this book, and for the spellings of the names of baseball people. It was silent, but enduring, help in the preparation of this book. Less silent, but equally helpful, were a number of individuals, in addition to the writers, who aided our task. Ed Gallagher conducted valuable research; David Nemec, in addition to writing his historical text, drew on his awesome baseball knowledge in commenting upon the essays; Bruce McCall, Lee Eisenberg and Liz Darhansoff provided counsel and criticism of all sorts; Austin Olney of Houghton Mifflin smoothed a few particularly rocky roads; Eugene Zepp of the Boston Public Library and John F. Redding, Librarian of the National

INTRODUCTION

Baseball Museum in Cooperstown, New York, were generous with their time and advice; George Rosenfeld challenged a few favored assumptions. Illustrative material was gathered with the help of the following sources: Nat Andrianni, United Press International; Bruce Brass, Wide World Photos, Inc.; Harry and Meredith Collins, Brown Brothers; Eugene Ferrara, The New York Daily News; Melvin Gray, The Bettmann Archive; Bob Jackson, Culver Pictures, Inc. Special gratitude goes to the memorabilia collectors Frank Driggs, Robert and Paul Gallagher, Larry Gladstone, Robert Lifson and Richard Merkin.

All of the above made assembly of the book even more pleasurable than could have been expected, which is saying a great deal. There is one thing, though, that they could not do, which is the one thing we wanted most: arrange for us to have another three volumes, another 1,000 pages, another 3,000 illustrations.

Finally, I would like to give credit to those responsible for the earliest roots of this project: John R. Tunis, whose books sent one seven-year-old to his bed at the mandated hour, happy so long as he was equipped with a flashlight spirited under the covers and an ear tuned to the approaching steps of a suspicious parent; and Walt Dropo, who hit a stunningly, preposterously, absolutely beautifully high fly into the left-field seats at Briggs Stadium 27 years ago, at the first game I ever attended. I have not stopped cheering since.

—D.O.

FIRST INNING: 1876-1900

The theory of the game is that one side takes the field, and the other goes in. The pitcher then delivers the ball to the striker, who endeavours to hit it in such a direction as to elude the fielders, and enable him to run round all the base lines home without being put out. If he succeeds a run is scored. When three players are put out the fielding side comes in: and after nine innings have been played the side which have scored the most runs wins the game. The rules are voluminous and minute. . . .

The attitude of the striker is not an elegant one, and the pitcher is allowed to keep the former's muscles too long on the stretch before actually delivering the ball. Base ball is a quicker and more lively pastime than the great English national game of cricket, which is the chief thing to be said in its favour.

—Encyclopedia Britannica, 1890

WHEN Alexander Joy Cartwright brought the Knickerbockers and the New York Nine to the Elysian Fields in Hoboken, New Jersey, on June 19, 1846, to play the first game of baseball, it was his impression that he was creating a sport that would be played by gentlemen of leisure for recreation and amusement. Within the short span of 30 years, however, the game had evolved to a point where it was seen by businessmen to have enormous potential for financial profit. With this aim in mind, several of them met at the Grand Central Hotel in New York on February 2, 1876, to form baseball's first major professional league out of the shambles of the old National Association, a loosely knit federation of teams that had come into existence in 1871 and had quickly run aground because of inept leadership, player drunkenness and the infiltration of gamblers. As an example of the association's weak structure, nearly half the 13 teams that were fielded in 1875 failed to play a complete schedule, and the competition was so unbalanced that the champion Boston Red Stockings had an .899 winning percentage, while no less than five also-rans finished below .200.

Before the gathering at the Grand Central Hotel dispersed, a constitution for the new federation was drafted and a decision made to call it the National League. Morgan Bulkeley, who later became a sen-

Alexander Cartwright, the closest thing to a "father of baseball," despite the Abner Doubleday myth. "The only thing Doubleday ever started," Branch Rickey said, "was the Civil War."

ator from Connecticut, was appointed the titular president, but the real leader was William Hulbert, the owner of the Chicago White Stockings. It was Hulbert who was most instrumental in determining the design of the new league and who would rule it with an iron hand through scandal, financial turmoil and franchise upheavals until his death in 1882. Hulbert's motives were not so much altruistic as

The Boston Club, 1874. Most of that season was spent in England, on a tour arranged by Albert G. Spalding (standing, with ball). The London *Post* approved of the Americans: "As is unfortunately not too often the case with our cricketers, they all were men who lead an abstemious and moderate life."

Harry Wright (L), organizer of the first all-professional team, was (said the Cincinnati *Enquirer*) "a baseball Edison. He eats base-ball, breathes base-ball, thinks base-ball, dreams base-ball, and incorporates base-ball in his prayers." His brother George (C) was the finest infielder of his era; he and Spalding (R) formed the nucleus of an 1875 team that finished 71-8, and of a sporting goods empire that flourishes to this day.

self-serving. At the conclusion of the 1875 season he had raided the champion Red Stockings and induced four of their stars—Al Spalding, Cal McVey, Ross Barnes and Deacon White—to sign contracts with his Chicago outfit; in addition, he had lured the Philadelphia Athletics' young slugger, Adrian Anson, to come west. Fearing that the National Association would expel the White Stockings for his piracy, he dodged a confrontation by forming a new league.

The charter members of the National League were Boston, Chicago, Cincinnati, St. Louis, Hartford, New York, Philadelphia and Louisville. On April 22, 1876, the fledgling operation played its opening game at Philadelphia, with Boston taking the measure of the home side, 6–5, before 3,000 fans. The winning pitcher was Joe Borden, who a year earlier had fashioned the first professional no-hitter; later in the 1876 season, Borden also recorded the first no-hitter in the National League. Borden had few other good days on the mound for Boston, and the Red Stockings were able to finish no better than fourth to Hulbert's club, which was captained by Spalding, the league's leading pitcher. No doubt the style of play in that initial major league season would have amused the modern fan. Gloves were disdained by fielders; batters had the option of calling for low or high pitches; catchers played behind the bat only with runners on base; and the league's top hitter, Ross Barnes, was so adroit at slicing hits that landed in fair territory and immediately caromed foul that he forced a rule change that autumn stating that for a struck ball to be fair it must stay within the foul lines until it passes a base or until it is fielded. Perhaps the most curious footnote of all in 1876 was the play of the Cincinnati club, which only seven years earlier had streaked to a record 56 straight victories. In their first National League season, minus most of their original stars, including George and Harry Wright and Cal McVey who had defected to wealthier clubs, the Redlegs finished dead last, winning only nine games and losing 56.

The Redlegs continued to languish the following season. Likewise, the Hartfords were in dire financial straits and had to play all their home games in Brooklyn. The struggles of these two clubs, coupled with Hulbert's decision to expel New York and Philadelphia for refusing to make their final road trips in 1876, placed the league's future in jeopardy. The climax came when Hulbert was faced with baseball's first scandal when he was presented with proof by the Louisville club that four of its players had conspired with gamblers to throw the pennant to Boston. Hulbert once more rose to the test and acted firmly, barring all four men from the league for life. As a consequence the Louisville

J. M. Ward, founder of the Brotherhood. *The Sporting News* called him "The St. George of baseball, for he has slain the dragon of oppression."

Grays—Wright, pitcher Monte Ward and right-fielder Jim O'Rourke—are in the Hall of Fame, and two others probably should be. One is Paul Hines, the first National League triple crown winner and also its first repeat batting champion. The second man, Joe Start, is remembered today mainly for the home run that brought Cincinnati's win streak to an end in 1869, but he was actually the game's finest early-day first baseman and a star performer for over two decades. Aged 34 when the National League was formed, Start was still active ten years later and retired with a .300 average and many early records. Several others who were high on the lists of statistical leaders in 1879 have also been largely forgotten. One was Will White of Cincinnati, the last pitcher to start and win every game in which his club was victorious; another was Boston pitcher Tommy Bond, only 23 in 1879 but even at that point the holder of 154 career wins. The game's first genuine slugger, Charley Jones, was yet a third: the home run king in 1879, Jones fell on bad times in 1880 and was arbitrarily blackballed by Boston owner Arthur Soden at the conclusion of the season after a contract dispute. Jones's plight was typical of an era in which every player, from the stars down to the lowest subs, ran the risk of being squeezed out of the league by whimsical owners who saw players as chattels, to be kept in line much like factory hands. Standing uninvolved for the moment but nevertheless carefully observing

franchise folded. When Hartford and St. Louis followed suit, Hulbert placed teams in Providence, Indianapolis and Milwaukee for the 1878 season. Already reduced to a six-club circuit, Hulbert's brainchild seemed headed for collapse when both Indianapolis and Milwaukee flopped. But the new Providence team quickly established itself as one of the league's finest, and when the Redlegs unexpectedly revived and narrowly missed overtaking Boston for the 1878 pennant, four new cities—Cleveland, Buffalo, Troy and Syracuse—put up the entry fee to come aboard Hulbert's listing vessel and were added to the 1879 schedule. Of the four only Buffalo, behind rookie pitcher Pud Galvin, was competitive; but the imbalance, to Hulbert's thinking, was outweighed by the fact that the league again had eight teams and could increase its seasonal schedule from 60 games to 84.

In a number of ways 1879 was the year that the National League first came into its own, and the Providence club made a large contribution. Led by George Wright, who remains today the only man ever to win a pennant in his only year as a manager, the Grays finished five games ahead of brother Harry's Boston charges. Three members of the

In 1875, Spalding and three teammates signed with Chicago. A Boston paper said they "have determined to desert...and will try to take the pennant to Chicago in '76." They did.

Cap Anson, early and late in his 22-year career. From 1876 through 1889, he never finished worse than sixth in the league in batting. He also was responsible for the signing of Mike Kelly, Billy Sunday and John Clarkson, among others.

these practices was the young Providence pitcher Monte Ward, who, before his time was out, would do much to revolutionize the whole player-owner relationship.

In 1880 Cincinnati tumbled into the cellar again. National League leaders were willing to tolerate the Redlegs' poor play, but when the club insisted on selling beer at its home games and leasing its park to teams that played on Sunday, Hulbert was persuaded to expel the Redlegs from the league. Their passing was viewed as good riddance.

Meanwhile, the White Stockings, with their rookie pitchers Larry Corcoran and Fred Goldsmith, had replaced Providence and Boston as the game's foremost club. In the four years since their last pennant, the White Stockings had rebuilt almost entirely and now featured an outfield of George Gore, Abner Dalrymple and Mike "King" Kelly that was the equal of any in the nineteenth century. But it was Adrian "Cap" Anson, the manager and first baseman, who provided the main spark. Still just 29 years old, Anson already had a

reputation as the best all-around player the game had yet known and was thought by Henry Chadwick and other early sportswriters to have another four or five years of top-level play left in him. No one could then have predicted that it would be not five but 17 years before Anson called it a career or that when he retired he would take with him statistics providing a strong case for his qualification as not only the greatest player of the last century but of all time. Playing his prime years in a period when the season schedule called for less than 100 games, Anson still managed to accumulate over 3,000 hits and 1,700 RBIs. Projecting his career totals over the 154-game schedule that did not come into existence until after he retired would bring him within easy range of almost every major batting record.

But while hitters of Anson's era suffered by statistical comparison to modern players due to the short schedule, pitchers feasted. Given a generous number of days off between games, the relatively untiring sidearm deliveries to which they were restricted and a 50-foot distance from the mound to home plate, most pitchers routinely posted season

Charles Comiskey, Billy Sunday, Pete Browning (L to R). Comiskey quit as Browns manager when the Players' League was formed: "I couldn't do anything else and still play square with the boys." Sunday abandoned baseball altogether for the higher calling of evangelism: "Goodbye, boys," he said, crying in a Chicago saloon, "I am done with this way of living." Browning never knew such contrition; a contemporary newspaper called him "Pietro Redlight District Distillery Interests Browning." He died in a Louisville insane asylum in 1905.

win totals between 20 and 50, depending on the quality of the teams behind them. In 1882 Jim Mc-Cormick, working for fifth place Cleveland, amassed 65 complete games; the following season John Coleman of Philadelphia set a record that will never be equalled when he lost 48 contests; and in 1884 Old Hoss Radbourn set the converse record by winning 60 times for Providence. These achievements, which seem incredible today, were accepted as routine in the 1880's, and only Radbourn's occasioned much comment; he had missed the early part of the season while under suspension for insubordination, and was not given the chance to go on his winning tear until Charley Sweeney, the club's first-line pitcher, had jumped the team in mid-season.

The National League's most serene campaign to date took place in the year 1881 when several clubs made substantial profits and last place Worcester finished only 23 games behind the pennant-winning White Stockings. But during the next year Hulbert died, and the league lost its exclusive monopoly on major league baseball when Cincinnati, Louisville and St. Louis—all National League castoffs—combined with outfits from Pittsburgh, Philadelphia and Baltimore to form the rival American Association. At the outset the quality of play in the Association was inferior to that in the older league, but its flamboyant operation (which included beer in all its parks, baseball on Sunday and halving the Na-

tional League's fifty-cent admission price) provided a sharp contrast to the tight-fisted, cadaverous image of the old-guard moguls. Arraying its players in gorgeous silks and showing no qualms about hiring blacklisted performers or raiding National League rosters for disenchanted stars, the Association soon attained parity, compelling the National League to keep pace by reinstating New York and Philadelphia and lopping off the weak-sister franchises in Troy and Worcester.

The Association originally relied on National League rejects like Will White and Charley Jones to attract fans, but by the end of its second year of operation it had developed many new stars of its own. Among them were Harry Stovey, Dave Orr and Pete Browning. Despite their positions as the Association's leading batsmen for nearly a decade, none of this trio is in the Hall of Fame; nor, for that matter, are any other performers who spent the majority of their careers in the Association. What this oversight suggests is that the game, deep into the twentieth century, still bears a lingering grudge inherited from old National Leaguers, who privately could not accept the Association as a true major league even after technically recognizing it as such. Ironically, in the only year that the leading players from both leagues played under the same banner—in the Players League in 1890—the top two batsmen were not King Kelly or Dan Brouthers or any of the many other future National League Hall of Famers but Browning and Orr, and the stolen-base leader was Stovey.

Efforts were made during the decade the Association flourished to match its pennant winners against those of the National League in a postseason series, but the results were always indecisive, largely because the series were so obviously designed by owners for maximum financial gain that neither the players nor the fans could be made to take them seriously. Adding to the confusion was the formation of the Union Association in 1884 by Henry Lucas, a St. Louis realtor who believed that baseball players were unjustly treated and who was determined to build a new major league without a reserve clause. Originated in 1879 by Arthur Soden, the reserve clause was first designed to bind only the top five players on each team but was soon expanded to include the entire roster. It was viewed by owners as necessary to prevent the wealthier clubs from corralling all the best talent. The players themselves recognized that something like it was needed to maintain a competitive balance. For those who still had lingering doubts, the example of the Union Association put them permanently to rest. In 1884, their one year of operation, the "Onions" lost money all down the line as the St. Louis Maroons, with the largest bankroll, purchased a team so powerful that it won a hideously lopsided pennant race (the team finished 94–19), and fans in all cities lost interest in the proceedings by the Fourth of July.

The lesson that owners in both the Association and the National League should have drawn from the "Onions" fiasco was that unfair practices against players would lead inevitably to further revolts, but instead, as soon as the Union threat was dispelled, the two leagues opted to impose a $2,000-salary maximum on players and eliminate all salary advances. To combat the owners, Billy Voltz, a minor league manager at Chattanooga, in 1885 formed the National Brotherhood of Professional Baseball Players, the game's first labor organization. Voltz held no sway among major league performers, and his place at the head of the brotherhood was soon assumed by Monte Ward. Ward, who was still a star pitcher and shortstop and the beneficiary of a legal education, prevented the owners from enforcing a ceiling on player salaries for the time being. It was an uneasy truce, however, and upon returning from an Australian tour after the 1888 season, Ward learned that in his absence Indianapolis owner John Brush had pushed through a rule limiting players' salaries according to their ability, with pay to range from $2,500 for a Class A player down to $1,500 for a Class E player. With Ward acting as their spokesman, the players rebelled vigorously not only at having their salaries limited but more, one might suspect, at the public grading of their performance.

When Ward was refused an audience with club owners to discuss the new rule, players from both

New York finished sixth in 1883, despite the presence of Buck Ewing, Monte Ward and Roger Connor (seated, in order, from third from R). Ward played 56 games in center field that year, five at third base, two at shortstop, one at second base — and pitched in 33.

Read "Jack Skelly, the Great Feather-Weight," in No. 84 of this Library.

NEW YORK FIVE CENT LIBRARY

Entered According to Act of Congress, in the Year 1892, by Street & Smith, in the Office of the Librarian of Congress, Washington, D. C.
Entered as Second-class Matter in the New York, N. Y., Post Office.   June 16, 1894   Issued Weekly. Subscription Price, $1.25 per Year.   June 16, 1894.

No. 85.   STREET & SMITH, Publishers,   NEW YORK.   31 Rose St., N. Y. P. O. Box 2734.   5 Cents.

King Kelly, the Famous Catcher;

Or, The Life and Adventures of the $10,000 Ball-Player.

BY BILLY BOXER, THE REFEREE.

KING KELLY, THE FAMOUS CATCHER AND ALL-AROUND BALL-PLAYER.

Celebrations of Mike "King" Kelly, and contemporaries. Kelly was an extraordinary hitter, baserunner, fielder, manager and carouser. On an English tour in the nineties, a reporter asked him if he drank while playing. "It depends," Kelly replied, "on the length of the game." Nash graduated to a long career as an umpire; Murphy worked in a brokerage house.

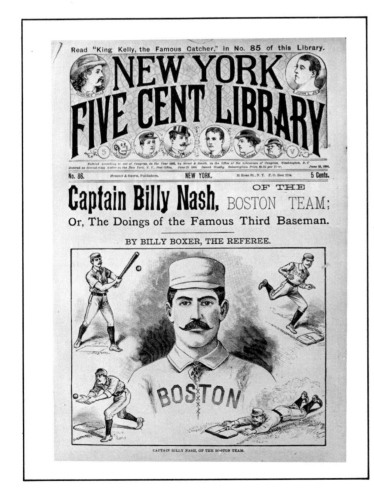

Kid Gleason, Tommy McCarthy, Hoss Radbourn (L to R). Gleason won 138 games as a pitcher through 1895; his arm worn out, he switched to second base and played another 14 seasons. McCarthy was, with Hugh Duffy, one of Boston's celebrated "Heavenly Twins." But to Duffy, "McCarthy was the heavenly one. He was the smartest ballplayer I ever saw." Radbourn won his 60 games in 1884 with a cricket-style pitching motion that included a running start.

leagues began meeting secretly during the 1889 season with Albert Johnson, the Cleveland street railway magnate who had shown himself sympathetic to their cause. With Johnson's help in influencing other capitalists to loan them money, the brotherhood began plans to build parks in all the National League cities and secede from organized baseball to form an enterprise owned and operated entirely by members from its own ranks and called, appropriately, the Players' League. The owners at first regarded the scheme as a pipe dream on the part of the Brotherhood, but discovered to their dismay in the early months of 1890 that the Players' League had successfully installed franchises in every National League city except Cincinnati and had enlisted most of the available stars. One notable exception was Anson, who by that time was part owner of the White Stockings. The Association, a bystander to much of the battle, nevertheless found its ranks so depleted that the Louisville club, a last-place finisher in 1889, won the Association pennant in 1890 and in the process became the lone major league team in history to rise from last place to first in the space of a single season. The thoroughly demoralized Association hung on through the 1891 season, but its demise had been signaled as far back as 1886 when Pittsburgh, one of its soundest franchises, had shifted to the National League, and Cleveland, Cincinnati and Brooklyn had later defected in recognition that the Association, now that its novelty and panache had worn thin, was bereft of the leadership necessary to make the league a long-term paying proposition.

The Players' League pennant was captured by Boston—managed by Mike "King" Kelly—while Brooklyn won the National League flag by retaining the core of the club that had triumphed in the Association in 1889. Neither of these events is much remembered, yet each was as remarkable in its own right as Louisville's climb to the top of the Association. The 1890 season was, in fact, the most intriguing of the nineteenth century. Kelly, himself a notoriously unmanageable player, was perhaps the

Moses Fleetwood Walker, the first black major leaguer, with Toledo in 1884. He was educated at Oberlin, as was his brother Welday, who also played for Toledo. After Cap Anson drew the color line, Welday wrote the President of the Tri-State League, George McDermott: "The rule that you have passed is a public disgrace."

Ed Delehanty, one of five Delehanty brothers to play in the majors. His .346 lifetime average is the fourth best in history. In 1902, he batted .376; the next year, *Sporting Life* headlined "DELE-HANTY DEAD. The Famous Player Finds His End in Niagara River. Put Off a Train at Fort Erie for Violent Conduct, the 'Only Del' Walks Through the Open Draw of a Bridge and Is Swept Over Niagara Falls." When his body was found, "about $1,500 in diamonds and $200 in money the deceased is known to have carried with him" had washed away with his clothing.

Anson and his 1888 Chicago club, which finished second to New York. Seated in front of Anson is the team mascot, Clarence Duval. Anson had just that year initiated his organized purge of black players in professional baseball. At least 25 minor leaguers lost their jobs as an immediate result.

least likely manager in history and certainly the least likely to win a pennant. Handed the reins of the Kansas City Association team the following year, he soon made a botch of the club and failed to last out the season. Brooklyn, meanwhile, remains the only franchise to win pennants in two different major leagues in successive seasons, and is one of only two National League clubs (the 1939-40 Reds are the other) to win consecutive flags without a single Hall of Famer on the active roster.

The Detroit Wolverines, 1888. Ned Hanlon (6) was the brains of the club and Dan Brouthers (7) its muscle. Champions the previous year, the club was so money-starved that owner F. H. Stearns engineered a 15-game series against the St. Louis Association team at the season's end.

Cleveland Spiders, 1892. "A milk-and-water, goody-goody player can't wear a Cleveland uniform," said manager Patsy Tebeau. After they lost a five-game play-off to Boston, historian David Voigt notes, one writer termed the Spiders "highly successful in the manufacture of nothingness, surrounded by an elliptical fence."

The three pennant winners of 1890 were not the only clubs of interest. Perhaps the oddest outfit of all that season was the Cleveland Players League entry, which numbered Pete Browning, the game's top hitter, and a 16-year-old rookie pitcher named Willie McGill, who the following season became the youngest 20-game winner ever. Poor fielding landed Cleveland in seventh place, and one of the leading malefactors was the club's shortstop, who turned in an .830 fielding average. As his bat work wasn't much

St. Louis Browns, 1888. This was Chris Von der Ahe's fourth consecutive pennant winner, but contention between owner and players soon saw the juggernaut stopped. Harold Seymour writes that "when Von der Ahe began to lose his grip..., he tried everything to raise money, converting his park into a honky-tonk with shoot-the-chutes, a merry-go-round, and a wine room, and advertised it as 'The Coney Island of the West.'"

better, many were dubious when in the following season the Phillies gave him their center field post between Hall of Famers Billy Hamilton and Sam Thompson and still kept him after he hit only .243. Within three years, however, he had made it abundantly clear that the Phils had not two but three future Hall of Famers in their outfield. It is now generally forgotten that his first job as a big league regular was at shortstop, but not much else about his career is. In spite of his inauspicious beginning, many still consider Edward James Delahanty the greatest right-handed hitter of all time.

By the end of the 1890 season Ward and the Players' League had the National League on its knees, but they failed to grasp the advantage they held and allowed Soden, Brush and other old-line owners to talk them back into the fold on the stipulation that they could return to their former teams without reprisal. Some slight concessions were won by the players as a result of the war, but in the main their rebellion accomplished little and had an unpleasant side effect on their cause. Following a dispute over the reassignment of Players' League personnel like second baseman Louis Bierbauer who were accidentally left unprotected on the "reserve list," the American Association began the year 1891 by withdrawing from the National Agreement and attempting to exist as an entity separate from the National League. Their twenty-five-cent admission fee proved insufficient to meet skyrocketing operating expenses, and by the season's end they were forced to fold. Baltimore, St. Louis, Washington and Louisville were absorbed by the National League, swelling its ranks to 12 teams, and for the remainder of the century the Nationals once more had a monopoly on major league play. To recoup financial losses owners began to slash salaries by as much as 40 percent once the 1892 season was under way. With only one major league now, the players had no alternative but to agree.

In an effort to stimulate fan interest and make the new 12-team circuit less unwieldy, a split season was played in 1892 for the only time in major league history. Boston, behind the pitching of Kid Nichols and Jack Stivetts, was an easy winner in the first half, while the Cleveland Spiders squeezed home ahead of the pack in the second half by acquiring John Clarkson to bolster their already overpowering pitching duo of Cy Young and Nig Cuppy. After an opening-game tie, Boston triumphed in four straight games in a postseason play-off that generated little excitement and served to underscore what observers had been noticing all season. Boston and Cleveland were not the only teams with outstanding pitching; every club was getting exceptional mound work. Dan Brouthers and Billy Hamilton were the lone hitters above .320, and only Brouthers and Sam Thompson were able to collect over 100 RBIs. Now that the 24 teams in existence since 1890 had been condensed into only 12, it appeared that the weaker pitchers had been weeded

A. G. Spalding proceeded from pitcher to manager to owner to, finally, monopolist. His baseballs ostensibly competed with those manufactured by Reach and by Wright and Ditson, when all three companies were in fact under Spalding control; by 1900, the man *Sporting Life* called "The Big Mogul" also headed the Bicycle Trust. In 1907, he organized the commission that conferred the crown of baseball creation on Abner Doubleday.

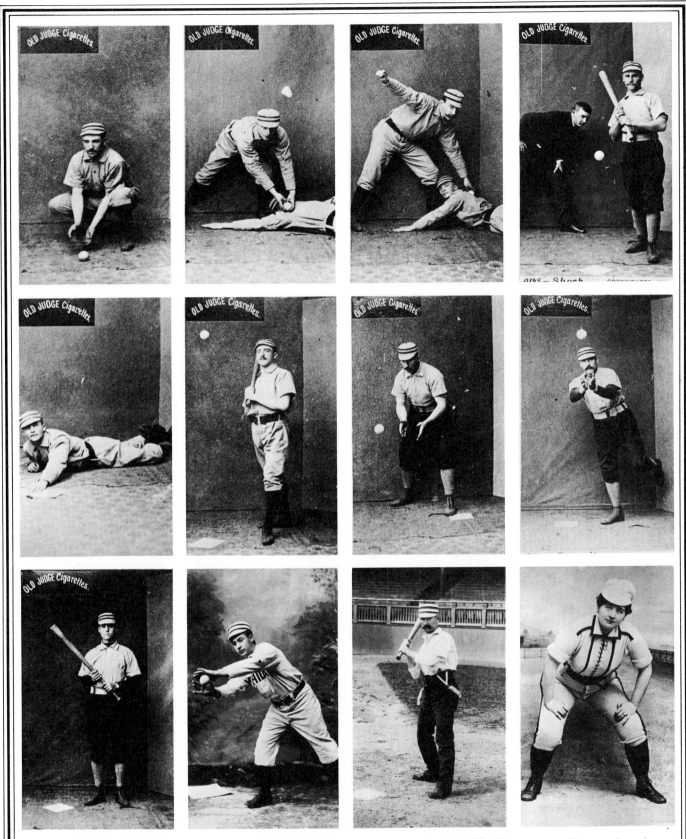

The first baseball cigarette cards were Victorian studio tableaux, stately and stiff. Pictures were first used on the blank cardboard stiffeners in cigarette packages in 1878. There is no ready explanation for the lady at lower right.

out and the batters were at a distinct disadvantage having to face on a daily basis pitchers like Cy Young and Amos Rusie. Proof of the sorry state into which the art of batting had fallen was offered by Cap Anson who hit only .272, Monte Ward who slipped to .265 and two-time batting champion King Kelly, down to an unbelievably dismal .189. A number of solutions were proposed, but none was nearly so radical as the one finally adopted a year later: the pitching rubber was moved back from 50 feet to 60 feet 6 inches. Seen as an experiment at first, it proved instantly successful; the geometry of the playing field has been the same ever since.

One problem that could not be solved by geometry was how to improve the franchises taken aboard when the Association closed its doors. All four brought up the rear of the league in 1892; the performance of the St. Louis Browns was particularly disquieting. The scourge of the Association throughout the late eighties under the ownership of Chris Von der Ahe, the game's first great sportsman, the Browns were now at so low an ebb that they hit a meager .226 as a team and were spared the embarrassment of a cellar finish only by the presence of Baltimore, a perennial weak link and the only club that had been in the Association every year of its existence and never won a pennant. Baltimore's situation was so tenuous in 1892 that the team went

through three managers before turning to a man who had floundered abysmally the previous year with Pittsburgh. A former National League outfielder, his only positive credit to date was playing on the champion Detroit Wolverines in 1887. He was Ned Hanlon, and during the decade between 1891 and 1900 Hanlon and Boston manager Frank Selee would account for every pennant in the National League. Despite ten pennants between them and the responsibility for developing more Hall of Fame players than any other two managers in history except John McGraw and Connie Mack, neither Hanlon nor Selee is in the Hall of Fame.

By winning 43 games in 1891 and 37 in 1892, the White Stockings' Bill Hutchison became the last pitcher to tally 80 victories in two seasons. In 1893, with the mound moved back ten feet, he fell to only 16 wins. Several of the top pitchers of the era were at least temporarily impaired by the increased distance, although Amos Rusie and Frank Killen actually appeared to improve. Granted, no one would ever again be able to pitch every day as had Radbourn down the stretch in the 1884 National League season, nor was anyone likely to match Mattie Kilroy's 513 strikeouts as a Baltimore rookie in 1886; but by the same token there was room now, with the extra ten feet, for pitching craftsmen to

The New York Metropolitans, 1888. This championship team was ostensibly managed by Jim Mutrie (C), although Buck Ewing (standing, extreme R) actually led the team on the field. Mutrie was responsible for watching the money, though, and coined the team's peculiar slogan, "We are the people!" Legend attributes to him a change in the team's nickname as a result of his boast, "My big fellows! My Giants!"

employ a wider assortment of deliveries. Teams were forced to deepen their pitching staffs and give more opportunities to rookies.

Of greater importance was the immediate acceleration in hitting. The league as a whole—led by the three Phillies outfielders, Hamilton, Thompson and Delahanty, who finished in that order at the top of the batting race—hit .280 in 1893, 18 points better than the highest *team* average a year earlier. When Pittsburgh finished second to Boston, one of the Pirates' owners, William Temple, was so excited that he promoted a postseason series between the first- and second-place teams. Called the Temple Cup Playoff, the series, sadly for its originator, did not begin until 1894, by which time his Pirates had slumped to seventh. The Baltimore Orioles, meanwhile, had risen phenomenally to the top of the league. In two years Hanlon, by a series of deft trades, had put together a team that hit .343 and averaged more than nine runs a game.

Over in New York, Monte Ward had coaxed Jouett Meekin from Washington to pair with Rusie on the Giant mound, and while this move was not enough to bring the Giants the pennant, it enabled them to rout the Orioles in four straight games for the first Temple Cup championship. Boston fans, disappointed when their team sagged to third place, were consoled in part when Hugh Duffy won the

triple crown while hitting a record .438, and the Phils, another length back in fourth, boasted an all-.400-hitting outfield led by Tuck Turner's .416. In a year when hitters captured all the attention, Rusie's ERA of 2.78, nearly a full run less than that of his closest rival, escaped notice. So did the departure of Cincinnati manager Charlie Comiskey at the season's close to take over the St. Paul franchise in the minor league Western Association, reorganized earlier that year by his friend Ban Johnson, a former sportswriter for the *Cincinnati Commercial Gazette*. National League owners had no way as yet of knowing it, but once again the seeds for a threat to their monopoly had first been sown in Cincinnati.

The Orioles continued their reign over the next two seasons, although they had to wait until 1896 to win their first Temple Cup. The winners of three straight pennants, Hanlon's men possessed probably the most potent offensive team of all time and were virtually as strong in the field. Their chief competitors in the mid-nineties, the Cleveland Spiders, had Cy Young, the game's most durable pitcher, and Jesse Burkett, the league's first repeat batting champion since Dan Brouthers in the early eighties. The Spiders were a cut below the Orioles in overall ability but matched them almost exactly

Boston Beaneaters, 1892. Even though the lettering on King Kelly's uniform indicated his distinct status in the game, he was by this time an old man of 34. He batted only .189 that season and two years later was dead of "typhoid pneumonia." Next to Kelly, out of uniform, is manager Frank Selee. He developed a signal system so effective that, according to Bill Dahlen, all the fielders knew exactly what their pitcher would throw next. At extreme right is John Clarkson. From 1885-1888, he won 160 games.

OLD JUDGE CIGARETTES Goodwin & Co., New York.

Kid Nichols in his last minor league season. In 1891 he began a string of seven consecutive seasons in which he won at least 30 games. He joined with Clarkson and Harry Staley to win 83 of Boston's 87 victories that first year.

been eased out of the league after being unable to purchase more stock in the Chicago club. Betrayed by Al Spalding, who had promised him a controlling interest in the White Stockings and then had reneged, Anson's statement upon leaving the game speaks reams for the atmosphere in which he played: "Baseball as at present conducted is a gigantic monopoly intolerant of opposition and run on a grab-all-that-there-is-in-sight basis that is alienating its friends and disgusting the very public that has so long and cheerfully given to it the support that it has withheld from other forms of amusement."

Anson's comments, intended as a warning to club owners that fans and players were growing impa-

in the roughhouse style of play that characterized the nineties and became an integral part of the legend of John McGraw, Hughie Jennings and other stars of the period.

Hanlon's team was still at its peak in 1897 but missed the pennant by two games when Kid Nichols steered Boston home in front with his seventh straight 30-win season. In the final Temple Cup Playoff the Orioles won in five games, making it three years out of four that the second-place team had easily triumphed. Oriole rightfielder Willie Keeler ended Burkett's grip on the batting title, hitting .424. Keeler was an anomaly among the Orioles. Small, quiet, his uniform always immaculate, he never rubbed his hands with dirt and refused to join his teammates in filing his spikes. A masterful place hitter and bunter, Keeler more than any other player bridged the gap between ancient and modern baseball.

In a sense the ancient era of baseball ended not with Keeler but with the retirement of Cap Anson in 1897. Though 46, Anson was still in perfect shape and probably would have played longer had he not

Tim Keefe. In 1889 the owners instituted a classification pay scheme, arbitrarily setting salary limits for every player. Keefe earned $5,000, highest in the National League. The year before, he had won 19 consecutive games in a period of six weeks.

tient with their practices, went totally unheeded. At the conclusion of the 1898 season Harry Vonderhorst, who owned controlling interests in both the Orioles and the Brooklyn club, shuttled Hanlon and several players from his Oriole powerhouse northward in the sensible belief that there was more money to be made in the New York area with a good team than anywhere else. Intrigued by the Brooklyn example, the Robison brothers, owners of the Spiders, bought the St. Louis franchise and transferred all of Cleveland's stars west of the Mississippi in time for the 1899 season. Syndicate ownership at the time was permissible under league statutes. Still, in searching for further ploys that would give them an edge over their competitors within the league, the moguls missed seeing the specter of competition that loomed huge outside their walls. Ban Johnson and Charlie Comiskey of the Western Association, still a minor league, were fixing watchful eyes on the internecine struggles in the National League and in particular those involving the franchises in financial trouble. Washington and Louisville were in the worst shape, but the disem-

Cy Young. Ogden Nash wrote:
Y is for Young
The Magnificent Cy;
People batted against him,
But I never knew why.
He had more wins, more losses, more complete games and more innings pitched than anyone else in baseball history.

boweled Spiders and Orioles were not far behind. When the Spiders ended the 1899 season with a .130 winning percentage, the poorest in modern history, NL owners voted hastily to pare their league to eight clubs and dispense with the four weaklings—significantly the same four franchises (substituting Cleveland for St. Louis, which had been infused with Cleveland's—and thus "National League"—talent) that had been absorbed from the old American Association.

The immediate beneficiary was Louisville owner Barney Dreyfuss, who was permitted to buy the Pittsburgh club and shift the cream from his Kentucky outfit to the steel city. The long-range beneficiary was none other than Ban Johnson. Denied an opportunity to consult with National League officials about plans to expand his Western Association, Johnson installed a team prior to the 1900 season in Cleveland, moved the St. Paul franchise to Chicago and announced his intention to change the Western Association's name to the American League and make it a major league enterprise. For the moment the National League felt utterly at ease in ignoring him. The 1900 season was the most successful in its 25-year history. All eight teams were financially and competitively solid. The Brook-

Amos Rusie. In 1894, from mid-July through New York's conquest of Baltimore in the Temple Cup series, Rusie and Jouett Meekin pitched every one of the Giants' games. The New York *Herald*'s O. P. Caylor wrote, "The Giants without Rusie would be like *Hamlet* without the Melancholy Dane."

lyn Superbas, winners of their second pennant in a row under Hanlon, appeared to be a strong entry for years to come. The Pirates, led by batting champ Honus Wagner, and the Phils, with their young second baseman Nap Lajoie, were both solid contenders. It seemed only a short while now before a National League pennant would fly for the first time in a Pennsylvania city. St. Louis also was finally making first-division overtures. Even the last-place Giants had experienced a resurgence after shortstop George Davis took over the managership in mid-season.

Following close on Wagner's heels in the 1900 batting race were two familiar names, Burkett and Keeler, and a new one, Elmer Flick, the Phils' latest outfield sensation. Flick was also the RBI leader, with teammate Delahanty a close second. Among pitchers Joe McGinnity, Jesse Tannehill, Cy Young, Bill Dinneen and Rube Waddell were the statistical leaders. Wagner, Lajoie, Keeler, Burkett, Flick, Delahanty, McGinnity, Tannehill, Young, Dinneen, Waddell and George Davis: three years later most of these names would still be high among the individual leaders, but only two of them, Wagner and McGinnity, would appear in the National League column. —David Nemec

Napoleon Lajoie, in a remarkable studio photograph made in 1901. When he jumped from the National League to the new American, a court order obtained by the Phillies barred him from playing in Pennsylvania. When Cleveland played in Philadelphia that season, Lajoie would spend the day hanging around Atlantic City.

TEAM:
The Old Orioles
By Robert W. Creamer

IN THE beginning there were the Baltimore Orioles.

Well, not really. There had been a lot of baseball and a host of lively teams before the Old Orioles raced to the center of the big league stage in the 1890's, but the Orioles were something special. They were for me, at any rate, and for others of my generation of baseball fan, even though we never saw them play.

They had gone out of existence more than 20 years before I was born, but they were the Titans of prehistoric baseball—history for me and other kids my age having begun in 1901, when the American League came into existence as a full-fledged rival of the older National League, and the "modern era" of baseball began. The lists of pennant winners in most of the baseball books and journals we had access to began with that year; an occasional listing might also include National League winners from the league's inception in 1876, but we didn't pay much attention to that. The magic number was 1901, the dawn of civilization. I could recite by heart the pennant winners in the American and National from 1901 on, and I could do the World Series winners from 1903 (when the Series was first played), always noting in passing that there was no Series in 1904 because John McGraw of the Giants refused to play the champions of the upstart new league. John McGraw was an Old Oriole. We knew that, too.

If we did not know precisely what the Orioles had accomplished, or when, we had heard of them. We knew they were *good,* that legend said they were the greatest team of all time until the 1927 Yankees came along (McGraw said they were better than the Yanks). I saw my first big league game in the summer of 1931, just after my ninth birthday, when my big brother took me to the Polo Grounds in New York to see a doubleheader between McGraw's Giants and the Brooklyn Dodgers. I have several vivid memories of that afternoon but the most vivid is that *I saw John McGraw.* I saw Wilbert Robinson, too, known as Robbie (or Uncle Robbie, or Uncle Wilbert), who was managing the Dodgers. As a nine-year-old baseball adept I knew that McGraw and Robinson were Old Orioles as well as I knew that Babe Ruth hit home runs and that Connie Mack's real name was Cornelius McGillicuddy. McGraw had played third base and was tough. Robinson had been the catcher and once got seven hits in seven at bats in a nine-inning game, a record that stood unmatched for more than 80 years.

They were genuine Old Orioles, they were there in the flesh and I gazed on them with awe. They were old men then. McGraw was 58, which seems relatively young now, but he had been managing the Giants for almost 30 years, he had snow-white hair and he was *old.* He was in his last full year as manager of the Giants. In 1932 he quit 40 games into the season—his resignation was headline news —and 20 months after that he was dead.

Robinson, 68, ten years older than McGraw and as genial as McGraw was bad-tempered, had been managing the Dodgers since before the first World War and was such a fixture in Brooklyn that the team was usually called the Robins. Newspaper headlines referred to the Robins as the Flock, and long years after Uncle Robbie's day, after the nickname "Dodgers" had regained the ascendancy, New York tabloid headlines still shouted, FLOCK BEATS JINTS. Nineteen thirty-one turned out to be Robinson's last season, too, and in 1934, six months after McGraw died, Uncle Robbie followed him to the grave. Few sagas have ended so abruptly.

I was acutely aware of McGraw and Robinson that day partly because of my grouchy little grandfather, who lived with us and smoked cut-up White Owl cigars in a corncob pipe and told me stories of playing shortstop on town teams when he was young. I was fascinated by old men. For me, McGraw and Robinson were archeological finds, living fossils proving the existence of a dead, distant past. For three decades sportswriters had been telling and retelling stories about the Old Orioles (most of them heard, it seems obvious now, from John

McGraw, Robinson and the revealed word. The friendship forged in Baltimore ended in 1913 when McGraw fired Robinson from his coaching staff. When Robinson took over Brooklyn, Abe Yager of the *Eagle* wrote, "Whether Robbie only reflects the greatness of McGraw or can go it alone is the question.... We shall let him work out his own salvation without interference or disfavor."

McGraw), and after I came into existence as a base-ball fan I must have read them all. They told about the hustling way the Orioles played the game, how rough and tough they were, how they played hurt ("We'd spit tobacco juice on a spike wound, rub dirt in it, and get out there and play," McGraw would say); how they invented the hit-and-run, the sacrifice bunt, the squeeze play, the double steal and other strategic ploys; how they'd scuff up a baseball or discolor it with tobacco juice to help their pitchers; how they'd cut corners running from first to third when the umpire's back was turned; how they'd hold a base runner's belt to delay his departure from a base; how they developed "inside baseball," the tight, close-to-the-vest brand of ball that scratched out a run or two and then protected it with strong pitching and deft fielding.

Inside Baseball became John McGraw's gospel, and he preached it incessantly, repeatedly citing the Orioles' example. It scorned the home run, the big hit. In a prototypical McGraw inning the batter would work the pitcher for a walk, steal second, be sacrificed to third and score on a squeeze bunt. Or would move from first to third on a hit-and-run and score on a fly ball. Or, having reached third, would score on a delayed steal. Tight baseball, scratching out runs.

In 1933, a year after McGraw had retired but while his presence and personality still permeated the game, at least in the National League, his Giants, now managed by Bill Terry and on their way to a pennant, defeated their archrivals, the St. Louis Cardinals, in a famous doubleheader. Old Giant fans still talk about that doubleheader, and I remember it well. The Giants won both games, 1–0 and 1–0. Carl Hubbell pitched an 18-inning shutout in the first game, and Roy Parmalee a nine-inning shutout in the second. It was the ultimate salute to McGraw's brand of baseball, the Old Oriole way of doing things: 27 innings of airtight pitching and defense, two little runs, two big victories.

But it was really a last hurrah for McGraw's game. At about the same time, my Uncle Bernie Kelly, my godfather, took me to a ball game. Uncle Bernie was a classic New York Irishman. He loved the city and he revered John McGraw. He felt uneasy away from the city (and, fittingly enough, eventually died in a subway car on the Third Avenue El after suffering a heart attack during a New York midsummer heat wave). Like Ring Lardner, who hated home runs, Uncle Bernie loved Inside Baseball.

When he discovered on one of his rare trips to our house "out in the country"—we lived in a sub-urb 15 miles from Times Square—that his 11-year-old godson was a baseball nut, he decided to take me to a game. He assumed I would want to see the Giants; I all but sneered. Despite my Polo Grounds debut I had been seduced by Babe Ruth and Lou Gehrig and was a Yankee fan. Uncle Bernie bit the bullet and took me to Yankee Stadium to see the Yanks play the Philadelphia Athletics. These were the Athletics of Jimmie Foxx and Mike Higgins and Mickey Cochrane, all those big, hairy-backed hitters. They scored 11 runs in the second inning. The Yanks came back with 10 in the fourth. The Babe hit a three-run homer in the eighth. The final score was something like 17–11, Yankees. I loved it. Uncle Bernie must have died. (Perhaps literally, come to think of it; he took that last subway ride only a year or so later, in 1934, the same year that McGraw and Robinson died.)

The Old Oriole idea passed away with those old men. The National League tried to stay with Inside Baseball but the big hitters in the American League turned the game around. Power dominated baseball and it wasn't until the 1950's, when the National had Jackie Robinson, Roy Campanella, Willie Mays, Henry Aaron and all the other hard-hitting black players, that it regained parity with and then superiority over the American. Lefty Gomez, the old pitcher who had basked in the glow of Yankee power when he was their ace in the 1930's, tried to show the National League the way. Toward the end of his career, trying to hang on in the majors, Lefty went to spring training with the old Boston Braves. One day, listening with amusement to his new National League teammates seriously discussing Inside Baseball, Gomez laughed. "Hey," he said, "don't you guys know John McGraw is dead?"

So the Old Oriole mystique faded away, to disappear almost completely in the 1950's when Baltimore returned to the major leagues after half a century of exile in the minors. The new Orioles effectively erased the memory of the Old ones.

But who were the Old ones, really? When *did* they play? What did they really accomplish? I knew some of the names: McGraw, Robinson, Wee Willie Keeler, Ee-Yah Hughie Jennings (he liked to shout "Ee-Yah!" a lot). I knew that McGraw played third, that Robinson caught, that Jennings, the shortstop, later managed the Detroit Tigers of Ty Cobb's era, and that Keeler, only five feet four inches tall, once hit in 44 straight games and when asked the secret of his batting skill had said, "I hit 'em where they ain't." Beyond that I knew little, except that even though baseball people persistently referred to them as McGraw's Orioles, the manager had been a man named Ned Hanlon. (Later Hanlon also managed the Brooklyn Dodgers, who were promptly sur-nicknamed the Superbas because at the time Hanlon took them over there was a popular vaudeville act called Hanlon's Superbas. Another time the Dodgers were dubbed the Bridegrooms, for the number of newlyweds on the squad. Bridegrooms, Superbas, Robins—it's a wonder the name "Dodgers" survived.)

But the team, the dynasty, the Old Orioles . . . what about that? I had to look it up, as Casey Stengel would advise his listeners, and to my considerable surprise I discovered that the Old Orioles were not a dynasty at all but a nova, a sudden manifestation in the baseball skies that flared brilliantly for a very short time and then disappeared.

Baltimore did not join the National League until 1892, and by 1900 it was gone again. The city did have a team in a second major league, called the American Association, starting in 1882, but it certainly did not distinguish itself. In their first eight seasons in the American Association the fledgling Orioles finished last, last, sixth, last, last, third, fifth, fifth. While such names as Cap Anson and Al Spalding and Old Hoss Radbourn and Orator O'Rourke and John Montgomery Ward and Tim Keefe and Buck Ewing and Mike (King) Kelly and Dan Brouthers and Pete Browning and Tip

O'Neill were ringing out from other cities, Baltimore had nobody. Oh, there had been a few good ballplayers—Tommy Tucker, a hard-hitting, hard-drinking first baseman who led the Association in batting in 1889: Matt Kilroy, a left-handed pitcher with terrific speed who won 46 games in 1887 and who a year earlier had pitched three no-hitters while leading the league in strikeouts—but none of those treasured names that stir the blood. Not yet.

In 1890, the year of the great player revolt, when dozens of players in the two established leagues jumped their teams to form a third major league, Baltimore did not have a team at all. Three major leagues, and no Orioles in any of them. The city's faltering American Association franchise had been shifted to Brooklyn, where it was one of *three* big league teams in that town. It faced stifling competition—one of its Brooklyn rivals won the National League pennant, the other finished second in the Players' League. Languishing in last place in its league and strangling to death, the franchise gave up in mid-season and crept back to Baltimore where, under the direction of Manager Billy Barnie (a longtime Baltimore favorite known alternatively as Blue Eyed Billy or Bald Headed Billy) it finished last again, 13 games behind the next-worst team.

The following season, with the player rebellion squashed and their league only a memory, a revived Baltimore team finished a distant but respectable third in the American Association. More important,

The 1896 Orioles. Front: Doyle, McGraw, Keeler, Pond; Middle: Brodie, Hoffer, Kelley, Hanlon, Robinson, Jennings, Reitz; Rear: Quinn, McMahon, Esper, Hemming, Bowerman, Clarke, Donnelly.

McGraw as a 16-year-old infielder in Olean, New York. "I could field the ball all right," he later recalled, "but on the throw I couldn't hit the first baseman or anything near him." In one game, McGraw committed nine errors.

While McGraw improved enough in two years to reach the big leagues in 1891 as a 121-pound 18-year-old, the Baltimore club featured men such as these. Top (L to R): Bill Shindle, survivor of a brief stay in Philadelphia (where he made an astonishing 119 errors, still a record, in 1890); Matt Kilroy, a genuinely good pitcher who nonetheless lost 100 games in four Baltimore years; Tommy Tucker, whose .372 average in 1889 was 118 points above the team average. Bottom (L): George Van Haltren, a fine hitter but a managerial flop: before his discharge in 1892, he had led the club to a 1-14 start; (C) Billy Barnie, "the bald-headed Eagle of the Chesapeake," who knew more about stock manipulation than about baseball. (R) The resistant object of their on-field exertions.

the nucleus of the Old Orioles (who were still yet to be) arrived in the city. Manager Barnie happened to own a part interest in the American Association's Philadelphia club (such conflicts of interest were not at all uncommon then), and when Philadelphia went bankrupt Barnie took a couple of its players in settlement. They were pitcher Sadie McMahon (christened John Joseph), who won 35 games for the Orioles in 1891 to lead the league, and Wilbert Robinson, who proved to be an outstanding catcher and a team leader, the Orioles' field captain, in fact. During that season of 1891 McGraw showed up in Baltimore, too: 18 years old, five feet seven inches tall, lean as a leather whip and just as mean. He got into 33 games, mostly at shortstop.

More changes followed. Baltimore's owner and president, a brewer named Harry Vonderhorst, fired Barnie and made an outfielder named George Van Haltren the playing manager. After the 1891 season, the American Association went out of business and four of its teams, including Baltimore, joined the National League to form a new, expanded 12-team circuit. The Orioles, perky after their third-place finish, entered the new league and the 1892 season with high hopes—and lost 14 of their first 15 games. Vonderhorst relieved Van Haltren of his managerial duties, though keeping him as an outfielder, and assigned Jim Waltz, one of his associates at the brewery, to run the club temporarily while he scouted around for a new manager.

Enter Ned Hanlon. He had been the centerfielder on the hard-hitting Detroit club of the 1880's. In 1889 he was traded to Pittsburgh, and in midseason became the team's playing manager. Hanlon was an opportunist. In 1890 he jumped with most of his key players to the Players' League team in Pittsburgh, and then in 1891, with the Players' League dead under him, he nimbly leaped back again, adroitly holding onto the manager's reins through each of the jumps. But midway through the 1891 season, with the Pirates in last place, he was fired. Still the team's centerfielder, he snapped a tendon in his leg on Opening Day of 1892 while chasing a fly ball in batting practice, and just like that his career was over. Pittsburgh released him a few weeks later, and a few days after that Vonderhorst made him the Orioles' manager. Within a year Hanlon had obtained a 20 percent interest in the Baltimore club and persuaded Vonderhorst to step aside and let him function as both manager and president of the team. He ran everything. Vonderhorst, a little put out by this turn of events, took to wearing a button in his lapel that he would point

to when people queried him about the ballclub. "Ask Hanlon," the button read.

Hanlon's arrival had little immediate effect. He took over a last-place team and it stayed last all season, the sixth time in its 11 years in the majors that it had finished in the cellar. But Hanlon was making moves, including one trade late in the season that would prove of enormous benefit to the Orioles in the seasons to come. He sent the experienced Van Haltren, who was batting over .300, to Pittsburgh for $2,000 and a 20-year-old rookie outfielder named Joe Kelley, who was batting only .239. While Van Haltren continued to be a good, useful ballplayer for another 11 years in the majors and ended his career with a lifetime average of .316, Kelley turned out to be one of the greatest, if not the greatest, of the Old Orioles. From 1894 through 1898, Baltimore's years in the sun, he did everything. He averaged .360 at bat, hit with power, batted in runs, stole bases, scored runs, fielded impressively and for four straight seasons didn't miss a game.

It was an astute deal, the first of several by Hanlon. In the off-season he signed a rookie named Heinie Reitz, a Chicagoan who had played minor league ball in California, and in 1893 Reitz quickly established himself as the team's second baseman. McGraw, no great shakes in the field but a terror on the bases, continued at shortstop, with a veteran named Bill Shindle, now 30 and in his eighth big-league season, at third. Robinson was behind the plate, though sharing his catching duties with two others (catchers were not expected to play every day), and Kelley was in center field. The leftfielder was a nondescript rookie named George Treadway who showed little promise but who turned out to be useful in the scheme of things. First base and right field were handled by a variety of players, one of them a taciturn youngster named O'Rourke, who was called Voiceless Tim in counterpoint to the more famous Orator Jim O'Rourke, now in the last year of his distinguished career.

Once again the Orioles began the season with high hopes, and once again the hopes were dashed. Although the team did improve tremendously, from 55 games under .500 in 1892 to only ten games under in 1893, it drifted along in the middle of the standings all season and finished a quiet eighth in the 12-team league.

Hanlon chafed. His team was not scoring enough runs and it was letting its opponents score too many. Hanlon was well aware of the significance of the new rule that had been put into effect that season, the radical lengthening of the distance between

Ned Hanlon. John McGraw wrote, in 1923, "Within a few days after his arrival Hanlon began making shifts. He took me from the bench and put me at second base. I was overjoyed and naturally thought him the best manager I had ever seen."

pitcher and batter from 50 feet to 60 feet 6 inches. (Modern baseball seems to have begun in 1893, not 1901.) The change had an immediate effect on pitching proficiency. The number of strikeouts dropped almost 50 percent between 1892 and 1893. Batting averages soared. In 1891 only nine players in the National League hit over .300; in 1894 there were 51. The overall league batting average, which had hovered around .250 for years, jumped to .280 in 1893 and to .309 in 1894. Runs came in great bunches: the record for the most runs ever scored in one season by one team was set by Boston in 1894 and still stands, even though the league played only 130 games that year. The second highest total belongs to Baltimore, also in 1894. Third highest: Philadelphia, 1894. And run totals remained high throughout the decade. Never mind John McGraw; the nineties were not a time of 1–0 ball games.

What Hanlon understood about this free-scoring game was that pitching had become relatively unimportant now that the ball was being hit more often. A few stalwarts, like the redoubtable Amos Rusie of the Giants, were able to adapt quickly to the longer distance, but pitching as a whole would take several seasons to adjust. Hanlon reasoned that if the ball were going to be hit more often, what

you wanted were smart batters who could hit hard, aggressive base runners who could move around and score, and deft fielders who could cope with the far greater number of batted balls coming their way. His 1893 Orioles, although an improving team at bat, were still nothing special, and in the field they were terrible. Only two other teams had allowed more runs. He moved to rectify this.

In June, 1893, the Orioles played a series of games in Louisville, where Hanlon became impressed by the fielding skill of the young Louisville shortstop. The rival manager turned out to be good old Blue Eyed Billy Barnie, and Hanlon worked out a deal with him, a trade that at the time seemed all in Louisville's favor. Hanlon gave up Voiceless Tim O'Rourke, who was hitting .363 at the moment, for the Louisville shortstop, who had batted .222 the year before and was hitting all of .136 at the time of the trade. The shortstop was Hughie Jennings. After the trade, even though Jennings was sick and then hurt and played hardly at all for Baltimore the rest of the season, a veteran baseball man named Jack Chapman, who had managed Louisville for years before being fired in 1892, said, "Louisville has made a great mistake in letting Jennings go." It was one of baseball's better predic-

Jennings and McGraw. In the off-season they taught baseball at St. Bonaventure College in exchange for academic instruction. After his baseball career ended, Jennings studied law at Cornell and practiced in Pennsylvania.

Willie Keeler. Sam Crawford told Lawrence Ritter that Keeler "choked up on the bat so far he only used about half of it, and then he'd just peck at the ball. Just a little snap swing, and he'd punch the ball over the infield. You couldn't strike him out. He'd always hit the ball somewhere."

tions. Jennings from 1894 through 1898 was one of the best shortstops who ever lived. He fielded brilliantly, ran the bases like a devil and batted .335, .386, .401, .355 and .328. Voiceless Tim's .363 average dropped rapidly in Louisville, fell further the next season and by 1895 he was out of the majors.

Toward the end of 1893 Hanlon found another piece to fit into his jigsaw puzzle. St. Louis had an outfielder named Walter Brodie, an ordinary hitter but a fine fielder. Brodie, called Steve after the famous Steve Brodie who had jumped off the Brooklyn Bridge, was having salary problems, a common complaint now that there was only one league and the owners were in the driver's seat again. St. Louis tried to trade him to various clubs for another player, without success. "That left me no alternate," the St. Louis owner said, "but to sell his release, because I was determined to have harmony in the ranks." Hanlon bought Brodie, paid him what he wanted, put him in center and moved Kelley to left.

Now he had two thirds of a superior outfield, but he still needed a rightfielder, and a first baseman as well. His eyes fell on Brooklyn. Early in 1893 Willie Keeler, 21, tiny, frail-looking, with only 34 games in the majors, fractured a bone in his ankle while playing for the Giants. Ball clubs did not keep injured players around very long in those days, and Keeler was released. Late in the season, his ankle healed, he returned to the big leagues with Brooklyn, where he got into 20 games and batted .313. The Dodgers also had a first baseman, one of the supreme sluggers of the pre-1900 game, the famous Dan Brouthers, a six-foot-two-inch, 210-pound giant. But Brouthers had been in the majors since 1879, was 36 years old and had played in only half of Brooklyn's games in 1893; he seemed near the end of his career.

Hanlon didn't care. He needed a hard-hitting first baseman and nobody hit harder than Brouthers. In Baltimore he hit a ball that, according to an old account, ". . . touched Mother Earth 60 feet from the fence on the outside of the grounds. Then it galloped up Calvert Street and assaulted a Blue Line car. . . ." A policeman retrieved the ball and returned it to the club, which had it gilded and kept as a souvenir.

So, in January, 1894, Hanlon pulled off the fourth and last of the shrewd deals that created the Old Orioles. He gave Brooklyn Bill Shindle, the veteran third baseman, and Treadway, the nondescript outfielder, each of whom had batted .260 that season, for Keeler and Brouthers. Brouthers played only one year for the Orioles before succumbing

to age, but in that season—1894—he batted .347, led the team in runs batted in and scored 137 runs. Keeler, playing a full season in 1894 for the first time in his career, batted .371 and scored 165 runs, and in his subsequent years with the Orioles batted .377, .386, .424 and .385. He averaged almost 220 hits a year during those five glorious seasons, stole almost 50 bases a year and scored an average of more than 150 runs.

Now Hanlon's masterpiece of a ball club was complete: Wilbert Robinson, catcher; Dan Brouthers, first base; Heinie Reitz, second base; Hugh Jennings, shortstop; John McGraw, in Shindle's place at third base; Joe Kelley, left field; Steve Brodie, center field; Willie Keeler, right field. Everyone but Brodie and Reitz is now in the Hall of Fame at Cooperstown. The No. 1 pitcher was Sadie McMahon, but Hanlon kept reaching around for others: Bill Hawke, Tony Mullane, Duke Esper, Kid Gleason. It didn't matter. This was a hitting team, and a fielding team.

The Orioles began the season against New York and Boston, the two best teams in the league, and won five games out of six. Boston, which had won the pennant three straight times, was undefeated when it played Baltimore, and the game went into the ninth inning tied 3–3. Then the Orioles exploded, scored 12 times and won 15–3. They went on to take 24 of their first 34 games and a firm hold on first place. They had arrived. Boston, still a powerful ball club—remember all the runs they scored that year—fought back but the Orioles, hitting hard, running bases insolently, fielding superbly, held onto the lead for three months. They did not invent the hit-and-run and the squeeze and the double steal and all those things—which had been in use in baseball for a decade—but they perfected them and used them to the hilt. And they hit—oh, how they hit. Their batting average *as a team* was .343. Only the Phillies that same year, of all the teams that ever played baseball, had a higher team average.

Keeler, Brodie, Brouthers and Kelley, who batted second, third, fourth and fifth through these early months of the season, were particularly phenomenal. In a 9–3 win over Cleveland in June they had 12 hits among them. In two victories over St. Louis a few days later, Keeler had 7 hits, Brodie and Brouthers 6 apiece, Kelley 4. The Orioles swept the hard-hitting Phillies 9–5, 18–14 and 18–11 and by June 25 had a four-game lead over Boston.

But in July, with Hanlon's new team still ahead of the more established, more highly respected clubs, umpire Tim Hurst was moved to declare,

Keeler, McGraw, Jennings and Kelley (clockwise from top L). The picture belies this testimony by McGraw on his old team: "We were in the field and the other team had a runner on first who started to steal second, but first of all he spiked our first baseman on the foot. Our man retaliated by trying to trip him. He got away, but at second Heinie Reitz tried to block him off while Hughie...covered the bag to take the throw and tag him. The runner evaded Reitz and jumped feet first at Jennings to drive him away from the bag. Jennings dodged the flying spikes and threw himself bodily at the runner, knocking him flat. In the meantime the batter hit our catcher over the hands with his bat so he couldn't throw, and our catcher trod on the umpire's feet with his spikes and shoved his big mitt in his face so he couldn't see the play."

"Baltimore is hitting over their heads. Jennings, Reitz, Brodie, young Keeler . . ." He predicted that when the inflated Oriole batting averages subsided, so would the team. A couple of weeks later Hurst seemed a brilliant prophet. The hitting had slowed down, and the Orioles were stumbling. Louisville beat them 6–0, 11–1. Robinson got hurt and went home to recuperate. Reitz was hurt. So was McGraw. Despite the tobacco-juice-and-dirt legend, the Old Orioles sat out games when they were injured. On July 24 Amos Rusie of the Giants shut them out 1–0 and the Orioles fell out of first place. By the end of July they were five games behind Boston.

Then they got it all together again. Robinson, Reitz and McGraw returned to the lineup and Hanlon shook up his batting order, a radical move in those more rigid times. He put McGraw in the cleanup spot, of all places (his .340 batting average was 27th in the league, only sixth best on the team), and the team began to move. Maybe it was McGraw's timely hitting that did it, or maybe it was simply the overpowering impact of Kelley, Keeler and Brouthers, who batted one-two-three ahead of McGraw, at the top of the Baltimore batting order. In a four-game series with Cleveland in August,

Kelley had 13 hits in 19 at bats, Keeler 10 in 19, Brouthers 10 in 17. The Orioles, leading the league in stolen bases, fielding better than any other team, won by such scores as 16–3, 19–12, 21–5, 20–1.

Boston tried to keep pace but the Orioles, off on a winning streak, squeezed back into first place on August 30 and kept on going. They won 18 straight games and 28 of their last 31 to win the pennant. Kelley hit .393 for the year, Keeler .371, the supposedly light-hitting Brodie .366. Except for Reitz at .303 (and Heinie had 31 triples and batted in 105 runs) every man in the lineup hit .335 or better. Brouthers drove in 128 runs. Kelley and Keeler each scored 165 runs, McGraw 156, Brouthers 137, Jennings and Brodie 134 each. The success-starved city of Baltimore saluted the champions with a tumultuous parade and a riotous demonstration during which 20,000 people snakedanced through the streets of the city. "I'm going to run for mayor," joked Hanlon.

But sourness followed, triggered mostly by McGraw, who had a genius for making enemies. He had been knocked down once in spring training by a rival manager after blocking a player on the basepaths. He did grab base runners' belts to slow them down as they passed, stood in their way deliberately

Brouthers and Robinson. McGraw's fondness for his old teammates led him to employ an older Robinson as his first lieutenant; Brouthers, along with Amos Rusie, was a watchman at the Polo Grounds when McGraw reigned there.

McGraw. "Around the circuit fans hated him, taunted him, called him 'Muggsy' to arouse his ire. They never failed in this, for he loathed the name. But it never was to their advantage to stir him to anger — for then he was cold and hard and tough, and there was no holding him and no stopping him, at bat or in the field." — Frank Graham

to make them run around him, stepped on their feet as he took throws at the bag. This did not make him terribly popular. When he would skip a base when the umpire's back was turned and take a shortcut between first and third or second and home, he was thumbing his nose at authority, acting the outlaw. Other Orioles followed his lead. Harold Seymour, in his monumental history of baseball, says they would run into a first baseman to knock the ball out of his hands, throw masks in the way of a runner heading home, jostle a catcher trying to handle a ball at the plate. *The Sporting News* said the Orioles were "playing the dirtiest ball ever seen in this country," and John Heydler, an umpire in the 1890's who later became president of the National League, said, "The Old Orioles were mean and vicious, ready at any time to maim a rival player or an umpire. The club was never a constructive force in the game. The worst of it was they got by with much of their browbeating and hooliganism." McGraw was the worst. He was called "the toughest of the toughs and an abomination of the diamond . . . a rough, unruly man . . . he uses every low and contemptible method that his erratic brain can conceive to win a play by a dirty trick."

McGraw got into the center of a controversy after the season ended, when the Orioles were slated to meet the New York Giants, who had come on strongly to pass Boston and finish second, in a new postseason series called the Temple Cup. The cup had been put up by William C. Temple, a stockholder in the Pittsburgh club, for a showdown between the first- and second-place teams. A players' purse from the gate receipts was to be divided: 65

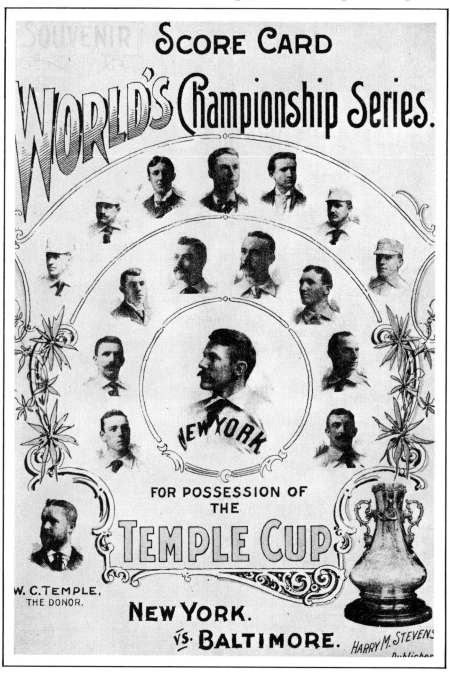

SOUVENIR

SCORE CARD

WORLD'S Championship Series.

NEW YORK

FOR POSSESSION OF
THE

TEMPLE CUP

W. C. TEMPLE,
THE DONOR.

NEW YORK.
vs. **BALTIMORE.**

HARRY M. STEVENS
Publisher

THE TEMPLE CUP

TWO-STEP   MARCH.

COMPOSED   BY

JOHN W.   CAVANAGH.

The Temple Cup.

DEDICATED TO OUR CHAMPIONS,

THE NEW YORK BASE BALL CLUB.

1. Park A. Wilson. 2. Charles A. Farrell. 3. George van Haltren. 4. Roger Conner (released). 5. Jouett Meekin. 6. Huyler Westervelt. 7. Amos Rusie. 8. W. H. Clark. 9. Lester German. 10. John J. Doyle. 11. John Ward. 12. M. J. Tiernan. 13. George S. Davis. 14. W. B. Fuller. 15. Edward Burke. 16. James Stafford. 17. W. H. Murphy.

New York's sweep of the first Temple Cup competition in 1894 capped great seasons for Meekin (rear, third from R) and Rusie (rear, extreme R), who won two Series games each, and closed the extraordinary career of Monte Ward (C, behind catcher's gear). Joe Tinker called Ward "a star outfielder, a brilliant infielder and a better pitcher than Radbourn. And he was one of the best base runners who ever lived." Ward batted as high as .372; won 163 games, including a perfect game in 1880, in less than seven years as a pitcher; registered a .562 percentage as a manager; founded the Brotherhood of Professional Base Ball Players; initiated the formation of the Players' League; earned a law degree at Columbia during his playing career — and, after retiring from uniform, became president of the Boston Braves and attorney for the National League.

The Baltimore playing field, 1897. The cost of its construction (a predecessor burned down in 1894) was used by Hanlon to justify tight reins on his growing payroll.

The 1898 Orioles, the city's last pennant winner for more than 70 years. In the 1920's, a New York *World-Telegram* reader told that paper's Joe Williams, "Individually, you haven't lost much in having missed seeing the Old Orioles. But collectively, oh, my dear scribbler, could you have seen them, your whole life might have been different."

percent to the winners, 35 percent to the losers.

The Orioles, led by McGraw, balked at the idea. Their salaries had ended when the season ended, and McGraw argued that the chance of ending up with the meager 35 percent losers' share wasn't worth the effort of playing. Monetary practicalities overcame professional confidence, and the Orioles decided they would not play unless there was a straight 50-50 split. Hanlon and Monte Ward, the Giants' manager, agreed to the 50-50 idea, but when William Temple heard about it he was infuriated and threatened to withdraw the cup. The managers agreed to return to the 65-35 formula, but several players on each team made private 50-50 agreements.

The Temple Cup games were played, but they were not an esthetic success. The Orioles, overwhelming favorites, played listlessly and lost four straight, 4–1, 9–6, 4–1 and 16–3. Vonderhorst said, "The whole Temple Cup business has been a farce." Temple was so outraged that he sold his Pittsburgh stock and left baseball. A newspaper condemned "the unsportsmanlike squeal of McGraw et al before the series commenced."

The Orioles came back to win pennants again in 1895 and 1896. In 1895 they played desultorily until August when, lying third, they began another late-season rush to the flag, winning 22 of 26 to take over the lead and 41 of their last 51 to win comfortably over second-place Cleveland. Despite William Temple's disenchantment, the Temple Cup series was staged again, and again the Orioles played like automatons, losing to Cleveland four games to one. In 1896 they were stronger, winning the pennant easily by almost ten games and whopping Cleveland four straight times in the Temple Cup. McGraw was less in evidence these two seasons. Laid low by tonsillitis and, later, by typhoid fever, he missed 35 games in 1895 and appeared in only 18 all season in 1896. Dan Brouthers was gone, Hanlon selling him shortly after the 1895 season began and using three different first basemen over the next four seasons. Reitz was injured much of 1895 and the versatile Kid Gleason, later a real-life character in Ring Lardner's Jack Keefe stories, filled in. Brodie began to fade in 1896 and was traded after that season.

But the heart of the club—Jennings at shortstop, Kelley in left field, Keeler in right—stayed intact from 1894 through 1898. These three, more than anyone else, kept the Orioles' reputation for winning baseball high. Even in 1897, when they finished second to Boston, the Orioles played superb ball.

Their second-place won-lost record was almost identical to their runaway pennant performance of the year before, and they beat Boston's pennant winners four games to one in the fourth and final Temple Cup series.

Boston beat out Baltimore again in 1898, but again the Orioles played good baseball. In fact, over the five-year period that began in 1894, five years during which they finished first three times and second twice, they had an overall winning percentage of .680. That figure, applied to a modern 162-game season, would translate to an average of 110 victories a year for those five years. The Old Orioles were indeed something special.

And, then, it was all over. The nova vanished. Hanlon and Vonderhorst worked out a stock-transfer deal with the owners of the Brooklyn club, a bizarre arrangement that left Hanlon and Vonderhorst with 50 percent ownership of Baltimore and 50 percent ownership of Brooklyn, and the Brooklyn owners with 50 percent of their own club and 50 percent of Baltimore. Hanlon, still president of Baltimore, resigned as manager in 1899 to become manager of the Brooklyn office of this odd combine, announcing as he did that he was switching Jennings, Kelley and Keeler to that club. He won the pennant with Brooklyn in 1899 while Baltimore, now managed by McGraw, sagged to fourth place.

Hanlon won again with Brooklyn in 1900, but before the season began the National League decided to reduce its membership from 12 teams to eight, and the Baltimore franchise was jettisoned. McGraw and Robinson, the only true Old Orioles still with the club, went off to play for sixth-place St. Louis. In 1901 the brand-new American League put a team in Baltimore and named McGraw to manage it, but it finished well down in the standings; in June of 1902 McGraw abandoned it and jumped back to the National to begin his saga as manager of the Giants. That was the last gasp. In 1903 the moribund Oriole franchise followed McGraw to New York to become the American League's entry there. The club was called the Highlanders at first but became somewhat better known later on as the New York Yankees.

Thus, the Old Orioles. They may not have been precisely what John McGraw said they were, but they were one hell of a baseball team. For five years they were the dominant force in baseball, a team whose stars peaked together, whose best years came at the same time. They all faded rather quickly once the glory years ended. Except for Keeler, none continued as a top star. McGraw's playing career ended before he was 30. Jennings's skills deteriorated rapidly; he took to playing first base instead of shortstop and showed little of his former glitter at bat and on the bases. Kelley turned to managing, and while he continued to play the outfield he was nothing special anymore. It was over, that's all.

It was a strange team, brought together by Hanlon's genius, fired up perhaps by the catalyst of McGraw's fury. How good were they really? Who knows? McGraw went to his grave insisting they were the best that ever was, but in 1927 Wilbert Robinson gave a different opinion. Interviewed during the World Series in which the Yankees of Ruth and Gehrig, Lazzeri and Dugan, Meusel and Combs, were crushing the Pittsburgh Pirates in four straight games. Uncle Robbie was asked how these Yankees would have fared against the Old Orioles. Robinson had had a bitter falling-out with McGraw years earlier, and his reply to that question in 1927 did nothing to heal the breach. "They would have beat our brains out," he said.

Long after joining the Giants, McGraw said of the Orioles: "Every year later on we had a reunion....It was like an old college football team."

SECOND INNING:
1901-1909

The fundamental reason for the popularity of the game is the fact that it is a national safety valve. Voltaire says that there are no real pleasures without real needs. Now a young, ambitious and growing nation needs to "let off steam." Baseball furnishes the opportunity. Therefore, it is a real pleasure.... That is what baseball does for humanity. It serves the same purpose as a revolution in Central America or a thunderstorm on a hot day....
A tonic, an exercise, a safety-valve, baseball is second only to Death as a leveler. So long as it remains our national game, America will abide no monarchy, and anarchy will be too slow.

—Allen Sangree, 1907

LATE in 1900 National League owners informed Ban Johnson that they were amenable to sitting down with him for a discussion of his upstart league, then kept him standing in the hall outside their meeting room for several hours and left him there when they adjourned. Johnson's reaction to this snub was to overthrow the National Agreement, under which all organized baseball operated, and declare open war by abandoning the regional concept of his league and installing clubs in the four eastern cities of Boston, Philadelphia, Baltimore and Washington. With the aid of disgruntled National League pitcher Clark Griffith, Johnson skimmed off enough talent that all eight American League teams began the 1901 season with a distinct "major league" flavor. Of the 182 players who contributed significantly to the American League's inaugural major league season, 111 of them were former National Leaguers.

The first to be hard hit by American League raiders were the Boston Braves, who lost Jimmy Collins, Chick Stahl and Buck Freeman to the crosstown Pilgrims, and the St. Louis Cardinals, robbed of John McGraw, Mike Donlin, Wilbert Robinson and their crack battery of Cy Young and Lou Criger. Because of the National League's stubborn refusal to raise its $2,400 salary ceiling, players on all its teams were readily susceptible to offers from Johnson's emissaries. Dreyfuss and other farsighted owners circumvented the threat by paying clandestine bonuses to their stars to retain their loyalty, but intransigents like Soden of the Braves and Andrew Freedman of the Giants chose to scorn the American League in the belief that it would soon collapse and thus allow them to reclaim their players as had happened after the Players League war. Between the farsighted and the stubborn within their own league were clubs with no particular stance like the Phils and Reds. Entering the 1901 season with their strongest club to date, the Phils lost Nap Lajoie to the fledgling Philadelphia Athletics but still managed to vie with the Pirates for the pennant deep into September despite having no better replacement for Lajoie than 34-year-old Bill Hallman, a .184 hitter. The Reds, also in search of their first National League flag, finished last but showcased Sam Crawford, the league's top slugger, and Noodles Hahn, whose 22 victories were the most by a pitcher for a cellar team until Steve Carlton won 27 for the Phillies in 1972.

Player-managers led both pennant winners in 1901. Though only 28, the Pirates' Fred Clarke already had five seasons as a manager under his belt,

whereas Clark Griffith, his counterpart with Charlie Comiskey's White Sox (who had stolen not only the Chicago National League entry's players but their nickname as well), had no previous bench experience. Griffith's club was nothing exceptional, and it ducked in under the wire because neither the Pilgrims nor the Athletics were able to sort out their talented pitching staffs until the season was nearly over. Establishing a set lineup was a problem common to all American League teams. The Orioles, with "Iron Man" Joe McGinnity and the best hitting in either league, finished only fifth when their Hall of Fame-studded roster proved incapable of playing as a unit under McGraw, and Cleveland went through 14 pitchers before deciding on a regular rotation. The Braves in contrast used just five pitchers in all of 1901, and the Phils got by with only six.

Critics of the American League cited Lajoie's easy capture of the triple crown as evidence that the AL product was inferior. Lajoie, they pointed out, had never even finished among the top five hitters in the National League. Buck Freeman's slugging with the Pilgrims was also viewed askance. Overlooked in the haste to malign the American League's showing was Freeman's 1899 season in the National League when he clubbed 25 homers (the most hit by any major leaguer until 1919, except for Ned Williamson's 27 for the 1884 White Stockings, all of them coming in fluky Lake Park, whose fences were so short that in every other season balls hit over them were declared ground-rule doubles). Other American League leaders were Cy Young in wins and ERA, Bill Keister in triples and Irv Waldron in at bats. The latter two are among the most mysterious figures to wear major league uniforms. Playing only one season—in 1901, split between Milwaukee and Washington—Waldron hit .311, score 102 runs and then disappeared completely. Keister's biography is even more baffling. He played five full seasons and parts of two others, never saw action for the same team two years in a row, never played the same position two years in a row and was dropped by the Phils after the 1903 campaign in which he hit .320 and led the club in RBIs.

What made the Keister saga so strange was that by 1903 the Phils were in desperate need of players. American League raiders had stripped them of almost every front-liner from their 1901 contender. The Phils resorted to legal steps in 1902 to recover their stars, and the Pennsylvania Supreme Court ordered Lajoie and others to rejoin them, but Johnson sidestepped the law by transferring Lajoie

Larry Lajoie. Ed Walsh said, "If you pitched inside to him, he'd tear a hand off the third baseman, and if you pitched outside he'd knock down the second baseman." Grantland Rice thought "a Lajoie with Cobb's speed might have batted .500."

LAJOIE
CHEWS
RED DEVIL
TOBACCO

Ask him if he don't

QUEEN CITY TOBACCO CO.
Cincinnati, O.

Rube Waddell. He drank, chased fire engines and regularly went to jail for non-support. But, said Branch Rickey, "When Waddell had control — and some sleep — he was unbeatable."

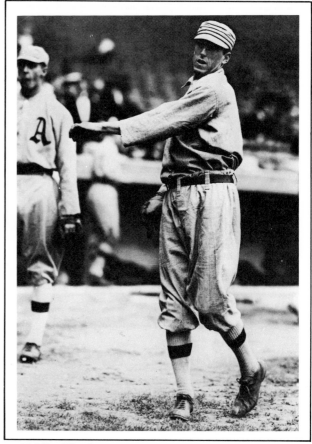

Eddie Plank. A 1901 graduate of Gettysburg College, Plank was as reliable as Waddell was not. Ty Cobb called him one of the five best pitchers in the years through World War II.

from the Athletics to Cleveland and keeping him out of Pennsylvania where he could be arrested. Johnson was not so successful in dealing with John McGraw. Owed $7,000 by the Orioles, McGraw bargained for his release from the club rather than reimbursement on the condition that he could take several of the Orioles' stars along with him to the Giants, who had hired him as their manager. When Joe Kelley left Baltimore to sign as skipper of the Reds and enticed Cy Seymour to accompany him, the Orioles suddenly lacked enough players to field a team. Johnson countered the National League's sabotage attempt by operating the Orioles for the rest of the season on league funds and stocking the club with players contributed by the other American League teams. At the season's close the Baltimore franchise was shifted to New York, where players for the new squad were pirated from the National League. By securing a foothold in the nation's largest city, Johnson convinced National League owners that peace at any price was essential. Soden and company at first proposed a merger similar to that offered the American Association after the 1891 season, but Johnson realized he held the upper hand and would accept no less than a treaty that acknowledged his league as major and allowed it to keep virtually all disputed players. In

return Johnson made only one important concession: he would not transfer the financially troubled Detroit team to Pittsburgh to compete with the Pirates.

The treaty came too late to arrange a "World Series" between the pennant-winning Athletics and Pirates. Pittsburgh's repeat champs won by an all-time record 27½ games over second-place Brooklyn and were one of the most powerful teams ever assembled. Wagner, Clarke and centerfielder Ginger Beaumont all hit well over .300, and each of the five regular pitchers won at least 16 games. The season schedule still only called for 140 contests, depriving the Pirates, who won 103, of a chance at the record 116 victories the Cubs would set in 1906. Connie Mack's Athletics by comparison had a season-long struggle with the St. Louis Browns, who had replaced Milwaukee in the league after 1901 and fashioned an instant contender by looting the rival Cardinals of no fewer than seven regulars. Even without Lajoie the Mackmen had the league's top scoring outfit, headed by Lave Cross who hit .342 and knocked home 108 runs. But it was the A's pitching that decided the issue, as their southpaw pair of Waddell and Eddie Plank won 44 games and Bert Husting chipped in a 14–5 record after being obtained from the Boston Pilgrims. Husting,

1903 World Series. The contract said that "the minimum price of admission shall be 50 cts. and the visiting club shall be settled with by being paid 25 cts. for every...ticket sold."

like Waldron a year earlier, dropped unaccountably from view after his outstanding season and never again played a single inning in a major league uniform.

The year 1903 is instantly remembered as the year the first World Series was played, the Pilgrims defeating the Pirates five games to three behind the pitching of Bill Dinneen and Cy Young. Missing from many books is the reason the Pirates lost. Quite simply, their magnificent pitching staff of the

year before had been seriously hurt by Sam Leever's arm injury and the defection of Jack Chesbro and Jesse Tannehill to the American League. In addition, Ed Doheny, the Pirates' temperamental left-hander, suffered a breakdown on the eve of the Series and had to be forcibly removed to a mental hospital. Doheny's violent departure was not the game's only tragedy that season. Under still-unexplained circumstances, Ed Delahanty, the Senators' prize acquisition from the Phils, had fallen to his death after an altercation aboard a train crossing

Lou Criger, Hugh Duffy and an unidentified man. Criger was Cy Young's personal catcher, traveling with Young from Cleveland to St. Louis to Boston. Duffy was manager of the Phils at the time this photograph was made, ten years after he hit his epochal .438.

John Peter Wagner. Ed Barrow said "there is no question that Honus Wagner was the best all-round ballplayer who ever lived." Among those who concurred were Sam Crawford, Bill Klem, John McGraw and Branch Rickey.

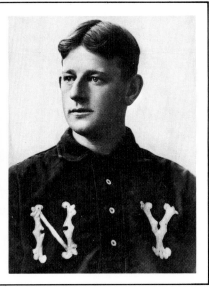

Cy Young, Dummy Taylor, Jack Chesbro (L to R). Young retired in 1912; he later said, "I guess it was about time. I was 45 years old. I never had a trainer rub my arm the whole time I was in baseball." Taylor, a deaf-mute, won 117 games in a nine-year career. He once was ejected from the Polo Grounds for insulting umpire Hank O'Day in sign language. Chesbro won 41 in 1904, but wild-pitched the winning run home the last day of the season, costing New York the pennant. His widow spent much of her life attempting to have the scorer's ruling changed to a passed ball.

Niagara Falls, and in the preseason, Tiger pitcher Win Mercer, who just days before had been appointed player-manager, committed suicide by gas inhalation in San Francisco. Events on the field were no less strange, particularly in Brooklyn, where at the season's end Ned Hanlon sanctioned a trade that sent Bill Dahlen, one of the game's best shortstops, to the Giants for a mediocre replacement and then failed to retain rookie right-hander Henry Schmidt, whose 22 victories represented the most ever by a modern-era pitcher playing only one major league season. But while Brooklyn was losing ground rapidly because of executive ineptitude, both New York and Chicago were on the rise. The Cubs (rechristened by a Chicago sportswriter commenting on the team's penchant for signing young players—"cubs"—to replace those stolen by the American League) were now managed by Frank Selee who had lost none of his touch despite failing health. Always sharp at spotting talent, Selee had replaced the aging infield with which the Cubs had begun the century with three speedsters named Tinker, Evers and Chance and was carefully building the most formidable pitching staff in the game.

In New York, McGraw avoided his mistakes with the Orioles and hired hungry young players like Art Devlin and George Browne to support his two mound aces, McGinnity and Christy Mathewson. Although no regular hit above .286, by 1904 McGraw's club was ready to replace the Pirates at the front of the National League when Dummy Taylor won 21 games to go with Mathewson and McGinnity's combined total of 68, giving the Giants a "Big Three" that won 89 contests and lost only 35.

In the first exciting pennant race of the new century the Pilgrims triumphed on the season's final day by besting the New York Highlanders in the opening game of a doubleheader when Jack Chesbro wild-pitched home the winning run in the ninth inning. The irony was that Chesbro, the winner of a modern record 41 games that summer, had almost single-handedly carried a club that had looked in the preseason to be one of the league's weakest. As McGraw and Giants' owner John Brush still did not recognize the treaty with the American League, the Pilgrims were deprived of an opportunity to play in their second straight World Series.

Chesbro was not the only American Leaguer to have a superb year. Cleveland's Nap Lajoie won his fourth straight batting title. His .376 average fell several notches below his league record .422 in 1901, but still stood 132 points above the league average, and his 102 RBIs and 208 hits were by far the most in the majors. Although no records were set by Lajoie, his 1904 performance might be considered the best, under the circumstances, by a hitter in this century. The "dead ball" era was already very much in vogue. In the first year that the two leagues went to a 154-game schedule, only one American League team, Cleveland, was able to average over four runs a game.

With the eight American League franchises now stabilized, patterns that would last for many decades had begun to emerge. The Senators for the second straight season had finished in the cellar; the White Sox had only one hitter who struck more than two homers; and Cleveland, the top hitting club in the league, also had the two stolen base lead-

John L. Sullivan and Jimmy Collins, 1904. Collins "was the first modern third baseman...coming in for bunts and playing an alert, mobile game." — Ed Barrow

ers and the ERA champ, yet could finish no better than fourth. In only their fourth year of existence, these three clubs had developed the character traits that would haunt them for many decades. Washington would never quite live down "First in war, first in peace, and last in the American League"; the White Sox would remain the "Hitless Wonders" until the century's eighth decade; and Cleveland, just once a cellar finisher in the league's first 68 years of existence and always adorned with statistical leaders and future Hall of Famers, would somehow contrive to win only three pennants. A fourth club, the Tigers, also made strides toward achieving

an identity in 1904 when Bill Yawkey (uncle and foster father of future Red Sox owner Tom Yawkey) bought the team and immediately improved it by obtaining Bill Coughlin and Germany Schaefer to shore up the league's poorest infield. The Tigers from then on would always have exceptional front office leadership, and upon bringing young center-fielder Ty Cobb up from the minors late in 1905 to play alongside Sam Crawford, they became instantly competitive.

American League clubs by no means had a monopoly on unwelcome character traits. Beginning in 1900 the Boston Braves, just two years earlier the

Jack Dunn, Sam Crawford, Harry Steinfeldt (L to R). Dunn was a fair pitcher, and occasional infielder, for Brooklyn and other clubs — but later a judge of talent who discovered Ernie Shore, Babe Ruth and Lefty Grove. Ty Cobb remembered Crawford as "the big dog in the meat house" when Cobb joined the Tigers. Steinfeldt, whose name did not fit the metric requirements of F. P. Adams's poem about the Cub infield, made a living performing with Al Field's Minstrels before entering baseball.

BALL PLAYERS

THIS NEW PATENTED

Reach Pneumatic

Head Protector

For Batters

Was designed by the largest makers of sporting goods, in your interest, and is thoroly practical in all respects.

PATENTED JANUARY 24, 1905

Price **$5.00** each

Every Ball Team Should Have One.

So many batters have been put out of the game by being struck in the head by pitched balls that the demand for some protection for the batter caused us to design this Pneumatic Protector which we know will prevent injuries of this nature.

It is not only the loss of the player's services that is involved, but his usefulness to a team is impaired even after he recovers, as he is timid when approaching the plate, which necessarily effects his batting.

Our Protector will restore the confidence of the player. It protects every part that is liable to injury. With the knowledge that he is thoroughly protected, the player will be as valuable to a team as he was formerly.

It will also inspire confidence in the timid batter who is afraid to hug the plate which is the secret of all successful batters.

FOR SALE BY

A. J. Reach Co., Philadelphia, Pa.

AND BY ALL SPORTING-GOODS DEALERS

Frank "Wildfire" Schulte was an unlikely customer for Reach's Head Protector. Charles Van Loan, describing a Cub victory, once wrote, "Schulte came home with the winning run like Balaam entering Jerusalem."

Ed Walsh. Sam Crawford described Walsh's spitter in *The Glory of Their Times:* "I think that ball disintegrated on the way to the plate and the catcher put it back together again. I swear, when it went past the plate it was just the spit went by." Charles Dryden said Walsh was the only man who "could strut while standing still."

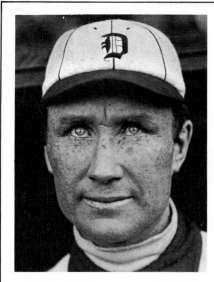

Hughie Jennings, Walter Johnson (as a rookie, 1907), Hal Chase (L to R). Jennings' calm managerial theory: "If you have to begin fining them, it's time to get rid of them." Johnson's impact was such that, after winning five games in his first season, he was picked on an all-time all-star team by Billy Sunday: "He is young and shown himself a wonder." Chase was accused of throwing games as early as 1909. Jim Price of the New York *Press* said of him, "He has a corkscrew brain."

proudest team in baseball, commenced a record for futility that resulted in only two pennants and one second-place finish in five decades. Their pitching staff in both 1905 and 1906 numbered four 20-game losers. One of them, Vic Willis, who set a twentieth-century mark by losing 29 games in 1905, escaped to the Pirates the following spring. Willis, probably the finest pitcher not in the Hall of Fame, lost 92 games over four years with the Braves. In Pirate livery he won 90 games over the next four seasons, then balked when traded to the Cardinals in 1910 and retired after that season. The Cardinals, one of the National League's strongest clubs in the century's second quarter, were easily its weakest up to

Kansas City Monarchs, 1908. Black baseball was a semi-professional affair early in the century. This part-time team consisted largely of former college athletes, including Tom and Ernest McCampbell (sixth and tenth from L). They were both physicians.

The Chicago Leland Giants of 1907 and the New York Lincoln Giants of the pre-World War I era. The Lelands were organized by Frank C. Leland (in suit), but dominated by Rube Foster (rear, extreme R). Honus Wagner called him "the smartest pitcher I have ever seen in all my years in baseball." He was also founder of the Negro National League. The Lincoln club boasted John Henry Lloyd (middle, C), who was the club's manager, and Spottswood Poles (rear, extreme R), the "black Ty Cobb."

Arthur "Bugs" Raymond. At 27 he won 27 games for the Giants, on a 2.47 ERA. At 29, fired by McGraw for drinking during a game, he was tending bar near the Polo Grounds. At 30, he was dead.

were other third basemen from the game's early years with even better credentials for entry. Deacon White—brother of Will, the Redlegs' early mound great—played on National League pennant winners in three different cities and retired at 43 after the 1890 Players League season with some 25 years of service as a professional and the distinction of being a member of both Chicago's fabled "Big Four" in 1876 and Detroit's in 1887. From Collins's own era were Tommy Leach and Lave Cross, the latter having held the record for most career base hits by a third baseman until it was broken by Brooks Robinson. Yet Cross and Leach have never come close to induction into the Hall of Fame; nor have two other dead-ball third-base artists, Bill Bradley and Harry Steinfeldt. Steinfeldt for years had the reputation of being the real catalyst on the Cub teams that featured Tinker, Evers and Chance, and it was his arrival from Cincinnati in 1906 that gave the Cubs the final ingredient they needed to break the

that point. After seeing their team finish second in 1876, National League fans in St. Louis were made to wait 50 years before their club ranked as high again. The 1908 version was one of history's dreariest outfits and personified at its worst the style of play during the dead ball era. Despite a staff ERA of 2.64, the Cardinals lost 105 games when they were able to cross home plate only 372 times, an average of less than two and a half runs a contest.

Since the inception of the Hall of Fame in 1939, those responsible for selecting its members have traditionally named the top performers at every position from each era. The notable exception has been third base. Of all third basemen retired before 1920 in the major leagues, only one, Jimmy Collins, is represented in Cooperstown, and a large part of his support came because he managed the Pilgrims, the first team to win a World Series. Collins was a fine player and deserving of selection, but there

Mordecai Brown. Asked if his curve was helped by his missing index finger, he said, "To know for sure, I'd have to throw with a normal hand, and I've never tried it."

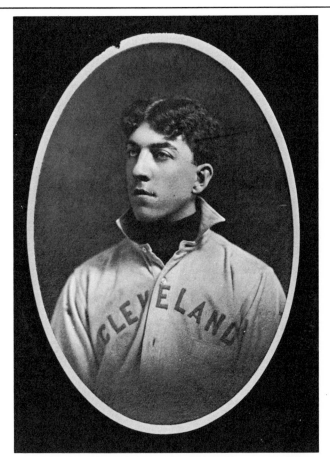

Addie Joss. He used a pitch described as a "false rise" to register a career ERA of 1.88, second lowest in history. Billy Sunday preached the sermon at Joss's funeral, and league stars played a benefit game that brought his widow $13,000.

The Series RBI leader, and also the Sox regular season leader, was George Davis, who once held the record for most career base hits by a switch-hitter. Like all the aforementioned third basemen, shortstop Davis is not in the Hall of Fame. Much of the reason is the acclaim that went to Tinker, Evers and Chance after they were immortalized in Franklin P. Adams's verse. Of the three only Chance was much of an offensive threat, and the poem's message to the contrary, the trio was far from being the era's top double-play combination or even its best infield unit. But in an age where the game's only medium was the newspaper, and sportswriters could make or break reputations with a stroke of the pen, Tinker, Evers and Chance became legendary, and half a dozen or so better infielders of their time have been shortchanged. Even Chance's nickname "The Peerless Leader" becomes suspect when it is taken into account that Selee constructed the backbone of the Cub team before ill health forced him to step down in 1905 and that Chance's later managerial endeavors with the Yankees and Red Sox resulted in abject failure.

As late as 1906, team nicknames were still determined more often by sportswriters than by the clubs

lock the Giants and Pirates had held for five years on the National League pennant. The league leader that year in hits and RBIs, Steinfeldt was also runner-up to Wagner for the batting championship and the top fielder in the game at his position.

In racing to 116 victories the Cubs made such a mockery of the pennant chase many missed noting that the second-place Giants, although 20 lengths back, won more games than the American League flag bearers that season, the White Sox, and that the Pirates, 23½ games out in third place, won exactly the same number. Accorded little chance in the Series, the White Sox won easily when Cub pitchers lapsed and allowed 22 runs in six games after recording an incredible staff ERA of 1.76 during the regular season. Led by Ed Walsh, the Sox held the Cubs to only nine earned runs—remarkable but nowhere near the record set the previous autumn by the Giants, who gave the A's only three runs, none of them earned, and blanked them four times, including the last three games in a row after Chief Bender of the A's pitched a shutout of his own in the second Series contest. Hitting star for the Sox was George Rohe, a career-long sub who was installed at third base on a hunch by manager Fielder Jones and led both clubs with 12 total bases.

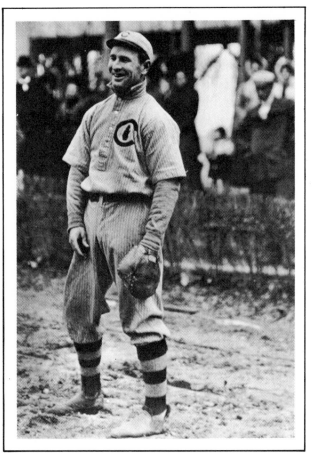

Frank Chance's career was cut short by repeated beanings. Joe Tinker may have explained it when he said, "Chance and McGraw were born to battle on baseball fields."

Johnny Evers and his son. Hugh Fullerton called him "a bundle of nerves with the best brain in baseball." The nerves failed him when he suffered a breakdown in 1911, and his intensity so affected his disposition that fellow players called him "The Human Crab."

themselves. The New York American League entry was called the Highlanders because the club played in Highland Park; Boston was a year away from the moment its owner would decide Red Sox was a more fitting name for a ball team than Pilgrims; Brooklyn was still called the Superbas even though Hanlon, who had been responsible for the nickname, was now managing the Reds; and Cleveland, depending on the mood of the day, was known as either the Blues or the Naps, the latter in honor of team star and manager Nap Lajoie. Cleveland fans were not above resorting to other, less flattering sobriquets for their club in 1906 when the Naps led the American League in every major department except games won. In a strange sidelight, Elmer Flick, their batting title winner of the year before, raised his average five points and yet did not finish among the top five hitters. Flick's .306 average in 1905 was the lowest to win a batting championship until Carl Yastrzemski's .301 in 1968, and when Wagner slumped to .339 in 1906 but still proved an easy batting champ in the National League, it was forecast that the game was in the throes of another downward hitting trend. Notions of moving the mound back an additional ten feet were quickly dispelled by the meteoric ascension of Ty Cobb.

In 1907 Cobb embarked on the first of his three successive seasons of World Series play as the Tigers squeezed past the Athletics in a rainy summer that saw the A's fall nine games short of playing a full schedule and the Tigers four. The A's actually lost fewer games than Detroit and could theoretically have won the pennant if the schedule had been completed, but little was made of this possibility at the time. Nor was much attention paid to Washington, who dropped into the cellar again after breathing seventh-place air in 1906; that year, the Red Sox had plummeted past the Senators after player-manager Chick Stahl committed suicide during spring training. It was still too soon for Washington fans to realize it, but their fortunes had been blessedly altered by an early season injury to reserve catcher Cliff Blankenship. Unable to play, Blankenship was sent by the club on a scouting mission and signed Clyde Milan, whose 88 stolen bases in 1912 would give Cobb a target to shoot at, and a young right-hander from an Idaho semi-pro league who would set marks that pitchers in both leagues would still be shooting at 70 years later. Walter Johnson won only five games in 1907—his first season—and five again in his last season two decades later, but the years between enabled him to log more victories than any other twentieth-century hurler.

Pitching was almost the entire game in the National League in 1907. Bob Ewing of the Reds tallied 333 innings and a 1.73 ERA that was memorable only in that it matched the ERA of the *entire* Cub staff. Orval Overall and Three Finger Brown were Chance's big winners, but Carl Lundgren, Jack Pfiester and Ed Reulbach among them allowed less than a run and a half a game. The Cubs seldom scored much more themselves; Steinfeldt, again the team RBI leader, totaled only 70. When Dave Brain of the Braves led both leagues in homers, the National League's premier slugger for the second time in three seasons was a man who never hit another home run in the majors. Back in 1905 Fred Odwell of the Reds had led the National League with nine homers, which represented all but one of his career total. Home runs off the dead ball were so rare that in 1908 the White Sox hit only three, and as late as 1909 Red Murray of the Giants was a league leader with seven.

Because a rookie named Fred Merkle erred in his baserunning one afternoon, the 1908 National League pennant race overshadowed that of the American League, but when put in full historical perspective, events in the AL appear more significant. With the lone exception of the slapdash Federal League finale in 1915, the 1908 Cleveland Naps are the only club ever to lose a pennant by a half-game margin. The rub was that Cleveland, by dint of playing a full schedule while the other contenders had postponements, entered the season's final day already eliminated from the race and had no choice but to helplessly watch the Tigers battle the White Sox in Chicago with the flag on the line. Had Ed Walsh bested the Bengals' Bill Donovan, the Sox would have won a pennant with a team batting average of .224. When Walsh, who had already worked in over 460 innings and won 39 games, proved too arm-weary to stem Cobb and company, the Tigers earned a second crack at the Cubs, and Cleveland sneaked into second place ahead of the Pale Hose on percentage points. The furor in Cleveland over losing a championship on weather mishaps belatedly led officials in both leagues to adopt a rule that all postponed games with bearing on a pennant verdict had to be made up.

The National League had no alternative but to order a makeup game when the Cubs and Giants ended the season deadlocked after the Merkle game had been ruled a tie. The fates conspired against Merkle on all fronts that season, for the Pirates played the Cubs on October 4 with a chance to eliminate both the Giants and Chicago and clinch the pennant themselves. After winning 5–2, the Cubs held a one and a half game lead on the Giants pending the outcome of New York's final three games with Boston. The odds were heavily against the Giants sweeping all three, but it happened. And when Jack "The Giant Killer" Pfiester beat the Giants in the makeup game, Merkle was doomed to wear the goat's horns for the rest of his life, and Johnny Evers once more became destiny's darling for having observed Merkle's failure to touch second base on Al Bridwell's apparent game-winning single and having called it to umpire Hank O'Day's attention. The final turn of the screw for Merkle was that on September 4, a few days before his boner, Evers had tried to have Warren Gill of the Pirates declared out by O'Day on a similar play. O'Day had refused at the time but realized upon reflection that Evers was correct in his argument that a runner who failed to touch the next base on a game-winning hit was subject to being a force out. Since the Gill incident was reported in many papers and since the doings of the Cubs and Pirates, the Giants' chief rivals all through the decade, should have been of prime concern to McGraw's men, the real goat in the affair was not Merkle, a 19-year-old simply following the lax custom of his day, but McGraw, for failing to alert his charges to Evers's ingenuity.

Lost in the flurry of season-ending twists was the brilliant pitching duel on October 2 between Ed Walsh and Cleveland's Addie Joss. Walsh was superb, surrendering only one run, but Joss was perfect. By not allowing a single base runner in a 1–0 game with the pennant possibly riding on every pitch, Joss gave the most exceptional pitching performance under pressure in history. Two years later, before succumbing to meningitis, Joss again threw a 1–0 no-hitter against the White Sox, this one only slightly less than perfect. Expiring while still in his prime years, Joss could not match the lifetime marks of other pitchers of his era but was the equal of any of them during the brief time he played, and his selection for the Hall of Fame in 1978 is among the most gratifying acts the Old Timers Committee has performed. Another unrecognized achievement in 1908 was Tim Jordan's home run crown. Jordan, also the National League homer king in 1906, was the sole Brooklyn batter to hit above .243 or knock in more than 39 runs. So dismal had become the club that began the century as the game's finest that it included four 20-game losers and hit only .213 as a team. Jordan's bat was all that kept Brooklyn from edging out the Cardinals of 1908 for the title of history's most punchless club. Performing for the future tenants of Ebbets Field were a centerfielder who hit .195, a leftfielder who knocked in only 18 runs and catcher Bill Bergen, who in 1909 posted the lowest average ever by a batting championship qualifier when he hit .139.

The Tigers held off the rebuilt Athletics long enough in the summer of 1909 to become the first American League team to win three pennants in a row. A lap behind were the Red Sox, totally remodeled since the days of Jimmy Collins and Cy Young, and the White Sox clung to fourth place when Frank Smith replaced the ailing Ed Walsh as the club's workhorse. Cleveland, close for so long, was suddenly an old team; New York had the *enfant terrible* Hal Chase and little else; and the Browns, after their strong start in 1902, had joined the Senators as the league's traditional doormats. In the National League almost the same situation existed. The Pirates rocketed back to the top after six years away, while the Cubs and Giants each finished over .600. Excepting the Phils, who had challenged in 1901 before being demolished by Ban Johnson's raiders, no other National League team had mustered even a mild pennant gesture since 1900.

One phenomenon that suggested the dead-ball era might be winding down was the sharp increase in 1909 in the use of relief pitchers, although it was not evident in the Series that fall. George Mullin, the Tigers' ace, went the route in all three of his starts, and Pirate rookie Babe Adams, who stunned everyone by winning three games including the decisive seventh contest, also did it without any help from his friends in the bullpen. During the regular season, however, pitchers in the two leagues had combined for 110 saves as contrasted to only 32 in 1901. It had been just three years since Jack Taylor of the Cubs and Cardinals had concluded a string of 139 straight complete games, but in 1909 the National League had only three pitchers who worked in over 300 innings and Three Finger Brown's arm was the only one to complete more than 30 games— standards that once had been used to separate the true pitcher from the dilettante.

By winning pennants in each of his first three seasons as a manager, Hughie Jennings of the Tigers set a standard that only Ralph Houk has matched (1961–1963) in the years since. With Mullin still at his peak and Cobb, that season's triple crown winner, with his best years still ahead of him, Tiger fans did not mourn unduly over their club's third successive failure to bring home a world championship. Surely before Cobb retired, they reasoned, there would be many more opportunities. Sadly, though, there was none. The opportunities went instead to two other young stars who first blossomed in 1909. Before both were done, they would play on championship clubs in not one but two American League cities, and each, as would Cobb, would feel the wind at his back from one of baseball's two largest twentieth-century scandals.

The parallels among Ty Cobb, Tris Speaker and Eddie Collins are many. Left-handed hitters, dazzling base thieves, outstanding fielders, they amassed over 11,000 hits among them, and dominated the game in the second decade of the century.

—David Nemec

Ty Cobb. "He was possessed by the Furies."
— Bozeman Bulger

PITCHER:
The Real Frank Merriwell
By Jonathan Yardley

HE CAME up at the turn of the century, throwing his first pitch for the New York Giants on the afternoon of July 18, 1900. He was a big right-hander—he stood six feet one and a half inches, weighed 195 pounds, and back home in Factoryville, Pennsylvania, they called him "Husk"—and he was still a kid, a month shy of his twentieth birthday. But he had tenacity, intelligence and the poise of the veteran that indeed he was, having refined his superb skills playing against older men in the tough town leagues of northeastern Pennsylvania. He had four pitches: a respectable if not explosive fast ball, a big curve, a change of pace, and a peculiar reverse curve that no one had seen the likes of. He called it his "fadeaway"—now we call it a "screwball"—and he could put it wherever he wanted.

His name was Christopher Mathewson. Over the years to come, as his fame spread and his legend grew, the sportswriters sought a heroic moniker for him and came up with "Big Six." It had nothing to do with his number: in those days ballplayers had neither numbers nor names on their jerseys. It had something to do with his height, or with a famous New York fire brigade, or with a powerful typographical union—no one seems to know for certain. But that was strictly for the headlines. To the fans, who loved him as they did no other player, he was simply "Matty." He was the golden god of baseball's true golden age.

Tradition has it that the golden age was the twenties, when Murderers Row stalked the land, home runs flew off every player's bat, and great screaming crowds filled the giant ballparks. Maybe so. But I'll take the game played before the war, a

Giant fans. Chief Meyers told Lawrence Ritter. "The Giants didn't even start home games until four o'clock. . . . The stock market didn't close until three and then two or three thousand people who worked down at Wall Street would take the elevated train up to the Polo Grounds. They were all good fans."

game that turned not on a single stroke of the bat but on the cumulative results of finesse, guile, savvy, "brains." In most essentials it was the game we know today—by the time Matty joined the Giants virtually all the rules of modern baseball had been established—but the conditions of play made it significantly different. The diamonds were rough and erratic and a player could expect the ball to take uncertain bounces; gloves were small and unsophisticated, designed more for protection than entrapment; and the ball, even after the rubber core was replaced in 1911 with cork, was heavy and dead. Long hits were rare, so pitchers could afford to let the opposition swing away and then ask the defense to go to work. The result was a fascinating combination of high batting averages and low earned run averages, high hit totals and low run totals. The game was decided on the field of play, not on the flight of the ball into the bleachers.

It was a game for which Matty was ideally suited. He was strong, so he could pace himself over the long innings and go the distance; of the 551 games he started over seventeen seasons he completed 434, an extraordinary percentage of .788. He had perfect control, so he almost never defeated himself; he averaged a mere 1.6 bases on balls every nine innings. He was intelligent, so he knew that a hit doesn't necessarily mean a run, that his fielders

could do the job behind him, and that he could stop the opposition when it counted; he permitted 7.9 hits every nine innings, but he allowed only 2.13 earned runs. And he was courageous. He liked to pitch in the moments when the game hung in the balance (he once wrote, or hired Jack Wheeler to ghost for him, a book called *Pitching in a Pinch*), so he could reach back for his best stuff and beat the batter man against man; his strikeout total of 2,502 ranks sixth in major league history (yet he wasn't known as a strikeout pitcher) and his victory total of 367 ranks fourth.

Of all these formidable assets, it was his control that most impressed his contemporaries. Here is the young Ring Lardner, writing in a strained attempt at the vernacular: "They's a flock o' pitchers that knows a batter's weakness and works accordin'. But they ain't nobody else in the world that can stick a ball as near where they want to stick it as he can. I bet he could shave you if he wanted to and if he had a razor blade to throw instead of a ball. If you can't hit a fast one a inch and a quarter inside and he knows it, you'll get three fast ones a inch and a quarter inside and then, if you've swung at 'em, you can go and get a drink o' water. . . . I ain't tryin' to make you believe that he don't never fail to pitch where he's aimin' at. If he done that, he wouldn't be here; he'd be workin' agin the angels in St. Pe-

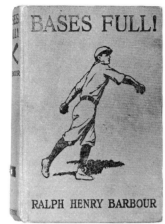

BASES FULL!

RALPH HENRY BARBOUR

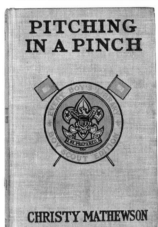

PITCHING IN A PINCH

CHRISTY MATHEWSON

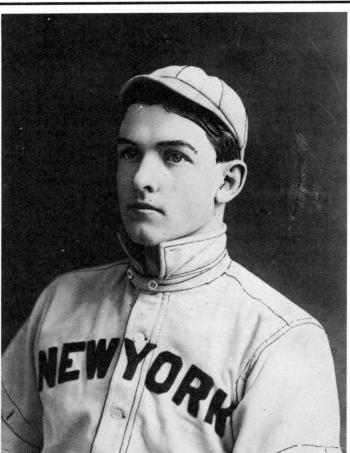

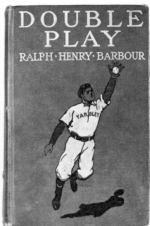

DOUBLE PLAY

RALPH·HENRY·BARBOUR

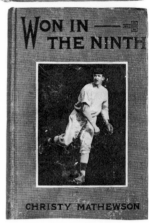

WON IN THE NINTH

CHRISTY MATHEWSON

In 1932, Gilbert Patten, who used the pseudonym Burt L. Standish, wrote, "For my hero I took the given name Frank to express one of his characteristics. . . . Merriwell was formed by a combination of two words, Merry—expressive of a jolly, high-spirited lad—and well, expressing abundant physical health. I've never heard of a person, living or dead, whose family name was Merriwell." But in Mathewson he had a model, as did Ralph Henry Barbour, who wrote 23 boys' baseball novels. Matty's own books were written by newspaperman John N. Wheeler.

Ring Lardner (L) and colleagues, all willing admirers of Mathewson. Virginia Woolf said Lardner "writes the best prose that comes our way." Those who challenged him included John N. Wheeler, Mathewson's ghost (standing, L) and, seated, Fred Lieb (second from L), Damon Runyon (third from L), Bozeman Bulger (C), and Grantland Rice (second from R). In foreground, (R), is concessionaire Harry M. Stevens.

The Polo Grounds, from Coogan's Bluff and from the right-field bleachers. "It's not the physical but the nostalgic quality of Coogan's Bluff that counts," wrote Milton Bracker. The view included little more than the shortstop, leftfielder, centerfielder and — before the game — Matty leading the team from the center-field clubhouse.

"Matty was the greatest pitcher I ever saw. He was the greatest anybody ever saw. Let them name all the others. I don't care how good they were. Matty was better."
—John Kieran

ter's League. But he's got ten to one better control than any guy I ever seen, and I've saw all the best o' them."

And here is Chief Meyers, who caught Matty for seven seasons from 1909 to 1915, quoted in Lawrence Ritter's classic oral history of early baseball, *The Glory of Their Times*: "What a pitcher he was! The greatest that ever lived. He had almost perfect control. Really, almost perfect. In 1913 he pitched 68 consecutive innings without walking a man. That record is still standing, I think. That season he pitched over 300 innings and I doubt if he walked 25 men the whole year. Same thing in 1914. I don't think he ever walked a man in his life because of wildness. The only time he might walk a man was because he was pitching too fine to him, not letting him get a good ball to hit. But there was never a time he couldn't throw that ball over the plate if he wanted to."

The greatest that ever lived? A considerable statement, one made of course with prejudice and affection. Certainly, though, there is evidence to back it up: the complete games, the bases on balls, the earned-run average, the strikeouts, the victories. And there is more. Three times Matty won 30 or more games in a single season, and nine times he won 20 or more. In five seasons his earned run average was under 2.00, and in the 1909 season it was a breathtaking 1.14. In 11 World Series games, when a pitcher is in the ultimate "pinch," he had an earned run average of 1.15 and completed ten games, two of them in extra innings; in the 1905 World Series he pitched three shutouts—one of the transcendent accomplishments of baseball history —and in the 1913 Series he pitched another one. His skill was matched by his durability; his career total of 4,777 innings puts him ninth on the all-time list, and only three of those ahead of him did all their pitching in the game's modern era.

He was a great pitcher by any standard, but if one is to seek a final judgment about such things he probably cannot be called the greatest. That is because one man stands ahead of him: Walter Perry Johnson. In large measure, as they always do in baseball, statistics tell the story: 413 victories (exceeded only by Cy Young's 509, more than half of which were gained before 1900); 532 complete games out of 666 starts (a percentage of .799); 5,923 innings pitched (third behind Young and a nineteenth century pitcher, Pud Galvin); and 3,499 strikeouts (ahead of everyone).

What is of even greater import is that while Matty pitched for John J. McGraw's Giants, contenders in all but three of his years with them and

league champions in five, Johnson pitched for the city that was "first in war, first in peace, and last in the American League." In Johnson's 21 years with the Senators, from 1907 to 1927, his record was 413 wins and 277 losses, a percentage of .599; the *team's* record was 1,559 wins and 1,609 losses, a percentage of .492. The Senators were in last place twice, seventh place five times; they won only two pennants, and those late in Johnson's career when his best stuff was gone. Matty's teammates were the likes of Roger Bresnahan, Art Devlin, Fred Snodgrass, Al Bridwell, Chief Meyers, Josh Devore and Larry Doyle. Johnson for most of his career had the backing of nondescripts and incompetents. It is true, of course, that to a great degree the Giants were powerful because they had Matty on the mound (*and* Rube Marquard, *and* Iron Man Joe McGinnity, *and* Hooks Wiltse, *and* Jeff Tesreau); but Johnson often accomplished what he did in spite of, not thanks to, his teammates.

Like Matty, Johnson was a gentleman; the two men admired each other for personal as well as professional reasons. But Johnson never caught the public's fancy the way Matty did; Matty had what we now call charisma, and that along with his remarkable performances made him into a legend. Few if any Americans of his day were so widely and deeply loved. Certainly no baseball player was, nor has any been since—not even Babe Ruth, who was loved in the way one dotes upon a large, boisterous, gifted but irresponsible child. Matty was worshiped. Men and women of all classes held him up as a model for their children, and no doubt secretly regarded him as one for themselves. In our national mythology he occupies a place alongside Frank Merriwell and Dink Stover: a flawless hero, a paradigm. That in point of fact he was not, that there was at least a narrow gap between myth and reality, only makes him more appealing: a true hero is rarely a saint.

It needs to be understood that until Matty came along, baseball had given the nation no real heroes. There were men whom fans admired for their surpassing skills—Cy Young, Honus Wagner, Cap Anson—but generally ballplayers were held to be a coarse and irresponsible breed. Most of them were country boys with rough manners, profane speech and little formal education. They spent much of their time on trains and in second-rate hotels, drank too much, and chased—or were chased by—women. If many American parents wanted their boys to grow up to be ballplayers, they kept it pretty much to themselves.

But then Matty joined the Giants, and he spar-

Walter Johnson. The tip that led Washington to sign him came in a letter: "He knows where he's throwing because if he didn't there would be dead bodies strewn all over Idaho."

kled like a diamond in a coal mine. To begin with, he looked like a Greek god; as E. E. Cummings wrote of Buffalo Bill, "Jesus he was a handsome man." His origins were not low but relatively lofty: his mother had some inherited money and his father was a gentleman farmer. Not merely had he gone to school, he had gone to college—at Bucknell, where he was a three-sport star, president of his class, a singer in the glee club, and a member of two literary societies. He was known to be scrupulously honest, he was shy and self-effacing, he spoke against the evils of drink, and he refused to play ball on Sundays. Even the pugnacious McGraw melted before his charm; he considered Matty the greatest pitcher the game had known, treated him as an equal instead of an underling, and once invited him and his wife to move into the McGraw apartment for an extended period—after which, Mrs. McGraw said, the two couples "were still on speaking terms." On the road with the Giants he stayed away from the Baseball Annies and sought milder, more elevated diversions. Hugh Fullerton, a Chicago journalist who knew him fairly well, described them:

"Christy Mathewson, who is one of the hardest players to find when not in uniform (also when he is playing), specializes in chess and when on the circuit spends his evenings at chess clubs playing the local champions. He plays cards well, but never when he can find a worthy opponent at chess or checkers."

If all this makes him out to be a prig, the happy truth is that he was not. "He was a good man," his wife said once, "a very good man, but he was not a goody-goody." His refusal to play Sunday ball had less to do with religious scruples than with a promise he had made to his mother—not a very meaningful one, either, since only three National League teams then played Sunday home games, and the Giants were not among them. He was known to take a drink, though certainly in moderation, and at various times he smoked cigars, cigarettes or a pipe. What most took for shyness and reserve, others took as coldness and aloofness. The journalist Fred Lieb has written: "He disliked having people —even teammates—close in on him. When a train carrying the Giants stopped at a smaller city, Mathewson, playing cards beside a window seat, would pull down the shade of the Pullman so that none of the people on the train platform could see him." Though he did not hesitate to capitalize on his role as college man among semi-literates, the fact is that he was not alone; other ballplayers of the day who had attended college included Harry Hooper, Eddie Collins, Davy Jones, Jack Coombs, Frank

The "boyish countenance and Apollo-like form" were also displayed on the vaudeville stage, in an act called "Curves," written by Bozeman Bulger. Chief Meyers and actress May Tulley co-starred.

Chance, Chief Bender, Chief Meyers, Ed Reulbach, Eddie Plank and Art Devlin. His demeanor on the field was not without flaw; baseball historian Harold Seymour reports that once, in Philadelphia, he slugged a lemonade boy who supposedly had insulted one of the Giants, splitting the youth's lip and knocking loose several of his teeth. He had a taste for showmanship off the field (like many of his contemporaries, he made off-season money in vaudeville) and on, as his old Chicago Cub rival Mordecai "Three Finger" Brown recalled in his autobiography: "I can still see Christy Mathewson making his lordly entrance. He'd always wait until about ten minutes before game time, then he'd come from the clubhouse across the field in a long linen duster like auto drivers wore in those days, and at every step the crowd would yell louder and louder."

But Brown's skepticism was the exception to the rule, inside the game and out. Once, during the 1914 season, when Matty's career was drawing to its close, a member of Boston's "Miracle Braves" is said to have taunted him during a game by yelling: "Attaboy, Milk Legs! Save the day!" To which his manager, George Stallings, sharply replied: "Lay off the guy. He's a monument to baseball." Fred Snodgrass, whom Matty could easily have treated with disdain after his infamous "muff" in the 1912 World Series, described him to Ritter decades later with abundant affection: "He was a wonderful, wonderful man, too, a reserved sort of fellow, a little hard to get close to. But once you got to know him, he was a truly good friend."

The one thing Matty didn't have much of was luck. On two of the most notable occasions in baseball history, his teammates let him down and brilliant pitching efforts went for nothing. The first took place late in the 1908 season, when Fred Merkle made his famous dash to the dugout instead of proceeding to second base; it cost Matty and the Giants not just the game, but the season, for the two teams ended in a deadlock and a play-off was required; the Cubs won it 4 to 2, as Matty was beaten by Three Finger Brown. Characteristically, Mathewson offered no alibis: "I don't believe Merkle touched second base," he said.

The pain of Merkle's historic boner was nothing, however, compared to what happened at Fenway Park in Boston late in the afternoon of October 16, 1912. It was the deciding game of a World Series between the Giants and Red Sox in which Matty had already suffered rotten luck: he went 10 innings in the second game, but Giant errors led to four unearned runs and the game was called because of darkness at a tie score of 6 to 6; in the fifth game

Merkle and Snodgrass. Mathewson called Merkle, after the "boner," "one of the gamest players that ever stood in a diamond"; after Snodgrass' "muff," Mathewson shouldered the blame for failing to call for the correct fielder on a critical foul pop.

Some Giants. Josh Devore (L) stole four bases in one inning in 1912; spitballer Jeff Tesreau (R) won 48 games in 1913-14; Roger Bresnahan (Below), a catcher speedy enough to bat lead-off, invented shin guards in 1907.

"Laughing Larry" Doyle (above L) said "It's great to be young and a Giant"; Chief Meyers (above R) represented the players in a dispute with league officials over distribution of Series money in 1911; Al Bridwell (L) would have had the game-winning hit against the Cubs on September 23, 1908, had Merkle touched second; Rube Marquard (R), purchased as a rookie for an unheard of $11,000. His speed prompted Joe Tinker to say, "You can't hit what you can't see."

Mathewson and son. In 635 games, 4,783 innings, Matty
was never once ejected by an umpire.

he gave up two runs, neither of them earned, and lost 2 to 1.

Now, with the championship on the line, Matty was pitching the game of his life against Boston's Hugh Bedient. As Tris Speaker, the great Boston outfielder, wrote about it in his autobiography: "The game quickly took the form of a magnificent pitchers' battle and I don't think Matty ever was much better than that autumn afternoon. He turned us back with machine-like precision for six innings and by that time the one run the Giants had scored in the third began to look awful big." But in the seventh Boston got lucky: a Texas Leaguer fell between two indecisive New York outfielders, and a pinch hitter doubled the runner home. Still, Matty was grinding them down—through the eighth, the ninth, into the tenth. The Giants got a run in the top of the tenth, and in the bottom of the inning "Snodgrass's Muff" and an unclaimed foul pop brought the Red Sox the championship. This is how Ring Lardner began his account of that game:

"Just after Steve Yerkes had crossed the plate with the run that gave Boston's Red Sox the world's championship in the tenth inning of the deciding game of the greatest series ever played for the big title, while the thousands, made temporarily crazy by a triumph entirely unexpected, yelled, screamed, stamped their feet, smashed hats and hugged one another, there was seen one of the saddest sights in the history of a sport that is a strange and wonderful mixture of joy and gloom. It was the spectacle of a man, old as baseball players are reckoned, walking from the middle of the field to the New York players' bench with bowed head and drooping shoulders, with tears streaming from his eyes, a man on whom his team's fortune had been staked and lost, and a man who would have proved his clear title to the trust reposed in him if his mates had stood by him in the supreme test. The man was Christy Mathewson."

It was the beginning of the end. Matty had good years in 1913 and 1914, but in 1915 his skills began to deteriorate sharply and his record fell to 8–14. Midway through the 1916 season, with his earned

Rube Marquard and son. Marquard was married for three years to actress Blossom Seeley. She performed a popular song of the day, "The Marquard Glide."

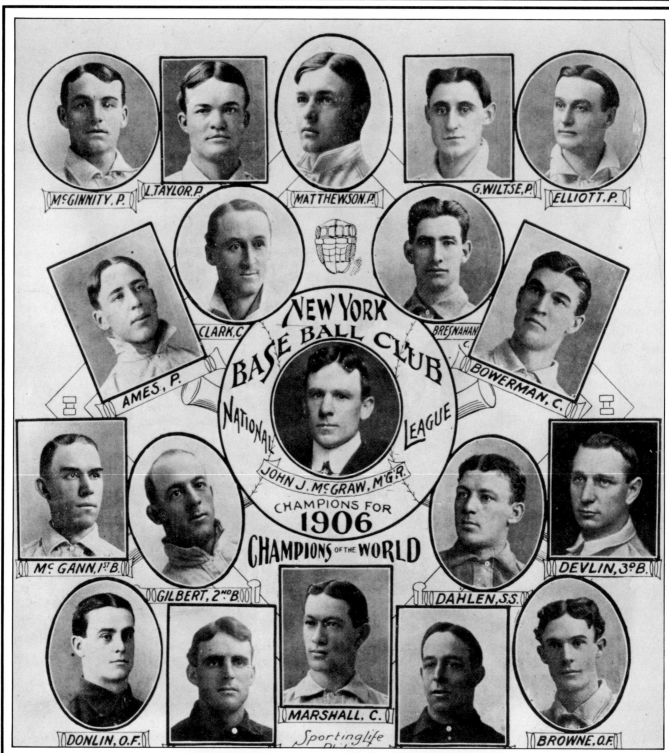

The first official World Series winners. Despite later protestations in behalf of the Orioles, McGraw said, "In my opinion, the Giants of 1905 can do anything the champion Orioles did — and have a shade on them, besides." Of the first five pitchers, McGinnity's 2.84 ERA was the highest. The offensive star was "Turkey Mike" Donlin (lower L), who had missed most of the 1902 season while serving a sentence for drunken assault. Years later, when night baseball was introduced in the minors, Donlin would say, "Jesus! Think of taking a ball player's nights away from him!" He was married to vaudevillian Mabel Hite.

Matty, McGraw, Joe McGinnity. In 1903, McGinnity three times in one month won both ends of a double-header. In 1904, he and Mathewson combined for a record 68 victories. And in the 1905 World Series, they gave up but 24 hits and 3 runs in a total 44 innings pitched. McGinnity hung on in the minors until he was 54.

In 1911, McGraw resuscitated the black broadcloth uniforms his team had worn when they beat Philadelphia in the 1905 World Series. His unerring sense of showmanship was no doubt related to his Broadway life: (R) McGraw with jockey Tod Sloan. In 1905, the two men opened a billiard parlor in Herald Square. (L) An opening day floral garland from the Lambs Club, of which McGraw was a devoted member.

McGraw's words to Cincinnati owner Garry Herrmann, when he offered him Mathewson as manager (L), were "You know he is my friend. But he can't pitch any more." Attempting to recover from the tuberculosis he contracted in the army (R), Matty returned to his home in Factoryville (C). The news service caption on this photograph was headed "'Almost well,' he says, flowers his diversion, baseball still his love — Matty comes home, his heart aglow." When players in the 1925 World Series donned black armbands (Bottom), and a memorial prayer was offered in Mathewson's behalf, K.M. Landis said, "Why should God wish to take a Thoroughbred like Matty so soon, and leave some others down here that could well be spared?"

run average up near 3.00 and his record at 3–4, McGraw worked out a trade that permitted him to go to Cincinnati as player-manager. He pitched only one game, which he won 10 to 8. The score against him persuaded him that he was through, and from then on he concentrated on managing. Like most star players, he was not very good at it; over two and a half seasons his Reds won 164 games and lost 176, and failed to finish in the first division.

At the close of the 1918 season Matty enlisted in the Army and, at war's end, was sent to Europe to join the Army of Occupation. He was terrified of the ocean and highly susceptible to seasickness, and on the way over became badly ill. His luck did not improve in Europe: somehow he was exposed to poison gas left over from the war, and it had a debilitating effect. By the time of his return to the States in 1919, tuberculosis set in.

Much of the rest of his life was spent in a sanatorium in the Saranac Lakes region of New York State. He did attend the 1919 World Series—where he sat in the press box with Hugh Fullerton, making notes on questionable play that seemed to confirm widespread rumors that the Series was fixed—and for a while he served as a coach with the Giants.

In the early twenties he came out of the sanatorium to become the largely figurehead president of the Boston Braves, but he did it against the advice of his doctors and it was more than his health could stand. He died on the night of October 7, 1925, at the age of 45.

The day of Matty's death the Washington Senators beat the Pittsburgh Pirates, 4 to 1, in the first game of the World Series. The winning pitcher was Walter Johnson. It is said that when he learned of Matty's death, Johnson turned pale and silent. The next day, all the players on both teams wore black armbands.

Eleven years after Matty's death, the Baseball Writers of America chose five men as the first inductees into the Baseball Hall of Fame in Cooperstown, New York. In the order of the votes they received, the five were Ty Cobb, Babe Ruth, Honus Wagner, Christy Mathewson and Walter Johnson. Plaques were cast in honor of each of them and placed in a room that year by year would slowly fill with other plaques honoring other men. The last line on Christy Mathewson's plaque reads: "Matty was master of them all."

MATHEWSON MEMORIAL ISSUE

Bucknell Alumni Monthly

Vol. X   November, 1925   No. 2

Christopher Mathewson, ex '02—1880-1925

My eyes are ever misty
As I pen these lines to Christy
Oh, my heart is full of heaviness today.
May the flowers ne'er wither, Matty
On your grave in Cincinnati
Which you've chosen for your final fadeaway.
     —Ring Lardner

THIRD INNING:
1910-1919

Why is baseball, you ask? Because it is like charity—it never faileth. It is always there, except on Mondays or wet grounds. And to the man who is too old to keep up with the attempt to civilize football, and too young to need so soothing a sedative as golf; who works hard when he works and wants to rest hard when he rests; who wants a drama that is as full of surprizes for the actors as it is for the audience; who wants a race that cannot be fixt like a horse-race; who is so genuine an American that he wants something to kick about without meaning it, and something to yell about that everybody around him will think more of him for yelling about— to that man baseball is the one great life-saver in the good old summer-time.

—Los Angeles Times, 1916

THERE is no more dramatic illustration of the change the financial structure of baseball has undergone than the price tag put on the Philadelphia Athletics' infield in the years between 1910 and 1914. The entire unit was then valued at $100,000. Today, the mere rumor that second baseman Eddie Collins might be available on the free-agent market would send the Steinbrenners and Krocs scurrying to the bank with moving vans. Yet by the end of 1914, when Connie Mack unloaded his high-salaried stars, he netted barely enough in exchange to stay solvent; for Home Run Baker he received virtually nothing.

Much of the same criticism that is leveled at Tinker, Evers and Chance can also be applied to the A's quartet. With the exception of Collins, all were somewhat overrated. Jack Barry, the shortstop, was a less than .250 hitter; Stuffy McInnis at first base had good but not extraordinary lifetime statistics; and Baker, although a solid third baseman for many years, had only five truly outstanding seasons as a hitter. Underrated are the contributions made by some other team members. Rube Oldring and Amos Strunk were two of the better outfielders of the era, and Jack Coombs won 79 games over three seasons before encountering arm trouble. Mack's own role has been tarnished over the years by his poor overall record as a manager and the long stretch in the American League doldrums that concluded his career, but his record from 1901 to 1914 is better than that of any other skipper over a like amount of time save the other two Macs, McCarthy and McGraw. Only a poor season in 1912 by Chief Bender and an incredible one by Smokey Joe Wood of the Red Sox prevented the A's from being his-

Ty Cobb. "Let him sleep, if he will," Connie Mack told his team. "If you get him riled up, he will annihilate us."

tory's first team to sweep five consecutive pennants.

The Cubs began the new decade by reclaiming the top rung in the National League when the Pirates once again failed to plug the first-base hole that had been created when Clarke misguidedly traded Kitty Bransfield in 1905. Awards for the most surprising teams went to the Phils, who broke .500 (largely because of leftfielder Sherry Magee, whose .331 average ended Wagner's batting cham-

"Cobb lived off the field as though he wished to live forever. He lived on the field as though it was his last day." — Branch Rickey

(Below) Cobb with Lajoie, joint recipients of the 1910 Chalmers Award, when the Browns tried to rig it for Lajoie. (R) Cobb with racer Brick Owens at Indianapolis.

"I was like a steel spring with a growing and dangerous flaw in it," Cobb said, late in his life. "If it is wound too tight or has the slightest weak point, the spring will fly apart and then it is done for." (R) Flanked by teammates Bobby Veach and Sam Crawford, 1915. Crawford said, "He sure wasn't easy to get along with."

McGraw and Mack, at the 1911 Series. "You have one of the greatest teams I've ever seen," the New York manager told Mack afterward. "It must be. I have a great team, too, but you beat us."

pionship monopoly), and the Yankees, piloted most of the way by George Stallings before Hal Chase took over late in September and brought them home second. Yankee emery-ball pitcher Russ Ford won 26 games, but the medal for bravery in the line of fire was earned by Walter Johnson for scoring 25 wins with the seventh place Senators. The American League batting championship, for the fourth year in a row, belonged to Cobb despite the skullduggery of Browns manager Jack O'Connor, who ordered his infielders to allow Nap Lajoie to bunt on them on the season's final day in the vain hope that Lajoie might overtake the much loathed Georgian.

Cobb was even more devastating in 1911, leading the league in every offensive department except home runs while hitting .420. Shoeless Joe Jackson of the Indians chased him hard before finishing at .408—the highest average in this century by a batting runner-up—and Vean Gregg, the rookie Cleveland lefty, led the league in both winning percentage and ERA, a rare double win for a pitcher with an also-ran. But the year belonged to the Athletics, who repeated as world champs by beating the Giants in the Series that earned Home Run Baker his nickname. Yet it was not so much Baker as Wildfire Schulte of the Cubs who demonstrated the impact of the livelier ball introduced the previous year. Schulte clubbed 21 homers, the most thus far in the century. Even Larry Doyle, who coined the phrase

Frank Baker's hitting, and a full house of pitchers, won the 1911 championship for Mack. That season marked the first of four straight in which Baker would lead the league in home runs.

"It's great to be young and a New York Giant," got into the act, banging 13 home runs, enough to have won the league crown in any previous year since 1899.

Explanation for the Giants' return to the top after a six-year absence could be found in Mathewson's recovery of form and the 24 wins of 21-year-old Rube Marquard. Another youthful pitcher, Phillie freshman Grover Alexander, set a modern rookie record by winning 28 times. The Braves, with no arms of consequence, young or old, registered a staff ERA of 5.08 and lost 107 games, although

rightfielder Doc Miller missed the batting championship by a single point and the Bostonians became the fifth major league club to enjoy the services of Turkey Mike Donlin. Donlin's frequent holdouts and attempts to combine a stage career with baseball kept him from the fame his gifted bat should have brought him. Even so, he was a batting runner-up at various times in both leagues and retired with a .333 average, probably a good 20 points less than what it would have been had he given the game his full attention.

One of the 1911 Series home runs that earned Baker his nickname. Fred Lieb, who saw him play, wrote in 1977, "If playing today, he would hit 40 home runs a year." But in ten years of dead ball play, he managed only 96 home runs.

Tris Speaker. "He has a voice like rumbling thunder, and his softest words sound like the growl of a mastiff." — A. H. Spink. His roommate, Joe Wood, said, "Nobody else was even in the same league with him." Speaker called the last game of the 1912 Series — the game of Snodgrass's muff — his greatest day in baseball.

The year 1912 was a season for one-year wonders. Cub third baseman Heinie Zimmerman, a steady run producer but no slugger and never again even a moderate threat for a batting championship, won the triple crown. And the Cubs' Larry Cheney nearly matched Alexander's year-old record by winning 26 games as a rookie. Over in Pittsburgh, Owen Wilson, who normally hit about 12 triples a year, chose 1912 to smack 36 and set an all-time record. In Cleveland, a rather more consistent performer, Joe Jackson, was setting the AL mark for three-base hits (later tied by Sam Crawford) at 26. Jackson had a second distinction that season: he was the only hitter to bat over .390 two years in a row and come away without the championship, as Cobb once more broke .400 en route to the sixth of his nine consecutive titles. But the only achievement that meant a pennant was Joe Wood's. His 34–5

The champion Red Sox of 1912. The little girl in the back row is Dorothy Wood. Her brother Joe is to her left. Larry Gardner (middle row, third from R) 36 years later remembered his Series-winning hit: "It meant four thousand twenty-four dollars and sixty-eight cents to me," he told Henry Berry.

Joe Wood. "Can I throw harder than Joe Wood? Listen, my friend, there's no man alive can throw harder than Smokey Joe Wood." — Walter Johnson. When an arm injury ended his pitching career, Wood played five years as an outfielder. His lifetime batting average was .283.

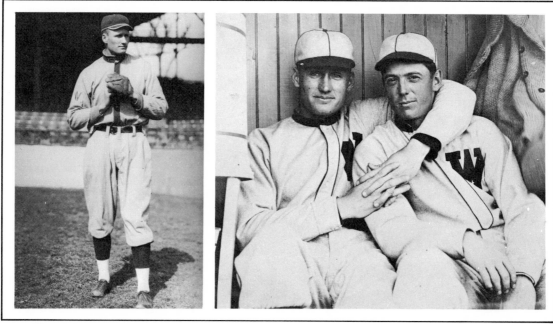

Walter Johnson, with Clyde Milan. "You never had to worry about a curve in those days from Walter, or a change of pace," Ty Cobb said in 1945. "Just speed, raw speed, blinding speed, too much speed." "Deerfoot" Milan stole 88 bases in 1912, 75 in 1913 — the only years Washington finished as high as second until 1924.

record included 10 shutouts, a 1.91 ERA and 35 complete games, figures that towered over those of every American League hurler except Walter Johnson. Wood, Tris Speaker, Duffy Lewis and Larry Gardner all emerged as stars in 1912 and brought the Red Sox home ahead of the astonishing Senators who finished second in Clark Griffith's initial season as their manager—the first time a Washington team in *any* major league had finished in the first division, much less as a runner-up.

The Giants had no record breakers in 1912 but again got good years out of all their regulars and a superb year out of catcher Chief Meyers. Although

the outcome of the National League race was never in doubt, Horace Fogel, one of the Phils' owners, was expelled for life by the league after making allegations that Roger Bresnahan of the Cardinals and other former Giant stars had rigged the season so that McGraw's men would win.

Fogel's notion was ridiculed at the time, but it should have sounded a warning note. In retrospect, there is little question that many games during the era—particularly those involving the Yankees and their suspect first baseman Hal Chase—were fixed. One of the most graceful fielders in baseball history, Chase nonetheless habitually posted the league's

Johnson winning the Chalmers as Most Valuable Player in 1913. It was perhaps the greatest single season any pitcher ever had: he won 36, losing only 7, with a 1.14 ERA and 243 strikeouts. He had 12 shutouts and pitched 56 straight scoreless innings. He also batted .261, including a 2-for-3 day as a centerfielder in the last game of the season.

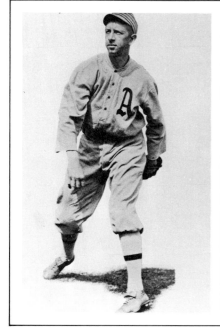  

Eddie Collins. He broke in under the name of Sullivan, in 1906 — a scheme devised by Connie Mack so Collins could keep his eligibility at Columbia. He played for a record 25 years.

Jim Thorpe. "Gee, he was an Adonis," Chief Meyers told Lawrence Ritter. "Built like a Greek god." His swinging bunt in 1917 enabled Fred Toney to win the famous "double no-hit" game over Hippo Vaughn.

Heinie Groh. He used his distinctive "bottle bat" to hit .292 in 16 National League seasons with the Giants, Reds and Pirates.

poorest fielding average at his position and displayed frequent lapses in games against tailenders. It is quite probable that many of those seemingly meaningless games, to which no one but gamblers paid much attention, were fixed by Chase; and even in his own day it was regarded as odd that the Yankee team, which had been second in 1910, could have slipped so badly that two years later it finished last.

No one has ever disputed the sincerity of the participants in the 1912 Series, however. For the first time since its inception, the world championship was not decided until the final pitch of the final game. In the first year that Fenway Park opened its gates, Boston fans saw Larry Gardner's sacrifice fly bring Steve Yerkes home with the winning run in a come-from-behind tenth-inning victory—made possible when Giant centerfielder Fred Snodgrass dropped a liner to open the rally, and Merkle and Meyers later let Speaker's pop foul fall unmolested.

A year later the Giants became the second National League team in the century to win three pennants in a row as Jeff Tesreau joined with Mathewson and Marquard to give McGraw three 20-game winners. The Phils, although a distant second, had both the league's top slugger in the refur-

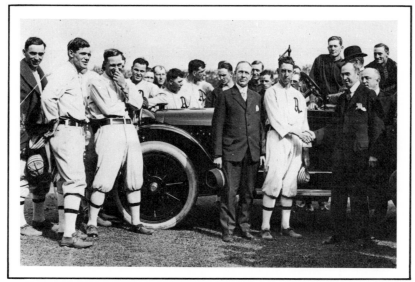

Eddie Collins wins the Chalmers for 1914. In 1943, Connie Mack was asked which of his players had been easiest to manage. "All my players, every one," he replied. "Especially Eddie Collins."

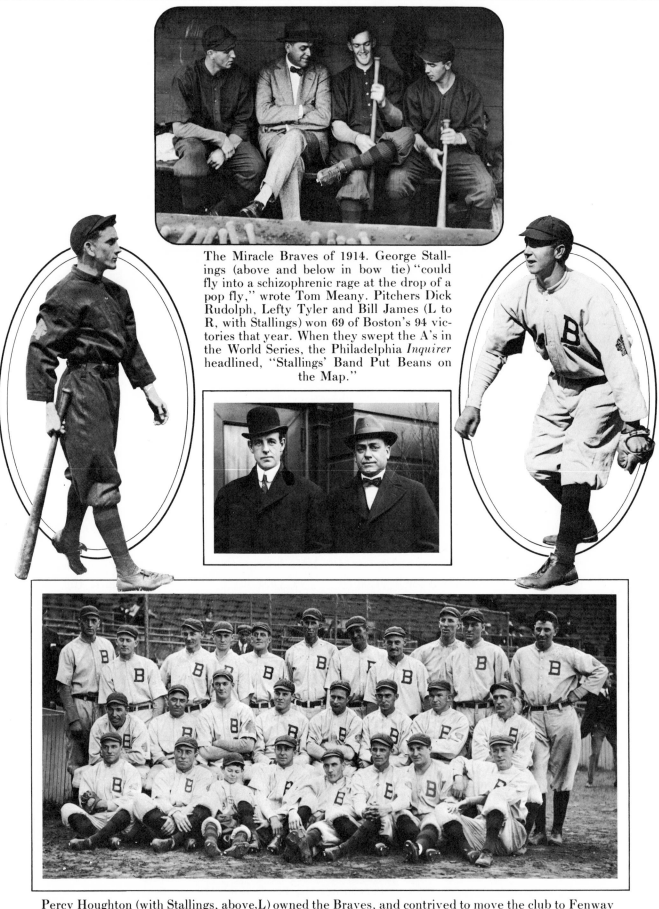

The Miracle Braves of 1914. George Stallings (above and below in bow tie) "could fly into a schizophrenic rage at the drop of a pop fly," wrote Tom Meany. Pitchers Dick Rudolph, Lefty Tyler and Bill James (L to R, with Stallings) won 69 of Boston's 94 victories that year. When they swept the A's in the World Series, the Philadelphia *Inquirer* headlined, "Stallings' Band Put Beans on the Map."

Percy Houghton (with Stallings, above,L) owned the Braves, and contrived to move the club to Fenway Park for the pennant rush (South End Grounds, where they usually played, seated only 7,000). Rudolph (above, R) was a control pitcher who occasionally used a spitter, but catcher Hank Gowdy (top row, third from R in team picture) said, "About the best you could say for it was that it was wet." Rabbit Maranville (above, L), wrote Meany, was "a midget with the arms and shoulders of a weight lifter." Late in his career, Maranville said "There is much less drinking now than there was before 1927, because I quit drinking on May 24, 1927."

bished Gavvy Cravath, up from a decade in the minors, and its leading winner in knuckle-baller Tom Seaton. At the other end of the spectrum the Cardinals replaced Bresnahan as manager with second baseman Miller Huggins but still tumbled into the basement. Aiding the fall were the league's losingest pitcher, Dan Griner (9–22), and two disenchanted outfielders, Rebel Oakes and Steve Evans, who played out the string that season while waiting for the minor Federal League to go ahead with plans to expand to big league status and dangle

lucrative contracts before current major leaguers.

In the American League the lone chord of consistency was struck by the Senators, who repeated their second-place finish of a year earlier. The Red Sox dropped to fourth after Joe Wood broke his hand, and the A's recaptured the top spot by using three young righthanders, Boardwalk Brown, Duke Houck and Bullet Joe Bush, to support the aging pair of Chief Bender and Eddie Plank. Had the Senators found a similar complement to Walter Johnson, they would have won the pennant with

(Top, L) Ernie Shore (L) and Grover Cleveland Alexander. Shore is remembered for the oddest perfect game in history: Babe Ruth was Boston's starter, but was ejected after walking the first batter. Shore came in, picked the man off first and retired the next 26 in a row. He might also be remembered for being the only man ever to lose a World Series game to the Philadelphia Phillies. Alexander, who beat him, had already won 118 games by the end of 1915, his fifth major league season. (Top, R) John McGraw and Pat "Whiskey Face" Moran, who was the manager of the pennant-winning 1915 Phillies (Bottom) and the 1919 Reds — the team that beat the Black Sox.

ease, for the Big Train in 1913 had the most awesome year of any pitcher in history. Not only did Johnson lead the league in every department, there was no one else remotely close. To fill out the days when Johnson had to rest, Clark Griffith used 23 pitchers over the season and got decent work only from rookie Joe Boehling. Between them, Johnson and Boehling had a 53–14 record, while the other 22 Senator pitchers came in at 37–50.

When the Giants again failed to win the Series, McGraw dealt for Reds' speedster Bob Bescher,

who once had a string of four stolen-base titles. But it was a Giant homegrown, George Burns, who finished as the league champ in both stolen bases and runs scored. Unfortunately for McGraw, the rest of his regulars had off years, clearing the way for the Braves to win. Much was made of the Braves' having been in last place on the Fourth of July, but their accomplishment was making up the 31½ games they had been off the pace in 1913. Improved pitching was the reason. By finding three unknowns —Dick Rudolph, Bill James and Lefty Tyler—

Babe Ruth. (Top,L) As a 16-year-old shortstop; (R, standing extreme L) as a 17-year-old catcher, both at St. Mary's Industrial School in Baltimore. (Bottom) As a 20-year-old pitcher for the Red Sox (L to R, Rube Foster, Carl Mays, Ernie Shore, Ruth, Dutch Leonard). It was his first full season and he hit four home runs in 92 at bats, when the league leader only had seven. "That's the first thing I can remember about him—the sound when he'd get a hold of one. It was just different, that's all."—Larry Gardner

Boston manager Bill "Rough" Carrigan (Top, L) holds the winner's check from the 1915 Series. Ruth considered him the best manager he ever played for. In three full managing seasons (1914-16) he finished second and won two consecutive championships; he then went into banking at age 33. Over a decade later, persuaded out of retirement, he sullied this extraordinary record by managing the execrable Red Sox clubs of the late twenties. Ruth appeared only once in the 1915 Series, as a pinch hitter, but in 1916 and 1918 would win three games and pitch 29 consecutive scoreless innings. In the team picture, the "Golden Outfield" of Duffy Lewis, Tris Speaker and Harry Hooper are first, third and fourth from L in the first row. Dutch Leonard (who would later accuse Speaker and Cobb of throwing games) is in the second row, second from R.

Benny Kauff. He led the Federal League in batting and stolen bases both years of its existence, then signed with the Giants. When he returned home to Middleport, Ohio, in 1916, the local paper reported, "He has made enough money to start a bank."

game to having one of its best. In the Series against the A's, tops in the American League in scoring, Stallings's trio was so effective that the A's could eke out but six runs while being swept in four games.

With the focus on the Braves, little was made of Dodger first baseman Jake Daubert's second straight batting title or the fact that the Dodgers, normally a dismal hitting club, had four of the league's top five hitters. Also passed over were the demise of the Indians, who finished in the cellar for the only time until 1969, when the majors went to two-division play; the 1.01 ERA posted by Dutch Leonard of the Red Sox (the closest any pitcher with over 200 innings has come to allowing less than a run a game); and the Cardinals' leap from the basement to third place after Huggins glued together a pitching staff even stronger than that of the Braves.

One factor in the Cards' climb was the Phillies' nosedive after Federal League raiders relieved them of Tom Seaton and their shortstop-second base combination of Otto Knabe and Mickey Doolan. As had happened the last time the Phils built a contender, an upstart league came along to ravage them. The Federal League, off its initial showing, looked to be a sturdy challenger to the two established circuits. Other teams besides the Phils suffered heavy casualties as the Feds went about forming their teams and took the field for the first time under a major league banner in 1914.

and in George Stallings a manager who knew how to use them, the Braves vaulted in the space of two seasons from having the worst pitching staff in the

Federal League Opening Day, 1915, at Washington Park in Brooklyn. Primary backers of the league were Harry Sinclair, later convicted in the Teapot Dome scandal, and Robert B. Ward, of the Tip Top bread fortune. During the court action that resulted from the war between the leagues, the presiding judge said: "Both sides must understand that any blows at the thing called baseball would be regarded by this court as a blow to a national institution." The judge was Kenesaw Mountain Landis.

Ty Cobb and Joe Jackson, 1914. Cobb's split-hand batting grip enabled him to move the top hand down if he wanted to pull, or push the bottom hand up if he wanted to go to left. Of Jackson, he said, "He just busted them and hoped for the best. He just did what came naturally." Jackson would take all of his bats to South Carolina with him every winter, insisting that bats, like ballplayers, did not like cold weather.

Bill Klem. For 40 years, he was the model umpire. Early in his career, when an inflamed John McGraw threatened to strip Klem of his job, the umpire replied, "Mister Manager, if it's possible for you to take my job away from me, I don't want it." Shortly before he died, he described a 1941 game in which "I walked away from the beefing ballplayer, saying to myself, 'I'm almost certain Herman tagged him.' Then it came to me and I almost wept. For the first time in my career I only 'thought' a man was tagged." Klem retired that afternoon.

Charles Hercules Ebbets opened his ballpark in Brooklyn (Top, L) in 1913. There was no grass in the outfield until midsummer. Rube Marquard and Chief Meyers (Top, R) helped Ebbets's team to its first pennant in 1916; Marquard had been released by McGraw the previous season, but went on to pitch ten more years. Casey Stengel (in profile, B) raised the flag at Brooklyn's Opening Day in 1916; as early as 1923, Damon Runyon would write, "The baseball land teems with tales of the strange didoes cut by Casey Stengel." The Brooklyn outfielders in their 1916 pennant year (Middle, L to R): Stengel, Jimmy Johnston, Hy Myers, Zack Wheat.

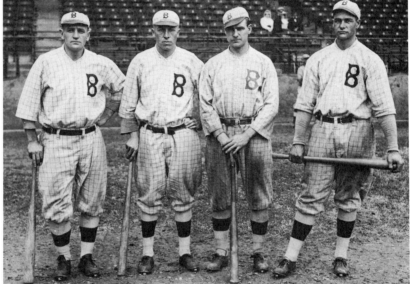

George Sisler. As a rookie in 1915, he was tried as a pitcher. He split his eight decisions, but one was a 2-1 victory over Walter Johnson. The one time he faced Detroit, Ty Cobb went hitless in five tries.

Eddie Collins. When he was sold to the White Sox, he took with him a Philadelphia salary of $14,500 — more than double what any of his Chicago teammates was making. He was barely on speaking terms with Swede Risberg, his shortstop, and was one of the few Sox who was clean in 1919.

When the Indianapolis Hoosiers—sparked by Benny Kauff, the Feds' answer to Ty Cobb—won in a tight race over the Chicago Whales, managed by Joe Tinker, and Knabe's Baltimore Terrapins, league owners were sufficiently encouraged to go after more big-name players for the 1915 season. Indianapolis was moved to Newark and Kauff was transferred to the Brooklyn Tip Tops so that the Federal League would have two clubs and their leading player in the New York area. Newark drew poorly, however, and the Tip Tops never were in contention. The Feds consequently failed to capture the media in New York and the national attention that might have been theirs for staging, in 1915, the wildest pennant race in major league history. By virtue of two postponed games that inexplicably were not made up, Chicago finished one percentage point ahead of the St. Louis Terriers and only four points ahead of the third-place Pittsburgh Rebels. The Terriers had won one more game than Chicago and thus stand as the only club to lead its league in victories and not win a pennant. Many Federal League owners wanted to tackle the two entrenched leagues for still another season, but court battles over disputed players had so depleted league resources that Fed president James Gilmore was open to peace overtures. Before the 1916 season, National and American League owners agreed to assume responsibility for unsettled Federal League contracts, permit two of their own franchises—the Cubs and Browns—to be bought by FL owners, and guarantee payment to assure the reimbursement of the investment of several others.

When the dust cleared, the Giants had come away with Kauff, the Cubs had landed Dutch Zwilling, the top Federal League slugger, and star defectors like Hal Chase, Ed Konetchy and Claude Hendrix had been embraced by their old teams. Unaccountably, other stars like Steve Evans, Ted Easterly, Vin Campbell and Rebel Oakes, still young and at the top of their game, were allowed to drift away from the majors. Campbell is an especially puzzling presence in a murky period. After vying for the National League batting championship in 1910, he waged a bitter holdout war with the Pirates the following season and was sent packing. Bobbing up with the Braves in 1912, he led the league in at bats and was third in runs scored yet once more was cut loose. In his two years in the Federal League, Campbell hit well over .300, only to vanish when the league folded, the owner of a .310 lifetime average at age 27.

One club the Federal League raiders left largely unscathed was the Giants. To McGraw's consternation, however, his team plummeted to the National League cellar in 1915. But there were consoling moments for the Little Napoleon. Larry Doyle won the batting championship (even though his .320 average was the lowest ever by a National League winner). A more important balm was the Giants' .454 winning percentage, the highest ever by a last place club. The league as a whole was so evenly balanced that the Giants finished just 14 games behind the second-place Braves, and the pennant-winning Phils scored only 73 more runs than the

John Henry "Pop" Lloyd. One of the first true giants of black baseball. Honus Wagner said, "I am honored to have John Lloyd called the Black Wagner. It is a privilege to have been compared with him."

Joe Williams. Robert Peterson, in *Only the Ball Was White*, reports that in 1914 Williams was 41-3 for the Chicago American Giants. In 1952, a Pittsburgh *Courier* poll named him the best pitcher in black baseball history.

poles in fielding and all eight pitching staffs had an ERA between 2.17 and 3.11. Above it all stood Grover Alexander, the winner of 31 games, and Gavvy Cravath, whose 24 homers broke Wildfire Schulte's twentieth-century mark.

The balance in the American League extended only down to the fourth-place Senators. As a further consolation to McGraw, his fellow tenants in the Polo Grounds, the Yankees, had no better winning percentage than the Giants, although they finished fifth. In the upper echelons of the league the Tigers became the first AL team to win 100 games and miss a pennant when the Red Sox scored their 101st win, eliminating a need to play three postponed games. Managed by 31-year-old Bill Carrigan, whom injuries had reduced prematurely to a backup catcher's role, the Sox survived an offensive breakdown when Babe Ruth racked up 18 wins in his first full season and led the club in homers despite having only 92 at bats. A breakdown on all fronts—after Eddie Collins and Jack Barry were traded, Home Run Baker sat out the season, and the Federal League plundered Chief Bender and Eddie Plank—doomed the A's to becoming the first and only team to win a pennant one year and finish last the next. The Indians also depressed their followers by trading Joe Jackson to the White Sox for three lesser lights, although one of them, Braggo Roth, led the league in homers, the first ever to do so while dividing the season between two teams. Almost the only notes of interest in the Series were that for the second year in a row a Boston team won,

Reds, the league's poorest offensive team. Somehow, in attempting to destroy their rival, the Feds had helped to achieve the goal that for years had eluded the greatest baseball minds: an almost perfect competitive balance. A mere 14 points separated the National League's worst hitting team and its best, eight points separated the two opposite

The St. Louis Stars, 1916. Frank Warfield (front, second from L) was an excellent second baseman whose career in black baseball was typical, in that he played for seven different clubs in 16 years. What was atypical was how, Robert Peterson reports, he ended the career of a contemporary player, Oliver Marcelle: Warfield bit his nose off in a fight.

Had this outfielder managed better than two hits in 22 at bats in a tryout with the Yankees in 1919, they might not have tried to buy Babe Ruth. The rookie, George Halas, found football rather more suited to his skills.

Waite Hoyt. "The secret of success as a pitcher," he said in 1927, "lies in getting a job with the Yankees." He won ten games in two seasons with the Red Sox, 157 in nine years with the Yanks.

and for the second straight year the winner played in the park of its crosstown rival. In 1914 the Braves used Fenway Park because it had a larger seating capacity than their own ancient structure. They returned the favor in 1915 by allowing the Red Sox to play in newly completed Braves Field, which had more seating than Fenway. But the event of 1915 that would have the greatest repercussions did not occur in the Series or even on the playing field. In mid-January two sportsmen, Colonel Jake Ruppert and Captain Tillinghast l'Hommedieu Huston, pooled their rather extensive capital to buy the New York Yankees.

Bill Carrigan is the lone manager to win back-to-back world championships without making the Hall of Fame. His 1916 Red Sox won the pennant over the White Sox by two games, but they needn't have had such a difficult time of it had Carrigan done what Ed Barrow would do upon taking over the club in 1918—put Babe Ruth in the outfield on days when he was not pitching. Ruth in 1916 was still exclusively a pitcher, and for that one season he and Alexander were the game's best. Alex's 33 wins enabled the Phils to improve their record a notch over the previous year, but they fell short of becoming the second Philadelphia team of the decade to hoist a repeat pennant when the Dodgers parlayed

Eddie Collins, Ty Cobb, Gen. John J. Pershing with Babe Ruth. From the Washington *Star*, July 21, 1918: "Base ball received a knockout wallop yesterday when Secretary Baker ruled...players in the draft age must obtain employment calculated to aid in the successful prosecution of the war or shoulder guns and fight." Nearly 250 players entered the service. Ruth, who was a reservist in 1918, was photographed with Pershing in 1924, when the player joined the New York National Guard.

Daubert, young outfielder Zack Wheat and a host of rejects from other clubs to win for their popular manager, Wilbert Robinson. For the third season in a row the National League leader was a dark horse, a team that had not won a pennant since 1901 and had seemed on paper to pose little threat. More so even than the Phils and Braves, the Dodgers appeared to have caught the rest of the league asleep, and when they fell decisively to the Red Sox in the Series, it was not expected they would be heard from again for a long while; the assumption was the Giants would once more assume command. In May of 1916 the New Yorkers reeled off a record 17 straight road victories, then topped that by winning 26 straight games in September. For the balance of the year, though, the team barely played .400 ball and had to settle for fourth place. Disappointed as Giant fans were, Cardinal supporters were even more despondent when their club again crumpled to last place. Huggins's crack pitching staff of 1914 was in total disarray, and only rookie third baseman Rogers Hornsby made the team interesting.

The other St. Louis club had a good-looking young infielder named Sisler and the league's RBI leader in Del Pratt. The pair were enough to boost the Browns over .500 for the first time since 1908.

Dropping below .500 by a scant three points were the Senators; in a normal year their 76–77 record would have brought them home fifth at worst, but 1916 was not a normal year. For their showing the Senators earned the honor of being the strongest *seventh*-place team in history. Forty games behind them, losing an American League record 117 games, straggled the A's, who had two capable pitchers, Joe Bush and Elmer Myers, with a combined 29–47 record, and 13 culls whose stats were 7–70.

In 1917 the two St. Louis clubs charted opposite courses. The Browns narrowly escaped the cellar despite no-hitting the champion White Sox on successive days, whereas the Cardinals bounced into third after shifting Hornsby to shortstop and watching him lead the league in slugging average. Over in Cincinnati there was cause to rejoice, as the fourth-place Reds had their best finish since 1905 and Edd Roush won the batting title with a .341 average. Strong relief pitching and the productive bats of Zimmerman, Burns, Kauff and home run leader Dave Robertson rendered the Giants an easy winner. The White Sox received excellent relief work from Dave Danforth, but the acknowledged staff leader was shine-baller Eddie Cicotte. Managed by Pants Rowland, the first skipper in the century to win a flag without big league playing

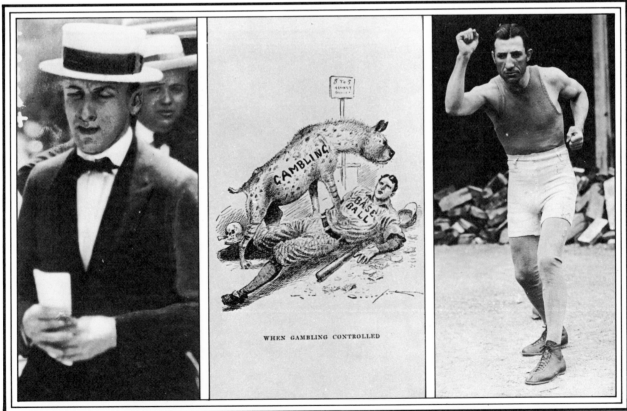

Arnold Rothstein (L) was the man who fixed the 1919 World Series; Abe Attell (R) was the former boxer who was his bag man. Although the Davenport cartoon between them, which dates from the first decade of the century, indicates that gambling's influence on the game was no novelty, the events of 1919 had an enormous impact on the nation. From *The Great Gatsby* — Nick Carraway has just met Meyer Wolfsheim, the man Fitzgerald patterned on Rothstein: "The idea staggered me.... It never occurred to me that one man could start to play with the faith of fifty million people — with the single-mindedness of a burglar blowing a safe."

experience, the Sox reversed 1916 positions with Boston. The Red Sox were still a strong club, but they found themselves caught short by Carrigan's resignation and the aftermath of Speaker's sale the previous year to the Indians after a contract dispute.

In the Series opener Cicotte outdueled the Giants' catch from the Cardinals, Slim Sallee, but the next nine days belonged to Sox right-hander Red Faber. He pitched four games and won three of them. Playing on his fourth world champion of the decade, Eddie Collins hit .409 and Jackson, Chick Gandil and Happy Felsch provided most of the Sox' slugging. A pre-Series injury to shortstop Swede Risberg forced Rowland to move Buck Weaver over from third base. Not unfamiliar with the position, Weaver had been the last fielder to make more than 70 errors in a season while playing there earlier in the decade.

The National Commission, a three-man body set up in 1903 to govern baseball, demonstrated that the game was ready to do its part for the national war effort by closing down the season on Labor Day in 1918. Consequently each of the 16 teams played fewer than 130 games, and the Red Sox won the American League pennant with only 75 victories. The abbreviated schedule created other oddities: Sherry Magee led the National League in RBIs with only 76, and not a single National League pitcher worked in over 300 innings. One who was not bothered by the short season was Scott Perry, who won 21 games for the last-place A's. Perhaps because Perry was never the same pitcher again, his feat has received scant mention in the history books.

With Jackson, Faber, Risberg, Felsch and Lefty Williams involved in war-related activities for much of the season, the White Sox bowed out of the 1918 pennant race early, leaving Cleveland and the Senators as the only hopes to contain the Red Sox. When Speaker, the Indians' new star, was suspended in August for assaulting an umpire, and Washington matched the Browns in ushering out the last vestiges of the dead ball by hitting only five team homers, Boston rode in on Carl Mays's arm and Ruth's bat. Now mainly an outfielder, Ruth tied Tilly Walker of the A's for the home run championship, then reverted to the pitcher's mound for the Series and extended the scoreless inning string he had begun in 1916 to 29⅔ before the Cubs caught up with him in the fourth game. Not much else went right for the Cubs in the Series. Hippo Vaughn gave up only three runs in the three complete games he pitched but lost two of them, and rookie shortstop Charlie Hollocher, so brilliant all season, was held almost totally in check by Mays and Ruth. Hollocher, the league leader in hits and

Say they made a great ball club and let it go at that.
Say it all once, a score of long years after.
Then, let it go at that...
—Nelson Algren, *Swede is a Hard Guy*

total bases, had lit a fire under an aging team that seemed even less pennant-worthy than the Dodgers two years earlier. But with the Giants suffering from the draft, the Reds experiencing erratic pitching and the even more erratic Hal Chase, and the Cardinals yo-yoing again into the basement after the Yankees lured away Huggins and Hornsby slumped to .281, the Cubs had a clear path to the top. Hollocher, like Scott Perry, the American League's surprise star, would never be much of a factor again. Emotional problems drove him to early retirement and eventual suicide.

Many fans were left with a sour taste by two player-management disputes late in 1918. Members of the Cubs and Red Sox voted to strike prior to the fifth Series game in a stab at resolving the long-standing dispute with the National Commission over the division of Series proceeds. The players eventually took the field with nothing settled, in part because they sensed the unfavorable publicity they would receive for striking in wartime, but more because Harry Hooper, acting as player-spokesman, perceived that Ban Johnson (whose support was needed by the players) had arrived at Fenway Park too tipsy to discuss the issues cogently.

The second dispute concerned Jake Daubert and Dodger owner Charlie Ebbets. When the season ended on Labor Day, Ebbets refused to give Daubert his full salary, claiming that Jake could scarcely expect payment for the part of the schedule that had not been completed. Daubert contested the case in court and won when it was ruled that it had been the decision of agents acting on Ebbets' behalf to curtail the schedule.

In a pique Ebbets then traded Daubert to the Reds, and Jake was again victorious when the Reds won their first pennant in 1919. Short on power, Cincinnati was solid in every other phase of the game. They had the league's top hitter in Roush and a trio of pitchers—Dutch Ruether, Hod Eller and the well-traveled Slim Sallee—who won 60 games among them. In the shortened 140-game postwar schedule only the White Sox had a triad of starters who won more. But the Sox' record was not as good as the Reds', and they had a lengthy battle with the Indians before prevailing. Still, they entered the Series as heavy favorites because of their superior hitting and the experience most of their regulars had acquired in winning the 1917 championship.

Typifying the thinking of the period, the 1919 Series was increased to the best of nine games by the same minds who had voted to improve baseball's image by shortening the regular season. When the

Sox lost in eight games, those in attendance who were wearing rose-colored glasses postulated that a rigorous pennant race had left them depleted, while the Reds had been able to conserve strength by clinching their title early. Others close to the scene, aware that the Sox' stars were notoriously underpaid by team owner Charlie Comiskey, quietly voiced alarm over some of the Series performances they had witnessed. Cicotte in particular was suspect for his pitching in the opening game, and the heavy battering Lefty Williams had sustained in all three of his outings also strained credibility. The facts would not filter through all the ugly rumors until late in the 1920 season, when eight members of the Sox would stand accused of having fixed the Series and be barred for life. Even then much of the full story remained buried, and with all the participants now dead it is doubtful whether many of the nagging questions that linger will ever be satisfactorily answered. How, for example, could Joe Jackson, not noted for his guile, be a willing accomplice to the fix and still manage to be the Series' top hitter? Was it possible that Buck Weaver, who had a great Series and his finest season ever in 1920 while supposedly playing under clouds of suspicion, was *not* lying when he said he had no part in the plot? Were Comiskey and Sox manager Kid Gleason to be believed when they denied having advance knowledge that a fix was in the works?

The entire 1919 season confronts the game's historians like a minefield. It is highly probable that the Series scandal was not an isolated incident of player reaction to miserly ownership but rather the tip of a huge iceberg. At the conclusion of the season Hal Chase and Heinie Zimmerman were jettisoned by McGraw and never appeared again in the majors. Lee Magee, suspected of conspiring with Chase to rig games for the Reds in 1918, was dropped by the Cubs. These three had long been part of the game's shady element, but there are strong intimations that few players of the period were simon-pure. In 1926 an event that threatened for a time to surpass even the Black Sox scandal surfaced when former Tiger pitcher Dutch Leonard revealed he had letters from Joe Wood regarding bets that Leonard, Wood, Tris Speaker and Ty Cobb had made on a game between the Tigers and Indians on September 25, 1919. Speaker and Cobb were at first persuaded to retire in exchange for having the matter swept under the rug, then decided to fight the charges. When Leonard refused to appear publicly to confront them, the issue died (although neither Speaker nor Cobb, both player-managers at the time, was ever offered a manager's post again), and word had it that Leonard's motive had been revenge for Cobb's having released him from the Tigers during the 1925 season.

By 1926 the game was back on an even keel, but it is chilling to think what might have occurred if Leonard's letters had come to light a few years earlier when Judge Landis, baseball's newly appointed first commissioner, had been engaged in a massive campaign to clean up the game and restore its image. Considering that Landis expelled players like Joe Gedeon, Gene Paulette and Jim O'Connell on allegations even less substantial than Leonard's, the possibility is strong that the game might have been shorn of two of its greatest stars just as it was about to enter its golden era.

Yet it was not the aroma of the 1919 Series that spelled the end of the National Commission and pointed up the need for a leader who was above the influence of the two leagues and their owners. Rather, it was Red Sox pitcher Carl Mays, who quit the club in mid-season, claiming the team did not try when he was on the mound. Owner Harry Frazee was requested by Ban Johnson to suspend Mays but instead sold him to the Yankees in the first of the many transactions between the two clubs that would result in the ruin for many years of both the Red Sox and the game's competitive balance. Johnson's inability to prevent the sale indicated he had lost the steel grip in which he held his league for two decades and prompted the more farsighted owners to begin a search for someone who could better protect their investments. Landis, who had attracted attention for his handling of the Federal League case a few years earlier while a judge, was the clear choice for commissioner. His actions did much to put the game back on solid ground, but his appointment came too late to block the sale of yet another of Frazee's stars whose actions would do even more for the game. In 1919 Babe Ruth demolished all then-existing records when he clubbed 29 homers and slugged at a .657 average, 27 homers and 313 points higher than the slugging marks of one Sammy Vick. Vick by rights should exist today in the same obscurity as Ira Flagstead, Merlin Kopp and other journeymen of the period at his position. Instead he is remembered for now and for always as the man Ruth replaced in right field for the Yankees. —David Nemec

Judge Landis. "His career typifies the heights to which dramatic talent may carry a man in America if only he has the foresight not to go on the stage." — Heywood Broun

MANAGER:
Mr. Mack and the Main Chance
By Wilfrid Sheed

BASEBALL fans make a number of strange sounds, but the only one that has been isolated and genetically identified with the game is the sound "boo." And the home of the boo, its very Cooperstown, is Philadelphia, which also by chance gave us Connie Mack, Mr. Baseball for half a century.

Philadelphians have always had a lot to boo about—besides Philadelphia itself (an enchanting city, but infinitely booable). They have had more losing teams than any three cities should be asked to endure. And many of these were provided by Mack, the somewhat different genius.

Mack served up only two kinds of teams: unbeatable and lousy. When I was a boy, he was going through one of his lean periods, which tended to linger a bit, like biblical plagues. The sun shone

and the infield sparkled like a dress shirt in that comeliest of stadiums, the old Shibe Park, but something was wrong. The players moved neither to right nor left; they hit not the curve nor the fastball, nor even the lowly change of pace. If they held the Yankees or Red Sox to single figures we lit bonfires—or rather, being what we were, we booed.

The soul of a fan in a losing city is warped by inches (it being a game of inches anyway, as my cliché adviser avers). At first, age nine in my case, you simply overrate the local heroes like everyone else and are baffled by their consistent inadequacy. By 10, you still believe the training camp reports swearing that everything will be different this year; by 11, you clutch like the local infielders at rays of hope—fairly good Aprils, split doubleheaders, two-game winning streaks; by 12, you believe nothing. You are marinated like Nolan Ryan's blister. You take to booing. Also, in those days, to running dementedly round the bases after the game and hook-sliding into home with three other fellows.

I don't know what happens after that, because I left Philadelphia the next year to start a new life as a Dodger fan. But many people went through whole adolescences of this, until the team itself left town out of kindness. By then, the thing had become self-perpetuating. The fans booed the players one by one into nervous breakdowns, until they became even more useless than before. Unless memory plays tricks, visitors were frequently spared, except from the eighth inning beer cans, which rained indifferently on whoever was standing in left field. The fans saved their fury for their own, and the bigger the better: Richie Allen of the Phils being the consummation, the best player, best booed.

Curiously, though, they never blamed the founder of much of this Beckett situation, the long-faced Irishman in the black suit who had not once but twice led them out of the Promised Land and into the desert: Mr. Mack, who only left the cellar in order to win occasional pennants; also, Mack the Knife, who dismembered two of the greatest teams of all time, in 1915 and again in '33, on the stated grounds that the fans were bored with success! As if they weren't bored with what they got in its place. Jehovah Himself never thought up a prettier punishment for smugness. Nine pennants were paid for with 16 last places.

Yet no one minded Mack. He was, at first glance, a funny sort of saint. In the "City of Undertakers," he dressed the part to the nines. Connie always seemed to be wearing black, or perhaps one of his festive dark grays, and his cadaverous length was usually stretched further by a derby or straw boater. In this mournful regalia he couldn't very well go out on the field, so he ran things from the dugout shadows, like an Irish city boss or, as I prefer to think, a renaissance cardinal. He wagged his scorecard as if it were a papal bull, and lesser men went running.

In short, he was a Presence. While other managers bounced around like monkeys in bloomers, or waddled to the mound with arthritic dignity, or even, as in the case of George Stallings of the Braves, offered to bust a puzzled Connie in the snoot, Mack himself sat stiff on his plank-wood throne, a man of respect, a figure from the past, but not one you laughed at—unless you craved a broken nose from one of his employees. He had, I'm told, an inner merriment (at least one got mortally tired of his "twinkling blue eyes" that lit up the *Evening*

Bulletin) which must have made you wonder who was laughing at whom. But most of all, he embodied the Game, he was a one-man shrine who preserved himself like a committee, and gave you a glimpse of what it must have been like in a sweeter time.

Only baseball with its layers of history could have produced such a figure. Connie was a good name for him. He had the look of a cheating minister or funereal card-sharp. When he set out in the eighties and nineties, ballplayers were considered lower even than actors, and Mack was the type who could get them into the hotel and assure you they were all good boys and get them out by moonlight. He boasted in later years of how he used to "tip the bat" when he was a catcher and he was also known to freeze baseballs overnight and to call for quick pitches while fixing his equipment—all devices necessary for keeping his scrawny frame in the big leagues, or what passed for them, for ten years or so.

Later, he had a special weakness for dim-witted roustabouts like Rube Waddell, the fire truck chaser, who were the very essence of baseball in those days, if you could get them to show up. His great team of 1929 was so foul-mouthed that the boys singed Judge Landis's ears in the commissioner's box and brought down an unprecedented edict to cease and shut up. The test of a manager was and is how much of this animal energy he can hold under rein, and Mack took the limit.

Baseball needed class, but it couldn't have handled a real saint. Mack was the perfect compromise. When he walked onto the field in 1905 to battle Muggsy McGraw's Giants, the two men repre-

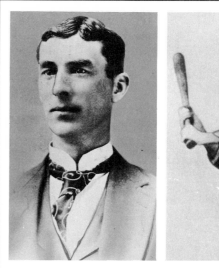

Young Mack. A club jumper in 1885, he joined the Players' League in 1890. "The purpose of our brotherhood," he said later, "was to protect the players. The group which...opposed us was interested in protecting the magnates."

Mack as young magnate. "Opportunity knocks at every man's door," he once said. "Don't let any skeptic tell you it doesn't come to everyone today, and here in America the opportunities are greater than ever before, if one has the good sense to seize them."

Space on top of houses adjacent to Shibe Park (which opened in 1909) was rented out by the buildings' owners; when Mack failed to stop the practice through legal action, he raised the height of the stadium wall.

sented baseball's two faces, dignity vs. the low life, pinstripe vs. bum, the world vs. Durocher, but in odd proportions. McGraw had class, too, of the old New York school of Dinty Moore's and Delmonico's, and he kept it under his hat; Mack wore his on his sleeve. But they were well-matched: McGraw never put one over on Mack and Mack never lorded it over McGraw. A beautiful pair of Irish actors, they could have made a great comedy team or political rivalry, with a twist of circumstance.

Judging from the amount written about the 1905 series and its re-runs in 1911 and '13, this rivalry captured the nation's imagination more than any other and gave it something to play with, a new kind of drama. Despite the manager's unearthly dignity, Mack's Athletics had been dubbed by McGraw himself the White Elephants, the dregs of the upstart American League, which McGraw's swaggering Giants would shortly put out of business for good. In fact, no five-game series was ever closer than the 1905 set. The difference was two men: Christy Mathewson, who won three, and Waddell, who didn't show up at all (he'd hurt his shoulder wrestling over a straw hat), and such small differences can be adjusted by time. When the teams met again in '11 and '13, the Athletics got even twice. Eddie Plank and Chief Bender were the executioners, and Mack issued his famous edict that "pitching is 75 percent of baseball" or 80 or 90— the number has floated free ever since, and oddly enough is never disputed, at whatever quotation. In

1911, Home Run Baker, who hit two of his namesakes, and six days of rain, made up the remaining percent. Mathewson's arm cooled off in the rain, and Mr. Mack had his first of five championships.

Suddenly he also had the first of his perfect teams. The $100,000 infield of Stuffy McInnis, Eddie Collins, Jack Barry and Frank Baker was the featured attraction, and the word was that they were almost too good for baseball. Mack acquired a reputation as the greatest teacher of fundamentals ever, and perhaps this gave him a Pygmalion or Henry Higgins complex, and he came to believe he could pass *anyone* off as a ballplayer. Because in 1914, he broke up his perfect teams as a man might smash a gold watch in a fit of temper. The A's had just contrived to lose four games out of four to the Miracle Boston Braves; and while the Braves had amazing momentum, there is hearsay reason to believe that Mack suspected his heroes of dumping the series. After his ace Chief Bender was strafed in the first game, Bender did not appear again, although Mack always called the Chief his greatest clutch pitcher. Remember we are just five years away from the Black Sox scandal, and the notorious Hal Chase would continue to throw games all over the place almost into the twenties. In fact, rumors of tank jobs filled the air in those pre-Landis years, and an upset on this scale had to worry the manager somewhat. Mack was fussy about his integrity, to such good effect that in 1927 he was able to refute Dutch Leonard's charges that Tris Speaker and

The heart of the 1910-1914 A's included pitchers (clockwise from Top L) Chief Bender, Jack Coombs, Joe Bush and Eddie Plank; the brains (C), Eddie Collins. A 1915 eulogy to the team in the Literary Digest said, "The Athletics had begun to look like a team that could not lose —the mythical team of which every fan has dreamed."

The 1911 World Series (Top) was the first to be filmed for commercial purposes. From the Pittsburgh *Post* of October 22: "The members of the National baseball commission, Ban Johnson, August Herrmann and Tom Lynch, were amused today when they learned that the players...had decided to make a firm demand for a share of the moving picture privileges." The A's hunchback mascot (front, R), Louis Van Zelst, was retained for "good luck." (Middle) The 1910 team was paced by Jack Coombs of Colby College (middle row, third from L), who won 30 games and, in the Series, won three more and batted .385. (Bottom) The 1913 A's rebounded from a third-place finish in 1912. Wrote Mack: "They quickly picked themselves up again and started out with a vengeance."

Before and after the fall. (Top, L to R): Stuffy McInnis, Danny Murphy, Frank Baker, Jack Barry, Eddie Collins — the $100,000 infield, plus one. Odd man out was Murphy, who was pushed to right field when Collins became a regular in 1909. The infield's aggregate batting average for the four years they played together was .319; for his part, Murphy hit .323 over the same period. (Bottom) Mack with some of the 1916 A's, the team that lost 117 games. Pitchers Jack Nabors and Tom Sheehan were 1-19 and 1-16, respectively. Nabors (he retired with a lifetime record of 1-24) once in a 1916 game held a 1-0 lead in the ninth. When two errors tied the score and put the winning run on third, he threw the next pitch over the backstop. "If they think I'd stand there in that sun and pitch another nine innings waiting for our bums to make another run, they're crazy," he told Sheehan.

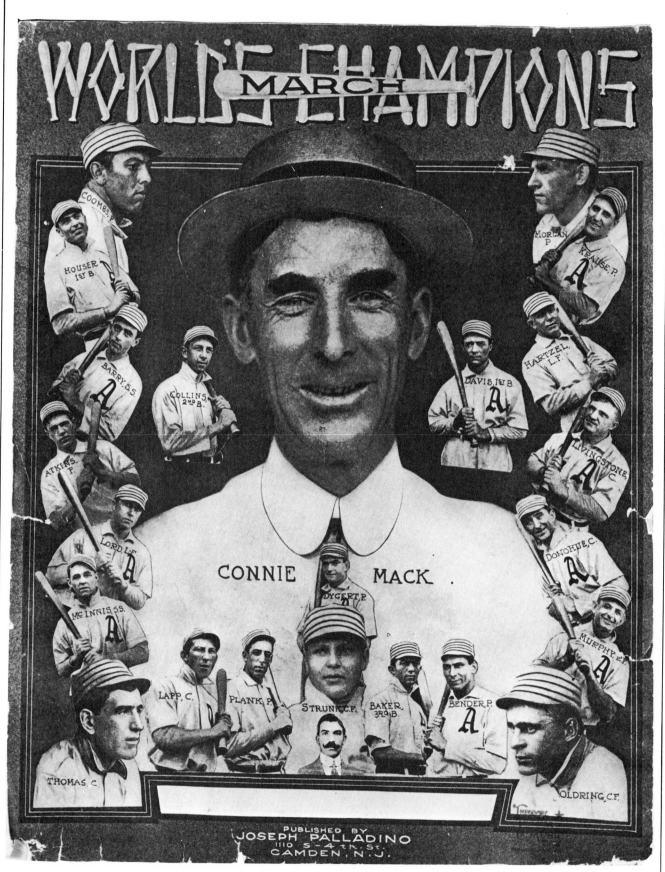

This sheet music celebrates Mack's 1910 champions. Missing from the lineup was Joe Jackson, who had been traded to Cleveland in the off-season. "Had Jackson...remained under the steadying influence of Mack," Fred Lieb wrote, "he might have avoided the tragedy and disgrace which befell him nine years later." Mack had, in 1909, offered to engage a tutor to teach Jackson to read and write.

Ty Cobb had thrown games back in 1918 (they had) simply by retaining them. And perhaps this legend of integrity began with the break-up of the 1914 team, not for excellence but for naughtiness.

They were easily raffish enough to throw a Series. That year, six of them were summoned by the IRS for failure to report their Series shares. And maybe half of them were playing footsie with the new Federal League, which was offering real money as opposed to Mack's wooden nickels. Connie's hold over his players should not be exaggerated. When Lefty Grove was later asked what it was like being managed by Mack, he said he didn't know, because he never paid any attention to him.

Which was a fair turnabout, because Mack never paid Grove or anyone else what *they* wanted, namely top dollar. Grove was reported at one time to be getting $30,000 a year, but he later told a writer that he'd never seen anything like that much. Mack groaned mightily over his payroll, but like that other saint, Branch Rickey, he would have traded his mother to keep it down to size. He deplored the practice of buying teams and stocking them with pricey players (as if stinginess were a badge of integrity), but he had nothing against selling teams and fielding bargain basement ones in their place. His 1916 team, which lost 117 games, is widely believed to be the worst team that has ever played the game, and I'll go along with that, because I can't see Connie settling for anything less. But I'll also bet that it had the smallest payroll.

Mysteriously, the pennant winners of '14 had contrived to lose $65,000, with a huge drop in reported attendance, and Mack got it back the quick way, by peddling star flesh, most notably Eddie Collins for a cool $50,000. Even thus refreshed, he was not able to meet the price tag of $25,000 that Baltimore owner Jack Dunn had put on Babe Ruth and Ernie Shore, a couple of promising young pitchers who might have helped a bit in the coming plague years.

Thus pain entered Philadelphia, and the A's became White Elephants after all. They proceeded for the next few years to match their manager's eerie detachment, looking either up at the League or down at it, but seldom being precisely in it. In 1915, the Phillies with Grover Cleveland Alexander won one of their rare National League pennants, but there was no trolley series, because the A's were nowhere to be found. And in '17 and '19, A's fans had to sit by slack-jawed as the great Eddie Collins helped the White Sox to two pennants, and ironically turned out to be one of the clean Sox, when that team changed color.

It has always been hard to swallow that the 1914 A's were really too perfect to get a decent game from anyone. The Red Sox boasted the immortal outfield of Tris Speaker, Harry Hooper and Duffy Lewis. Detroit had Ty Cobb and Sam Crawford; Chicago, Buck Weaver; Cleveland, Joe Jackson: in fact, an All-Star American League team of that year would have matched the best of any era without needing a single Athletic. Yet the fable endured of perfection blighted and came in very handy when Mack did the exact same thing in the thirties: sold a super team for straight cash because they were too good for this world.

It certainly wasn't the high price of black suits that made him do it. Unlike Clark Griffith, the Scrooge of Washington, Mack wasn't consistent enough to be called a miser. He did home-grow another great team in the 1920's, in his little victory garden, but what made it great was the purchase of the aforementioned Grove from Baltimore in the International League for the record amount of $100,600. The obtainment of Cobb and Speaker, on the other hand, was probably for straight gate-

Mack's Mascot Says Connie Will Win Another Pennant by Developing Youngsters

Hyman Pearlstone, Big Booster From Palestine, Tex., Here En Route to Join Athletics on Annual Summer Cruise, Declares Man Who Has Won Six Flags in American League Will Come-Back as a Contender by 1919—Has Followed Connie Since 1906 and Saw Development of Collins, Baker, Barry, McInnis, Schang and Other Philly Stars.

Hyman Pearlstone. This Texas banker was Mack's biggest booster. "In three years," he said in 1915, "Mack will be back in the first division, and he'll win a pennant in five." Mack's decimated team didn't emerge from the cellar until 1922.

The Second Coming, with disciples. By 1929, the A's were back on top; Mack was accompanied (at L) by coaches Kid Gleason (L) and Eddie Collins (R). His son Earle (at R, in uniform, with Mrs. Mack and Connie Jr.), was the "assistant manager." In 1950, the patriarch wrote that Earle "started about 1913 and played his first game as catcher.... At bat he got a single and three-bagger and outhit any man in our club that day." His father failed to mention that those were the only major league hits Earle ever got. Besides, the game was in 1910.

appeal—a penny-wise move tantamount to hiring Buffalo Bill, which may have cost him the pennant in 1928. For once his policy of developing cheap young players was suspended, and Bing Miller and Mule Haas had to watch the two old gentlemen creaking around the outfield a few times too many.

The passing through of Cobb may have had another subtle effect on Mack's fortunes, because in '28, Ty introduced the players, and perhaps the manager, to the pleasures of the stock market, just in time for the Crash. This must have given Mack's payroll fits, as he proceeded to win three pennants in a row with a team of busted investors.

Those years, 1929–31, are the glories of Mack's career: without them, he would belong squarely in the limbo of Hughie Jennings and Fred Clarke and other minor divinities of the first quarter century. But to challenge the lordly Yankees of Ruth and Gehrig and take them three in a row—what manner of strange old man was this? A mere two years before, the Yankees had fielded their greatest side ever, and if Ruth had slipped a hair since then, Gehrig certainly hadn't, and now the great Bill Dickey was on hand to announce a whole fresh dynasty. Yet the A's beat them without breaking a sweat. They were not only good but ferocious: "Bucketfoot" Al Simmons, who worked himself into a homicidal rage against pitchers before going up to bat; Jimmie Foxx with his sleeves cut off so that his very muscles might subdue you ("how much air do they hold, Jimmie?" asked Ted Lyons; "35 pounds" answered Foxx); Black Mike Coch-

rane, perhaps the fastest *running* catcher who ever played and the most competitive, and the best; and the towering, glowering Grove, so unfathomably angry in defeat that his teammates couldn't go near him. Luckily, defeat seldom happened: in 1931 Grove went 31–4, but ripped his shirt and three lockers to pieces after one of the four losses—a 1-0 fluke that ended a 16-game winning streak. And these were just the Hall of Famers. The rest of the squad included such names as George Earnshaw and Rube Walberg (pitchers) and Jimmy Dykes (third baseman) that were still magic in the sour-apple forties, and was strong at every position. Yet again, it was not really in a class by itself. The Yankees beat it at almost full strength in 1932, and Mack didn't dismantle it for good until that winter.

"Philadelphia bankers force Mack to sell," said the headlines. A loan of $400,000 had apparently been called in abruptly. What had gone wrong this time? The '32 team claimed a loss of $500,000, and Mack chaffered about the payroll and the cost of stadium renovation—although few fans would have traded Jimmie Foxx et al for a paint job. Rumor inevitably started in Philadelphia that Mack and/or his sons Roy and Earle had taken a bath in the market and in real estate and that "someone" in the front office (*Baseball Digest,* 1943) was investing the petty cash; and the question was raised whether Mack would dare to show his face on opening day, 1933.

He not only did, but he marched all the way to the flagpole, eyes front and shoulders straight like

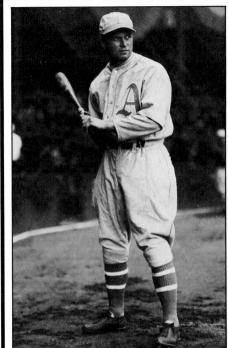

(Top) Jimmie Foxx (L) joined the A's as an 18-year-old on a tip from Frank Baker; he hit .667 in his ten-game tryout in 1925. Jimmy Dykes (C), picked off a Philadelphia sandlot in 1918, worked for Mack, as player and manager, for 28 years. Mickey

Cochrane (R) was the entire reason for Mack's purchase of the Portland club in 1924. Mack's bankroll was furnished by Ben Shibe (Middle) and his family; their money came from the A. J. Reach Co., yet another arm of the Spalding Trust.

Among the pitchers Cochrane handled so adeptly were Rube Walberg (L), who was, said Ed Barrow, "not always too co-operative mentally," and Howard Ehmke (R), whose glory in the first game of the 1929 Series almost disappeared when he gave up two quick runs in the final game; it was Walberg who came in to get the win. (C) The 1928 outfield of Al Simmons, Tris Speaker and Ty Cobb. Speaker was 40, Cobb 41; Simmons said, "If this keeps up, by the end of the season I'll be an old man myself."

Mack and Robert Moses Grove. Grove, wrote Robert Smith, "was quick to take offense, to see insults where none was meant....He had no apparent use for his admirers." But Mack, Grove told Donald Honig, "was just like a father to everyone."

Grove and Cochrane in Japan, after Mack's 1933 housecleaning. "I do not have to remind you," he said in 1950, "of those dark days when the banks closed down." Tom Yawkey alone gave Mack $400,000 to lighten the gloom.

In 1946, age 83, and three years later, as "Chief for a Day" in Meriden, Conn. "Champions," he told John Tunis in 1943, "cost money." In the last 16 years of his career, Mack's teams finished last ten times.

a Sinn Fein leader defying British bullets. It was enough. He never had to appear again. Whatever else we booed in Philadelphia, which included even each other at times, we never booed the man who had made the long march to the flagpole and back.

The long Mack twilight had begun. His vaunted gift for spotting talent proved to be nothing special. Doc Cramer, Bob Johnson and Wally Moses were good, but not great hitters, and he couldn't seem to spot pitchers at all. Unlike Branch Rickey, who could grow a cheap star under an expensive one any day, Mack could no longer either buy them or develop them the old way. He never got much of a grip on the farm system idea, which Rickey had invented in the twenties, and his shavetails from Toronto and elsewhere were just ballplayers, the kind you see all over—replaceable, anonymous, forgettable.

But still he hung on, like some old chieftain who knows he will die if he quits. By the late 1940's, fresh rumors began to float that he was losing his finer marbles, that he couldn't remember his players' names, that Al Simmons really ran the team from the third base coaching box. It was hard to tell, because the game-to-game management was so wooden and featureless that it could have been coming from anywhere. Only the occasional rank mistake suggested that our leader was dozing.

Yet those were the years when the legend grew the most. The surprise starting of the aged Howard Ehmke in the '29 Series was exhumed and seen as pure genius; the 10-run inning in the same Series was all Mack's doing now. The inability of his pitch-

ers to hold Cardinals on base in '31 was no affair of his. All was Ehmke and Bender and the infield of 1914. The modest achievements any man might rack up in 50 years sparkled brightly in the dung heap of Philadelphia baseball.

Mack is also a chapter in the history of the sporting press. Reporters were kindly in those days, as well they might be since the club frequently picked up all their tabs; and Mack was the most obliging man in the business. Writers' interests are not necessarily fans' interests, and last place teams are quite endurable for them if the copy keeps coming. In return, writers would cover up whatever there was to cover up. If they could throw a blanket over Ruth's excesses, they could hide anything. I have it on good authority that when Jackie Robinson's Dodgers were due to play an exhibition with the A's, old Mack was less than enthusiastic about having "the Nigger" along. But the writers were off doing pieces about Ehmke and the 10-run inning.

As for the financial structure which had forced Mack to gut his team yet later left a handsome trust fund for his five daughters—that was Mr. Mack's business. You don't examine a saint's books. He was free to give whatever reasons he chose for breaking up his teams, until Mack's excuses became official history. Outside of his shadowy partner Ben Shibe (and presumably his sons) nobody knew *what* the rigid Mack was sitting on all those years. No reporter of the period seriously probed him, because he was famous for his integrity. And why was he famous for it? Because they said so.

Bobby Shantz, who played for Mack in 1949-50, told Donald Honig that Mack "wasn't able to handle the ball club very well....Sometimes you'd have to wait and wait for a sign to come."

Eddie Joost at the 1949 All-Star Game, flanked by Red Sox Ted Williams, Dom DiMaggio and Birdie Tebbetts (L to R). His 23 home runs were more than any of the A's had had since 1941.

(C) Al Simmons and Mack. "When he signals for an obviously wrong move," Bob Considine wrote in 1948, "Al Simmons turns his back on the old man...and calls for the right move." (Bottom) Ferris Fain (L, at L, with Gus Zernial) was the best hitter on Mack's last teams, but led AL first basemen in errors five times; Buddy Rosar (R), who was an adequate hitter, in 1946 became the only catcher in major league history to play an entire season without a single error.

Baseball is, of course, whatever the public thinks it is. For instance, when Branch Rickey brought Robinson into baseball, he too was canonized. Yet he had a number of most practical reasons. World War II had flooded the northern cities with potential black fans; black groups had been pushing hard for sports integration during the war, and already pro football was sliding into it with much less fuss (maybe because helmets make blacks less noticeable); and Rickey was grabbing himself a dynasty of pennant winners, at the cost of some wear and tear on Robinson's nerves.

Okay, it still took courage for Rickey to do it, and Rickey could make anything he did seem like a branch of religion. But what one savors about Rickey is still the slight whiff of hypocrisy, the sense of the pious rogue who does well by doing good, and that's what one liked about Connie Mack. Because he did it on even fewer actual good works than Rickey. *Why* did he have such a reputation for integrity? Because he looked as if he should. Because the closest he got to swearing was when he said to Jimmy Dykes "and nuts to you too, Mr. Dykes." (Not swearing is the pinnacle of virtue in baseball.) Because the sport, having rashly proposed itself as the national pastime, has always clutched at anything that could pass for statesmanlike. Because the players worshiped him.

At the end, as he sat senile and glassy-eyed through a 1954 old-timers' game, the players introduced themselves to him with an appearance of reverence that only stopped short at kissing his ring. He didn't recognize any of them, but it didn't matter. They thought they were shaking hands with Baseball.

Mack had long since ceased influencing the game in any practical way. Some said that he was a prisoner of his sons Roy and Earle, who kept him there for dynastic purposes (since no one would ever bad-mouth Mack himself, his sons came in for a lot of this and came to seem like very dubious fellows. Rightly or wrongly, someone has to redress the balance of virtue in a family). But it was nice to have him there on any terms because he tickled the imagination. Born in the Lincoln Administration, and still staggering through Eisenhower—he was like a tree with initials on it from the Garden of Eden.

As a feisty young catcher, Mack had been active in what passed for a players' association and had even taken part in a species of players' strike in the 1880's. After his death, his team with its strange history ran afoul of a more streamlined Players Association. Charlie Finley, the professional bad boy, whose horns had replaced Mack's halo as the A's symbol, found the new free-agent rule posing the same kind of threat that the Federal League had in 1914. And he reacted exactly the same way.

In a ghostly re-run, he broke up the team—because of low attendance, putative stinginess, restless players and the owner's conviction that he could build a great new team anytime he wanted to. And as in '14, the players made their own deals where possible, and the A's did not get their money's worth.

It is to be supposed that Mack would not have cared for Finley's vulgarity and carny approach to baseball, but I wouldn't bet on much more than that. Baseball is a game of appearances, of slyness and bluff, and Connie's blue eyes might have twinkled in his mortician's face to see a new kind of actor go through the old motions. The man who brought gloom to Philadelphia and the one who broke hearts in Kansas City and Oakland are brothers under the skin and form a weird continuity of their own. The main difference, and let old-timers shed a tear over this if they choose, was that Cornelius McGillicuddy was always a gentleman about it.

"I'm not quitting because I'm too old. I'm quitting because I think the people want me to."
— Connie Mack, October 18, 1950

FOURTH INNING:
1920-1929

We do not trust cashiers half so much, or diplomats, or policemen, or physicians, as we trust an outfielder or a shortstop. The light which beats upon him would do very well for a throne. The one thing which he is not called—many things as he may be called for his blunders—is sneak or traitor. The man at the bat, cheer him or hoot at him as we may, is supposed to be doing his best. . . . All may be fair in love and war, but in sport nothing is fair but the rules.

—The Nation, 1920

THE 1920 Cleveland Indians were the first team in the century to have three men register 100 RBIs. As a unit they hit .303 and led the league in runs scored. One of their pitchers, Jim Bagby, was the last American League right-hander until Denny McLain to win 30 games, and two others won 20. Nevertheless, in order for them to bring home their first pennant by a scant two games, their chief rival, the White Sox, had to lose almost their entire regular lineup late in the season, and the Indians had to find a last-ditch replacement for their own star shortstop, Ray Chapman, the only man ever killed in a major league game. After 20 years of frustration and near misses, Cleveland finally won the AL title. It was the season Babe Ruth hit 54 homers and slugged a record .847. It was the season that for the first time in history a team—the White Sox—had four 20-game winners. It was the season that the usually impotent Browns and Senators hit .308 and .291. It was the first season that the two St. Louis infielders, Hornsby of the Cardinals and Sisler of the Browns, won batting titles and the last season that Ed Barrow managed the Red Sox before becoming business manager of the Yankees. It was also the last season that a league home run leader would have fewer than 20, or that Wilbert Robinson would manage a pennant winner.

Robinson's Dodgers looked no better in 1920 than they had in 1916 but won with ease when Red pitchers floundered and the Giants were caught in the transition between the old guard of Larry Doyle and Art Fletcher and the new, represented by Ross Youngs, Frankie Frisch and George Kelly. The season was not without the Dodgers' usual quota of madcap developments. Joe Oeschger of the Braves for the second time in two seasons found himself locked in a marathon game against the Dodgers when he battled Leon Cadore to a 1–1 tie in 26 innings on May 1. On April 30, 1919, almost a year earlier to the day, Oeschger, then with the Phils, had gone 20 innings against Dodger ace Burleigh Grimes in a 9–9 game. Oeschger's record of 46 innings in two starts without a decision is nearly as esoteric as that set by Dodger rookie Jack Sheehan, the most marginal player ever to participate in a World Series and the only one to record as many Series career hits as regular season career hits—two.

It was predictable that a Series involving the game's most ill-starred team, and its zaniest, would not be dull; but of course no one could have anticipated that the Indians, in winning, would hit the first Series grand-slam homer, the first Series homer by a pitcher, and pull off the only unassisted triple play in Series history. All took place in the fifth game, with the contest tied at two games apiece, and left the Dodgers so shell-shocked that they were scoreless from then on.

Over the winter the Yankees resumed their systematic rape of the Red Sox roster by slipping the financially strapped Frazee enough cash to obtain Waite Hoyt and Wally Schang, giving them the

Bill Wambsganss (L), Elmer Smith. Wambsganss told Lawrence Ritter, "the only thing anybody seems to remember is that I once made an unassisted triple play in the World Series. . . . You'd think I was born the day before and died the day after." Smith had one other notable accomplishment besides the first Series grand slam: in 1921, he made seven consecutive extra-base hits — a record that still stands.

(Top, L) Ray Chapman, killed by Carl Mays's pitch, August 17, 1920. From the *Washington Star:* "So terrific was the blow that the report of impact caused spectators to think the ball had struck his bat. Mays..., acting under this impression, fielded the ball which rebounded halfway to the pitcher's box, and threw it to first base to retire Chapman." (Top, R) Stan Coveleski. Each of his three wins in the 1920 Series was a five-hitter. (Bottom) The 1920 champion Indians. Their armbands memorialized Chapman. Catcher Les Nunamaker (rear, extreme L) in 1914 threw out three men stealing in one inning.

Eppa Rixey (L), Pie Traynor. In 1921, Rixey allowed but one home run in 301 innings pitched; he won 266 games in his career despite spending all of it with the Phillies and the Reds. Traynor was so aggressive a fielder, said Charlie Grimm, that "he'd scoop everything off the field — grass, dust and gravel — and fling it over to first with the ball. It was like a sandstorm."

battery they needed for a pennant. Ruth's slugging dropped a point in 1921 to .846, but he broke his own year-old homer mark by soaring to 59 and Sam Thompson's 33-year-old RBI record by knocking home 170 runs. Even so, the Indians hung close to the Yankees until late September and finished with a record almost identical to that of the National League's pennant-winning Giants, who overcame a wide lead by the Pirates with a late surge.

The Yankees opened the first subway Series by shutting out McGraw's sluggers two days in a row. On the third day the Giants unleashed 20 hits and thereafter coasted to the championship in eight games. Other National League champions were Hornsby and teammate Austin McHenry, who finished one-two in slugging average and one-three in the batting race. McHenry's steady improvement each year had coincided with that of the Cardinals. By 1921 he was the league's foremost leftfielder, and the team fell just short of overhauling the Pirates for second place. Favored by many for the 1922 pennant, the Cardinals experienced yet another setback in their long climb to the top when McHenry went home ill in mid-season and died before the year was out.

It was left to the other St. Louis team to stir fans along the Mississippi in 1922. Slowly building for several years around Sisler, the Browns displayed an outfield of Baby Doll Jacobson, Ken Williams and Jack Tobin; the best hitting catcher of the era, Hank Severeid; and a young second baseman, Marty McManus, whose 109 RBIs made the Browns the first team in history to have four men over the 100 level. The club failed to capitalize on an opportunity for a fast start, granted them by Judge Landis when he suspended Ruth and Bob Meusel of the Yankees for the first month of the season because of an illegal barnstorming tour the previous fall, and they trailed the Yankees until July. Taking a slight lead into August, the Browns dropped a crucial series to the Yankees in St. Louis and never recovered, ultimately losing the pennant by a single game. Nevertheless, the 93 victories they tallied in 1922 were the most in Brown history.

St. Louis fans were not left holding an empty bag, however. Hornsby and Sisler both took batting titles with averages over .400, and Ken Williams deposed Ruth as home run and RBI leader. Approaching his 36th birthday, Ty Cobb became the second man in the century to top .400 and miss a batting championship when he hit .401 (Sisler's mark was .420), up 12 points from the year before when he had been runner-up to teammate Harry Heilmann. Cobb, Heilmann and Bobby Veach formed an outfield in Detroit even more explosive than that of the Browns. Indeed, six teams had outfields comprised entirely of .300 hitters, and the Pirates had so much hitting depth that they could afford to platoon Reb Russell, a former pitcher, who in just 60 games drove in 75 runs. The "rabbit" ball—put into play by the American League in 1920 and adopted by the National League a year later to seize upon the interest in home runs that Ruth had generated—had raised batting averages some 25 points over 1919 and was reflected even more sharply in pitching statistics of the era. For the first time in history the National League did not have a single ERA qualifier under 3.00 in 1922, and

Sammy Vick. In 1919 he was the right fielder for the New York Yankees. He told Marshall Smelser, "A rabbit didn't have to think to know what to do to dodge a dog.... The same kind of instinct told Babe Ruth what to do and where to be." When Ruth (inset) replaced him in right field in New York, Vick was soon off to Boston, and out of baseball a year after that.

Waite Hoyt. The "Brooklyn Schoolboy" was originally signed by John McGraw as a 16-year-old, and by 21 was the mainstay of the Yankee pitching staff. He sang at the Palace, painted, wrote, and said, "Wives of ball players, when they teach their children their prayers, should instruct them to say: 'God bless mommy, God bless daddy, God bless Babe Ruth! Babe has upped daddy's pay check by 15 to 40 percent!"

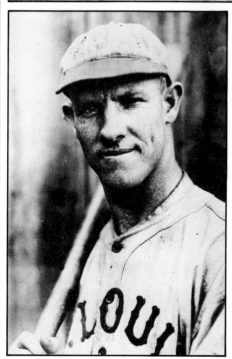

(Top, L) Hub Pruett. He had a lifetime record of 29-48 with a 4.63 ERA — but Ruth batted only .182 against him, striking out 15 times in 30 at bats. (Top, R) Babe Ruth, Judge Landis, Bob Meusel (L to R). Landis suspended the two Yankees for one month in 1922, for illegal barnstorming. Said Landis of Ruth, "In this office, he's just another player." (Middle) Giant outfielders Casey Stengel, Bill Cunningham, Ross Youngs, Irish Meusel (L to R), 1922. The next year, when Stengel hit an inside-the-park home run in the Series, Damon Runyon wrote, "People generally laugh when they see old Casey Stengel run." Youngs died of Bright's disease in 1927. (Bottom, L) Austin McHenry, too, died tragically; he hit .350 for St. Louis in 1921 and was dead of a brain tumor a year later. (R) Eddie Rommel. He was the father of the modern knuckleball, using it to win 19 as a starter and another eight in relief for the 1922 A's, who won but 65 games. In 1932 he allowed 29 hits in one extra-inning game, a record.

Rogers Hornsby. He was originally signed for $400; by 1926, he owned 15 percent of the Cardinals and was arguably the greatest hitter ever, combining average with power as has no other man. In his three .400-plus seasons, Hornsby averaged 35 home runs; his is the second highest career batting average and seventh highest slugging average. He holds single-season batting records for three different clubs. He was also deeply disliked, a cold and outspoken man who was, wrote Dave Egan, "born to be a target," forever losing managerial jobs because of his bluntness and his profligate gambling. (He knew no other vices; he would not even attend movies, fearing for his batting eye.) Still, as Clyde Sukeforth told Donald Honig, "when he had a bat in his hands, he had nothing but admirers."

George Sisler and (inset) Harry Heilmann, who traded batting titles in the early 1920's. Sisler, wrote Robert Smith, "spent ten years building up the fiction that he could not hit a high inside pitch. He used to strike out on such pitches occasionally, just so he could count on having pitchers throw them to him in tight spots." Heilmann, wrote Ken Smith, "was not a good fielder or...thrower, and there were several faster players in every game he played. He was a hitter, for a pure and simple fact."

A BASE-BALL MIRACLE.

only Red Faber beat that figure in the AL the previous year. Faber was working for the seventh-place White Sox, yet managed to win 25 games. In 1922, Ed Rommel outdid Faber and everyone else by scoring 27 wins, the most in the majors, for the seventh place Athletics.

In the second subway Series in a row, four pitchers divided the four Giant victories among them. The same pattern had existed during the regular season when the Giants had become the National League's first champion without a 20-game winner. As if to confound the theorists who have always maintained that no team can win without strong pitching, the Giants went on to hoist a third pennant in 1923 and yet a fourth in 1924 with one of the most mediocre staffs in the game. Remarkably, during the club's record string of four consecutive pennants, its sole 20-game winner was Art Nehf in

1921, and in the final two years of the string, no Giant could win more than 16.

The best pitching in the majors in 1923 belonged to the Reds. Staff leader Dolf Luque had 27 wins, and both Eppa Rixey and Pete Donohue broke the 20-game barrier. So strong was their pitching that the Reds finished second despite scoring the fewest runs of any team in the league except the Braves. The Cubs, jinxed by injuries since winning their pennant in 1918, lost Ray Grimes, the previous year's batting champion runner-up, and had to resort for a time to using young catcher Gabby Hartnett at first base. Only the presence of the Phils and Braves—pennant winners less than a decade ago but now consigned to being the league's dregs for some 20 years—made the Dodgers and Cardinals seem respectable. First baseman Jimmy Bottomley's .371 average in his debut as a regular removed

Judge Landis, 1923. He was a fan before he became commissioner. He was appointed, said Will Rogers, because "somebody said, 'Get that old boy who sits behind first base all the time. He's out there every day anyhow.' So they offered him a season's pass and he jumped at it."

Beginning in 1922, Ring Lardner earned about $17,000 annually from the syndication of a comic strip based
on his baseball short stories. Asked who the model was for the unforgettable Jack Keefe, Lardner wrote,
"There are no ballplayers left whom they haven't guessed, from Noah to Bucky Harris, and I may as well
give the correct answer. The original of Jack Keefe is not a ballplayer at all, but Jane Addams of Hull House,
a former Follies girl."

(Top, L to R) Walter Johnson, his pitching grip, Muddy Ruel; (Middle, L to R) Goose Goslin, Firpo Marberry, Joe Judge; (Bottom) the wedding of Bucky Harris. "I never saw a day in baseball like that of October 10, 1924," Ruel said. That was the day Johnson pitched four shutout innings in relief as the Senators won their first Series in the twelfth inning of the seventh game. Ruel had two hits in the entire Series, but both came in the last game, and he scored the winning run; Judge hit .385 for the Series; Goslin had three home runs; Marberry saved two games and gave up only one earned run in four appearances — and Harris won a championship as a 28-year-old rookie manager. He would win another pennant in 1925, yet only once more in 27 years as a manager would he finish higher than third.

Johnson at Daytona Beach, 1926, and accepting a Lincoln at the opening of the 1924 Series. His opponent in the first game, Art Nehf, said, "Walter was so nervous I felt sorry for him.... When we shook hands for the photographers, his hand trembled." Johnson, 20 years later, said, "I was 36 years old and that's pretty far gone to be walking into the last game of the Series." In 1925, he would appear in his second — and last — Series and win two games. Then, in the seventh game, wrote James Harrison, "with mud shackling his ankles and water running down his neck, the grand old man of baseball succumbed to weariness, a sore leg, wretched support and the most miserable weather conditions that ever confronted a pitcher."

Dazzy Vance (L), Zack Wheat (R). Vance, said Johnny Frederick, "could throw a cream puff through a battleship." He didn't win his first big league game until he was 31; he won the last of 197 when he was 44. Wheat, who hit .316 in 18 seasons in Brooklyn, in his last year there hit the "longest" home run in major league history: crippled by a charley horse rounding first, he sat in pain on second base for five full minutes before he completed his home run trot.

some of the sting from Card manager Branch Rickey's gift of Jack Fournier to Brooklyn, where he hit .351 and knocked in 102 runs. Rickey, soon to become known as a cunning trader, had done poorly thus far in his ventures in flesh-peddling. His most interesting swap to date had come between games of a 1922 doubleheader between the Cards and Cubs, when he arranged for Max Flack and Cliff Heathcote to exchange uniforms in time to appear in box scores for both teams on the same day.

While the National League's second-division clubs traded to keep their fans interested, the Yankees continued to deal with a vengeance, receiving Joe Dugan and Herb Pennock, additional gifts from the Red Sox. No less than seven of the 13 players who formed the Yankee front-line cadre in 1923 had once worn Red Sox uniforms. In exchange for them, the Sox had received exactly one man (Norm McMillan, a .253 hitter) who played regularly in 1923. The Tigers and Indians, with no realistic hope of competing for the pennant, skirmished between themselves all season for second place, the Tigers winning by half a game. George Uhle of Cleveland was the league's top winner, however, and aided his own cause by hitting .361. A lifetime 200-game winner, Uhle continued to be a valuable pinch hitter after his arm faded, and he retired in 1936 with the highest career batting average by a pitcher in over 500 games.

After disappointing twice in a row in the Series, Ruth finally got untracked in 1923. The rest of the Yankees joined him in pummeling Giant pitchers and brought home the club's first world championship. Satisfied at last, Ruppert, Huston and manager Huggins let the winter pass without a single trade of consequence, although one must imagine they threw a covetous glance now and then at Howard Ehmke, who won 20 games for the last place Red Sox, hurled a no-hitter and missed a second consecutive no-hitter by the margin of a controversial scorer's decision on a ground ball that eluded his third baseman. Had the Sox kept Joe Dugan around a while longer, there likely would have been no controversy. Dugan in 1923 happened to be the best-fielding third baseman in the league—but for the Yankees.

When spring training began in 1924, Senator outfielder Sam Rice was 34 years old. He was stolen-base king in 1920, but his speed in recent years seemed to be slipping. Likewise Walter Johnson, nearing 37, had won only 17 games in 1923, and shortstop Roger Peckinpaugh, a boy wonder in 1914 when he had briefly managed the Yankees, had recently passed his 33rd birthday. The Senators, in a word, were an *old* team and were expected to decelerate sharply after contending for over a decade without ever quite being able to mount a concerted challenge. They had always lacked a steady run producer and a pitcher who could team with Johnson.

Out of nowhere they got both in 1924 when Goose Goslin, a bare .300 hitter the year before, became the first Senator to be the league's RBI leader, and Firpo Marberry shattered all existing relief records by compiling 15 saves. Moreover, Johnson came back with 23 wins, and Peckinpaugh and the new boy wonder, player-manager Bucky Harris, easily topped the league in double plays. But the icing was the "return" of Sam Rice who hit .334 and led the league in hits. Clicking on all cylinders, the Senators astounded their followers by dethroning the Yankees and becoming the third of the four "virgin" clubs in the American League to win a pennant in the 1920's.

Welcome as the Senators' victory was, it lacked the drama of the Giants' triumph in the senior league. As expected, the Giants were closely pressed all season by the Pirates but wound up having to fight off a late challenge by the Dodgers that missed by only a game and a half. With Dazzy Vance and Burleigh Grimes finishing one-two in pitching honors, Fournier leading in homers and Wheat finishing runner-up to Hornsby for the batting championship, only the lack of a dependable shortstop separated Robinson's men from McGraw's.

But being a runner-up to Hornsby in 1924 meant finishing some 50 points behind him; the Rajah hit for the highest average in the century, .424. Even more than Ruth, Hornsby and four-time American League batting champ Harry Heilmann profited from the rabbit ball now in use. Hornsby's performance during his first four seasons suggested he had potential as a hitter but gave no inkling he would average nearly .400 from 1920 to 1925 and sweep all six batting titles. Heilmann failed to show much at all in his early years. As late as 1920, his sixth season, he hit only .309, while the other stars of the era were well over .350. But a year later he became the first right-handed hitter since 1904 to win an American League batting championship and started a string of seven consecutive seasons over .346. Hornsby and Heilmann were similar in style. Although they could hit with power—Hornsby in 1922 was the first National Leaguer to clear 40 homers—they were primarily line drive hitters. When the peppier ball forced outfielders to spread out and play deeper, both were able to take full advantage of the gaps created.

A less obvious beneficiary was Sam Rice. Playing in mammoth Griffith Stadium, whose outfield walls were so remote that the Senators went without a home run champion until 1958, Rice grew so adroit at utilizing the increased space between outfielders that at age 40 he could still hit .349 and account for 207 hits. Rice made the mistake of retiring in 1934 while 13 hits short of 3,000. By failing to reach that magic figure, which assures rapid Hall of Fame selection, Rice had to wait until he was in his seventies before being inducted—as did another, earlier Sam (Sam Crawford, who retired with 2,964 hits). Heilmann also was inexplicably made to cool his heels while committee members went about honoring Tinker, Evers, Chance and others whose contributions were much less than his. Harry was kept waiting too long; he died in 1951, the year before the committee suddenly realized that Cooperstown was still without the last right-handed batter to hit over .395.

Ty Cobb and Judge Landis. Landis cleared Cobb and Tris Speaker of Dutch Leonard's game-fixing charge largely because Leonard would not attend a hearing on the matter. Wrote Fred Lieb, "Ballplayers who knew of Cobb's terrible temper told me that Leonard was afraid to come...for fear that Cobb would tear him apart physically." When Landis cleared him, Cobb said the Judge "sure took his time getting to the truth."

(Top, L) Wally Pipp. (Top, R) Lou Gehrig, 1922. (Bottom) Gehrig in high school (middle, third from R). On June 2, 1925, Pipp (who had hit .295 and led the AL in triples the year before) asked to be excused from a game because of a headache. His replacement had played on a national championship high school team but earned his scholarship to Columbia as a football player (and by taking a special six-month preparatory course to pass academic muster). There, the *New York Times* called him "the best college player since George Sisler." He dropped out after two years to sign with the Yankees.

"The boy picked up a bat — one of Ruth's, by some curious chance — and advanced to the plate. He was obviously nervous, missed the first two pitches, then bounced one weakly over second base. Then he hit one that soared into the right field bleachers, high up, where only Ruth had ever hit a ball.... He hit another ball in there — another — still another. His nervousness had slipped from him now. 'That's enough,' Huggins cried. He turned to the players. 'His name's Gehrig,' he said, and walked slowly behind the hulking figure of the youngster toward the dugout. The players looked after them in silence." — Frank Graham

The Senators won again in 1925, the year of Babe Ruth's famous stomachache. Tumbling to a .290 average and only 66 RBIs, Ruth was made to shoulder most of the blame for the Yankees' descent to seventh place; but the real culprits were ineffective Yankee pitchers and the thoughtless Red Sox, who were now so awful that they had no one Ruppert and Huggins could snaffle up to fill a gaping shortstop hole. With Ruth ailing, teammate Bob Meusel took the slugging honors. And rookie Lou Gehrig replaced Wally Pipp at first base.

While the Red Sox were occupying last place for the first of a record six straight seasons in 1925, those former doormats, the A's, moved up to second. A melding of young talent, including Al Simmons, Mickey Cochrane and Lefty Grove with standbys Ed Rommel and Bing Miller, gave Mack what appeared to be a dynasty that would rival his 1910–1914 clubs. In the interim, McGraw's own dynasty became one of the past when Pittsburgh's crew of "free spirits" bolted to an early lead and was never caught. Second baseman Eddie Moore was the lone Pirate regular below .300; and while the pitching staff yielded no 20-game winners, Bill McKechnie could choose from five solid starters, including Jughandle Johnny Morrison, who doubled

as the league's top relief man.

The Pirates had no relievers, however, who could match Washington's Marberry, and they fell behind in the Series three games to one. As no team had ever rallied from such a deficit in World Series play, the Senators appeared to have a lock on their second consecutive world title. But the luck that had brought them victory over the Giants in 1924 on Earl McNeely's famous "pebble" grounder suddenly deserted them, and the Pirates pulled out the Series with a 3.54 staff ERA, the worst to date by a winning club. The final game evolved into a contest between Pirate second-line relief pitchers and stubborn Bucky Harris, who refused out of sentiment to remove Walter Johnson and insert Marberry to hold a lead. In consequence, Johnson absorbed a nine-run pounding, while the Pirates' Red Oldham, who had managed only one save all season, held the Senators in check to end the series. Playing in a losing cause, Joe Harris set a seven-game Series mark when he slugged .880. The record stood until 1972.

Now manager of the Cardinals, Hornsby saw his average sag to .317 in 1926 and that of teammate Jimmy Bottomley fall to .299. That those two figures were good enough to support a pennant winner

Brooklyn outfielders, 1928. Jigger Statz, Rube Bressler, Gink Hendrick, Ty Tyson, Babe Herman, Max Carey (L to R). John Lardner wrote, "Floyd Caves Herman, known as Babe, did not always catch fly balls on the top of his head, but he could do it in a pinch. He never tripled into a triple play, but he once doubled into a double play, which is the next best thing." When Herman returned to Brooklyn in 1945 as a pinch hitter, eight years after he last played in the majors, he tripped and fell over first base on his first hit. Statz was the only man in baseball history, other than Ty Cobb, to collect more than 4,000 career hits. More than 3,300 of them, however, were made with Los Angeles of the Pacific Coast League, for whom Statz played for 19 seasons. Carey—born Maximilian Carnarius—was the most prolific base stealer in NL history until Lou Brock.

Joe Sewell. He broke in as a replacement for Ray Chapman, in 1920. In a 14-year career — during which he averaged .312 — Sewell would strike out only 114 times. In 1929 he played 115 consecutive games without striking out.

was largely attributable to three factors: the continued decline of the Giants; batting averages of .222 and .191 by Max Carey and Clyde Barnhart, the two men the Pirates employed in centerfield between Kiki Cuyler and rookie sensation Paul Waner; and Cincinnati's inability to find hitters to go with Bubbles Hargrave, the first catcher in history to win a batting championship, and rookie Cuckoo Christensen, his runner-up, who came within three points of being the most improbable batting leader ever. (Christensen played 57 games the next season, and then disappeared.) In the most evenly balanced race since 1915 the Cards won with a .578 percentage, finishing two games ahead of the Reds and just seven in front of the fourth-place Cubs, instantly back in contention after dropping to the cellar the previous year.

American League competition was no less even,

with the lone exception of the Red Sox. The sixth-place Tigers finished just 12 games behind the pennant-winning Yankees and had three of the league's top four hitters, two of whom—Bob Fothergill and leader Heinie Manush—had not been good enough a year earlier to break into the Bengals' all-.370-hitting outfield. In the Yankees' immediate tracks were the Indians, spearheaded by strikeout ace Uhle and Joe Sewell, the shortstop who was achieving fame as the man who never struck out. Sewell in 1926 had an "off" year when he fanned six times, twice more than he had in 1925.

By winning the first pennant in their history the Cardinals were the popular favorites in the Series and gained immortality when they won in seven games behind 39-year-old Grover Alexander, back on top after a decade of toiling for second-rate teams. Alexander's two complete game wins and seventh-game save eclipsed Card shortstop Tommy Thevenow, the Series' leading hitter, who hit a homer in the second game that was truly remarkable; he played 12 more years in the majors without ever hitting another. Legend has fixed Alexander's strikeout of Tony Lazzeri as the act that ended the Series, but this actually came in the seventh inning. The game actually ended when Ruth was caught trying to steal second base with two out in the ninth inning and Meusel at bat.

In 1927 the A's had seven Hall of Famers on their club, won 91 games, had a .303 team batting average, and yet were never in contention. They were matched against the Murderers Row team from the Bronx that won a league-record 110 games, and

Lloyd Waner (L) and Paul Waner (R), flanking their parents and sister. Lloyd struck out almost as infrequently as Joe Sewell — in 1941, as a part-time player, he came to bat 219 times without fanning once. Buddy Hassett quoted Paul's theory of hitting: "He said he just laid his bat on his shoulder and when he saw a pitch he liked he threw it off."

The site of Yankee Stadium, the completed structure, and the man who made it possible, with his constituents. Jacob Ruppert purchased the land — in full view of the Polo Grounds, from which his team was being evicted — for $600,000. "Some thought it should be named Ruth Field," wrote Robert Creamer, "but Ruppert insisted it be called Yankee Stadium.... The only area in the ballpark named after Ruth was the right-field bleachers, where most of his home runs landed. It was commonly known as Ruthville." Ruppert said, "Yankee Stadium was a mistake. Not mine, but the Giants'."

"Ruth filled the parks by developing the home run into a hit of exciting elegance. For almost two decades he battered fences with such regularity that baseball's basic structure was eventually pounded into a different shape."
—Lee Allen

Aspects of Ruth: Facing page. (Top) In a publicity still, with Lou Archer, from *Babe Comes Home;* at a House of David exhibition game. (Middle) With Graham McNamee; with Amelita Galli-Curci and Franklin D. Roosevelt, 1920. (Bottom) With Yankee mascot Ray Kelly; at his second wedding, 1929. This page: (Top, L) With Gehrig; (Bottom, L) with Gehrig and agent-entrepreneur Christy Walsh; (Bottom, R) with one of his two adopted daughters.

"He was a parade all by himself, a burst of dazzle and jingle, Santa Claus drinking his whiskey straight and groaning with a bellyache caused by gluttony. Babe Ruth made the music that his joyous years danced to in a continuous party.... What Babe Ruth is comes down, one generation handing it to the next, as a national heirloom."—Jimmy Cannon

a Babe Ruth whose 60 homers were four more than the total hit by *any* of the other seven teams in the league. The Yankees for a change also had strong pitching, as Hoyt, Pennock, Urban Shocker and rookie Wilcy Moore all had big seasons. Hall of Famers Hoyt and Pennock both pitched for years without much distinction for other clubs, and it is reasonable to surmise neither would have a plaque in Cooperstown today if he had not had the good fortune to be traded while still in his prime to the Yankees.

Ruth's season-long pursuit of the home run record all but buried Gehrig's new RBI record of 175 and the exciting batting duel between Heilmann and Al Simmons that was not resolved until the season's final day, when Heilmann went six for eight in a doubleheader against the Indians to overtake Simmons for the crown and miss a .400 season by a single hit. The National League batting race for the first time in history was a struggle between two siblings, the Waners, with Paul winning and Lloyd finishing third behind Hornsby, who had been swapped to the Giants for Frisch after a falling-out with Card owner Sam Breadon. The Waners, Pie Traynor and Glen Wright—an erratic fielder but one of the strongest run producers ever to play shortstop—gave the Pirates such outstanding hit-

ting that they hardly missed Kiki Cuyler. Cuyler was benched in mid-season by manager Donie Bush for refusing to bat second in the order, believing he was more effective in the third slot. Still, Pittsburgh had to wait until the season's final day before clinching the pennant; the Giants and Cardinals had both stayed close all through September. Each benefitted from the Hornsby-Frisch deal, the Cards gaining speed and the Giants obtaining a hitter who could team with Bill Terry, but it was the contributions of two ancients that nearly brought them the pennant. For the Cards, Alexander became the first National Leaguer to be a 20-game winner after age 40; and the Giants' 35-year-old George Harper batted .331, filling a right-field gap that the tragic illness of Ross Youngs had left.

Decimated in the Series in four straight games, the Pirates ended the season demoralized. It would be 33 years before the club that had won five pennants in a quarter century would win another. Two other eras also came to a close in 1927. Ban Johnson, reduced in power by the appointment of Judge Landis and in recent years little more than a figurehead, resigned as American League president, and Garry Herrmann, who had been chairman of the National Commission during its heyday in the teens, quietly left his post as president of the Reds.

The 1928 Yankees. They were preparing to meet the Cardinals, to whom they had lost in 1926 when 39-year-old Grover Alexander had dramatically emerged from a hangover to strike out Tony Lazzeri (rear, third from R). After that game, Alexander rebuffed a reporter: "How do I feel? Go ask Lazzeri how he feels." This time, the Yankees would win in four straight, outscoring St. Louis 27-10. Middle row, second from left, is Leo Durocher; Earle Combs, who coined the term "Five O'Clock Lightning" to describe the late-inning heroics of Gehrig and Ruth, is at rear, extreme right.

Art Shires had the publicity skills of Dizzy Dean but he had neither the charm nor the baseball talent (though he did hit .291 in four seasons with the White Sox, Senators and Braves). He called himself "Art the Great" and tried to combine a boxing career with one on the diamond. "His self-chosen role," wrote Robert Smith, "was to assert that he could do anything, outshout the loudest shouters, beat the best boxers, wrestle the strongest wrestler to the ground. The fact that he could do none of these things only mildly mitigated his paper success." He did once manage to knock out his manager, Lena Blackburne.

(Top) Al Schacht and Nick Altrock (L and R, front) extended their on-field clowning into the off-season with this touring basketball team. The players included (rear) umpire Dolly Stark (third from L) and one-time Dodger Snooks Dowd (second from R), a second baseman who could not make the throw to first; he opened the 1926 season for Brooklyn and was given his release two days later. Although Schacht managed only 24 major league decisions as a pitcher with the Senators, his playmate Altrock was a three-time 20-game winner for the White Sox. (Bottom) Heinie Manush (L) and Paul Waner (R) with friend, in a benefit show. Waner, who wrote the skit, was an Oklahoma farm boy who read Seneca in his spare time; Manush had a lifetime .330 average and was so out of place when he arrived in Brooklyn near the end of his career that he was respectfully called "the club pro" — he may have been the only one there.

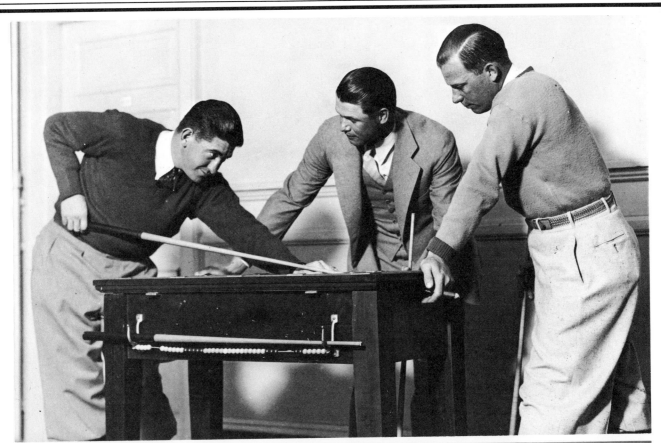

At leisure. (Top) Mickey Cochrane, Jimmie Foxx, Jimmy Dykes (L to R). Connie Mack wrote in 1950 that women often asked him if they should permit their sons to be professional ballplayers. He would reply, "Yes, it is a healthful and honorable profession.... I should say that the habits of ballplayers are on as high a level as those of men in any other pursuit of life." (Bottom) On the set of *Slide, Kelly, Slide*. Miller Huggins complained that Bob Meusel's attitude "is one of just plain indifference." Withal, he was a .309 hitter. Interviewing the silent Lazzeri, said one writer, "is like trying to mine coal with a nail file and a pair of scissors." His power was unobtrusive too: in 1930, he had 121 RBIs on only nine home runs. Casey Stengel said Emil "Irish" Meusel — Bob's older brother — was the best right-handed hitter in the National League, after Hornsby.

(L to R) Heinie Manush, George Kelly, Edd Roush. Manush spent seven years in the minors after he finished his big league career. In Cincinnati, Roush often called pitches, signaling the catcher by the position he took in center field. Kelly was at first an enormously unpopular replacement for Hal Chase with the Giants, but his consistent power soon brought him acceptance. All three are in the Hall of Fame.

The year 1928 saw the finish of yet another chapter, when Cobb and Speaker made their last appearances in major league uniforms, and the third member of their once dominant batting trio, Eddie Collins, was relegated to pinch-hitting duties. Strangely enough, all played for the A's, who once again had seven Hall of Famers and once again lost out to the Yankees. Philadelphia made a close race of it but came up short when age slowed Cobb in the final weeks and Mack could not make up his mind where to place the booming bat of 20-year-old Jimmie Foxx in the lineup. In third place—the last time they would finish that high until 1944—were the Browns, with little going for them but Heinie Manush and two 20-game winners, General Crowder and Sam Gray. The Red Sox, with nothing at all going for them, finished last again despite having lured Bill Carrigan out of retirement to manage.

The other Boston team became Hornsby's third stop in as many seasons. With the club for only that one year, he became one of their two twentieth-century batting champions while the team was in Boston. Playing beside him was the league's fourth-best hitter, George Sisler, but the rest of the club was so awful that these two greats could not keep it from losing 103 games. The Phils, losers 109

Chicago American Giants. They were Negro League Champions in 1926 and 1927. Manager "Gentleman Dave" Malarcher (Middle, fourth from L) told Robert Peterson about playing, travelling and living circumstances in the black leagues: "They were conditions which I could not continue to bear." He left baseball in 1934 to pursue a career in real estate. Pitcher Willie Foster (Top, fourth from L) was pioneer Rube Foster's half-brother. He later became dean of men at Alcorn College.

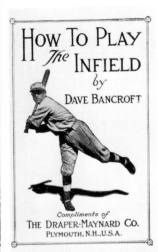

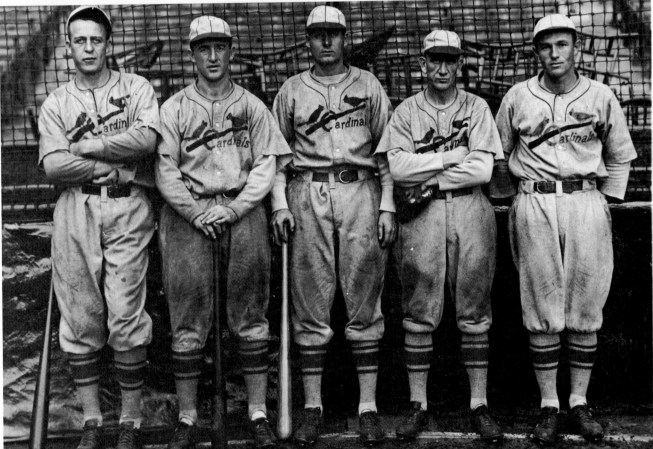

(Top, L) Cardinal mascots — child and man-child. The freakish mascot was a creature of baseball superstition; the best known, Eddie Bennett of the Yankees, was a middle-aged hunchback whose hump Yankee hitters would touch for luck before batting. (Top, C) Rabbit Maranville with his father, 1928 Series. As manager of the Cubs in 1925, he once went through the team sleeping car at 2 a.m., shouting "There will be no sleeping on this club under Maranville management." It was his only year as a manager. (Top, R) Author Dave Bancroft — Beauty Bancroft, he was called — was sent to the Braves by John McGraw "to do something big for my old friend Matty," who was Boston's president. McGraw called Bancroft "the best shortstop in baseball, without a doubt." Jim Bottomley, Frankie Frisch, Tommy Thevenow, Rabbit Maranville, Andy High (L to R). Bottomley came to the Cards' attention by writing a letter proclaiming himself big league material. He had six straight 100-RBI seasons, and in 1924 had a record 12 RBIs in one nine-inning game.

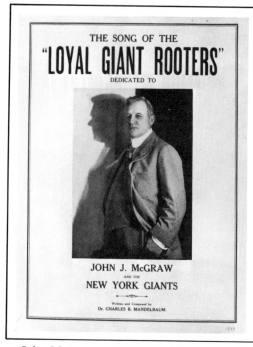 

John McGraw, celebrated; Mel Ott, his last cause for celebration. By the late twenties, said Bill Terry, McGraw "was the type fellow who would call all the pitches until you got in a spot, then he'd leave you on your own." Ott caused no trouble but, John Lardner wrote, "McGraw operated the biggest stable of sleuths outside Scotland Yard" to keep his other players in check.

times for rookie skipper Burt Shotton, were even more ghastly. Third baseman Pinky Whitney was their sole bright spot, although Chuck Klein, a late-season replacement for the aged Cy Williams, hit .360 in 64 games and quickly demonstrated an aptitude for caroming hits off the short right-field wall in Baker Bowl, the Phils' idiosyncratic home park.

Winning 25 games in September, the Giants came from far behind and missed beating out the Cardinals by only two games. The Giants had stronger hitting than the Cards and the league's top pitcher in Larry Benton, but Bottomley's slugging and the steadying influence of newly acquired shortstop Rabbit Maranville made McGraw a loser again in his attempt to claim one last pennant before retiring. For the second year in a row the National League entry came out of World Series play empty-handed, as Ruth and Gehrig between them set virtually every batting record for a four-game Series.

In the late twenties the Cubs, Braves and Phils made an absorbing study in their contrasting approaches to maintaining a major league franchise. After falling into the cellar in 1925 (albeit by only a half-game margin), the Cubs began the following season with three rejects from other clubs—Riggs Stephenson, Hack Wilson and Charlie Root—who made them immediately competitive again. When they obtained the disgruntled Kiki Cuyler from the Pirates a year later for Sparky Adams, a good player but scarcely in Cuyler's class, the fiber was present for their 1929 pennant winner. The Braves

and Phils could probably have had all four of these players for the asking but opted instead to go for former stars like Sisler, Maranville, Joe Dugan, Clarence Mitchell and Virgil Barnes, who were near the end of the line but still had some box office appeal. Illustrating the penurious and inept manner in which the weaker franchises of the period faced the problem of entertaining their fans, Braves owner Judge Emil Fuchs traded Hornsby in 1929 so he could manage the club himself, and the Phils, already one of the best hitting teams in the majors, acquired still another batsman, Lefty O'Doul, from the Giants in the off season—while ignoring the development of a pitching staff that over the next two seasons would be the worst in the game's history. Meanwhile, the Cubs happily took Hornsby off Fuchs's hands, and later pried Zack Taylor away from him to replace the ailing Gabby Hartnett. The two helped manager Joe McCarthy win the first of his nine pennants.

Once Mack decided Foxx's best position was first base, the A's had no trouble winning their first pennant in 15 years. Like the Cubs, the A's were a franchise that knew how to get maximum mileage out of limited financial resources, but in another way the A's were totally unique. Of the eight front-liners on the 1929 team only Bing Miller had previously played regularly elsewhere, and Jack Quinn was the only one of the six pitchers with over 100 innings who did not win his first major league game in an Athletics uniform. But Branch Rickey's notion of building a farm system to breed young play-

(Top, L) Andy Cohen (L) and Rogers Hornsby. Cohen, Hornsby's untried replacement when the latter was traded from New York to Boston after the 1927 season, started off hot, and one New York paper ran a daily box demonstrating his statistical superiority to Hornsby. "That's a lousy trick to play on the kid," Hornsby said. "I ain't hitting now, but when I start I'll lose him." He would outhit Cohen by 113 points that year. Cohen said, "It is hard for fans to believe a guy named Cohen can play ball." (Top, R) Charlie Root, who won 201 games for the Cubs, and who may or may not have given up a "called" home run to Babe Ruth in 1932. (Bottom) The 1929 Cubs. They were the victims of Howard Ehmke and the ten-run inning in the Series; "everybody in Chicago was mad," wrote Warren Brown, "and kept getting madder."

ers was beginning to take hold, and the A's were the last dynasty to be molded exclusively by the once common practice of purchasing promising players from minor league clubs.

Grove, Rube Walberg and George Earnshaw carried Mack's pitching load during the regular season, but his surprise choice for the Series opener was 35-year-old Howard Ehmke. Using mostly off-speed deliveries, Ehmke kept the Cubs so off-balance that he struck out a record 13 batters and won 3–1 over Root. Four days later, ahead 2–1 in games, the A's overcame an 8–0 Cub lead in their legendary 10-run seventh inning, highlighted by Mule Haas's three-run homer. Haas homered again in the ninth inning the following day to tie the Series finale and set the Cubs up for Miller's double, which decided the issue. Seldom much of a slugger, Haas hit only .161 in the Series, and Ehmke never won another big league game after his Series masterpiece.

The decade ended sadly for the Yankees when Miller Huggins took ill and died in September. Overpowering just two short years earlier, the team was on the downswing by 1929 and had only one league leader—Ruth, in homers and slugging average. The Indians, strong throughout the decade, were still holding their own at its end, but their sister club in Ohio, which had also begun the decade strongly, was at its lowest ebb. Seventh in 1929, the Reds were as bad off for the moment as the Phils and Braves. Worst off were the Red Sox, who scored the fewest runs of any team during the 1929 season while playing in a park that was nearly as friendly to hitters as Baker Bowl.

The Red Sox and Reds both had even worse times ahead of them in the next decade, but by its end they would be back among the top clubs again. In 1939 the Braves and Phils would still be vying for the cellar, having progressed not an inch in over 20 years. —David Nemec

Honus Wagner as Pittsburgh coach. In his late years, wrote Robert Creamer, he would "swipe baseballs and trade them for beers." Wrote Robert Smith, "The new customers yelled for longer and longer hits and for faster and faster pitching. Who cared about a single run, a single dollar or the life of a single man?"

SERIES:
Pepper Martin vs. Philadelphia, 1931
By Red Smith

PEPPER Martin looked like an outsize bird of prey. When he ran he took flight, wings beating, beak splitting the wind, and when he stole a base he swooped down on it with a predator's headlong dive. "The Wild Horse of the Osage," he was called by Harrison J. Weaver, trainer of the St. Louis Cardinals, and the sobriquet caught on during the 1931 World Series when this upstart from Oklahoma stole Mickey Cochrane's drawers in broad daylight.

It was possible to stuff John Leonard Martin into city clothes but his natural plumage consisted of dungarees and a work shirt open at the throat, no socks or underwear. He had a love affair with midget racing cars that lasted a year or so, but in his heart he believed the only way God intended man to travel was in a pickup truck, with a shotgun hung crosswise behind the driver's head and a brace of bird dogs in the rear.

"Pepper Martin looks so honest," said Fresco Thompson, a contemporary in the National League, "and when he talks he sounds so honest and the fact is he is so honest that if you could get him in with you on a con game you could take all the money in the world."

In 1931 Martin was a rookie centerfielder with the Cardinals, a rookie of 27 who had been knocking around in baseball for seven years, mostly in the St. Louis farm system. He had spent the summer of 1928 polishing the Cardinals' bench, used almost exclusively as a pinch runner, and the next year he was back in the minors. In 1930 he batted .363 for the Rochester farm in the International League, but the Cardinals regarded an average like that

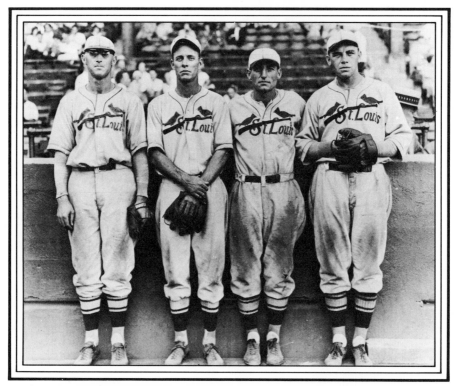

(L to R) Chick Hafey, George Watkins, Pepper Martin, Wally Roettger. Among St. Louis' first four outfielders in 1931, only Watkins (.288) hit under .300. Of the pull-hitting Hafey, Fred Lindstrom said, "It sure will be difficult for third basemen to get insurance while that guy is in the league."

coolly. In 1930 all Cardinals, meaning everybody in the batting order, hit over .300. The regulars ranged from .303 for Taylor Douthit to .373 for George Watkins, and on the bench were people named Ernie Orsatti, .321, Gus Mancuso, .366, Showboat Fisher, .374, and Ray Blades, .396.

Even so, they had to close with a devouring rush to win the pennant in 1930. They were 12 games back in fourth place behind the Cubs, Giants and Dodgers as August ended. By the time they got to Brooklyn on their last eastern trip they were in second place, half a game behind the Dodgers. On the eve of the first game in Ebbets Field, Bill Hallahan smashed his right hand in a taxi door. He was up most of the night while Doc Weaver applied hot and cold packs, and the next afternoon he went out to pitch with his left hand against Dazzy Vance.

The game was scoreless through the ninth inning. Hallahan had a no-hitter for eight, and at one point he retired 20 batters in a row. In the top of the tenth a single by Douthit and a double by Andy High gave the Cardinals a run, but in their half the Dodgers filled the bases with one out.

Al Lopez hit a ground ball that almost hopped over little Sparky Adams at shortstop, but Adams snatched it out of the air and threw to second where Frank Frisch pivoted and fired to first a breath ahead of Lopez for the double play. The Cardinals were in first place to stay, but something was lack-

ing. Hallahan knew what it was. It was his roommate, Flint Rhem.

Scheduled to pitch the second game in Brooklyn, Rhem hadn't shown up in the hotel the night Hallahan smashed his hand, and he didn't show up the night after the first game. He surfaced the next day with an interesting explanation: he had been kidnapped by Brooklyn gamblers and forced at gunpoint to drink whiskey as long as he was conscious. This was 1930, when the clammy hand of Prohibition was on the land, and you had to know somebody to *buy* a drink in Brooklyn.

Years later, one Jay Hanna Dean remarked casually that he had accompanied Rhem on his adventure without his absence from hotel or park being detected. Maybe so, maybe not. No one will ever know the truth, but it is a fact that Dizzy Dean did make that eastern trip with the Cardinals and it is true that he could have defected without being missed. A rookie fresh from St. Joseph, Missouri, by way of Houston, he was along only to pitch for batting practice. He was long and loose and gangling, with arms too long for his jacket and a look of ineffable gratitude in his eyes if you said, "Hello, Diz."

After the pennant was safe, Dean closed that season by beating Pittsburgh, 3–1, with a five-hitter. That winter he paid a visit to Branch Rickey, the Cardinals' vice president. For at least two hours,

Martin with string of quail. Roy Moore, Martin's teammate with Houston in 1929, said, "Old Pepper goes out on the prairie and scares up a bunch of rabbits. He runs along with these rabbits. He reaches down and feels the sides of these rabbits. If the rabbit is a bit thin he lets him go...if the rabbit is nice and fat, old Pepper picks him up and puts him in his bag."

In 1928, when the Yankees swept the Cardinals 4-0 in the Series, St. Louis's pitchers included (Top, L) Clarence Mitchell, Grover Alexander and Jess Haines (L to R). Mitchell was 37, Alexander 41, Haines 34. Making his first appearance in 1930, on the last day of the season, was (Top R) Jay Hanna Dean, age 19. He beat the Pirates on a three-hitter. (Bottom) Branch Rickey, who built one pennant winner as another faded, was, wrote John Lardner, "a man opposed to Sunday baseball except when the gate receipts exceeded $5,000."

Dizzy Dean, 1934. He didn't appear in the 1931 Series; he had been relegated to the minors that season after a spring training altercation with Gabby Street. "If Dean is going to worry anybody this year," Street said, "it'll be the manager of Scottsdale or one of the other farms."

the door to Rickey's office was closed. When at last it opened, the vice president emerged wearily. He was in shirtsleeves, collar unbuttoned, bow tie undone, hair disheveled.

"Do you know what that—that busher said to me?" Rickey said. "He told me, 'Mr. Rickey, I'll put more people in your park than anybody since Babe Ruth.' That—that country jake! Judas priest, if there were one more like him in baseball, I'd get out of the game!"

The evening would come when Rickey's family, at dinner at home in St. Louis County, would be startled to hear the head of the house mumbling over his soup.

"I'm a man of some intelligence," Rickey told himself. "I've had some education, passed the bar, practiced law. I've been a teacher and I deal with men of substance, statesmen, business leaders, the clergy. Then why—" the voice rose— "why do I spend my time arguing with Dizzy Dean?"

Still, the fact is that the man who had discovered Dizzy and brought him to the Cardinals was none other than Wesley Branch Rickey, a gifted judge of talent who was almost solely responsible for building a bankrupt franchise to supremacy in the National League.

Loquacious, polysyllabic and adroit, Rickey could elevate circumlocution to the level of fine art. Some men in baseball were daunted by his mind; they never went into discussion of a player trade without fear of being hornswoggled. "Keep your mouth shut, your hands in your pockets and don't drink," was the advice of one.

In a sometimes rowdy company, Rickey was a total abstainer. He was steeped in the old-style religion, and because he was a razor-sharp operator who refused to play ball or even visit the park on Sunday, he was often pictured as a sanctimonious

fraud. His observance of the Sabbath was not a pose and was not, as was widely believed, due to a promise to his mother, nor did he consider Sunday baseball sinful. When his devout and devoted mother raised no objections to his seeking a career in professional baseball—the equivalent, in rural Ohio in 1902, of selling his soul to the devil—he told himself that this was the least he could do to show his respect and love. He kept the promise to himself, even when it got him fired from his first major league job as a catcher for Cincinnati.

He caught for the St. Louis Browns and briefly for the Yankees, coached baseball at Michigan and doubled as president and field manager of the Browns. He then joined the Cardinals when they were so poor they took spring training at Washington University in St. Louis, unable to travel south.

As vice president of the Cardinals, Rickey reasoned that since the club couldn't afford to buy players, the only alternative was to grow them. To make connections with minor league clubs where raw talent could be sent for development, he invented the "working agreement," whereby he would help to staff a team in the minors in exchange for first call on that club's players at the end of the season.

To gather the raw material, he set up tryout camps for free agents. These three-day workouts were conducted in various parts of the country, and kids without ties in professional ball were invited to the camp nearest their homes to display their talents to a jury of scouts. The first camp uncovered Ray Blades, a youth from Mt. Vernon, Illinois, with scorching speed afoot. He batted .301 over 11 years with the Cardinals and managed them for two seasons. Years later a young redhead named Albert Schoendienst showed up from Germantown, Illinois. Red Schoendienst, a magnificent second base-

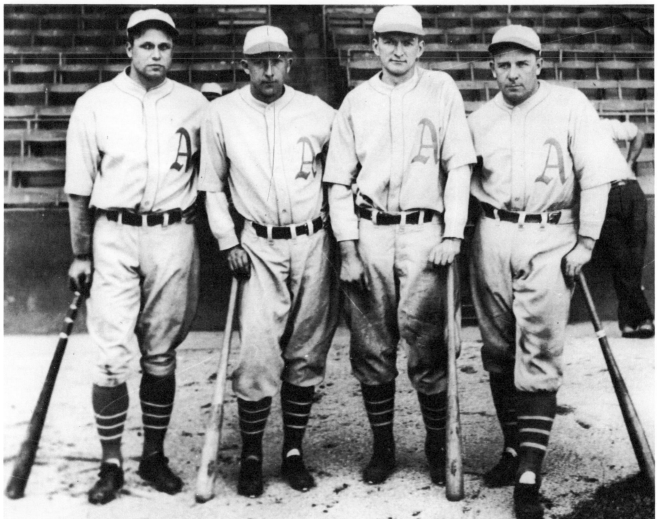

(Top) Philadelphia pitchers, 1931. (L to R) Hank McDonald, Lefty Grove, Rube Walberg, Lew Krausse, Ed Rommel, Jim Peterson, Roy Mahaffey, Waite Hoyt. This was the third straight year Grove led the majors in winning percentage, ERA and strikeouts. Krausse's son, Lew Jr., would pitch for the A's from 1961-69. (Bottom) Philadelphia infielders, 1931. (L to R) Jimmie Foxx, Max Bishop, Joe Boley, Jimmy Dykes. Dib Williams played in Boley's place in the Series. It was Lefty Gomez who, trying to decide how to pitch to Foxx, told Bill Dickey, "I'd rather not throw the ball at all."

man, played for the Cardinals in 14 of his 19 seasons and managed the team for six years. Hundreds of others, including Dizzy Dean, emerged from the tryout camps.

In 1919 Rickey saw a knuckleball pitcher named Jesse Haines work for Kansas City. He had to borrow the $10,000 it cost to buy him, but after 18 years with the Cardinals, Haines wound up in the Hall of Fame. More significantly, Haines was the last player the Cardinals bought for more than a quarter of a century. Rickey's farm system supplied all the others who won pennants in 1926, 1928, 1930, 1931 and 1934.

Winning the pennant in 1930, the Cardinals found Connie Mack and the Philadelphia Athletics waiting at the pass. This was the team that had smashed the Chicago Cubs in five games in the 1929 World Series, winning one game with a ten-run assault in the seventh inning when Chicago had a shutout, 8–0. The Hall of Fame awaited Lefty Grove, Mickey Cochrane, Jimmie Foxx and Al Simmons, and accomplices like Bing Miller, Mule Haas, Jimmy Dykes, Max Bishop and Joe Boley were not far behind them. They rubbed out the Cardinals, four victories to two.

Taylor Douthit was a dazzling fielder who may have been a shade slower at 30 than at 21. Probably he would have been forgiven for this if he hadn't been a resourceful bargainer who had worked up to a salary level of $14,000. With the Great Depression nearing rock bottom, this lent a special charm to a farmhand who could hit .363, could run like a striped ape and would give an arm and leg for $4,500.

So, early in 1931, Douthit was traded to Cincinnati and Pepper Martin took his place in center field. He batted an even .300 while the Cardinals breezed to their second successive pennant. Getting there, they found the Athletics already in possession of their third championship and looking more formidable than ever. Grove had won 31 games, George Earnshaw 21 and Rube Walberg 20, and Simmons led major league hitters with an average of .390.

The World Series opened in St. Louis with Grove beating Paul Derringer, 6 to 2. Derringer was a towering rookie who rocked back on the mound with his front foot two stories high, then came whistling over the top. He had earned the starting assignment by winning 18 games, but the Athletics worked him over rudely. Meanwhile the

Taylor Douthit, Pepper Martin. Martin became a regular when Douthit—who had missed only two St. Louis games in three years—was traded to Cincinnati. Rickey made the deal on Friday, to be announced on Monday; Douthit made eight straight hits over the weekend.

Series combatants. (Top, L) Frank Frisch and Eddie Collins; (Top, R) Jim Bottomley and Al Simmons; (C) Gabby Street and Connie Mack; (Bottom) Burleigh Grimes (L) and George Earnshaw (R). Grimes, wrote John Kieran, "always looked like a man who was about to commit assault and battery when he threw the ball." Earnshaw was so angered by Martin's base-stealing that he wanted rookie Joe Palmisano to replace Cochrane behind the plate.

Cardinals made 12 hits off Grove, who that evening displayed a broken blister on the middle finger of his left hand.

Nobody paid much attention to the fact that three of the St. Louis hits were made by Pepper Martin. He rapped Grove for two singles and a double, and after one of the singles he stole second. In the first World Series game of his life, he was serving notice of his presence.

The next day Hallahan shut Philadelphia out on three hits. In his first time at bat, Martin lined a single to left and when Simmons slipped fielding the ball Pepper scoured around first and went into second on his face. As Earnshaw pitched to Jimmie Wilson, Martin took off like the thief he was, diving into third ahead of Cochrane's throw. Wilson flied out and Martin scooted home with the first run.

That was in the second inning. In the seventh, with Hallahan protecting his one-run lead, Martin singled and promptly stole second. He took third as Wilson grounded out. Then with Charley Gelbert at bat he broke for the plate. Gelbert laid down a bunt. Earnshaw pounced on the ball and made a backhand flip to Cochrane but the toss was high and Martin slid home beneath it.

The suicide squeeze made it 2–0. Hallahan would have been home free except for a bizarre bit of confusion that came to be known as "Wilson's boner."

Opening the ninth inning, Hallahan walked Foxx. Bing Miller flied out, Dykes walked and Hallahan got a called third strike past Dib Williams, the shortstop. With two out and runners on first and second, Jimmy Moore batted for Earnshaw and the count went to one ball, two strikes. Hallahan broke off a curve, and Foxx broke for third base. What prompted him to steal was a secret Jimmie took to the grave, for the run he represented was worthless by itself and, in the circumstances, risking the game's final putout was a mortal sin.

Hallahan's pitch came in low and broke down. Moore swung, missed, and threw his bat away. Guided by the animal instinct of a catcher, Wilson threw to third to cut off Foxx. Jake Flowers leaped high for the ball, came down and crouched for a sweeping tag but Foxx had slid in safely. No matter; Moore had struck out. Flowers's first impulse was to fling the ball into the stands in celebration but it occurred to him that Hallahan might want the ball as a souvenir. And now Eddie Collins, a

Paul Derringer, Lefty Grove. Two years earlier, Heywood Broun had written, "When danger beckoned thickest it was always Grove who stood towering on the mound, whipping over strikes against the luckless Chicago batters." In the 1931 Series he beat Derringer twice; the latter's luck was such that, with Cincinnati in 1933, he finished 7-27 on a 3.30 ERA.

Philadephia coach, came racing in from his station at third base shouting to Moore, who was trudging toward the dugout.

Clutching Moore by the shoulders, Collins gave him a shove toward first base. Puzzled but obedient, Moore trotted to the bag. Now Collins was talking to Dick Nallin, the chief umpire. Fans were on the field and Cardinals were converging on the mound to congratulate Hallahan when Nallin made his ruling: the third strike on Moore had not been fairly caught but had bounced into Wilson's mitt; the catcher should have tagged Moore or thrown him out at first instead of throwing to third.

Instead of a 2–0 shutout, Hallahan had the bases filled with two out and Max Bishop at bat.

"A guy I didn't like to pitch to," Hallahan said later, "a smart little hitter who generally got the bat on the ball. 'Camera Eye,' they called him."

Hallahan turned up the steam. Bishop popped a twisting foul toward the visitors' dugout, where temporary boxes had been built out from the grandstand. Jim Bottomley, the first baseman, stretched over a dozen heads, caught the ball, lost his balance and disappeared in a tangle of cash customers. The series was tied at one victory each.

There was a day off for travel (by special train then) followed by a day of rain. Something happened that rainy Sunday that would have made headlines but it didn't get out until Frank Frisch mentioned it years later. Crawling out of bed that morning, Frisch felt a stab of pain in his lower back that brought him to his knees. He crawled to the telephone to summon Doc Weaver. The Cardinals' second baseman had lumbago and all the trainer could do was apply heat and tape him up. Playing the last five games strapped up like a mummy, Frisch finished the series with two doubles and five singles, drove in a run, scored two and handled 35 chances in the field without error.

Instead of headlines about Frisch's misery, the papers carried items like this in *The New York Times*: "PHILADELPHIA, Oct. 5—President Hoover will receive a cordial welcome when he arrives for tomorrow's World Series game, for his presence in the park invariably has served as a good omen for the Athletics. The President will occupy the same box at Shibe Park from which he watched the Athletics defeat the Cardinals last year and the Cubs in 1929."

Mr. Hoover's welcome turned out to be warm, but not exactly cordial. His arrival set off a wave of booing that spread and swelled and became an impromptu chant: "We want beer! We want beer!" The President sat with his hands folded over his abdomen and watched Burleigh Grimes pitch a no-hitter for seven innings, a one-hitter until he had two Athletics out in the ninth and wind up with a two-hitter, 5–2, after a two-run home run by Simmons.

As for Martin, in the second inning he singled off Grove, sending Bottomley from first to third,

Harrison J. "Doc" Weaver. The Cardinal trainer joined the club in 1927 and served 28 years. He patented a device for hay fever sufferers, the "nasal filter"; introduced knit underwear to replace sliding pads; and concocted a preposterous hand signal, used on opposing teams, called the "inverted triple whammy."

Jimmie Foxx, Chick Hafey, Al Simmons (L to R). "My gall bladder was in awful shape," Burleigh Grimes said later. "It would hurt even more when I'd look at Simmons, Foxx and some of those guys." Hafey, St. Louis's best hitter, did not intimidate the A's pitchers in the Series; he managed only four singles.

dashed to third base on Wilson's single to right and scored St. Louis's second run on a sacrifice fly. In the fourth, with Chick Hafey on first, he sliced a double to the wall in right, and scored behind Hafey on a single by Grimes. Thus he was involved in four of the Cardinals' five runs, but by some oversight he neglected to steal anything.

He made up for that the next day, racing down to second ahead of Cochrane's despairing throw the first time he got on base. This was in the fifth inning and his single was the first hit off Earnshaw. Big George allowed only one more hit, a double into the left-field corner by—who else?—Mr. Martin. Earnshaw's 3–0 victory squared the series again.

Not only Cochrane, Grove and Earnshaw were aware of Martin's presence now. In four games he had captured the public as few individuals can do in a team game. It wasn't only his bold larceny on the bases that excited the crowds, or his batting average of .643. It wasn't just his reckless headfirst slides. It was more the sense of joy that characterized his play and somehow communicated itself to spectators.

"Which one is Martin?" newcomers asked on entering the park. Crowds followed him in the streets, swirled about him in the hotel lobby.

The rich and famous in sports today are not necessarily the most approachable. Autograph hunters who queue up in restaurants while the soup grows cold have driven some of them underground. In Pepper Martin's time if you wanted to see a visit-

ing ballplayer you went to the team's hotel and there was your man sitting in the lobby waiting for someone to drop a newspaper. Money being short, the great ones accepted public adulation as part of their rewards, and made themselves available. So there was Martin in the lobby of the Benjamin Franklin with a pack of admirers making small talk.

"Pepper, you're a .300 hitter batting over .600. How do you explain it?"

"I don't know. I'm just taking my regular swing and the ball keeps hitting the fat part of the bat."

"Mr. Martin, how did you learn to run the way you do?"

"Well sir, I grew up in Oklahoma and out there, once you start running there ain't nothing to stop you."

In the fifth game it was Hallahan against Waite Hoyt. His first time up, Martin smashed a long liner to Simmons in left, driving in Andy High with the first run. In the fourth inning he beat out a bunt. When he came up in the sixth with Frisch on second, a man in the press box said to Sid Keener of St. Louis:

"He's done everything up to now—bunt, single, double, steal everything in sight. The only thing left is to put it up there in those seats."

So Pepper hit it on a line into the upper deck in left. In the press box Keener came to his feet making small, strangled sounds. The score was now

Pepper Martin and his wife Ruby during the Series. After the fourth game she said, "He's always been a hero to me. When we were in grammar school I stood on a soapbox to cheer for him.... Now when the crowd starts to yell for him my eyes get misty."

(Top) Martin scoring in fourth inning of the third game; (Bottom) stealing third, second inning, second game.

(Top) Martin scoring under Cochrane in seventh inning of second game; (Bottom) greeting Frisch after fifth game home run.

The benighted Mickey Cochrane, and the exploits of his nemesis. Lee Allen suggested the confrontation was symbolic in that Depression year: Martin, the man of the people who went to his first training camp in a boxcar, had outfoxed Cochrane, a college man, affluent and worldly (and who was said to have lost a fortune in the stock market crash).

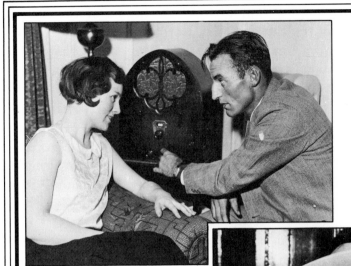

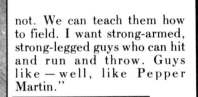

Martin at ease, at arms and at home. Charlie Barrett, a scout on Rickey's staff, was asked what the Cardinals look for: "Hard guys," he said. "I don't care whether they can field or not. We can teach them how to field. I want strong-armed, strong-legged guys who can hit and run and throw. Guys like — well, like Pepper Martin."

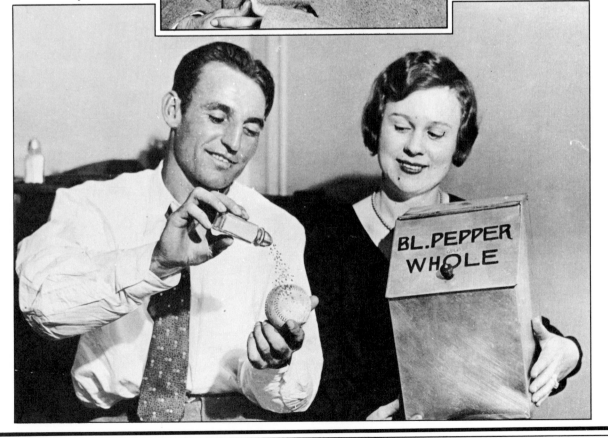

3–0. Philadelphia made a run in the seventh, Martin singled another home in the eighth, and one more St. Louis run made the final score 5–1.

Departing for St. Louis, the players had to struggle through mobs in the Broad Street Station. In the throng, Judge Kenesaw Mountain Landis caught sight of Martin. There was a good deal of ham in the baseball commissioner, and here was a ready-made audience. "Young man," he bawled, "how I'd like to be in your place tonight!"

Pepper compared salaries. "Well, Judge," he said, "$4,500 against $65,000—I'll swap you."

In 18 times at bat, Martin had made 12 hits, a World Series record. He would not get any more, but his year's work was by no means done.

Back in St. Louis, two four-run innings made the sixth game easy for Grove, 8–1. Thus the series was tied for the third time when Grimes opposed Earnshaw in the seventh game. In the first inning the Cardinals got runners on second and third with Martin coming to the plate. Earnshaw let go with a wild pitch that let one run score. Martin walked and stole second immediately. A third strike got past Cochrane and a second run came home. Had Martin stolen Cochrane's cool along with everything else?

Given two more runs in the third inning, Grimes pitched a shutout until the drama of the occasion got the better of him. Lord Burleigh never was one to wait in the wings while other and perhaps lesser mortals held the stage. For any ordinary assignment, he made up like a Mexican bandit with a two-day beard darkening his frown. An established spitball pitcher—those who specialized in the moist delivery before it was outlawed were allowed to keep on using it—he made opera out of bringing the ball to his mouth and ostensibly loading it up before every pitch. He snarled a good deal, showing yellow teeth.

He had been bothered by recurring symptoms of appendicitis that summer but the discomfort hadn't demanded an operation. Now, protecting a 4–0 lead in the eighth inning, Grimes began to clutch his side and grimace. He had a turn at bat in the bottom of the eighth and he scorned to let someone else hit for him. Trudging to the plate, he waved his bat weakly three times, purposely striking out to save himself for the last desperate stand on the mound.

He didn't know how desperate. He got two men out in the ninth but it cost him two runs. With Athletics on first and second, he made way reluctantly for Hallahan.

The batter was Max Bishop, the same pesky hitter who had challenged Hallahan away back there

In 1934 and again in 1936, Martin tried pitching. He gave up two hits and one run in four innings. He spent 1933-35 as St. Louis' regular third baseman and returned to the outfield in 1936, making occasional starts at first, third and shortstop.

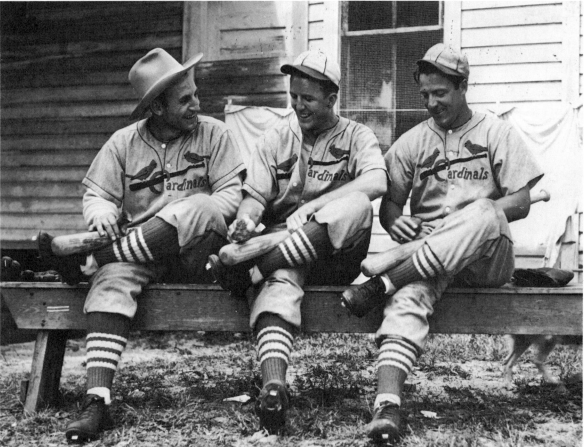

By 1936, Martin was acknowledged leader of the Gas House Gang, so named by Frank Graham of the New York *Sun*. (Top) Martin plays for teammates (L to R) Ripper Collins, Joe Medwick, Spud Davis, Ed Heusser and Heinie Schuble. Heusser once criticized Medwick for failing to chase a fly ball; Medwick knocked Heusser cold, right in the middle of the game. (Bottom, L to R) Martin, Terry Moore, Medwick, at spring training, 1936.

after Wilson's boner. The count went to three balls, two strikes. Hallahan fogged one. Bishop hit a fly that settled in the glove of John Leonard Martin.

Pocketing $4,467.59 as his share of the loot, Martin took off on a vaudeville tour at $1,500 a week. Clarence Lloyd, the Cardinals' traveling secretary, was assigned to go along as guide and father confessor. Clarence told Pepper about tipping. Maybe it was all right, he said, for an ordinary ballplayer to leave a dime after dinner, though even a rookie ought to come up with a quarter. But for a World Series hero, never anything under a half-dollar.

Officially welcomed by the mayor of Chicago, Martin received not the key to the city but a pocket-size medallion bearing the city seal. Later at the hotel, a bellman accepted a tip and turned away. "Oops!" Pepper said. "Just a minute. Come back."

For fifty cents he bought the medallion back.

When the tour ended, Martin was offered five additional weeks for a total of $7,500. "Hell," he said, "I ain't no actor." And he turned his face toward Oklahoma.

He had 13 years in the majors and then tried managing teams in the minor leagues. As leader in Miami, he was suspended for reasoning with an umpire while clutching that dignitary firmly by the throat. This was a crime too heinous for the league president. The case went up to the baseball commissioner, Happy Chandler.

Confident that there must be some mitigating circumstances, Chandler adopted a conciliatory tone. "Tell me, Pepper, what were you thinking when you had that man by the throat?"

"I was thinking," Pepper said, "that I'd choke the son of a bitch to death."

The Martin family, 1934. "Pepper Martin may not be a great outfielder or a great infielder. But he is a great baseball player...." — Grantland Rice

FIFTH INNING: 1930-1939

In a moment they were pressing round him in a swarming horde, deafening the ears with their shrill cries, begging, shouting, tugging at his sleeves, doing everything they could to attract his attention, holding dirty little scraps of paper toward him, stubs of pencils, battered little notebooks, asking him to sign his autograph....
For a moment Nebraska stood looking down at the child with an expression of mock sternness; at last he took the outstretched notebook, rapidly scratched his name across a page, and handed it back. And as he did so, he put his big paw on the urchin's head and gave it a clumsy pat; then, gently and playfully, he shoved it from him, and walked off down the street.

—Thomas Wolfe, 1938

CHUCK Klein, in his second full season, hit .386, slugged at .687 and collected 40 homers, 170 RBIs and 250 hits. In an average year Klein would have led the majors in all of these departments, but there was nothing average about 1930. That season Klein failed to lead the National League, much less the majors, in a single one of the five main hitting departments! Never again would the game experience so extraordinary an interlude, as magnates tried to circumvent the Depression and its inroads on attendance by livening up the ball once again, this time to a point where only one National Leaguer who batted over 400 times (Hod Ford of the Reds) hit under .250, and Dazzy Vance was the lone National League ERA qualifier to better 3.76. Statistics were slightly more sane in the American League, but even there, three men slugged over .700 and only the Red Sox failed to average over four runs a game. The Phils, on the other hand, crossed the plate about six times per contest and had three regulars who hit over .340, yet finished in the cellar when their pitchers compiled a whopping 6.71 staff ERA.

Amid the barrage Lefty Grove stood unscathed, the major league pitching leader in almost every department and the winner of two Series games. When George Earnshaw also won twice, the A's glided to the world championship over a Cardinal club that had a .300 hitter at every position and three utility men who hit .374, .366 and .396. Best

Hack Wilson. The fly ball he lost in the sun in the '29 World Series made him a goat, and despite his prodigal hitting the next year, Chicago fans would throw lemons on the field when he came to bat.

batting marks of all in the National League belonged to Bill Terry, who hit .401, and Hack Wilson, who set the NL homer record with 56 and the major league RBI record with 190. Both of these hitters had teammates like Mel Ott and Kiki Cuyler who slugged with equal élan, and it is not easy to explain why the Cardinals won out. No Redbird pitcher completed more than 14 games or won more than 15, and among the starters only Burleigh Grimes had a decent ERA. Hidden beneath the

(L) Chuck Klein and Bill Terry; (R) Kiki Cuyler. Klein in 1932 was the last man to lead his league in home runs and stolen bases in the same year; in 1930, playing caroms off the right field wall in the Baker Bowl, he amassed a record 44 assists, frequently throwing runners out at first. In 1954, the taciturn Terry, told he was elected to the Hall of Fame, replied, "I have nothing to say about it." Donie Bush benched Cuyler for the 1927 pennant stretch and the Series, for insubordination; when the season ended he was virtually given away to the Cubs, for whom he twice batted over .350.

Hack Wilson, Babe Ruth, Lou Gehrig (L to R). Wilson was 5'6" tall, weighed 190, and wore a size 5½ shoe and a size 18 collar. Warren Brown wrote, "Wilson was a high ball hitter on the field, and off it." After his epochal 1930 season he was paid more than any ballplayer but Ruth; soon quarreling with new manager Rogers Hornsby, he was dealt to Brooklyn, where he was paid but $16,500. Al Drooz said, "Gin was his tonic." Wilson was out of baseball by 1935. When he died in 1948, a $350 grant from the National League was all that saved him from a pauper's grave.

Bill Terry and Frank Frisch (L); Billy Herman (C); Joe Cronin (R). When Frisch managed the Gashouse Gang he said, "A sense of humor helps." Herman told Donald Honig, "I was a serious-minded player, and I didn't go out of my way to make friends." It was appropriate; Rogers Hornsby, his first manager, spoke to Herman only in grunts. Cronin was MVP at 24, a manager at 27, a general manager at 42 and, finally, President of the American League.

welter of bizarre pitching statistics were the signal bullpen contributions of Hi Bell and Jim Lindsey, just enough to give the Cards a two-game edge over the Cubs.

Milt Gaston continued to be the most luckless pitcher in history, when for the second time he became a league loss leader. A reliever as a rookie for the Yankees in 1924, Gaston went to the Browns the following year and led the club in wins. It was the last time during his 11-year career that he played for a team that broke .500; and when he left the majors in 1934, after a 6–19 record for the last-place White Sox, he took with him a .372 winning percentage that ranks as the worst ever for a pitcher in over 250 decisions.

Klein "slumped" to 31 homers and 121 RBIs in 1931 but won league honors in both departments after some of the hop was removed from the ball. The Cards and A's both repeated easily as league champs, setting up a rematch in the Series. This time it was the turn of Grimes and Bill Hallahan to win two games apiece, but the real difference was Pepper Martin. Martin hit .500, stole five bases and ended matters with a two-out, two-on catch of Max Bishop's liner in the ninth inning of the seventh game. Hit hard in the Series, Grove still managed to win twice and continue his onslaught on pitching records of the era. His 31–4 mark and .886 winning percentage were the best ever for a pitcher in more than 30 decisions. The Yankees under Joe McCarthy, who had been quickly snatched by Ed Barrow

when the Cubs fired him late in 1930, finished as a remote also-ran to the A's but received 21 wins from Lefty Gomez. Red Ruffing, obtained from the Red Sox for Cedric Durst in a steal that recalled Harry Frazee's days in Boston, had trouble adjusting to being with a winner his first year in New York, and Washington nearly crept into second ahead of the Yankees with a club rebuilt around shortstop Joe Cronin. Another shortstop, rookie Luke Appling, began 20 years of futility with the White Sox. No other player in the game's history would play for so long with a club that was never once in contention.

Leo Durocher. In St. Louis he was the "All-American Out" — but his fielding and his attitude ("Show me a good loser, and I'll show you an idiot") won ball games.

(Top) Lou Gehrig, subject, and Babe Ruth, photographer, 1932. The next year Ruth mildly criticized Gehrig's mother; they never spoke again. (Bottom, L) By 1932, Ruth was periodically out of uniform due to injury or illness. "He merely has disciplined his appetites and desires," Paul Gallico wrote. "He never got over having them." (Bottom, R) His last home run, hit for the Braves on May 25, 1935, was the first ball ever to clear the roof at Forbes Field. Guy Bush, who was pitching for Pittsburgh, said, "I never saw a ball hit so hard....He was fat and old, but he still had that great swing."

In the National League, Chick Hafey of the Cardinals won the batting title over Terry and Jim Bottomley by a fraction of a point, and the Phils for the first time since the days of Alexander had one of the league's top winners in Jim Elliott. Jack Quinn of the Dodgers became the oldest player to be a leader in a major category when at 47 he recorded 15 saves, many of them while pitching to rookie catcher Ernie Lombardi. Between Lombardi and Willie Keeler, who had been a teammate of Quinn's with the old New York Highlanders, Quinn in 1931 bridged a gap in baseball history that spanned 55 years—from 1892 to 1947.

It will always be a moot issue whether Babe Ruth called his shot in the third game of the 1932 Series. Similarly, the reason Rogers Hornsby was fired in August as Cub manager by owner Bill Veeck (father of the future owner of the Indians, Browns and White Sox) remains puzzling. Held down to a non-playing role by injuries, Hornsby at the time had his club ahead of the strong-hitting Pirates and the Dodgers, who were getting one final breath of good play from such ancients as Lefty O'Doul, Dazzy Vance, George Kelly, Hack Wilson, Glen Wright and Jack Quinn (who broke his year-old record by again, now aged 48, leading in saves). For the only time in the 32-year period between 1918 and 1950, both the Phils and the Braves contrived to play .500 ball in the same season; the Giants proved so dis-heartening that McGraw turned the club over to Terry; the Cards slipped, in spite of the injection given their pitching by the arrival of Dizzy Dean; and the Reds, for the second season in a row, brought up the rear of the league.

The American League was also in a time of transition. Gehrig and Ruth both had good years in 1932, but a new slugging king, Jimmie Foxx, outdistanced them. The Red Sox, weary of poor hitting, did an about-face and dealt for Smead Jolley and Dale Alexander. These two improved the club's attack a fraction but were such liabilities in the field that the Sox lost a team-record 111 games. The year 1932 would be the last time, however, that the Red Sox would finish in the cellar or score the fewest runs in the league.

Back on top the following season, after nearly a decade without a pennant, were the Giants and Senators. A scant three years after the greatest hitting display since 1894, the ball was so de-energized that only one Giant hit .300, and Klein led in slugging with just 28 homers and 120 RBIs. A triple crown winner that season, Klein lost the MVP award to Carl Hubbell after having won it the previous year. Traded to the Cubs in 1934, Klein at last had an opportunity to play with a contender but suffered a series of setbacks and was never the same player again. Still, he is the lone hitter who averaged .320 on over 2,000 career hits and remains outside the Hall of Fame. A forlorn figure as an

(L) George Raft, the actor, had been a batboy for the old New York Highlanders. (R) Al Schacht pitched for three years, then clowned for nearly 50. In 1945, he wrote, "I have become a household word. Whenever I enter a town, a courier gallops madly through the streets and shouts, 'Hey, girls — Al Schacht's in town!'"

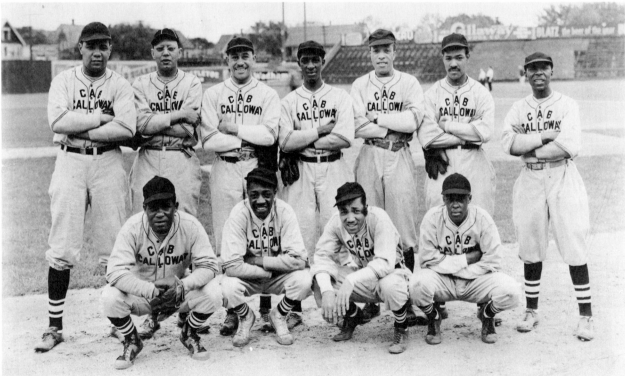

The affinity of show people for baseball was not confined to hero worship. (Top) Louis Armstrong's "Secret Nine," 1931. Armstrong, who sponsored the team, is at extreme right. (Bottom) The Cab Calloway band's team included bassist Milt Hinton (rear, C) and Calloway himself (on Hinton's right).

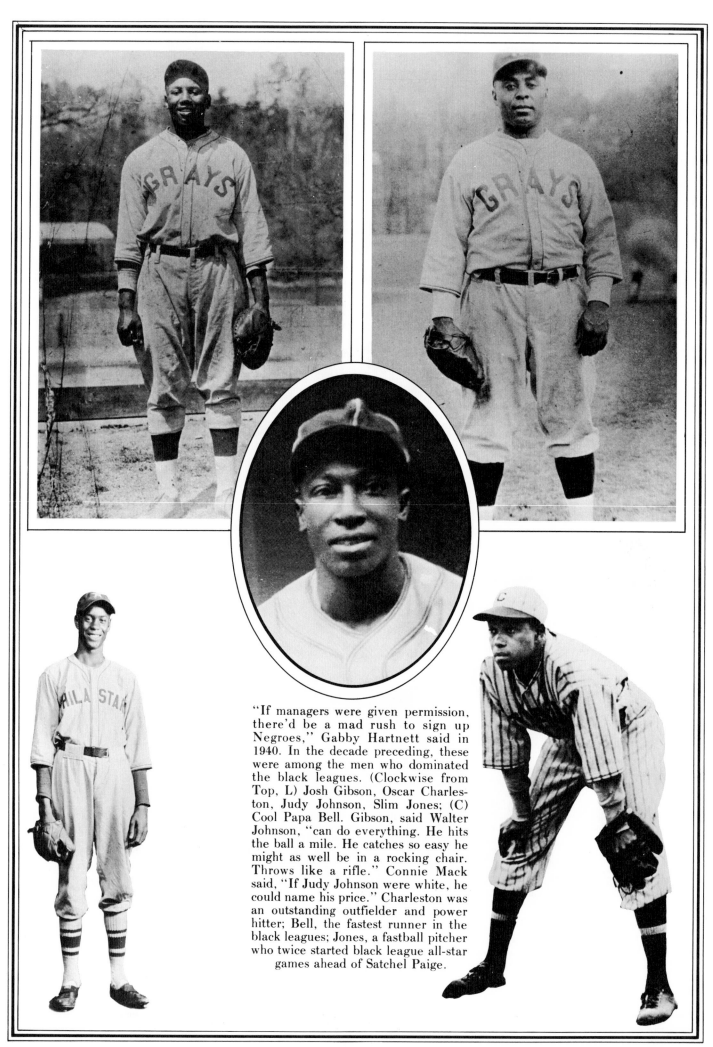

"If managers were given permission, there'd be a mad rush to sign up Negroes," Gabby Hartnett said in 1940. In the decade preceding, these were among the men who dominated the black leagues. (Clockwise from Top, L) Josh Gibson, Oscar Charleston, Judy Johnson, Slim Jones; (C) Cool Papa Bell. Gibson, said Walter Johnson, "can do everything. He hits the ball a mile. He catches so easy he might as well be in a rocking chair. Throws like a rifle." Connie Mack said, "If Judy Johnson were white, he could name his price." Charleston was an outstanding outfielder and power hitter; Bell, the fastest runner in the black leagues; Jones, a fastball pitcher who twice started black league all-star games ahead of Satchel Paige.

(Top) Homestead Grays, 1931. Cumberland Willis Posey (in sweater, L) was a former college basketball player who took over the team in 1916 and remained a dominant figure in black baseball until his death in 1946. His players included Gibson (rear, fourth from R), Charleston (rear, second from R) and an aged Joe Williams (rear, C). (Bottom) Pittsburgh Crawfords, 1932. Organized by Gus Greenlee, who signed many of the Homestead stars (Gibson, rear, in jacket; Charleston, rear, extreme R), the Crawfords also boasted pitcher-catcher Ted "Double Duty" Radcliff (front, extreme R) and 26-year old Satchel Paige (rear, second from L). Said Paige: "The Crawfords played everywhere, in every ball park. And we won, won like we invented the game."

occasional pinch hitter for the Phils during the war years, Klein was so shopworn by then that few recalled he was the last National Leaguer to register 200 hits five seasons in a row and the only player ever to total over 120 RBIs in each of his first five full seasons.

Another triple crown winner in 1933, Jimmie Foxx, also ended his career with the wartime Phils in a sad manner. Hopelessly outclassed by the rest of the league, the Phils tried to attract what few fans they could by using Foxx as a pitcher on days when his aging legs were too weary to play first base. Foxx was still at the pinnacle of his game in 1933, but three other stars were beginning to fade. Traded to the White Sox by Mack, Al Simmons became the last American Leaguer to tally 200 hits five years running, but he never had another 200-hit season. Grove marked his final year with the A's by leading the league in wins for one last time, and Ruth had his final season as a .300 hitter. Like Klein, Wilson, Foxx and Gehrig, his four great slugging rivals of the era, Ruth also ended his career on a downbeat when he went to the Braves in 1935 and thus had the dubious distinction of playing for the worst National League team of the first half of the century just eight years after playing for the American League's best.

While many of the great names that had made baseball the national pastime were fading by the early thirties, new ones were sprouting everywhere to take their place. By 1933 many observers saw Bill Dickey as the game's premier catcher. Arky Vaughan had given the Pirates yet another name in their long tradition of great shortstops. The Cardinals quickly moved back into contention behind the hitting of first-year regular Joe Medwick. And when rookie Hank Greenberg appeared, second baseman Charlie Gehringer at long last had a compatriot who could help him lead the Tigers out of the morass in which they had been since 1909.

When asked in the 1934 pre-season to assess the chances of his rivals, Bill Terry paused a moment when he came to the Dodgers, then said, "Is Brooklyn still in the league?" Sixth in 1933, the Dodgers showed no improvement the following year under freshman manager Casey Stengel; but as far as the Giants were concerned, by the season's end Brooklyn was the *only* team in the league. In first place for 127 days during the season, the Giants entered the final two games of the schedule tied with the Cardinals and were knocked off twice in the Polo Grounds by the Dodgers. Meanwhile Paul and Dizzy Dean were beating the Reds.

In the American League it was a summer for G-men as Gehrig won the triple crown, Gomez became the league's top winner and Gehringer, Greenberg, Goose Goslin and Gee Walker boosted the Tigers to a pennant over the injury-ridden Yankees. The Senators, after providing the Giants with

Paul Dean (L) and his brother. "Paul Dean was not like Dizzy, except in appearance and pitching skill. Dizzy talked. Paul listened. Dizzy wisecracked. Paul laughed. Dizzy was a great comedian. Paul was his best audience. Each was the other's hero." — J. Roy Stockton

(Top) Dizzy Dean being carried from the field in the 1934 Series; (Bottom) in a promotion at the Baker Bowl. "The funny thing about [the] cliche-ridden version of Dean's life," wrote Tristram Coffin, "is that it is essentially accurate." Let his latter-day view of the Cold War, as quoted by Al Silverman, serve here: "I'd get me a bunch of bats and balls and sneak me a couple of empires and learn them kids behind the Iron Curtain how to tote a bat and play baseball.... And if Joe Stallion knowed how much money they was in the concessions at a ball park, he'd get outta politics and get in a honest business." Around the same time, Dean gave a lecture at Southern Methodist University, entitled "Radio Announcing I Have Did."

Mel Ott. He never played a day in the minors, nor in any other uniform but that of the Giants. When John McGraw took him on as a 17-year-old, he said, "No minor league manager is going to have a chance to ruin him." The 5'9" Ott hit 511 career home runs.

Lou Gehrig, 1935. When he married in 1933, it was over the objections of his mother, to whom he was deeply devoted. Pete Sheehy, Yankee clubhouse attendant, said, "He'd be the first one dressed and on home to his momma." Bill Dickey told Maury Allen, "He just went out and did his job every day."

(Top) King Carl, Mountain Music, Prince Hal — Hubbell, Cliff Melton and Schumacher (L to R). During Hubbell's extraordinary strikeout string in the 1934 All-Star game, Frank Frisch said, "I could play second base 15 more years behind that guy. He doesn't need any help." Heywood Broun wrote, "During the reign of Hubbell, first base itself is a Marathon route." (Bottom) The 1938 Yankees. Joe McCarthy (front, arms folded) said, "Give a boy a bat and a ball and a place to play and you'll have a good citizen." One of McCarthy's boys, Jake Powell (front, second from R), went out to get Hank Greenberg in 1936 on a play at first and broke Greenberg's wrist.

Mel Ott, JoJo Moore, Joe DiMaggio, Lou Gehrig (L to R), 1937 World Series. Eddie Brannick, of the Giants' front office, called those Yankees "window breakers." Despite Ott, Moore, Hubbell and the other Giants, Frank Graham wrote, "The Giants simply had nothing with which to combat successfully the American League champions."

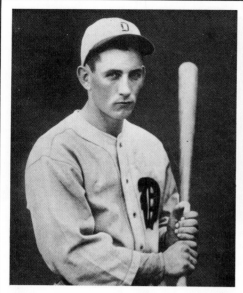

Charlie Gehringer (L), Hank Greenberg (R). Gehringer was called "The Mechanical Man"; Satchel Paige called him the best white hitter he ever faced. Said Ty Cobb, "He'd say hello at the start of spring training and goodbye at the end of the season, and the rest of the time he let his bat and glove do all the talking for him." Gehringer did say of Greenberg, "Hank loved to drive those runs in."

little competition in the 1933 Series, sagged to seventh place, the biggest tumble since 1915 for a defending pennant winner. For the first time since 1918 the Red Sox finished in the first division, justifying the expense and energy devoted to their improvement by their new owner, Tom Yawkey.

The Series went the full seven games, but the final contest was decided early on when the Cardinals scored seven times in the third inning. In the top of the sixth, Medwick's hard slide into Tiger third baseman Marv Owen nearly resulted in a riot, and enraged Tiger fans pelted Medwick with fruit when he tried to take the field in the home half of the inning. Judge Landis, who was in attendance, wisely ordered Medwick removed from the game for his own protection, but the incident had no bearing on the outcome; the Cards went on to win 11–0 for the most one-sided victory ever in a Series finale.

The National League's last 30-game winner in 1934, Dean won 28 for an encore; but his Gas House teammates were not up to the challenge presented by the Cubs, who went on a 21-game winning streak in September, the longest since the Giants' tear in 1916. Favorite victims of the Cubs and indeed everyone in the league were the Braves, defeated an astounding 115 times. After dangling a fourth-place finish in front of their fans in 1934, the Braves had the league's top slugger in Wally Berger but so little by way of a supporting cast that Ben Cantwell, one of the better pitchers of the era, had a 4–25 record. Only two years earlier, Cantwell had been the first Brave since 1921 to win 20 games.

Tiger supporters finally witnessed their first world championship when Detroit overcame an early Se-

ries injury to Greenberg and bested the Cubs in six games. The most notable feature of the Series was the Tigers' ability to override the anemic contributions of Marv Owen and sub Flea Clifton, whose presence in the lineup was necessitated by Greenberg's injury. Between them, Owen and Clifton went one for 36 and drove in one run. For their victory the Tigers took home individual Series shares of $6,544.76, the highest until 1948. Taking home nothing for their efforts were the Senators, who finished sixth and hit fewer homers as a team than either Greenberg or Foxx, the coleaders. Still,

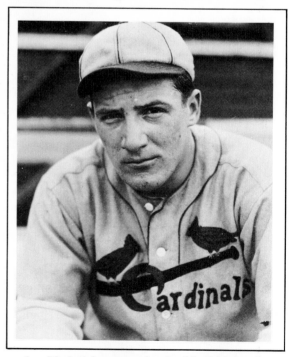

Joe Medwick was such a bad-ball hitter that in the 1934 All-Star game, he jumped and hit a homer on a pitch so high that Bill Dickey said he couldn't have caught it.

Detroit pitchers, 1935. Mickey Cochrane (second from L) managed, and caught, Schoolboy Rowe, Eldon Auker, Tommy Bridges and Alvin Crowder (L to R). Rowe, with 24 wins, led the staff. His celebrity earned him a national radio interview, during which he turned to his wife—while still on the air—and asked, "How'm I doing, Edna?" In the Series, the Cardinals repeatedly yelled the same phrase from the bench whenever Rowe was on the mound.

Senator second baseman Buddy Myer managed to drive in 100 runs and win the batting title by going four for five on the season's final day, while Joe Vosmik of the Indians was protecting what seemed a safe lead by sitting out the first game of a doubleheader. Alarmed when they learned of Myer's torrential finish, the Indians inserted Vosmik in the second game, but his one for four output cost him the title by a single point. The irony was that if Vosmik had sat out the second game as well, he and Myer would have ended in an exact tie for the championship.

As might be expected, the strongest second-division team in the pre-expansion era belonged to none other than the Indians. In 1936, while in the process of winning 80 games, they had Earl Averill, the league hit leader and batting runner-up, RBI champ Hal Trosky and 20-game winner Johnny Allen, yet finished fifth. With Greenberg disabled again, Schoolboy Rowe a sore arm victim and player-manager Mickey Cochrane suffering a nervous breakdown, the Tigers posed no threat to the revamped Yankees, who had five men over the 100 RBI mark and received the first of Ruffing's four straight 20-win seasons. Rookie Joe DiMaggio's bat was one of those over 100 RBIs, but it was his throwing arm that proved the major surprise. DiMaggio played left field for much of the season, and, in a feat rare for that position, led all American League outfielders in assists.

Luke Appling's .388 average not only led the

Hal Trosky, Earl Averill, Joe Vosmik, Roy Weatherly, 1936 (L to R). In time they all left Cleveland, which could only come close to winning pennants. When Weatherly was traded to the Yankees in 1943, he said, "I don't have to tell you that every ballplayer's prayers are directed toward New York and a job with the Yankees."

(Clockwise from Top, L) Red Ruffing, Johnny Vander Meer, Lefty Gomez, Johnny Allen. Ruffing won 273 games, and was one of the best hitting pitchers of his day; in 1941, he had one RBI every four at bats. Vander Meer would lose more games than he would win, but his consecutive no-hitters in 1938 insured his fame. "As I look back at it now," he said in 1943, "those days are the haziest period of my life." Gomez had a personality as ample as his ability. As a minor league manager, he was coaching third when two of his runners ended up on that base. Wrote Roy Blount, "Lefty took a quick look, gave a terrible yell and joined them all with a slide from the coaching box." Allen was as ill-tempered as Gomez was not; in 1942, he beat up umpire George Barr in the middle of a game, over a balk call. Still, Allen's talents were substantial: in his first six years, he won 85 and lost only 30.

Site of the 1938 Series. It had — and has — no lights because P.K. Wrigley, who wanted to be nice to the neighbors, would only put them up if the standards could be disguised as trees.

American League but was the highest by a shortstop in the century. That year also saw the century's highest average by a catcher in enough at bats to qualify for a batting title when Babe Phelps of the Dodgers hit .367. Remarkably, Dickey that same season was hitting .362, the top figure by an American League catcher. One final batting record was set by Woody Jensen of the Pirates, who officially came to the plate 696 times, the most by anyone playing a 154-game schedule.

The Giants received a pitching record from Carl Hubbell, who ended the season with 16 straight wins and lifted the club into the first subway Series since 1923. When Hubbell won the opener, the Giants seemed ready to make a contest of it, but the Yankees scored a record 18 runs in the second game and never trailed again. Unpopular Jake Powell, who had broken Greenberg's arm in April by crashing into his glove hand at first base on a routine play, was the hitting star.

In 1937 the Browns bore a resemblance to their powerhouse of 1922, when each of their three outfielders hit better than .325 and Harlond Clift led all third basemen in slugging, but a cursory look at their pitching staff abruptly scotches the similarity. Last in every pitching department, the club got only eight saves from its bullpen and had as its top winner Jim Walkup, who turned in a 7.38 ERA. In contrast, the White Sox were presented with a record-breaking 18 saves by Clint Brown and finished third with their best club since 1920. Studded with individual leaders, the Tigers led the majors in hitting, but their pitchers skidded without Cochrane's guidance after his playing career was ended in May by a near-fatal beaning. After debuting the previous summer with 15 strikeouts in his first start-

Gabby Hartnett, Bill Dickey in front of brother George, Ernie Lombardi (L to R). Hartnett, wrote John Carmichael, "was the official noisemaker of the Cubs." Bill Dickey, said Charlie Gehringer, "made catching look easy"; hitting was no problem either — he batted .313 over a 17-year career in which he played no other position but catcher. George was eight years younger, his lifetime average 109 points lower. Lombardi is the only catcher to win two batting titles — and he did it as the slowest man in baseball, stealing but 8 bases in a 1,853-game career.

(Top) Van Lingle Mungo (L), said Leo Durocher, talked "like Edgar Bergen doing Mortimer Snerd from the bottom of a well....And he drank a bit. Anything." Including, Leo insisted, hair tonic. (C) Emil "Dutch" Leonard, who would become part of the only all-knuckleball starting staff in baseball history, in the early forties. (R) Bobo Newsom, who was traded 16 times in a 20-year career, serving five different terms with the Senators. (Bottom) Zeke Bonura (L). He was a .307 career hitter, but in 1939 he grounded into five double plays in two games. Astonishingly, he led AL first basemen in chances per game three years running. (C) Wes Ferrell won 20 games six times, and hit over .280 five times. (R) Ted Lyons. "For 21 years Lyons pitched as though the White Sox were in pursuit of the pennant," Ken Smith wrote. "It was a game of make-believe." In his career in Chicago, only once did the White Sox come within eight games of first place.

ing assignment, Cleveland's Bob Feller ran into arm trouble in 1937 yet still finished fourth in strike-outs in the league. The Indians' Johnny Allen held most of the attention, however, when he took a 15–0 record into the season's final day. By losing his last start, Allen missed an opportunity to become the first winning percentage leader in history to post a perfect 1.000.

The Yankees made it five world championships in their last five tries by routing the Giants and their rookie 20-game winner, Cliff Melton, in a dull Series. The Braves became the first team in 34 years to have *two* rookie 20-game winners when Lou Fette and Jim Turner, a pair of career minor leaguers on the dim side of 30, between them led the league in shutouts, ERA and complete games. A broken toe in the All-Star game ruined Dizzy Dean's season and eventually his career, but team-mate Joe Medwick won the triple crown—the last National Leaguer to do so—and another Cardinal, Johnny Mize, was right behind him in most hitting departments.

All through the summer of 1938 Pittsburgh looked like a miracle club. The Waners weren't hit-ting, none of the starting pitchers could win con-sistently and only rookie Johnny Rizzo was able to knock in runs. Yet the Pirates began September with a seven-game lead over the Cubs and still led by a game and a half going into the final week of the season. Entering Wrigley Field for a three-game series, the Pirates lost all three contests, the *coup de grace* being a twilight home run by Gabby Hartnett, with two out in the ninth inning of the second game, breaking a 5–5 tie. It marked the third time in 30 years that the Pirates had lost at the wire to the Cubs, and the last time until 1960 that they would make a sustained pennant bid.

The National League in 1938 consisted of seven teams that were almost dead even. Only the Phils lost more than 80 games, and the Cubs in winning got exceptional seasons from none of their hitters and little help from Charlie Root and Larry French, who had been expected to shoulder a major portion of the pitching load. But Bill Lee and Clay Bryant combined for 41 wins. Lee was the league's best in ERA, wins, percentage and shutouts and carried the Cubs almost single-handedly down the stretch. Much of the recognition that should have been his went, however, to Johnny Vander Meer of the Reds, who threw two successive no-hitters, the second coming against the Dodgers in the first night game in the New York area. Vander Meer's timing couldn't have been more perfect. Not only did it draw attention to his own abilities but it established night baseball as an exciting and profitable venture for owners desperate to elevate attendance during the tag end of the Depression.

The focus on Vander Meer also served to re-acquaint fans with his team, which revived in 1938 from five cellar finishes earlier in the decade and placed fourth after fleecing the Phils of Bucky Walters and witnessing a batting title for Ernie Lombardi, the second catcher—and, interestingly, the second *Red* catcher—to win one. Meanwhile, publicists who grew bored with writing about Vander Meer had only to journey to the northern part of Ohio, where Bob Feller set a modern record by striking out 18 Tigers in a game, and then move on around Lake Erie to Detroit, where Greenberg was making a furious run at Ruth's home run record (he ended with 58) and depriving Foxx, who hit 50 himself, of his second triple crown.

Two slugging rookies received a large share of the press coverage in 1939. One, Charlie Keller, finished well up in the batting race and helped somewhat to buoy the spirits of his Yankee teammates after the tragic departure of Lou Gehrig. But the Red Sox were lifted even more by the arrival of Ted Williams, who led the league in RBIs and nearly beat out Harlond Clift for the lead in walks—an extremely rare win for a rookie, who traditionally is seldom given the benefit of the doubt by umpires on close pitches and whose batting eye is rarely so well trained.

In the National League in the decade's final season, two first basemen—Mize and Frank McCormick—led the hitters, and McCormick's teammates, Bucky Walters and Paul Derringer, totaled 52 wins and brought the Reds their first pennant in 20 years. One of the keys to the Reds' triumph was their second base-shortstop pair of Lonny Frey and Billy Myers. Neither was the league's best at his position, but together they formed a much stronger combination than any of the other contenders could put on the field. The outstanding pairing in the game, however, belonged to the Red Sox, who had Bobby Doerr and Joe Cronin. Solid at every position except catcher, the Red Sox nevertheless finished 17 games back of the Yankees when, for the second year in a row, none of their pitchers was strong enough to work 200 innings. On the surface,

Bob Feller. He struck out 15 in his first major league start, at age 17. He struck out 17 three weeks later, pitched an 18-strikeout game when he was 19, had his first no-hitter at 21 and won 107 games before he turned 22. Ted Williams said, "He had more stuff than anybody."

this statistic might not appear to mean much, but it looms significant when a study of the game reveals that since 1876 no team has won the pennant without at least one pitcher appearing in 200 innings. The Yankees of 1939 are an illustration. The club had pitching problems all season, and McCarthy never was able to establish a set rotation. No less than eight pitchers made 11 or more starts, and most are far from being among the era's important contributors. Throughout, however, Red Ruffing continued to take his regular starting turn and put in his usual quota of 200-plus innings. With Ruffing as a stabilizing force and Johnny Murphy coming out of the bullpen to score a record 19 saves, the Yankees were never in trouble after mid-July and could probably have threatened their own league record for wins if they had felt more pressure from the other contenders.

DiMaggio, in winning his first batting championship, became the last right-handed hitter to clear the .380 mark, and teammates Dickey, George Selkirk and Joe Gordon all had over 100 RBIs. McCarthy's offense was so potent that the club scarcely felt the effect of having two .230 hitters in their infield. When for the second year in a row the Yankees swept the Series in four games, giving them four consecutive world titles, more and more owners began installing lights in their home parks in an attempt to stimulate fans—and to disguise the lack of competition their teams offered the Yankees on the field. —David Nemec

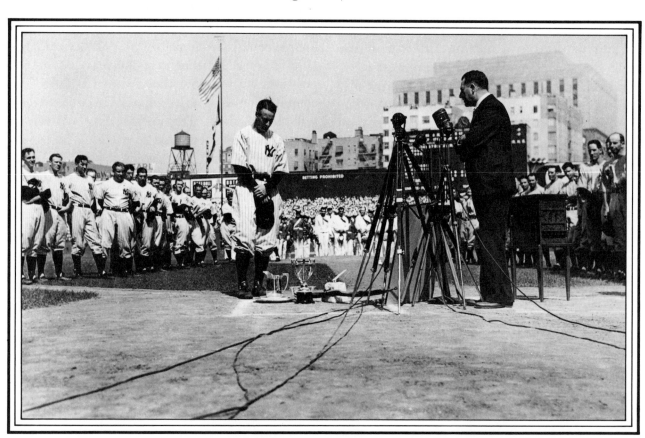

Lou Gehrig, July 4, 1939.
"Idol of cheering millions
Records are yours by the sheaves.
Iron of frame they hailed you
And decked you with laurel leaves."
—John Kieran

LEGEND:
How DiMaggio Made It Look Easy
By Roy Blount, Jr.

A TERRIBLE vision of 20 years from now: TV-commercial fans in their thirties and forties are gathered around reminiscing about the truly great ones. Crazy Eddie. "What's the Story?" Jerry. John Cameron Swayze for Timex. Various Alka-Seltzer pheenoms. Margaret Hamilton the cleaning lady. Madge the coffee-shop waitress. Mr. Whipple the tissue-squeezing grocer . . .

"But *none* of them," says one of these fans, "was as good as Java Joe. Old silver-haired DiMaggio.

"And he couldn't just do the coffee maker, he did the bank too—DiMaggio could do it all. *And make it look easy.* You never knew where he was coming from, he was always just *there.* Understated. Calm. Sure. Saying, 'How would you like to retire on $949,036.43?' In that great voice. That great

suit. That smile that said, 'I'm not selling you, I'm telling you.' Your Swayzes, your Whipples, they come and go. But there'll never be another DiMag."

None of the other fans offers any argument.

I suppose a number of young people did come to associate DiMaggio with baseball, to some extent, in '78, when he was widely publicized as the man whose consecutive-game hitting streak Pete Rose astonishingly came within 12 games of matching. But earlier in that season, Rose mentioned to a young autograph-seeker how much he used to covet DiMaggio's signature when he was a kid.

The kid gave no sign of recognition.

"Joe DiMaggio," Rose said. "You know, Mr. Coffee."

"*Oh,*" the kid said then.

It was even in "Peanuts." Charlie Brown yelling from the mound, "Joe DiMaggio never complained about playing ball on a hot day!"

Lucy yelling back from the outfield: "Who was Joe DiMaggio?"

"One of the greatest outfielders who ever lived, that's who!"

"I thought he just drank coffee," Lucy replies.

The irony of it. *Cloy Mattox* (1929 A's, 3 games, lifetime average .167) had, as they say, a cup of coffee. *Monte Pfyl* (1907 Giants, 1 game, .000). *Garton Del Savio* (1943 Phillies, 4, .091). *Goat Anderson* (1907 Pirates, 127, .206). *Bruce Barmes* (1953 Senators, 5, .200). *Bert Yeabsley* (1919 Phillies, 3, no batting average).

Joe DiMaggio ought to be identified with ambrosia. He is probably the greatest ballplayer alive, and the greatest centerfielder ever. He played in 13 seasons and 10 World Series, was the class of the Yankees in times when the Yankees outclassed everybody else. He averaged .325 for a lifetime, and 28 home runs a year, although one of his knees was bad and he had ulcers and for a good while there every time he put his weight down on either heel it was like he stepped on a nail. Baseball's vastest turf, Yankee Stadium's center field, he held in the palm of his hand, and when he shifted the ball to the other hand, to throw, he ruled whatever might be going on in the infield.

You don't hear of DiMaggio making diving tumbling circus catches. DiMaggio wasn't performing in a circus out there. He glided from wherever he was waiting to wherever the ball was going. No, that's not right. Gliding implies an element of drift, and of joyous show. From what one is told by eyewitnesses, DiMaggio didn't glide, he proceeded. He segued. He *always* seemed to be waiting, not pursuing. "Jolting Joe" was a misnomer: never was there a player whose movements entailed fewer discernible jolts.

Say the Yankees are leading the Red Sox 4–3 at home in the top of the ninth, two out, bases loaded, this game could mean the pennant and some Sock hits a shot to right center, runners all going and 50,000 Yankee fans on their feet, it looks like the coolly overbearing home side has blown a lead, when, just before the ball can intersect with the turf, DiMaggio has it in full stride and he's striding right on at the same speed with the same lack of expression across the infield and into the dugout, game over, Yankees win, crowd overwhelmed, DiMaggio gone.

"He never offered the appearance of either gaiety, or anger, or tremendous effort. His smile was self-conscious, his manner withdrawn to the point of a chill.... Joe was not one to burst into transports of either joy or rage—at least in public." — Robert Smith

During DiMaggio's first spring training, in 1936, Dan Daniel wrote, "Here is the replacement for Babe Ruth." The Yankees proceeded to win four straight World Series. (Top) DiMaggio, Frank Crosetti, Tony Lazzeri, Bill Dickey, Lou Gehrig, Jake Powell, George Selkirk. (Middle)

DiMaggio at the Polo Grounds, 1936 Series. (Middle, R) With Carl Hubbell, 1937. (Bottom, L to R) Selkirk, Charlie Keller, Tommy Henrich, DiMaggio, Frenchy Bordagaray, outfielders on the 1941 team that resumed possession of the championship.

More championships. (Top) Joe McCarthy, Col. Jacob Ruppert, Lou Gehrig, Tony Lazzeri (L to R) and DiMaggio, drinking the Colonel's beer in 1937. Lazzeri was young Joe's protector but it was a strange relationship: reporter Jack Mahon told of watching the two men, and Frank Crosetti, sit absolutely silent for 80 minutes in the lobby of St. Louis's Hotel Chase. Then DiMaggio cleared his throat. "What did you say?" Crosetti asked. "He didn't say nothing," snapped Lazzeri. "Shut up." The silence resumed. (Bottom) 1950 Series. DiMaggio's tenth-inning home run had won the second game for Allie Reynolds (L). Gene Woodling is behind Joe, Jerry Coleman at right.

Where have you gone, Joe DiMaggio, as Simon and Garfunkel asked in the sixties. "Joltin' Joe has left and gone away."

DiMaggio, who figured in a Hemingway novel, married Marilyn Monroe and was celebrated in another hit song in the forties: "Joltin' Joe DiMaggio . . . we want you on our side . . . glorified the horsehide sphere. . . ."

Now glorifying a bank and coffee.

There isn't even much of a film record of DiMaggio the great ballplayer. Inquiries at the Baseball Hall of Fame and at the Major League Films library fail to disclose a single clip of the Yankee Clipper sailing to where a fly ball falls. Major League Films does have Series highlight films of the forties in negative form, and in these there may be some representative DiMaggio catches. But the developed DiMaggio footage there and at Cooperstown is all batting and running, and not really very much of that.

We see DiMaggio taking several productive swings—big clean liquid strokes, full-bodied but not bursting or corkscrewing, founded on that commanding stride growing out of that crotch-stretchingly spread-out stance (whose lines unfortunately are obscured somewhat by the blousy knickers of the period). But no fielding, and no moments as prolonged as any of his commercial messages.

Two DiMaggio screen glimpses stick in the mind, and in both cases the focus is on his right foot. After Brooklyn's Al Gionfriddo makes his famous catch of DiMaggio's 415-foot drive in the sixth game of the '47 Series, DiMaggio is shown rounding second, looking down and kicking the dirt disgustedly.

And in a clip of Ernie Lombardi's famous "snooze" in the 1939 Series, when the Reds' catcher watched the ball roll away from him long enough for a winning run to score, we see (because the narrator reminds us) who it was who scored the run —DiMaggio, sliding abruptly through the frame, no part of him distinctly visible except his foot swiping across the first base corner of the plate just beyond the reach of the belatedly recovered Hartnett. It is the best slide I have ever seen: a blur, dirt flying, that foot, DiMaggio gone.

Watching these snippets of film is frustrating. In Arlene Croce's book on Fred Astaire and Ginger Rogers there is a frame of them dancing on the upper corner of each page, so that if you flip through the pages smoothly enough, they come alive. But my copy of the book is bound unevenly, so that Fred and Ginger skip and lurch and hop—magically enough, to be sure, but I want to capture the whole flow, what's in between. I felt the same way when I watched those DiMaggio films.

There should be available to every American household a video cassette of DiMaggio sighting and homing in on and catching up with and then annexing a long fly ball. (Or, since the attraction seems to have been mutual, of a long fly ball doing all those things to DiMaggio.) You could put it on when you have the blues, the way you put on a

With Connie Mack, 1938. "It has been aptly said that while Ruth was the Home Run King, Gehrig was the Crown Prince," Mack wrote. "Joe DiMaggio must therefore have been heir-apparent."

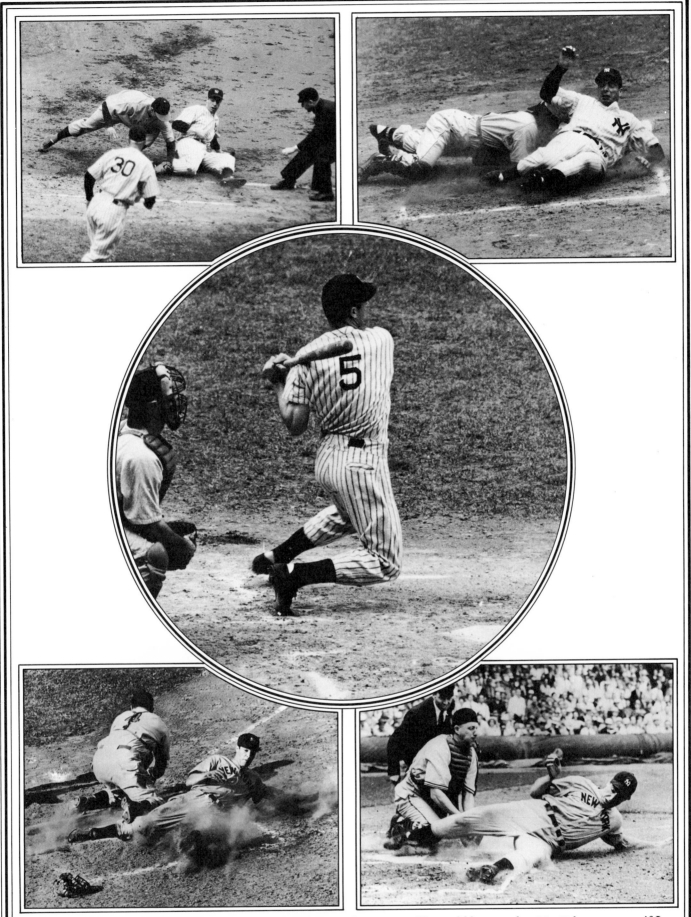

Joe McCarthy said DiMaggio was "the best base runner I ever saw. He could have stolen 50, 60 bases a year if I had let him. He wasn't the fastest man alive. He just knew how to run bases better than anybody. I don't think in all the years [he] played for me he was ever thrown out stretching." His victim at the lower left is Ernie Lombardi, tardily recovering from his inexplicable "snooze" in the 1939 Series. As for his hitting, DiMaggio himself said in 1949, "There's no skill involved. Just go up there and swing at the ball."

Billie Holiday record.

Except that you might feel unworthy around such a cassette. In 1941, the year of his 56-game streak, DiMaggio struck out only *13* times while hitting 30 home runs, driving in 125 runs and batting .357. Has anybody ever had over twice as many home runs and almost ten times as many RBIs as strikeouts in a season? Neither Babe Ruth nor Ted Williams nor Ty Cobb nor Stan Musial nor Rogers Hornsby ever came close. Tommy Holmes had nine Ks, 28 home runs and 117 RBIs in 1945, the year of his 37-game hitting streak, but that was the only slugging year Holmes ever had. In his career, Holmes struck out only 122 times, but he also had only 88 home runs. DiMaggio had nearly as many lifetime home runs (361) as he did strikeouts (369). Today's sluggers typically whiff three or four or five times as often as they hit one out.

The year of DiMaggio's streak was the year I was born. Ten years later, I was watching DiMaggio, on TV, being congratulated in the dugout after his last home run, in the '51 Series, in his last year as a player. It struck me even then as a more graven-in-stone occasion than I was likely to witness again. It must have been the same year when I received a jolt while reading a pictorial biography of DiMaggio. There was a photograph of what looked like a young kid, and at first I thought the legend hand-printed in white ink across the bottom of this photo said "JOE DIMAG, 10, SAN FRANCISCO SEALS, .398."

"Uh oh," I thought. At the time I was 10 myself and planning a career in baseball immortality. I thought, "Joe DiMaggio was hitting .398 in the Pacific Coast League when he was 10, and here I am hitting .086 in Little League." Somewhat later, I realized that there was a "G" between "DIMAG" and "IO" that was obscured by a white patch in the photograph.

But DiMaggio remains an intimidating figure to me. And to everyone else I know who is aware of who he was. Sidney Zion, a New York political reporter who says he would not be impressed to meet any President since Lincoln, once found himself in the same restaurant as DiMaggio. A woman friend blithely approached the Clipper and asked if he would allow Zion to meet him. DiMaggio, who was probably enjoying one of an impressive lifetime total of free class-eatery meals (in San Francisco, they say he has *never* been known to buy a drink

Yankee Stadium, June 30, 1951. Joe (L) and, four innings later, his brother Dom (R). He was not "better than his brother Joe, Do-min-ic DiMaggio," as the Boston song insisted, but he did have a lifetime .298 batting average, and Ted Williams told of fans in the left-field seats at Fenway Park suggesting that Williams should pay half Dom's salary.

In 1934, with the San Francisco Seals. The year before — his first season as a professional — he batted .340. A month into the '34 season he injured his knee and all but one of the scouts who had been dogging him lost interest. The Yankees' Bill Essick purchased his contract for $35,000, but the Seals' owner insisted on keeping DiMaggio through 1935. He hit .398 that year.

(Top, L) Ernie Sulik, Mike Hunt, Joe DiMaggio (L to R), 1935. (Top, R) In his rookie season in New York, DiMaggio was presented the preceding season's Pacific Coast MVP Award by Joe E. Brown. (Bottom) In 1933, at 18, he assembled a 61-game hitting streak, prefiguring 1941. Lefty O'Doul, who was Joe's last manager in San Francisco, told Lawrence Ritter, "In 1935 I had Joe DiMaggio in right field and won the pennant. Sold him to the Yankees...and the next year I finished next to last."

Dom and Joe, and brother Vince (inset). Vince, the oldest, had an arm as strong as Joe's and hit for occasional power — but in ten NL seasons led the league in strikeouts six times. Dom — "he looked like an assistant professor of biology," Fred Lieb wrote — had little power but was a superb fielder and spray hitter. The two younger DiMaggios were All-Star game teammates six times.

for anybody else), said sure. Zion had to be dragged over to the table. He stared at DiMaggio for a moment with his mouth open and then blurted, "Joe, you gave me such thrills!" Zion is still embarrassed that he actually said such a thing. But not *ashamed*.

I talked to DiMaggio once. I was doing a story about Danny Cater, then playing for Oakland. Cater's only nickname was "Carter," from his name's being so often spelled that way in box scores. Finding it hard to build much of a portrait around this cognomen and the fact that Carter hit a lot of looping liners to various fields, I approached DiMaggio, who was putting in a year as an Oakland vice-president and coach.

I did not say, "Joe, will you give me a quote"—even though I was unaware at the time that DiMaggio once said, "I can remember a reporter asking for a quote, and I didn't know what a quote was. I thought it was some kind of soft drink."

I did, however, say "Joe." I eased into a seat next to him on the bench, during batting practice. I don't think I let all my weight settle on this dizzying perch, and I felt sorry to see him dressed in a green-and-yellow uniform and huge white shoes, in the service of Charlie Finley, and I felt presumptuous using his first name, but sportswriters can't say "Mr. DiMaggio," or even "O Clipper." I asked him whether he could tell me anything about what made Cater such an effective hitter of looping liners to various fields.

"You'd better talk to the manager about that," he said.

That's all. He stared straight ahead toward the batting cage. So did I. I still had much of my weight on the balls of my feet. "I've . . . already talked to the manager," I said after a moment. To that, DiMaggio had no response at all. In retrospect it occurs to me that it would have been no more than civil for DiMaggio to say something like, "Well, I'm sorry, I don't have anything to say about Danny Cater, but I wish you well in your researches; good-bye now, I'm busy gazing out over the diamond."

He didn't say that, though. He didn't say anything. I rocked slightly on the balls of my feet and on those of my ass for a few moments, and then I passed out of DiMaggio's life. This was DiMaggio, and I figured he had reasons for not chewing the fat.

One reason he may have had for not talking to me was that I was working at the time for *Sports Illustrated,* a magazine which he had once considered suing for $5 million or so. Some time in the middle sixties *SI* printed in its Scorecard section an item sent in by a volunteer stringer in Sacra-

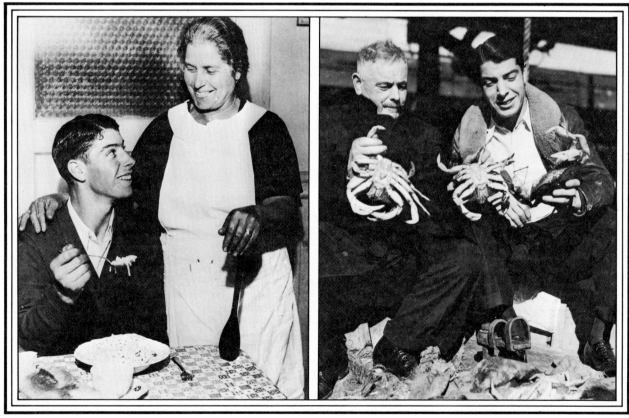

In his mother's kitchen, on his father's crab boat. "'I would like to take the great DiMaggio fishing,' the old man said. 'They say his father was a fisherman. Maybe he was as poor as we are and would understand.'" — Ernest Hemingway, *The Old Man and the Sea*

(Top, L) With 17-year-old Bob Feller. "Feller tried everything against him," Jim Hegan told Maury Allen, "high, low, inside, outside, curve, fastball. Nothing helped. He just hit everything Bob threw up to the plate." (Top, R) With Ted Williams, 1941 All-Star game. "I was always conscious of the other guy," Williams said after he retired. "Usually the other guy was Joe DiMaggio." (Bottom, L) In 1936, with Jake Powell (L) and George Selkirk (R), who had the misfortune of inheriting Babe Ruth's uniform number. (Bottom, R) With Dolf Camilli, 1941 Series.

Mel Harder. He was the one pitcher in the
AL DiMaggio could not hit. "I guess I'm
just grateful I had good luck against him.
It kept me around for a long time."

mento. According to this stringer, DiMaggio had
gone to the racetrack at Del Mar instead of to
Candlestick Park on opening day of the baseball
season, and at the track DiMaggio had explained,
"Baseball bores me now." For some reason no one
checked this item before it ran.

Right after it was published, Edward Bennett
Williams called the magazine to say that his client,
DiMaggio, had never said such a thing, he had not
been at Del Mar that day, had in fact been at
Candlestick, and might have been damaged by
Sports Illustrated several million dollars' worth.
SI Assistant Managing Editor Jack Tibby and
Staff Counsel John P. Dowd were assigned to avert
the suit. They invited Williams and DiMaggio to
lunch in New York at the Hemisphere Club. Di-
Maggio declined to attend, but sat in Williams'
East Side apartment drinking beer and watching
television as Tibby, Dowd and Williams skirmished
over lunch and four rounds of vodka martinis until
almost 4 p.m.

Then the three of them went to the apartment,
where DiMaggio sat glowering. Another *SI* legal
heavy, who had been standing by outside the apartment building, came in right after the main force.
He was wearing, recalls Tibby, "a three-piece Wall
Street lawyer suit with vest chain and Phi Beta
Kappa key."

"Just slip off that jacket and vest," Dowd told
this attorney, "and play barman. There's an apron
behind the bar." The attorney served drinks and
sat, at a distance, in silence.

Williams told DiMaggio that *SI* was abashed

and would print a retraction. No response. Then
Dowd, renowned for his drinking-and-defusing operations, moved in on the Clipper.

Dowd had grown up watching Yankee games.
He told DiMaggio how honored he was to meet him
and then reeled off 13 or 14 DiMaggio plays that
burned in his memory—all of them certifiable never-
to-be-forgottens, but none of them standard golden
moments he could have researched somewhere for
the occasion.

"DiMaggio's frozen scowl relaxed to deadpan,
then to a smile, finally to chuckles," Tibby recalls.
"He remembered those plays, too. Edward Bennett
Williams worked his face like Joe." Joe didn't sue
after all.

I guess that's how I should have approached Di-
Maggio when I had the chance to talk to him. I
could probably have found a suitably dressed lawyer to divest himself and tend bar, but it would
probably have gone against any lawyer's sense of
fitness to do all that without being paid for his time,
and where was I going to get that kind of money?
And I was too young to have the memories! And
DiMaggio was not going to bring up those moments
himself. He performed them. That was his end of it.

The terrible thing about DiMaggio's commercials
is that he looks so good in them. That's what people
say to him when they see him in the flesh. "You
look good, Joe," they say. Before the ceremonies
preceding the first game in the renovated Yankee
Stadium, I watched for about 10 minutes as at least
a dozen strangers came up to him and said, "Joe,
you look good." Then they would go away saying
to each other, "Don't he look good?"

If DiMaggio ever visits the Louvre, the Venus
de Milo probably waits until they are alone and then

(L to R) Batboy Tim Sullivan, DiMaggio, Tommy
Henrich, Red Rolfe. Henrich, Red Smith wrote, "got
more pure joy out of baseball than any other player I
ever knew." He also got a $25,000 bonus from the Yan-
kees when Judge Landis declared him illegally covered
up by the Indians.

leans toward him and whispers, "Joe, you look good." And DiMaggio probably smiles, not very committally, the way he smiled at the people at the Stadium, and moves on to exchange a level glance with the Winged Victory.

You assume that DiMaggio knows he looks good, that he's always known it. But they say that when he returned to the bench after his cuts he'd say to fellow Yankees, "How . . . how did I look up there? Did I look okay?"

"You looked good, Joe," his teammates would assure him. And he would keep on, often in spite of great pain, carrying his team and living up to his image. "He knew he was Joe DiMaggio," said teammate Lefty Gomez, "and he knew what that meant to the country."

In his commercials DiMaggio looks extremely distinguished and perfectly natural. When Tom and Nancy Seaver pitch aluminum siding side by side on the tube it is at least faintly embarrassing (will Seaver ever stop looking like a chubbyish California kid with a bent for public relations?), but DiMaggio looks as if he were born to the role of corporate spokesman and gizmo-endorser.

"Joe!" I want to cry out to him. "One bank is pretty much the same as another, isn't it? And I can tell you two or three better ways to make coffee!"

He never did talk much to the press, or to anybody else, apparently. He traveled for four days by car with Tony Lazzeri and Frankie Crosetti from San Francisco to his first Yankee spring training without saying a word, except, when they asked him to do some driving, that he didn't know how. That same year he sat silently with his foot in a drastically overheated diathermy machine until his foot was burned and blistered, "a sickening sight," according to a teammate.

He never even talked to Marilyn Monroe much. At their divorce proceedings, she testified he would sink into black moods and when she tried to find out what was wrong he would say, *to Marilyn Monroe,* "Leave me alone." You can talk all you want about that 56-game hitting streak, but that is a record that some day could conceivably be broken. No one else could play Garbo to Marilyn Monroe.

His confidants and relatives will not be interviewed about him. No one knows what he does when he isn't being recognized in ballpark ceremonies or catered to in pro-am golf matches or

Joe McCarthy and Ed Barrow; DiMaggio ending his 1938 holdout. After DiMaggio's epochal 1941 season, according to Al Silverman, Barrow said, "There's a war on, Joe. The country's in bad shape. We're going to have to cut you $2,500." Barrow himself wrote, "Joe DiMaggio held out for $50,000. I got up to $30,000 and we finally settled for $32,500. Mrs. Barrow told me to give it to him. She was always on the side of the ballplayers." Over 13 seasons, DiMaggio earned $704,769 in salary.

filmed for commercials or sighted in restaurants. And yet here is this enigma sharing with us his faith in this bank and this coffee machine.

Ah Capitalism! Ah Television! Ah Unjolting Joe!

The best profile of DiMaggio is Gay Talese's in *Esquire* in 1966. *"You're invading my rights,"* DiMaggio told Talese when he tried to interview him. Talese was able to learn, anyway, that Di-Maggio among friends says things like, "Look at *that* tomato!"

From early magazine stories one learns that, as a young player, DiMaggio had a habit of responding to questions about what he'd been up to by saying, "Oh, I've been nonchalantly meandering down the pike," and that his favorite radio star was Bing Crosby, to whom he referred as "Bingaroo." None of this seems edifying. The only biography of DiMaggio that I know of is Maury Allen's *Where Have You Gone, Joe DiMaggio,* which received no assistance from its subject and whose opening sentence is, "I was fifteen when I first touched Joe DiMaggio."

Tony Triolo, a *Sports Illustrated* photographer, once spent an evening with DiMaggio in the piano bar of the Yankee Clipper Inn in Fort Lauderdale. DiMaggio had come in with a mutual friend, who was delighting DiMag with a knowledge of obscure Cole Porter tunes. DiMaggio was very loose and laughing and kidding around.

"What did you say to him?" I asked Triolo.

"Well, I didn't really say things *to* him, directly. I would talk to him by saying things to his friend. You know what I mean? I couldn't believe it. I was there with Joe DiMaggio. I kept looking at his hands. You know what I mean?"

At old-timers' games, Mantle and Ford and all those guys may be in the dressing room with everyone looking up to them, but when DiMaggio comes in they join in the circle that forms around the Clipper. DiMaggio did not like it when the '78 Yankee old-timer affair was dominated by Billy Martin's bows to thunderous applause at the announcement that he would return to manage the team in 1980. DiMaggio reportedly told Yankee owner George Steinbrenner, "If these things are going to be like this, I'm not sure I want to continue coming."

"I would consider not having them," Steinbrenner replied contritely, "if you don't continue coming."

DiMaggio is the only person whose displeasure over improprieties in the providing of his World Series tickets can make headlines.

But couldn't he be making more of a contribution to American life? Ted Williams is not what you would call a natural-born ambassador of goodwill, but he is out in the world coaching the Red Sox occasionally and impressing Doris Kearns, biographer of Lyndon Johnson, with how much he reminds her of Johnson. The first time I met Williams he thrust an imaginary bat in my hands, seized my hips, told me to swing and then told me how I swung wrong. "Larger than life, his sunglasses held on by what appeared to be a piece of fishing line and his voice audible at Sullivan Square, Theodore Samuel Williams hit Fenway Park late yesterday afternoon not unlike the manner in which the Marines hit Anzio," reported *The Boston Globe* in June of '78. DiMaggio seems beyond "larger than life." If just once something pertaining to him would be visibly held together by fishing line.

Not that DiMaggio has always been regarded as impeccable. When he was a young player his teammates occasionally called him "Cruiser" for the way he fielded, but mostly they called him "Dago." When he held out (a) for $25,000 in 1938, and (b) for somewhat more in 1942 (the Yankees offered him a $2,500 cut after his epochal '41 season), Yankee general manager Ed Barrow accused him publicly of being greedy when so many Americans (though not Barrow) were (a) starving, and (b) fighting a war at low pay. These contretemps with management caused DiMaggio to be booed about as regularly as he was cheered. When he returned in '46 from three seasons' worth of Army service, a sportswriter falsely reported that he had avoided combat by faking stomach ulcers. It was not until 1949, when he was an elder statesman still playing wondrously with well-publicized hurts, that the boos disappeared entirely.

Even the beauty of DiMaggio's feelings for Marilyn Monroe, on whose crypt he has six red roses placed three times a week (and he *may* be the ex-husband who has made inquiries about the still-vacant crypt next to hers), has not gone entirely unsullied. In 1958, a woman accepted $7,500 out of court in settlement of her suit against DiMaggio and Frank Sinatra, in which she alleged that she had been seized with acute hysteria when, in 1954, those two near-mythic figures and some other people broke down her door and shone lights in her eyes. In '57 Sinatra had testified, according to *The New York Times,* that "he had remained in his parked car some distance from the scene until the former ball player and some friends returned a few minutes later, mentioning 'the wrong door'." Joe had been trying—just a few days after their

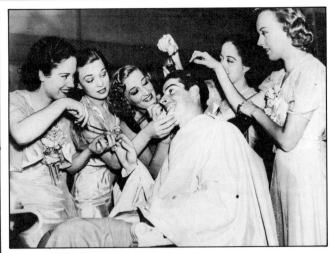

DiMaggio had a brief career in the movies: a small part in, and a great deal of publicity photography (L) for, a vehicle called *Manhattan Merry-Go-Round*. On the set, he met 19-year-old Dorothy Arnold (with Joe, R), who became his first wife, "the luckiest catch I ever made." Phil Rizzuto gave Maury Allen a reason for their eventual divorce: "I guess Joe was tough to live with."

divorce—to surprise Marilyn afield.

Marilyn is the subject DiMaggio most particularly refuses to talk about. What is he going to say? Why in the *world,* one wonders, would such a proudly introverted man marry Marilyn Monroe? Either he thought America expected it of him, or it was a case of "Look at *THAT* tomato!"

But then why in the world would DiMaggio ever give the press any cooperation on any subject, after what *Life* magazine did to him in May of 1939? Joe was just getting established as a superhero, but had had the temerity to hold out the year before for $25,000. Even if you bear in mind that Luce publications in those days were known to employ phraseology such as "Leon Blum, the Jew President of France," and that Italy in those days was an Axis power, it is still hard to believe that this story appeared (under the byline of one Noel F. Busch):

"Italians, bad at war, are well-suited for milder competition," the story observed.

"Although he learned Italian first Joe, now 24, speaks English without an accent, and is otherwise well adopted to most US mores. Instead of olive oil or smelly bear grease he keeps his hair slick with water. He never reeks of garlic and prefers chicken chow mein to spaghetti . . . .

"Joe DiMaggio's rise in baseball is a testimonial to the value of general shiftlessness . . . .

"His inertia caused him to give up school after one year in high school."

He is "lazy, rebellious and endowed with a bad stomach."

There is a reference to "squirrel teeth."

"Joe, who has not yet sublimated his appreciation of the opposite sex to the point of a courtship [huh?], admires [Lefty] Gomez for his *savoir-faire* and copies his manners."

The story is not framed as debunkery. It's just casually insulting. Beneath a photograph of DiMaggio and Joe Louis a caption reads: "Like Heavyweight Champion Louis, DiMaggio is lazy, shy and inarticulate."

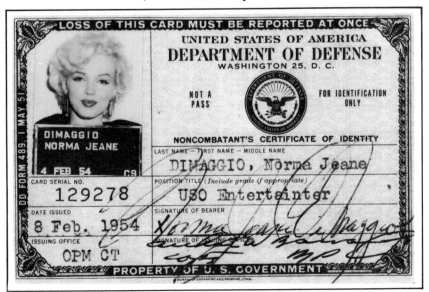

Beneath a photograph of DiMaggio being mobbed by autograph seekers: "Autograph-seeking children mob DiMaggio. . . Like other celebrities, DiMaggio sometimes cynically signs a pseudonym."

Beneath a photograph of Joe's parents in the new house he bought for them: "Mrs. Rosalie DiMaggio and Joe DiMaggio Sr. find their new magnificence somewhat depressing."

Beneath a photograph of DiMaggio listening to a cash register in his restaurant: "Joe listens to cash register, for publicity purposes. Posing for such absurd pictures is part of DiMaggio's job."

Beneath a photograph of DiMaggio posing as a crab fisherman: "Posing as a crab fisherman like his father is often unavoidable for Joe. He hates fish and fears crabs."

All this about a man who in later years was referred to in the *Times* as "a man whose very being exudes pure class." Such a story would drive anybody into looking dignified for a living.

One other thing in the *Life* story, in reference to DiMaggio's efforts to squeeze from the Yankees more money for himself and his family: "Unfortunately for the DiMaggios, the US national game is run according to strictly Fascist lines."

Strong words, *Life*! But it's true that the great DiMaggio was never a free agent. Never a free spirit, never a freewheeler, never a man with freedom of speech.

He was only free from the hitches, jerks and flutters that normal flesh in motion is heir to. And as long as that eerie and for the most part agonizing freedom persisted in his joints, he lived up to it—a freedom of physical continuity so pure that it couldn't be preserved in discrete images. We have, blink, him swinging, we have, flash, him sliding, we have, surely, rolled away in a reel somewhere, him intercepting unaccountably a long fly ball. We have him popping up for a bank and a coffee maker.

Whatever has gone on in between is gone.

"You saw him standing out there and you knew you had a pretty damn good chance to win the baseball game." — Red Ruffing

SIXTH INNING:
1940-1949

I honestly feel it would be best for the country to keep baseball going. There will be fewer people unemployed and everybody will work longer hours and harder than ever before....
Here is another way of looking at it—if 300 teams use 5,000 or 6,000 players, these players are a definite recreational asset to at least 20,000,000 of their fellow citizens—and that in my judgment is thoroughly worthwhile.

—Franklin D. Roosevelt, 1942

IT BEGAN with a pennant race that was decided by a pitcher so lightly regarded his vital statistics were never listed in the *Baseball Register*. It ended with two pennant races that were not resolved until the final day of the season. It was a decade that saw eleven different teams play in the World Series and all of the remaining five finish in the first division at least once. It was the most competitive ten-year period in the history of the game, and a strong case can be made that it was also the most exciting. It was the last decade in which the game would have a .400 hitter or a pitcher who completed more than 35 games in a season. It was the first decade in which a pennant race ended in a dead heat, and it happened not once but twice and conceivably could, with an ever-so-slight reordering of events, have happened several times more.

It was, at bottom, a time of breathlessly swift transition, a shift in the space of a few short years from a game that for nearly a century had been played exclusively by members of one race, in natural light and in front of live audiences, to one that would feature men of all races, who generally would be seen under artificial light and at distances of thousands of miles by people who had never visited the cities represented by the teams now appearing in their homes, much less climbed the ramps of the stadiums in which they played. Yet, during the war, there were moments when the level of play reached

Ernie Lombardi (L), Willard Hershberger. After his long career ended, Lombardi managed a living on welfare, then as a Wrigley Field press box attendant. His Cincinnati backup, Hershberger, had a .316 career average when he committed suicide midway through the 1940 season.

so low an ebb that many purists would have preferred the game be suspended for the interim, and by the end of the decade matters stood precisely as they had ten years earlier. The Yankees were ascendant once more and on the edge of establishing a new dynasty—this one more dominant than any in the past.

But for an unexpected interruption by the Tigers, the Yankees would have begun the decade with a string of five consecutive pennants. Detroit and Cleveland battled down to the last Saturday of the

The 1940 Tigers. Floyd Giebell, who pitched the game that won the pennant, was not even around long enough to qualify for the picture. Al Benton (second row, second from L) and Bobo Newsom (third row, extreme R) were both around long enough to pitch both to Babe Ruth and Mickey Mantle.

1940 season with the Tigers holding a one-game lead. Desperate for an able arm to counter Bob Feller, already a 27-game winner, Tiger manager Del Baker dipped his fingers into his hat and came up with a 30-year-old right-hander who had only two major league victories: Floyd Giebell, today a footnote in trivia books at best—except in Cleveland, where mention of his name still brings a light shudder to anyone over fifty. In a script that would have made Hollywood wince, Giebell beat Feller and clinched the pennant for Detroit. He not only beat him—he beat him 1–0. It was not just the most important game of Giebell's life—it turned out to be the *only* important game of his life. He never figured in another decision in the major leagues.

In some ways, the Indians were fortunate to come as close as they did. Manager Ossie Vitt spent the season putting down a series of insurrections that culminated when all 25 players presented a petition to team president Alva Bradley demanding that Vitt be fired. Eventually he was, but not until the season was over and the Indians had earned a reputation as crybabies. It would be another eight years before the Indians would make another pennant bid; and then, in a final bit of irony, their season would once more come down to a game in which they found themselves pitted against a pitcher destined never to win another game in the major leagues.

As for the Yankees, they finished third, a scant two games off the pace, and narrowly missed overhauling the Tigers after pitcher Tiny Bonham was recalled in early August from Kansas City. Summoning Bonham was an act the Yankees would have preferred to avoid; it was tantamount to a public admission that their once-proud pitching staff was in disarray. Yet Bonham proved so effective that the Yankees probably would not only have won their fifth pennant in a row if he had been recalled earlier in the season but, as events turned out, eight straight pennants between 1936 and 1943.

The Reds, winners of their second straight pennant, were the National League entry in the 1940 Series. But the final standings reflect none of the tragedy that engulfed Bill McKechnie's team and threatened for a time to ruin their season. On August 3 in Boston, Willard Hershberger, a second-line catcher who was filling in for the injured Ernie Lombardi, committed suicide in his hotel room while despondent over his role in a losing game that afternoon. In September the screw turned another notch when Lombardi was injured a second time. On the eve of the Series McKechnie was forced to bring Jimmie Wilson, the old Cardinal star, off the coaching lines and activate him. Wilson was 40 years old and hadn't caught a full game in three seasons. Employing Wilson in the Series, McKechnie was rewarded when Jimmie hit .353 and was instrumental in bringing the Reds their first untainted world championship. Despite the heroics of Wilson, the Reds were something less than a great team. They

Bob Feller (seated), after his 1940 Opening Day no-hitter. Two months later, Cleveland players initiated the "Crybaby Rebellion" to oust manager Ossie Vitt (third from R, behind man with glasses), who had shouted at Feller, during a bad outing, "Look at him! He's supposed to be my ace! I'm supposed to win a pennant with that kind of pitching!" Vitt was fired at season's end, and never managed again.

Ted Williams, five years before John Lardner wrote, "By the time the press of Boston has completed its daily treatment of Theodore S. Williams, there is no room in the papers for anything but two sticks of agate type about Truman and housing, and one column for the last Boston girl to be murdered on a beach."

remain the only modern-era club to win back-to-back pennants without having a single Hall of Famer in their lineup.

Another star of the period who would miss out on the Hall of Fame was Pete Reiser. After a solid but unspectacular rookie season in 1940, he emerged the following year as the youngest batting championship winner in National League history. Many who saw Reiser in 1941 still maintain that he would have been one of the greatest centerfielders ever if he could have been kept free of injuries. Still indelibly imprinted on the memories of all who followed baseball in the forties are photographs of him lying unconscious at the base of an outfield wall after crashing into it in pursuit of a drive, and for those too young to have seen him, he has assumed over the years an almost mythic stature.

Exactly how good was Reiser? It will never be possible, of course, to gauge what kind of career he might have had if he had not been so frequently injured. Perhaps the closest parallel is Charlie Hollocher, the Cub shortstop of 20 years earlier. Yet there are also parallels in a more modern era. Al Kaline, who won a batting title when he was only 20 and never won another, was also diminished by injuries. So was Tommy Davis. In Reiser's own era, Terry Moore was severely hurt in a collision

with an outfield wall in 1938, and numerous players such as Mickey Cochrane and Moose Solters were never the same after beanings. But the prewar game was one of abandon, of reckless machismo, of hurrying back into the lineup as soon as possible after an injury, as did Dizzy Dean. It is easy in hindsight to wonder why Leo Durocher didn't plant Reiser on third base, a position he played adequately, when it grew apparent that his manner of outfield play put his future in jeopardy; but Reiser himself has said he has no regrets. He was simply playing the game the only way he knew how.

In any event, Reiser's hitting in 1941, along with the addition by trades of Kirby Higbe and Mickey Owen, gave the Dodgers the cast for their first pennant winner in 21 years. In point of fact, not a single regular on the club was a product of the Dodger farm system. Joe Medwick came from the Cardinals, Dolf Camilli from the Phils, Cookie Lavagetto from the Pirates and Pee Wee Reese from the Red Sox' Louisville farm team. The Yankees, meanwhile, had returned to the head of the American League with the addition of Phil Rizzuto and the return to form of Dickey and Gomez. The pennant race itself provided no drama, but fans in both leagues were gripped for large portions of the season by two batting feats the likes of which may never be seen again. The one that received the most attention was Joe DiMaggio's hitting streak. After DiMaggio was finally stopped at 56 games, it remained only a formality to award him the MVP at the end of the season.

Luke Appling. In his 20-year White Sox career, they never finished higher than third. Fortunately, wrote Warren Brown, Appling "was completely relaxed at all times, winning or losing."

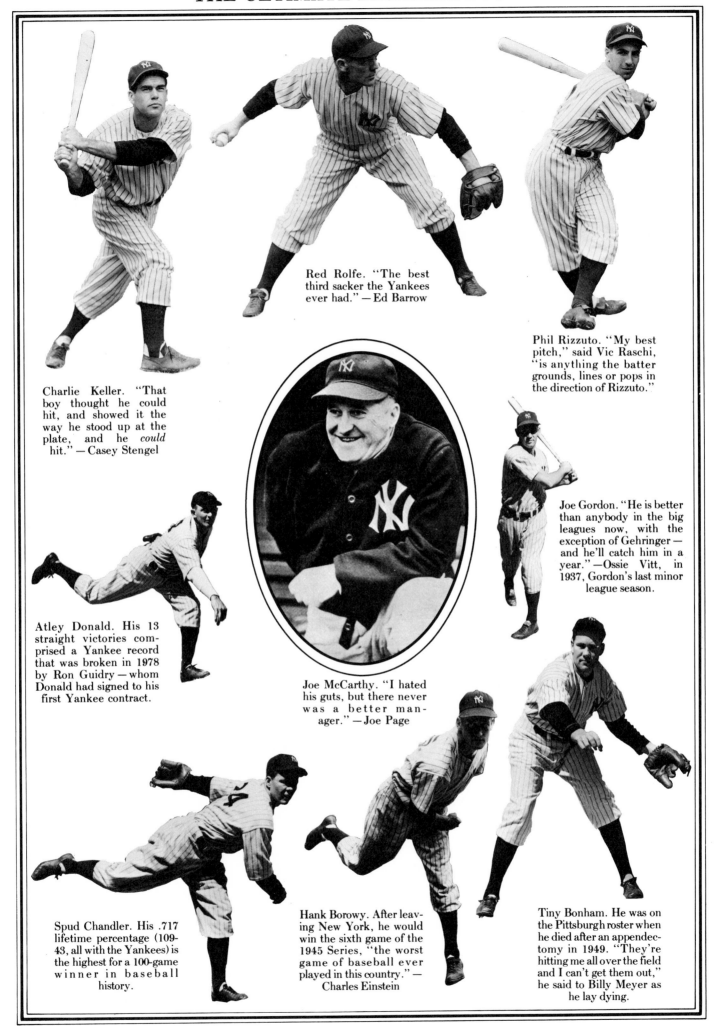

Charlie Keller. "That boy thought he could hit, and showed it the way he stood up at the plate, and he *could* hit." — Casey Stengel

Red Rolfe. "The best third sacker the Yankees ever had." — Ed Barrow

Phil Rizzuto. "My best pitch," said Vic Raschi, "is anything the batter grounds, lines or pops in the direction of Rizzuto."

Atley Donald. His 13 straight victories comprised a Yankee record that was broken in 1978 by Ron Guidry — whom Donald had signed to his first Yankee contract.

Joe Gordon. "He is better than anybody in the big leagues now, with the exception of Gehringer — and he'll catch him in a year." —Ossie Vitt, in 1937, Gordon's last minor league season.

Joe McCarthy. "I hated his guts, but there never was a better manager." — Joe Page

Spud Chandler. His .717 lifetime percentage (109-43, all with the Yankees) is the highest for a 100-game winner in baseball history.

Hank Borowy. After leaving New York, he would win the sixth game of the 1945 Series, "the worst game of baseball ever played in this country." — Charles Einstein

Tiny Bonham. He was on the Pittsburgh roster when he died after an appendectomy in 1949. "They're hitting me all over the field and I can't get them out," he said to Billy Meyer as he lay dying.

(Top, L) Joe Nuxhall as a 6' 2" junior high school pitcher. Two months later, on June 10, 1944, he pitched for the Reds. He told William Mead, "I walked five, gave up two hits and I think a wild pitch. I was just scared to death. Finally, [Bill] McKechnie just walked out and said, 'Well, son, I think you've had enough.' " (Top, R) Walker Cooper (L), Morton Cooper. Their father died early in the morning of October 6, 1943; that afternoon, the Coopers were the winning battery in the second game of the World Series. (Bottom) Christy Walsh had been a cartoonist before becoming the first full-time "sports agent." He returned to cartooning just long enough to help promote *Pride of the Yankees*, the film of Lou Gehrig's life.

The second feat—Ted Williams's .406 average—did not seem quite so remarkable at the time. It had only been 11 years, after all, since Bill Terry had last cracked the .400 barrier, and in the decade before that, .400 averages had been almost commonplace. As a result, Williams received nowhere near the superlatives DiMaggio did. Few pointed at his season on-base average of .551, which will likely stand forever as a record, and fewer still noted that his batting average for the *entire* season was only two points lower than DiMaggio's during the hitting streak.

Mickey Owen's missed third strike is the most remembered moment of the 1941 Series. Had Owen held Hugh Casey's final pitch to Tommy Henrich, the Dodgers would have evened the Series at two-all. Not so well remembered is that with a break or two, the Dodgers could have swept the Series in four games. The opener was lost when Reese, who was carrying the tying run, made an ill-advised attempt to advance to third on Jimmy Wasdell's foul out. In the third game—won by the Yankees 2–1—Freddie Fitzsimmons had to be removed while working on a shutout after being struck in the leg by a line drive in the seventh inning.

The perverse luck that befell the Dodgers in the 1941 Series pursued them over the next decade. Although they won three pennants, they could as easily have won seven. In 1942, for example, despite winning 104 games and holding a 10½ game lead in mid-August, they wound up second to the Cardinals. Billy Southworth's team was infused by the sudden rise to stardom of Mort Cooper, who scored the first of three successive 20-win seasons, and the play of two rookies, Stan Musial and Johnny Beazley. Musial's .315 average was anticipated off his minor league record, but Beazley's 21 victories were not. Returning from the service in 1946 after three seasons away from the game, Beazley could not regain his rookie form and won only nine more games before ending his career.

Prior to the 1942 season there was doubt whether the game would be allowed to continue in view of the war effort. Finally, in response to a written request from Judge Landis on how baseball could serve the nation, President Roosevelt issued his famous "green light" letter, stating that he felt it would be best for the country to keep baseball going, with overage and underage players as well as service rejects. The Yankees, easy repeat winners in the American League, were relatively untouched as yet by the draft. The Cardinals too still had a full complement of regulars and took the Series in five games. After the season, Branch Rickey surprised everyone by resigning as the Cards' general manager and joining the Dodgers as a replacement for Larry MacPhail, who was now a lieutenant colonel in the army. Rickey's switch would have little initial impact; the powerhouse he had been building in St. Louis would go on to win three more pennants in the next four seasons, while the war frustrated his efforts to reconstruct a Dodger team that had been hard hit by the draft.

Russ Derry, Danny Gardella, Nick Etten (L to R). "The game being played on the field in 1944 was recognizable," wrote Douglass Wallop, "but many of the players were not." Of these three, Etten was the closest thing to a real ballplayer; when he went from the Phils to the Yanks in 1943, he said, "Imagine a man in that environment [the Phils had lost 109 in 1942] hearing that he had been sold to the Yankees!"

Never one to leave the scene quietly, Ted Williams won the triple crown in 1942 before entering the service, but he was once more denied the MVP award when the writers chose Joe Gordon. In the National League, Ernie Lombardi became the last man to win a batting title with fewer than 400 at bats, and Johnny Mize took slugging honors after being inexplicably traded by Rickey to the Giants. Mort Cooper was voted the National League MVP after winning 22 games, but another 22-game winner, Tex Hughson, received no special accolades, despite having the finest season by any Red Sox pitcher since Babe Ruth.

It was still baseball pretty much as normal in 1942, but by the following World Series, with so many stars now in the service, only the uniforms were the same. This time it was the Yankees' turn to overwhelm the favored Cards in five games. The Series was a dull climax to a remarkably dull season that saw two one-sided pennant races. Attendance was down in most cities, and sportswriters were making dire forecasts on the game's future. After being exposed to Williams and DiMaggio, who could become aroused by Bill Nicholson and Nick Etten, to name only two performers who had done little before the war but now were suddenly stars? It was thought that if Williams were still around, he would hit not .400 but an easy .500. What was not a cause of much speculation, and certainly should have been, was the reason why so many greats whose careers were not interrupted by the service failed to dominate the game during the war years. Mel Ott, Joe Medwick, Ernie Lombardi, Rudy York, Stan Hack, Bob Elliott, Lou Boudreau and Frank McCormick all played throughout the war, and none did any better against wartime pitching than the Nicholsons or Ettens, who were regarded as worthy of major league uniforms only by default. It is possible that the game was not as diluted during the war as is generally believed. If that is the case, then a fresh look must be taken at the careers of those who rose to stardom during the war, and whose achievements were afterward dismissed as having come against mediocre opposition.

The leading example is Hal Newhouser, the only two-time MVP winner not in the Hall of Fame. Newhouser's totals for the seasons of 1944 and 1945 —54 wins, 14 shutouts and an ERA close to 2.00— surpassed those of all American League pitchers over a like period since Lefty Grove. After the war Newhouser went on to have two more 20-win seasons, including a 26–9 record in 1946 and a league-leading 21 victories in 1948. Over the course of the decade he won 170 games, the most by any pitcher active during that period. Even conceding that Feller would undoubtedly have won more had his career not been interrupted by the Navy, the neglect into which Newhouser has fallen seems sad and unfair.

Among the clubs least affected by the draft were

Johnny Mize, Hal Newhouser, Phil Cavarretta (L to R). Mize hit a home run in every major league park of his era. Of Newhouser, Bill Dickey said, "As far as the Yankees are concerned, we'd rather face anyone else." Cavarretta, wrote Warren Brown, "in all the years he has been with the Cubs, and they are many, has been kept grabbing for...a regular place in the lineup in which to light and remain." He batted .292 in his 20 years as a Cub.

the St. Louis Browns, the lone franchise in either league to enter the century's fifth decade still in search of its first pennant. When the Browns' drought finally came to an end in 1944, there wasn't a baseball figure in the country who begrudged them their moment, although many saw it as symbolic of the depths the game had reached. And in truth the Browns that season were the weakest entry, with the possible exception of the 1973 Mets, to win a pennant. Only Mike Kreevich, who hiked his average to .301 on the season's final day, kept the Browns from being the first flag winners in history without either a .300 hitter or a 20-game winner. Tied with the Tigers on the last morning of the season, the Browns won by beating the Yankees with Sig Jakucki—back in the majors after retiring six years before with an 0–3 lifetime record—while Tiger ace Dizzy Trout was losing to Washington. Many considered it the ultimate mockery that a pitcher of Jakucki's caliber was chosen for so important a contest, and much was made of the fact that it was his last major league victory. Sig Jakucki—his winning, his mere presence in a big league uniform—became in time the final thread in the blanket under which purists tried to hide the wartime game. How quickly Floyd Giebell had been forgotten!

The Series was an anticlimax for the Browns but not for St. Louis fans, who were seeing both of their clubs in World Series action. It was the last Series played by two teams using the same stadium, and it could have been the first Series broadcast by Dizzy Dean if Judge Landis had not ruled that Dean's

quaint homilies and grammatical distortions were too undignified for a national audience. It was one of the Judge's last decisions—he would die before the opening of the 1945 season—and represented for some an even more curious chapter than the one that had followed the 1943 season, when he barred William Cox, the Phils' owner, from baseball for betting on his own team. No one has ever ascertained whether it was Cox's gambling associations or the image of incredible foolishness he projected by betting on a team with only one first-division finish in the last 25 years that the Judge found most unpalatable.

On the eve of the 1945 World Series, Warren Brown, a Chicago sports editor, was asked whether he fancied the Cubs or the Tigers. His reply that he didn't think either club was capable of winning has become over the years an epitaph for the last wartime season; yet it was in many ways the most intriguing year of the decade. It was the last season that wartime travel restrictions were in effect, making it necessary for all the teams to train north of the Potomac River and, with the exception of the two St. Louis clubs, east of the Mississippi. It was the only season since the inception of the All-Star game in 1933 that no such contest was held. It was, furthermore, the only season in the last 60 years that a league slugging leader posted an average under .500, or that a home run leader struck out fewer than 10 times. It will readily be remembered by everyone as the year a one-armed outfielder and a one-legged pitcher played in the majors, and it

(L) Jackie Robinson, J.G. Taylor Spink, Burt Shotton (L to R). In 1942, Spink's *Sporting News* editorialized, "Clear minded men of tolerance of both races realize the tragic possibilities [of baseball integration] and have steered clear of such complications, because they realize it is to the benefit of each and also of the game." (R) Dan Daniel, in addition to his duties in New York, wrote 5,000 words weekly for Spink. Jerome Holtzman said Daniel "was once described, and accurately so, as the Arnold Toynbee of baseball."

will readily be remembered by Chicago fans as the last time the Cubs won a pennant.

What conclusions are to be drawn from the roll call of the wartime oddities? The obvious ones are that Warren Brown knew what he was talking about and that the experts who undervalue the feats of Hal Newhouser may have good reason after all. Yet the fact remains that pitchers like Claude Passeau, Jack Kramer and Paul Derringer pitched for decent teams during the war without winning 20 games; that Mel Ott hit only .234 against wartime pitching in 1943; that all three of the game's top shortstops—Marty Marion, Eddie Miller and Lou Boudreau—were active throughout the war, and while their fielding was as dazzling as ever, only Boudreau made any significant offensive contributions. It is likely that the brand of baseball witnessed during the war was not as bad as historians have made out. For along with the Irv Halls and Russ Derrys, thrown into the breach and then quickly discarded when the war ended, there were many like Eddie Mayo and Ken Raffensberger who were given reprieves after earlier flops and went on to successful postwar careers. There was also a 28-year-old minor leaguer who was beckoned by the pitching-hungry Indians in 1943; he was only fair during the war, but afterward he got a little better and managed to hang around long enough to compile 182 victories. His name: Allie Reynolds. And there was a 27-year-old infielder who was hauled up from the minors by the Cubs after Lou Stringer was drafted. He too impressed no one during the war—and didn't win a regular job until 1945, when the Dodgers began realizing there might be more to him than met the eye. He couldn't hit much, he didn't field all that well, but over the next five seasons he

played on pennant winners in three different National League cities and wormed his way onto several All-Star squads. His name: Eddie Stanky.

Those fans who had stayed away from ballparks in droves during the war years lined up to buy their tickets early in 1946, in the expectation that the game they remembered would soon be restored. It didn't happen. For while the war overseas had been won, another kind of skirmish was in progress on the home front. The names of Jorge Pasquel and Hector Racine, never before heard in America, were suddenly household words. Pasquel was threatening to pirate away many of the game's existing stars, while Racine was serving notice that the game would soon have new ones—and of a different color than any of the previous variety.

Jorge Pasquel, late in 1945, was still only a wealthy customs broker in Mexico who had a financial interest in the Mexican professional league south of the border and a patriotic desire to improve it. A chance meeting that winter at Al Roon's gymnasium in Manhattan with Giant outfielder Danny Gardella provided him with a way both his interests could be served. Soon, Gardella and several dozen other performers such as Mickey Owen and Sal Maglie had been induced to play in Mexico. When Vern Stephens, the Browns' slugging shortstop, threatened to join them, owners looked in desperation to Happy Chandler, the former senator from Kentucky who had replaced the late Judge Landis as commissioner the previous season. Chandler thus far had not inspired much confidence. His failure to intervene in 1945 when the Yankees somehow contrived to waive Hank Borowy, a front-line pitcher, out of the American League and into the

Some Brownies, 1944. (L to R) Nelson Potter, George McQuinn, Vern Stephens, Mike Kreevich. In 1935, total home attendance for Browns games was less than 82,000; in 1933, they once played before an audience of 34 people. Finally, in the last game of 1944, they had their first sell-out in 19 years. Stephens and McQuinn were part of an all-4F infield; the club assigned a priest to accompany Kreevich and keep him sober; Potter's two errors on one play in the Series kept the Browns from winning the first three games and, probably, the championship.

Pete Gray. His manager, Luke Sewell, told William Mead, "He didn't belong in the majors, and he knew he was being exploited." Mike Kreevich quit, his ego dashed when he was replaced by the one-armed outfielder. Gray never held another job of any kind after his last minor league season in 1949. Yet, Mark Christman said in 1976, "The fans still remember Pete Gray, because he was incredible."

hands of the pennant-bound Cubs, was taken as a sign that he was merely a stooge for the wealthier clubs. Chandler acted with dispatch on the Mexican issue, however, and ruled that all players who had not returned north by his deadline were automatically suspended from organized baseball for five years. The ban stuck until 1949 when a flurry of legal suits, most of them instigated by Gardella, forced Chandler to allow the wayward sheep to return to the fold.

By then it had developed that most of them were not needed, for the rosters of many teams were filled with names that until three years earlier had been allowed to appear in box scores with major leaguers only in exhibition play. Hector Racine was not really the man responsible for that, but it was he, acting in his capacity as president of the Montreal Royals' team in the International League, who called the historic press conference on October 23, 1945, to announce that organized baseball was no longer the province of one race—and to introduce the man who would be a candidate for an infield position with the Royals the following spring: Jack Roosevelt Robinson.

What has transpired since that day is history—and to the game's eternal discredit, all too recent history. What is not yet history, at least not in a way that permits a full perspective to be taken, are the contributions of Branch Rickey to the sport of baseball. Seen by many present-day executives as an Aaron Burr figure who traitorously forced them into expansion in the late 1950's by his efforts to start a civil war within their ranks over his proposed Continental League, he was not much more sanguinely regarded in his own day. Players who were buried in the vast farm systems of his teams loathed him. Fellow general managers who were continually being bilked of their talent or conned into purchasing his culls distrusted him. Fans misunderstood him; they believed, when he took over the Pirates in the fifties and failed miserably, that the game had passed him by. And in a sense they were right. Rickey was a man who worked, schemed and connived to build winning teams simply for the sake of being associated with a winner. A great baseball mind, Walter O'Malley has called him, a master at judging talent, but ultimately a disaster to have in your front office because . . . well, because for God's sake you couldn't make any money with the man! The great sport of baseball, that was the picture Rickey had of the game. When the camera angle changed and baseball passed from view as a sport and became a business, he was out of his element.

It is somewhat numbing to think that if the Dodgers had merely concluded the seasons of 1946, 1950 and 1951 with victorious games rather than losing ones, they would have won nine pennants in 11 years, including five in a row at one point. Of the three hairline misses, only 1946 could have been

Jorge Pasquel (C), flanked by (L to R) Danny Gardella, Mickey Owen, an unidentified Mexican League manager, Bobby Estalella and Alex Carrasquel. Gardella sued baseball for reinstatement when the men who jumped to Mexico were blacklisted. He settled out of court, and in 1950 he was granted a chance to return: he played one game with the Cardinals, and his career was over.

considered an upset if the Dodgers had won. On paper the Cardinal team that beat them was far superior. Even so, both clubs finished the regular season deadlocked, and for the first time in major league history a playoff was needed to determine a pennant winner. Minus Pete Reiser, who had broken an ankle three weeks earlier, the Dodgers were easy prey in the two-out-of-three play-off.

In the American League in 1946, the expected duel between the Tigers and Yankees never materialized, and the Red Sox breezed to an easy win. Hank Greenberg, who had returned from the service the previous season in time to clinch the pennant with a grand-slam homer in a surreal rain-delayed finale, picked up where he had left off before the war and led the AL in homers and RBIs. In the process he became the first American Leaguer to collect more than 40 homers on less than a .300 average. This dubious feat would soon become commonplace in the proliferation of the swinging-for-the-seats syndrome that overtook the game in the fifties, but the Tigers regarded it as proof that Greenberg was slipping and sold him to the Pirates. On the mound, Feller, Newhouser and Boo Ferriss were all 25-game winners, the last time either league would have more than one 25-game winner in a season. Feller also struck out every American Leaguer who qualified for the batting title at least once,

ending with a strikeout total that for a time would be considered a modern record. A more thorough check in later years of 1904 box scores revealed that Rube Waddell still held the record with 349, but the controversy would continue to rage until Sandy Koufax made it irrelevant. Stan Musial easily collected his second National League batting championship. In the American League, Ted Williams was outgunned by an obscure Washington first baseman named Mickey Vernon who had never before hit .300 and whose .242 average two years later would be the worst in the majors among first-base regulars. Vernon's hitting in 1946 was the lone bright spot for the Senators in the last half of the decade, and it made up in part for their disappointment the previous summer over missing the pennant when rookie centerfielder Bingo Binks forgot his sunglasses and lost a fly ball in the sun—costing the Nats a game that could have brought them into a championship tie with the Tigers.

The long-awaited confrontation between superstars Musial and Williams came a cropper in the Series when Musial hit only .222 and Williams, plagued by the Cards' use of a shift invented earlier that year by Boudreau to counteract Williams's pull-hitting, managed a paltry .200. As a result, the role of Series hero was vied for by Bobby Doerr and Boo Ferriss of the Red Sox and Harry Brecheen

A black all-star team in Venezuela, in 1945. "Among those who planned the brief stay in Caracas," Roy Campanella (rear, second from L) wrote, "was a good-looking, well-built young fellow from the Kansas City Monarchs.... He was a good hustling ballplayer who could hit the ball sharply and run like a deer." Jackie Robinson is in front, extreme left.

When Jackie Robinson (inset below) broke the color line on Opening Day of 1947, he was asked if Johnny Sain, who started for the Braves, was the best pitcher he had ever faced. "I hit against Bob Feller (above) on the exhibition tour," Robinson said.

Stan Musial. In 1964 Warren Spahn said, "This season will be different from all the others I've spent in the big leagues; Stan Musial will no longer be there. He enriched the game with his incomparable skill....Once Musial timed your fastball, your infielders were in jeopardy."

Rip Sewell. He used his blooper pitch — the Ephus — up to 15 times a game. Whitey Kurowski would spit at it every time Sewell threw it to him.

Warren Spahn. "Hitting is timing," he said. "Pitching is upsetting timing." He won more games than any left-hander in history.

Johnny Sain. He spent four years in the Class D Northeast Arkansas League before the Braves noticed him. He would win 20 four times.

Clint Hartung. When he came up, they said he could hit, he could pitch, he could run. But by 1951, Thomas Kiernan wrote, "The Hondo Hurricane had been reduced to an ordinary drizzle."

Larry Jansen. One of the foremost post-war practitioners of the slider, he was 21-5 as a Giant rookie in 1947.

Ewell Blackwell. On June 22, 1948, he was two outs from matching Johnny Vander Meer's consecutive no-hitters, when Eddie Stanky singled through the box.

Dizzy Trout. He "came by his nickname quite naturally," wrote Irv Haag. In 1944, he won 27 games, starting 40 and relieving in nine more.

Ralph Kiner. Enos Slaughter said he could score on a fly hit to Kiner 30 feet behind third; still, Kiner led the NL in home runs each of his first seven seasons.

Lou Boudreau. Rud Rennie wrote, "He can't run and his arm's no good, but he's the best shortstop in the game."

Mickey Vernon. "I've faced the best in the world just about," Satchel Paige said, "but I never could get Mickey out."

Satchel Paige. In the middle 1930s, Dizzy Dean called him the best pitcher alive; in 1948, as a 42-year-old rookie, he was 6-1 with the champion Indians; in 1953, at 47, he pitched in 57 games for the Browns. Of his own remarkable face, Paige said, "We seen some sights, it and I."

Lucky Lohrke. His career was distinguished only by his nickname: in the minors, he missed a team bus that crashed, and in the service was bumped from a plane that met a similar fate.

Larry Doby. Arnold Hano wrote, "He knows what a center fielder can do." He also hit well enough to lead the AL at various times in home runs, RBIs, runs and slugging.

Hoot Evers. A steady .300 hitter in the late forties, he suddenly lost it, and wound up finishing his career in six different cities his last three years.

George Washington Case was the only man to lead the majors in stolen bases five straight years.

Johnny Rucker. Said Bill Terry in 1940: "We may be looking at the start of the career of one of the greatest ball-players we've ever seen." In 1941, Rucker hit .288; in 1942, he was in the minors.

and Enos Slaughter of the Cards. Brecheen won three games, the first left-hander ever to do so in Series play, but Slaughter took the hero's mantle when he scored the run that won the Series by coming all the way home from first base on Harry Walker's wrong-field hit in the eighth inning of the seventh game. Walker was officially credited with a double, but most observers still contend it was no more than a long single. There is also some question as to whether Red Sox shortstop Johnny Pesky hesitated unduly with the relay throw from the outfield in his hand—but there is nothing about Slaughter's dash left open to dispute. Somewhat blurred over the years is the fact that it was performed by a man playing with an elbow that had been broken in an earlier Series game. An inheritor of the Gas House ethos of the thirties, Slaughter continued to play in the same headlong fashion until his retirement 13 years later at 43.

Although the Giants finished only fourth in 1947, they were *the* team that year. Not only did they amass 221 homers, surpassing all then-existing records, but in spring training they had the most vaunted rookie pitcher to come along in decades and a slugging rookie third baseman fabled for being the only member of his minor league team to survive a catastrophic bus crash. At the season's end they had the first rookie to win 20 games in the National League since 1942 and the top rookie slugger in all of baseball. They did not have the Rookie of the Year, however; that honor went to Jackie Robinson. And, oddly, the names of neither of their two rookie sensations matched those of the pair who had been so highly touted in the spring. Whereas Clint Hartung had been expected to score big on the mound in the Polo Grounds, it was Larry Jansen, a 27-year-old Coast League refugee, who stood the final test. And the fabled Lucky Lohrke proved only average, while a less-heralded rookie who won out over all competition in center field went on not only to have a fine lead-off season but to hit four years later "the shot heard around the world." Bobby Thomson . . . Larry Jansen . . . Jackie Robinson. Enough freshman talent in themselves to make 1947 a year to remember—but they were only the frosting on the cake. Pittsburgh had Wally Westlake. The Yankees unveiled Yogi Berra. Red Sox fans were enamored of Sam Mele's .302 debut. Clevelanders fell even more in love with Dale Mitchell's .316 bat. And the A's were quite happy with their new first baseman, Ferris Fain.

But the three names that come quickest to mind in recalling the 1947 season belonged neither to rookies nor statistical leaders but to a trio of marginal veterans who would never again appear in a major league box score after the 1947 Series: Bill Bevens, Cookie Lavagetto and Al Gionfriddo. Among them, they saved a sloppily played Series and made it seem, in retrospect, to have been a week of constant drama. All were on stage in Ebbets Field in the ninth inning of the fourth game. Bevens, holding a 2–1 lead, was one out away from the first no-hitter in Series history. Gionfriddo occupied second base, having just stolen it after being inserted as a pinch runner. With first base open, Yankee manager Bucky Harris ordered Bevens to walk Pete Reiser, violating the first rule of baseball and deliberately putting the potential winning run on base. For this crime against the game's logic, both Bevens and Harris paid dearly; Dodger manager Burt Shotton called the next scheduled batter, Eddie Stanky, back to the bench and replaced him with a man who had made only 18 hits all season and had already failed several times as a Series pinch hitter. But Cookie Lavagetto doubled home the tying and winning runs, making Shotton look like Merlin and leaving on Harris's face an egg stain so indelible that he was fired the following season for finishing third and replaced by a man who in nine seasons as a major league manager had never finished better than fifth.

Such was the way the design that was to be baseball's for the next 15 years took form. Harris, already engaged in a running battle with Larry MacPhail, Del Webb and Dan Topping—the trio who had bought the Yankees near the end of the war—was sharply criticized by them for walking Reiser and thereafter could do no right in their eyes. Shotton, acting as a lame duck replacement for Durocher, who had been suspended before the season for alleged conduct unbecoming the game, could no longer do any wrong. A year later, when Durocher continued to annoy Rickey and left Brooklyn to join the Giants, the job became Shotton's to keep. As for Bevens and Lavagetto, they were released at the end of the season. Gionfriddo was also soon gone, but not before he made the play that immortalized him—his catch of DiMaggio's drive in the sixth game. If ever a man made his own opportunity for immortality it was Gionfriddo when he stole second base off Bevens. For the way events played out, if Bevens had been allowed to pitch to Reiser and had gotten by him, the Yankees would have wrapped up the Series in five games.

If 1975 stands out as the recent season that revived baseball and made it once again the national pastime, 1948 marks the game's previous peak. Over the three preceding seasons, six different teams had played in the World Series, all three Series had lasted the seven-game limit and both leagues had enjoyed pennant races that had gone right down to the wire. The war years already seemed an interlude of the dim past; all 16 franchises looked solid for the moment, and even the A's had broken .500 the year before for the first time since 1933. The Braves also had broken .500—had managed, in fact, to come in third, their best finish in 31 years—but no one expected any more from them. The Cardinals and Dodgers were still the class of the National League, and the Red Sox, after duping the Browns out of Vern Stephens, Jack Kramer and Ellis Kinder, were expected to challenge the Yankees for supremacy in the American League.

In 1948 two teams won pennants for the first time in 28 and 34 years respectively and became the seventh and eighth different winners in a row; the American League had its only pennant playoff until 1978; and a team drew 2,000,000 fans for the first time. It was the year of the Redman, and it was largely the work of two men. One, Billy Southworth, is the only twentieth-century manager to win more than three pennants and not make the Hall of Fame. The other, Bill Veeck Jr., is not enshrined either. Many of the players who were pivotal in the events that summer have been Hall of Famers for some time, and one of their number, Lou Boudreau, made it almost entirely on the basis of his achieve-

ments in 1948. The last player-manager to win a world championship, the last shortstop to hit over .350, the *only* shortstop to have the best fielding average in his league nine years in a row—those were only the tangibles. It is likely that no other player has ever had so remarkable a season under pressure as Boudreau did in 1948. Yet if the Browns had not dealt Stephens to the Red Sox before Veeck could complete his own negotiations for the shortstop, Boudreau would have played that season in St. Louis, Cleveland fans would have picketed Veeck's park instead of flocking to it and the game would not have received the transfusion it needed to sustain it throughout the Yankee dynasty that was only a year away.

Both Veeck and Boudreau were imaginative but stubborn men who could coexist only when conditions were perfect, and in Cleveland in 1948, they were. A year later, when they were something less, Boudreau wanted out and Veeck was already plotting to sell the franchise he had built into the most profitable in baseball so he could take Satchel Paige and move on to the Browns—an even more desperate challenge than the one that had greeted him when he took over the sagging Indians after the war. The climate in Boston, meanwhile, was one of utter harmony as fans there envisioned an MTA Series and Boston's first world champion since 1918. The fantasy was rudely shattered by Boudreau and left-hander Gene Bearden. Bearden beat the Red Sox in the pennant play-off by kayoing their sur-

Joe Page, Casey Stengel, Yogi Berra (L to R). Page, said Stengel, "could get the fire out quick. He just came in and blasted the ball in there." He called Berra his second best ballplayer, behind DiMaggio but ahead of Mantle, even though "he's a man who looks funny in a uniform." Describing his own career to a Senate committee: "I became a major league manager in several cities and was discharged. We call it discharged because there was no question I had to leave."

prise pitching choice, Denny Galehouse, in Fenway Park, the most impossible structure in all of baseball for a visiting left-hander to win in. The Indians then leveled the Braves after a momentary setback in the Series opener, when Boston's Phil Masi scored the game's only run after being apparently picked off second base (a scenario that probably did more to trigger the minds that gave us the "instant replay" than any single moment in sports history).

None of the names that topped the individual charts in 1948 were surprises, but Philadelphians had a rare treat when for the second season in a row, both the Phils and A's placed a hitter in the top five. The A's furthermore won 84 games, their best show since the days of Foxx and Grove. As for the Phils, it was enough that they managed to win two more games than the cellar-dwelling Cubs. Imagine, the Phils actually winning more often than the Cubs! That hadn't happened since 1917.

On July 8, 1949, those fortunate enough to have tickets that day to see the Dodgers play the Giants in Ebbets Field saw something that had never happened before when Hank Thompson stepped up to bat against Don Newcombe. For the first time a black pitcher was opposing a black hitter in a major league game. It was only right that it took place in Brooklyn, where scarcely more than two years earlier the first black player in this century had emerged from a major league dugout in a major league uniform. On October 9, 1949, Dodger fans experienced a rougher form of justice when for the third time in the decade the Dodgers bowed to the Yankees in a World Series. What a jinx! Now even that *clown,* who'd been more responsible than anyone for the Dodgers' image of zany ineptitude in the thirties, was coming back to haunt them.

The "clown" had already haunted a lot of people that season. His return to the major leagues in 1949 caused lifted eyebrows everywhere. Had the Yankees snapped? Here was Casey Stengel, who only once in nine seasons as a big league manager had finished above .500, now sitting at the controls of a club that had not finished below .500 in 24 years. What was the plan? The Red Sox were first to learn that the plan, as far as the rest of the American League was concerned, was even more invidious than the one Ed Barrow had hatched in 1930 when he grabbed Joe McCarthy the moment the Cubs took their eyes off him. Coming into Yankee Stadium on the last weekend of the season, the Red Sox held a one-game lead and needed only to win either of the last two games to clinch the pennant. How could they miss? They had the two top winners in all of baseball. They had four .300 hitters (Williams, Pesky, Dom DiMaggio and Bobby Doerr) and the last two men in the American League to knock in over 150 runs in a season (Williams and Stephens). They even had Joe McCarthy! The Yankees, on the other hand, did not have a single batting title qualifier who hit above .287, and only one man who'd been healthy enough to

After beating the Red Sox in Yankee Stadium to win the 1949 pennant, Stengel said, "I want to thank all these players for giving me the greatest thrill of my life." His opposing manager, Joe McCarthy, was offered condolences for losing the pennant in the final game. McCarthy replied, "But we had 153 games to win it in."

play more than 130 games. No contest.

And it wasn't. The Red Sox never had a chance.

Still, the Yankee victory in 1949 seemed the last gasp of an aging warrior. The Dodgers, Red Sox, Cardinals, Tigers and Indians appeared to be the teams that would enter the fifties with the brightest prospects. Philadelphia fans were carrying their heads higher than at any time since 1913, the last occasion both of their teams had broken .500. The Phils incredibly had won 81 games for a manager no one had ever heard of, and the A's had come up with their first 20-game winner in 17 years, Alex Kellner, a rookie. Both St. Louis clubs had rookie stars, too, in Roy Sievers and Eddie Kazak. It was the Cards' hope that Kazak could come back from an injury he had suffered on the eve of the All-Star game, and the hope of the National League in general that something could be done about that All-Star game—and soon. The NL team hadn't won since 1940.

In the 1949 contests for individual honors, Williams missed becoming the only man in history to win three triple crowns when he lost the batting championship to George Kell by two-tenths of a percentage point. Lefties Mel Parnell, Preacher Roe and Warren Spahn were the outstanding pitchers, while two right-handers were conspicuous by their absence among league leaders: Johnny Sain slumped to 10 wins, and Ewell Blackwell, idled by kidney trouble, could manage only five. Two other right-handers were also absent from individual honors lists, but no one much noticed; neither had aroused any great expectations off his 1948 season. In 1949, one sported a lackluster 11–7 record; he'd once been considered promising but now, a few months shy of his 30th birthday, he had a career record of 83–94. The other man was a much battered 15–15 in his second season; just 23, he still had hopes, but the only pitching category he seemed likely ever to excel in was giving up home runs.

By 1976 both would be in the Hall of Fame. Their names were Early Wynn and Robin Roberts.

—David Nemec

Babe Ruth and Yogi Berra, 1947. "The only real game in the world, I think, is baseball.... You've got to start from way down, at the bottom, when you're six or seven years old. You can't wait until you're 15 or 16. You've got to let it grow up with you, and if you're successful and you try hard enough, you're bound to come out on top, just like these boys have come to the top now." — Babe Ruth

PLAYER:
Enos Slaughter, On His Toes
By Tom Wicker

W HEN Billy Southworth came to Martinsville, Va., in 1935 to look over St. Louis Cardinals farm-hands playing in the Class D Bi-State League, he spotted a stocky young outfielder with one glaring weakness and one promising statistic. The kid was hitting a mediocre .275—but more than a third of his hits were going for extra bases. So he hit with power; but to Southworth's experienced eye, he looked too slow of foot for the major leagues. Southworth took the rookie aside and told him he'd have to learn to run. Get out there in the outfield, he said, demonstrating a proper running stride, and start running on your toes. Get off that flat-footed gait or you're going home to plant some more tobacco.

To Enos Bradsher Slaughter, aged 19 and a short jump away from semi-pro ball and the Cavel Man-ufacturing Company team in his native Roxboro, N.C., that was a life or death choice. Not that $75 a month was much of a fortune even in Depression days, although room and board in Martinsville came to only five dollars a week. It wasn't even that the big leagues, if he could make it that high, offered something nearer wealth, although it was certainly a better deal than the hardscrabble life on a Person County tobacco farm, like the one on which Slaughter had grown up.

It was rather that baseball *was* life to Enos Slaughter—a fact not particularly unusual in his generation of ballplayers, most of them farm boys or slum kids, at a time when the game was truly the national pastime. It was a leisurely era before technology and affluence pushed American life so near hysteria, in the last years before the old game became modern big business.

To be cut in 1935 would have been worse than merely the end of a professional career, even as bad as that would have been: condemnation to semi-pro, with its cheap uniforms, skinned infields, smelly locker rooms (if any). It would have been worse than that, because making it in baseball in 1935 was not just fun and money in the pocket but living up to a myth.

So young Slaughter took Billy Southworth at his word, went to the outfield and started running on his toes; he ran and he ran and then he ran some more. Just four days after Southworth's ultimatum, Enos Slaughter went down the first-base line in *four steps fewer* than he had ever before. If a man worked at it, he observed, he could make himself do more than he had thought he could do; that was baseball, and that was America.

In 1936, the Cards sent the Tar Heel rookie with the newly developed speed to the Columbus, Ga., Redbirds of the Class B Sally League—not a bad jump in one season. At Columbus, the home dugout was set back a long way from the base line. In an early game, Slaughter came running in from the outfield to the line; then he walked to the dugout.

Manager Eddie Dyer met him at the steps. "Son, if you're tired," Dyer said, "we'll try to get you some help."

Enos Slaughter never walked to the bench again —or to his position, or to first base if a pitcher gave him a base on balls, or anywhere else on a baseball field. Dyer later taught him the strike zone and how to throw home on one bounce, but running became Slaughter's obsession, partly to keep his legs in shape, mostly because he believed it was part of the game that was his life. A ballplayer ran, because if he didn't he was out—out at first, out at home, out of the game, out of place in baseball.

So on October 14, 1946, when Enos Slaughter took a steal signal from Eddie Dyer, it was nothing unusual for Slaughter to be off and running; that was his style. But this time he wasn't running in the outfield at Martinsville or across the old ballfield at Columbus; this was Sportsman's Park in St. Louis, the big time—in fact, the eighth inning of the seventh game of the World Series. Enos Slaughter, on first base with a single to center, represented the go-ahead run and perhaps the championship of the world.

The score was tied—the Cards 3, the Boston Red Sox 3—when Slaughter led off the home eighth with his hit. He had watched impatiently from first as Bob Klinger retired Whitey Kurowski and catcher Del Rice, playing for the injured Joe Gara-

Billy Southworth (L), Eddie Dyer (R). "I've learned considerable since I was manager of the Cardinals in 1929; now I think I am ready," Southworth said when he replaced Ray Blades in 1940. Dyer, his successor, had won eight championships in 14 years as a minor league manager.

In 1975, Enos Slaughter told Donald Honig: "In 1937 they promoted me to Columbus, Ohio.... Ended up leading the league with .382. I was making all of $150 a month then. Branch Rickey was probably the most knowledgeable man that was ever in baseball, when it came to spotting talent. But he didn't like to pay out money. He'd go into the vault to get you a nickel change."

Some Red Sox, 1946. (L to R) Bobby Doerr, Dom DiMaggio, Johnny Pesky, Rudy York, Ted Williams. Only York had ever appeared in a Series before, and none would ever play in one again. In 1954, earning $150 a month as a forest fire fighter, York said, "I've heard thousands cheer for me, like the time I hit the home run that beat the Cardinals in the first game in 1946. I've been rich."

giola. Then, with Harry Walker at the plate and Klinger concentrating on the third out, Dyer, in the Series in his first year as a big league manager, flashed the steal sign.

Slaughter got his usual jump and was tearing for second at high speed, running on his toes, when the left-handed Walker popped a weak fly into center field. Rounding second, cutting his turn short and charging for third, Slaughter saw from the corner of his eye that Leon Culberson was moving to field the ball and that shortstop Johnny Pesky was already running out for a possible relay. To Slaughter, the ball Walker had hit looked like a "dying seagull"; he saw it was going to fall in front of Culberson and the thought flashed through his

mind, *I can score on this guy*.

The inning before, the Red Sox had tied the game when Dominic DiMaggio, with runners on second and third, doubled into right field off relief pitcher Harry Brecheen. But DiMaggio had pulled up lame at second with a torn muscle in his leg; Culberson, his replacement, was no DiMaggio in center field and Slaughter knew Culberson's arm was weak. And now, putting his head down, charging around second and digging hard, Slaughter knew what no one else in Sportsman's Park knew—that he was going all the way home.

Third base coach Mike Gonzalez gave no signal at all ("I think he was flabbergasted," Slaughter says) as the runner began to make the turn toward

Some Cardinals, 1946. (L to R) Joe Garagiola, Dick Sisler, Whitey Kurowski, Slaughter, Stan Musial. Although the Cardinals in spring training were "bursting at the seams with red-hot talent," they entered the Series as 10-3 underdogs. They nonetheless became the first team to beat Boston in a World Series. Five other NL teams had tried.

Harry Walker (Top, L) got the hit; Johnny Pesky (Top, R) took the relay; Roy Partee (Bottom, R) came up the line for the throw. Joe Garagiola (Bottom, L), Partee's St. Louis counterpart, hit .316 in the '46 Series and, said Yogi Berra, "played the best ball of his life." It was arguably the only good ball he ever played. Marty Marion (C), on the other hand, was called by Bill Dickey "a regular floating ghost." He was such an outstanding fielder that, in 1944, he was named Major League Player of the Year despite a .267 batting average and only six home runs.

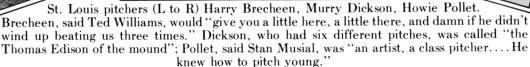

St. Louis pitchers (L to R) Harry Brecheen, Murry Dickson, Howie Pollet. Brecheen, said Ted Williams, would "give you a little here, a little there, and damn if he didn't wind up beating us three times." Dickson, who had six different pitches, was called "the Thomas Edison of the mound"; Pollet, said Stan Musial, was "an artist, a class pitcher.... He knew how to pitch young."

home with no sign of slowing. Behind him, Culberson fielded Walker's hit and threw to Johnny Pesky, still coming out with his back to the infield. Pesky's play was orthodox; Walker had singled with a man on first, and even with Slaughter's jump on the play, the sensible expectation was that he would pull up at third.

So when Pesky took Culberson's throw, he turned *toward second,* cocking his arm to throw, against the remote possibility that Walker would try to pick up an extra base. By then, the wide sleeves of his old-style baseball shirt flapping like wings, Slaughter was around third—hitting the bag at full speed with his left foot, as he had learned to do long before in the minors—and striding on his toes for home, with 36,143 fans standing and screaming him on.

Just as Pesky set himself for a possible throw to second, he caught sight of Slaughter tearing toward home. He reacted quickly enough, but from a disadvantage. He was set for a throw to second and had to shift quickly to his right to make the throw home, a move that would put any right-hand thrower somewhat off balance. Probably as a result, Pesky's peg was short, and it was late.

Red Sox catcher Roy Partee had to come out into the infield in front of the plate to field the ball. Slaughter, racing down the base line at top speed, could have scored standing up, but he didn't. He slid across the plate, climaxing one of the great individual plays in World Series history not with

an unnecessary bit of showboating but with an Enos Slaughter trademark. He *always* slid into every base but first, no matter how badly he had a throw beaten, because Enos Slaughter knew he would never be a better ballplayer than the legs that carried him around the bases and over the outfield, and he had seen too many other players go lame— little Dom DiMaggio just the inning before—by having to pull up sharply, from top speed, in order not to overrun a base. He believed it was safer to slide.

So Slaughter turning third, Pesky's fatal "hesitation" (although Slaughter has always defended the shortstop's turn toward second as the proper play in most circumstances), the hurtling slide home all passed into the bottomless repository of baseball lore. There was more drama to come, as there often is in a World Series game; in the Red Sox ninth, Brecheen gave up singles to Rudy York and Bobby Doerr, then forced three straight batters to hit the ball on the ground for infield outs, no one scoring. The Cat became the ninth pitcher in Series history to win three games (he had won two complete games previously, one of them the day before) and the first since Stan Coveleski of the Indians in 1920.

But with that head-down, game-winning, 270-foot dash from first to home on a weak single (Walker did go on to second and got a softhearted scorer's "official" double for his dying seagull), Slaughter became *the* Series star and one of base-

Slaughter scores, October 15, 1946; Roy Partee lunges for Johnny Pesky's throw. Pesky told Henry Berry, "I would have needed a rifle to nail Slaughter."

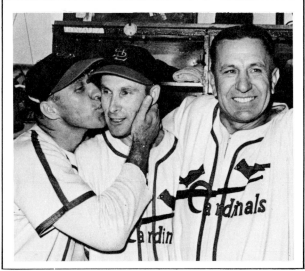

Slaughter, Harry Brecheen, Eddie Dyer (L to R), after the sixth game, 1946 Series. Before the game, Dr. Robert Hyland examined Slaughter's ailing arm and said, "You've got such a bad hemorrhage that if you get hit again the chances are I'll have to amputate your arm." Slaughter replied, "I guess we'll have to take that gamble."

ball's most memorable heroes—if not quite one of its certified immortals. When all else about the 1946 Series, a cliffhanging upset for the Cards, has been reduced to bloodless statistics, Enos Slaughter's break for home will be remembered, retold, elevated into the kind of myth baseball and America love the most—a story of individual effort, "hustle," playing hard, putting out the extra effort that wins the day.

And if the making of that play actually began far away and 11 years earlier in Martinsville with a desperate rookie trying to teach himself to run on his toes, the play itself was not an isolated moment. However orthodox Pesky's handling of the situation, he should have known by then—as Slaughter had known about Culberson's weak arm—that with Enos Slaughter on base and the game and Series possibly at stake, *something* out of the ordinary was likely to happen.

That could have been learned in the fourth game of that same Series, played in Fenway Park. In the sixth inning of the fourth game, the Cards leading 7 to 1, the Red Sox had loaded the bases with one out and had Cardinal pitcher George Munger (who had got out of the service only in August) on the ropes after a walk and singles by Doerr and Pinky Higgins. Hal Wagner ripped into a Munger pitch and, as Arthur Daley wrote in *The New York Times,* ". . . Rudy York was on third when Hal Wagner's towering smash backed Slaughter to the bullpen. York tagged up and raced home, knowing he couldn't be headed off. A throw was so impossibly far that it wouldn't even be attempted. But Slaughter, who never gave up on anything, threw

out York at the plate.

" 'What kind of ball do those fellows play?' asked the flabbergasted Rudy. 'No one else would even have attempted that throw'."

Now that quote from York probably should be taken with a grain of salt, since it doesn't sound like any ballplayer of the day, or any day, let alone Rudy York, and since Arthur Daley just naturally loved Enos Slaughter. Another time, Daley wrote: "On the ballfield he [Slaughter] is perpetual motion itself . . . he would run through a brick wall, if necessary, to make a catch, or slide into a pit of ground glass to score a run." But Slaughter's remarkable throw to take the Red Sox out of a possible big inning can't be questioned; there it is in the box score, under "double plays"—"Slaughter and Garagiola."

Arthur Daley also frequently told a story about the fifth game of that Cards-Sox series. A pitch from Joe Dobson caught Slaughter in the elbow, causing agonizing pain. Slaughter "stoically pattered down to first," Daley recalled in a column nearly 20 years later. Then he attributed to Slaughter a quote that may be as fanciful as the supposed words of Rudy York the day before: " 'I wouldn't give nobody the satisfaction of knowin' I was hurt,' said this Spartan."

Quote or no quote, Enos Slaughter promptly stole second base with his arm still wracked with pain. But the Cards lost that day, to return to St. Louis down three games to two. That night on the train, the Cards' team doctor packed the injured arm in ice and told Slaughter he was through for the Series.

"The fellers need me," Slaughter said, or so Daley reported. "No matter what you say, I'm playin'."

So in the sixth game he singled home a run in the winning rally, and in the seventh he dashed to glory. In neither game did the Red Sox try to run on him—the throw to double York at the plate had convinced them he had a gun for an arm, and he never let on that Dobson's pitch had incapacitated it for the rest of the Series. That year, Enos Slaughter was 30 years old, having lost what probably were his three best years physically to the Army Air Corps; the Cards were paying him less than $25,000.

Enos Slaughter's baseball career was destined to last through 1959, a startling 24 years from its beginning in Martinsville. From 1938 on, he was a big leaguer, playing 19 seasons—he was in the Air Corps in 1943, 1944 and 1945—with the Cards, the Yankees in two different tours, the Kansas City Athletics and the Milwaukee Braves. Slaughter was 43 years old when he ended his last season—typically playing hurt, after hitting a foul ball off his own foot, as Milwaukee finally lost the 1959 National League pennant to Los Angeles in a play-off.

He might have hung on another season or two—into his fourth decade of major league ball—as a pinch hitter, but in 1960 Slaughter took a fling at managing (with Houston, then in the American Association).

He retired with a lifetime batting average of exactly .300 for those 19 big league seasons, and given his total of 2,383 major league hits, it's not inconceivable that if he hadn't lost those three vital years to the Air Corps (when he was 27, 28 and 29 years old), he'd have reached the rarefied level of 3,000 hits.

A power hitter, but not a home run-or-strikeout muscle man, Slaughter blasted 148 triples and 413 doubles, as well as 169 home runs, thus maintaining for his career the old Martinsville pace that had first caught Billy Southworth's eye—more than a third of his hits were for extra bases. And in almost 8,000 at bats, he struck out only 538 times.

On the pennant-winning Cardinals of 1942 ("by far the best team I ever played on," he says today. "We had everything, we just felt we could beat anybody . . ."), Slaughter led the league in hits with 188, led the club and was second in the league with a .318 average and starred in the World Series the Cards won from the Yankees, hitting a home run in the fifth game.

In the Cards' pennant-winning year 1946, coming out of his three years in service, Slaughter hit .300 and led both leagues in runs batted in with 130. In 10 consecutive All-Star games, Slaughter hit .381 for the National League, and when St. Louis traded him to the Yankees in 1954, of all players then active in both leagues, only Stan Musial had more hits, 2,223 to 2,064, and only Ted Williams of the Red Sox had batted in more runs, 1,298 to 1,148.

When the Yankees traded Slaughter to Kansas City in 1955, he was 39 years old; he hit .315 for the Athletics, playing most of the time, and was voted the team's "most popular" player in a year

The 1942 Cardinals. Frank Graham wrote, "The Yankees have finally found a team they can't frighten half to death just by walking out on the field and taking a few swings in batting practice. The Cardinals haven't been around and they don't read the papers; the chances are they don't even know these are the Yankees they are playing." The St. Louis starting lineup averaged 26 years of age, the youngest ever to win a Series. Slaughter is seventh from left, middle row.

(Top) Stan Musial, who broke in as a replacement for the injured Slaughter in 1941. (Middle, L) Cardinal broadcasters, Johnny O'Hara and Dizzy Dean (L and R) flank Mort Cooper, who chewed aspirin on the mound to dull the pain in his arm. (Middle, R) Slaughter, John Beazley, Whitey Kurowski (L to R). Kurowski's right arm was missing three inches of bone as a result of a childhood injury. (Bottom) Walker Cooper, Kurowski, Creepy Crespi (L to R). Crespi's career was hurt when he broke his leg in an army ball game; it ended when he broke it again in a hospital wheelchair race while convalescing.

when he took the field—still running—for his 2,000th game.

The next year, at 40, Slaughter was hitting .279 and had played in 90 games—today's brittle stars, take note—when the Yankees sent cash and Bob Cerv to the Athletics (for delivery in 1957) to get him back a week before the September 1 World Series eligibility deadline. The Yanks released Phil Rizzuto to make room on the roster, whereupon Slaughter played six Series games, hit a game-winning three-run homer in the third game and wound up the Series batting .350, including two of the Yankees' five hits off that other indestructible, Sal Maglie, during Don Larsen's perfect fifth game.

But Slaughter, for all his success on the field, never had any financial luck. That year, for example, the Yankees (who won the Series in seven games) voted Rizzuto a full share of the winners' swag, or $8,714. Slaughter was supposedly due only a half-share, but second baseman Jerry Coleman went to Commissioner Ford Frick and asked on behalf of the other players that Slaughter's cut be raised to a three-quarter share. Frick agreed and Slaughter took down $6,536. Yankee clubhouse steward Pete Sheehy got a three-quarter share, too.

At 41 and 42, Slaughter then put in a couple of solid years with the Yankees—.254 in 96 games in 1957, plus .250 in five World Series games against the Braves; then .304, mostly as a pinch hitter with 138 at bats in 77 games in 1958, with another Yankees-Braves Series following.

Late in 1959, still making a contribution to the Yankees, nearly bald by then but still running on and off the field and weighing only three pounds more than the 188 he had hustled along the Martinsville basepaths 24 years earlier, the 43-year-old Slaughter fouled a pitch off his own foot and was out for a week. Then Casey Stengel asked him how he'd like a shot at his sixth World Series; the Yankees were out of the running in the American League, but over in the National Milwaukee, in a stretch race with the Dodgers, needed a left-handed pinch hitter.

The Yankees hadn't bothered to X-ray Slaughter's injured foot; he recalls that he "hobbled" into general manager George Weiss's office and protested, not the proposed deal, but that his foot might prevent him from helping the Braves. Weiss telephoned John McHale of the Braves with the injury news; but McHale told Slaughter, "If you can swing the bat, we can get a runner for you."

So at an age at which almost all his contemporaries were retired, unable to run in his trademark style, but dead game and still eager to play ball,

Enos Slaughter went back to the National League, to his fourth club, to another pennant race, and in his first game delivered a pinch-hit single against Bob Purkey of Cincinnati.

The Braves made it through a last road trip to a dead heat with the Dodgers, but lost the play-offs in two games, and Slaughter finished his playing career on a downbeat. Milwaukee took an 8–4 lead into the home ninth of the second game in the Dodgers' temporary home, the infamous Coliseum, a converted football stadium with a short left-field wall that made Fenway Park look like a pitcher's haven. The Dodgers scored five runs in that ninth inning and it was all over. If some heroics of his could have saved it for Milwaukee, as so often they had for St. Louis, that would have made a better ending; but Enos Slaughter's long day was done at last.

Maybe they still play his kind of tough, shrewd baseball in 1978—Thurman Munson of the Yankees comes to mind, and so does Lou Piniella's smart handling of a crucial hit to right field in that year's Yankee-Red Sox play-off game. Piniella couldn't see the ball in the sun but pretended he was making the catch; that held up baserunner Rick Burleson between second and first long enough so that when the ball dropped, Piniella could grab it and fire to third in time to halt Burleson at second. That could be a story about Slaughter, but few play that hard or smart today, and certainly not for the kind of small change Enos Slaughter was paid throughout his career.

From the start, he had given baseball all he had, but baseball gave him little in return except the fun of the game—admittedly no small reward. Even in the fall of 1934, when on the recommendation of Fred Haney, a baseball writer for the Durham, N.C., *Herald,* the Cardinals invited him to a tryout camp in Greensboro, general manager Branch Rickey made it clear that young Slaughter would have to pay his own expenses if the club didn't sign him.

After his 1937 season in Columbus, Ohio, of the American Association—the highest minor league classification—Slaughter thought his league-leading .382, 27 home runs and 122 runs batted in were worth something more than the $150 a month he'd been paid. Hadn't those statistics made him the MVP? Eddie Dyer was later to recall the heyday of the minor leagues and the farm system as a time when "if you needed help you could reach down to Columbus, Ohio, for a broad-tailed kid named Slaughter who was hitting .382."

So Slaughter went to the top. "Mister Rickey," he asked when the season was over, "how about a bonus?" Forty years later he remembered with a chuckle how Rickey "jumped down my throat and said the older fellows had been talkin' to me, puttin' ideas in my head."

No bonus, naturally. And when Slaughter went up to the Cards in 1938, it was for the munificent sum of $400 a month—not for 12 months, of course, but for the five and a half months of the major league season. The old Gas House Gang was breaking up (Dizzy Dean had just been traded to the Cubs), but some of Slaughter's teammates were legitimate stars—Johnny Mize, Joe Medwick, Pepper Martin, Terry Moore ("the greatest defensive centerfielder I ever played with. . . . I've never been back to the wall at no time that he wasn't there to tell you how much room there was and what base to throw to. . . ."). Catcher Bill DeLancey was a particular hero to Slaughter; after a bad case of tuberculosis, DeLancey played in 1940 with only one lung.

Even now, Slaughter professes not to know what any of these fabled ballplayers were being paid—although on the Cardinals of those years it couldn't have been much ("we didn't make no money with the Cards, they all said we was hungry ballplayers"). Back then, he insists, money wasn't much talked about and "nobody ever talked salary in the clubhouse"—maybe because no one had anything much to brag about. Today, with free agents and million-dollar contracts, the publicized jealousies of such as Billy Martin for the monstrous salaries of such as Reggie Jackson not only dominate the headlines but some clubhouses, too.

Slaughter hit .350 for the first three months of his first big league year, then tailed off to .276, an average that would earn a rookie a fat contract in 1978—and which brought him up to $600 a month for the 1939 season, when Ray Blades's Cards finished second; that year, the young outfielder hit .320 and led the league in doubles. That was worth $750 a month to the Cardinals for 1940, and Slaughter responded with an early-season batting tear.

Then came an Eastern road trip that he recalls as if it were yesterday, but not with pleasure. "I left St. Louis hittin' .371 and came back hittin' .216. I went three for 82, the worst slump I ever had" (perhaps not least because of a personal nemesis, one Jumbo Brown, a 295-pound relief pitcher for the Giants, who knew how to get Slaughter out).

That season the Cards were in the race all the way and once Slaughter shook his slump, he was a leading factor in another second place finish, finally

batting .306 for the year. He hit a solid 311 in 1941, and on the great 1942 team could pocket $9,000 for the season, plus a Series winner's share.

Slaughter played that Series as an enlisted man in the Air Corps, having signed up in August, and spent the next three years on what sound like some pretty good service ball clubs at Lackland Air Base, Hickam Field in Hawaii and in the southwest Pacific—where the players often had to build the field before they could play their morale-building exhibitions for the GIs. Birdie Tebbetts, Joe Gordon, Howard Pollet, Taft Wright, Ferris Fain, Tex Hughson—Slaughter remembers playing with or against them all, once on Iwo Jima just after its capture.

He came out of the service to give several great years to the Cardinals and in 1949 he hit .336 and led the league in triples, which earned him a $25,000 contract for 1950—the best he ever had. That season, he batted .290 ("a guy'd own a franchise, he hit that much today") and the niggardly Cardinals proceeded to hand him a 10 percent pay cut.

But baseball was beginning to change and TV was waiting in the wings to wipe out the minors and the farm systems and change the atmosphere and traditions of the game. Night World Series competition in the chill of October, for example, would have been unthinkable before TV; so would players who'd had their basic experience not at Martinsville or Columbus but at Arizona State and Southern Cal. Not far ahead were designated hitters, interchangeable parts for pitching staffs, uniforms gaudy as those of a marching band, rugs for playing surfaces and a time when a hangnail or a wounded ego could become a major factor in a pennant race.

Above all, television put money—big money—in the pockets of owners and players alike, and its largesse ultimately permitted free agentry to make capitalists out of second-string outfielders. But Enos Slaughter, who played his 19 major league seasons without an agent or a holdout, just missed the fat years; as they came in, he was past his prime.

Still, when the Cards traded him to the Yankees in 1954, he wept; *The New York Times* ran a picture of one of baseball's celebrated hard guys with his face in his hands. Even though St. Louis president August Busch blustered that he hated to trade "one of the greatest baseball players in the history" of the Cards, but had to in order to build a younger team, and manager Eddie Stanky mealy-mouthed that "a champion baseball player is going to a champion baseball club," the truth was apparent. Slaughter spoke it through his tears.

"I've given my life to this organization, and they

Facing page: (Top) Frenchy Bordagaray, Fiddler Bill McGee, Lefty Weiland, Rip Collins, Pepper Martin (L to R). Martin's "Mudcat Band" was at the heart of the team Slaughter had joined in 1938. "I just kept my mouth shut," he told Donald Honig, "and kept my eyes open." (Bottom) By 1941, Slaughter was established on a team that included (L to R) Terry Moore (who could, said J. Roy Stockton, "throw a ball into a bucket at a hundred yards"), Coaker Triplett and Don Padgett. This page: The early fifties. (Top, L) Slaughter with Eddie Stanky (C) and Red Schoendienst (R); (Top, R) with Stan Musial, whom he succeeded as St. Louis's "outstanding sports figure" in 1952. (Middle, L) Slaughter's last day as a Cardinal; (Middle, R) with Casey Stengel. Stengel said, "Some of my players think he's a show-off. That's because every time they see him he's running." He made this catch (L) when he was 41.

let you go when you're getting old."

That is also the story of baseball, the dark side of the myth, and in Slaughter's case, even the Russians recognized it. In *Soviet Sport,* the Soviet Union's leading sports magazine, the Slaughter trade was singled out as an example of "flesh-peddling in disregard of the player's wishes and rights . . . a typical example of beer and beizbol. The beizbol bosses care nothing about sport or their athletes but only about profits."

Right on, in 1954, and another of the reasons for free agentry today, as well as the fact that the Slaughter deal could not now be made without his consent. But he might not have vetoed it even if he could have, and not just because it got him away from the one pitcher who seemed to have his number, Carl Erskine of the Dodgers; but because for all his fire and dash on the field, in the clubhouse Enos Slaughter was a company man. He never caused trouble for the club, never groused about his paycheck, never gave anything but his best for whatever he was being paid. And it never occurred to him to do anything else.

So he went to Casey Stengel when he reported to the Yankees during a series in Washington, and told the manager he was ready to give him 100 percent; no doubt Stengel already knew that, but when the 38-year-old Slaughter added that he wanted to play regularly (at a time when the Yankee outfield consisted of Mickey Mantle, Hank Bauer and Irv Noren, with Gene Woodling and Bob Cerv in reserve), Stengel told him: "My boy, you play when I tell you to play, and you'll stay up here a long time."

Slaughter did; and Stengel, he says, played him against the "tough clubs" and especially against "the tough lefthanders," because for some reason the left-hand hitting Slaughter feasted on left-hand pitching; over his career, he hit better off lefties than off right-handers. One of his special pleasures is that, at 40, he hit the marvelous Billy Pierce "pretty good," and Herb Score, too. He was playing the outfield for the Yankees the day Gil Mc-Dougald's line drive hit Score in the eye and doomed his career—a memory that puts Slaughter in mind of a young pitcher he recalls only as "Slayball" who in the early fifties was hit in the eye by a line drive and injured so badly his eyeball was

(L) In 1954, after an on-field brawl with Walt Dropo, who had seven years, seven inches and 40 pounds on Slaughter; (R) with Kansas City; and (C) finally, with Milwaukee. On September 29, 1959, in the seventh inning of a pennant play-off against the Dodgers, Enos Slaughter came to bat in the major leagues for the last time. With Milwaukee leading 4-2, and two men on base, he popped out; Los Angeles went on to win the pennant in the bottom of the twelfth. The pitcher who retired him was Chuck Churn, who was four years old when Slaughter began his professional career.

"hangin' out on his cheek." But "he pitched the next year in Double-A," which to Enos Slaughter was the natural order of things. ("Slayball" was actually Bobby Slaybaugh, who indeed lost his eye in the accident—and who nonetheless attempted a comeback the following year.)

After his seasons with Kansas City, Slaughter didn't want to come back to the Yankees, where he feared he'd play less, and he was saddened to be the cause of Rizzuto's release; but baseball was still his life and he flew dutifully to Detroit, where at the age of 40 he went five for nine playing both ends of a Sunday doubleheader on his first day back under Stengel's command. In those last seasons, the Yankees paid him $18,000 a year, more or less.

After his last stand with the Braves, he went off to manage at Houston in 1960. His team finished third and Slaughter was released; after he paid his own way to the minor league meetings in 1961, he was signed to manage Raleigh (not far from Roxboro) in the Class B Carolina League. That was a farm club of the embryonic Mets and at the Mobile, Ala., training base, Slaughter looked over his "talent" and bluntly notified the higher-ups: "They ain't even Class D players."

He was told rather indignantly that he had at least 15 major league prospects on the Raleigh roster; as it turned out, he took just one of the 15 back to Raleigh, and that year 52 different Met farmhands, he says, paraded through the Raleigh clubhouse, all going nowhere, like the club itself. At the end of the season, Slaughter was released again.

That was the last of organized ball for one of its most dedicated performers; the myth was finished with him. He was never again offered a job, despite innumerable applications over the next few years. Maybe he was too demanding for today's ballplayers; he wouldn't have understood a player begging off the All-Star game with a sore toe. Or maybe he was too hardbitten for jetset owners and youngsters who hadn't been happy to get $75 a month playing baseball in order to get out of the tobacco fields. Maybe his talent evaluations were too merciless for his bosses.

To an interviewer's suggestion that maybe baseball also feared that a rural Southerner of his generation couldn't deal with blacks, he snorted: "Long as they produce for me I don't care if they're red." He'd had blacks at both Houston and Raleigh, he said, and had no trouble, and he'd managed to bridge baseball's lily-white years and the coming of the blacks in the fifties.

In 1970, Duke University's athletic director, Eddie Cameron, hired Slaughter to coach baseball at a school where it was a secondary sport. He had no scholarships to offer, and often lost his best players to a rule that football scholarship men could play baseball only in conference games. Still, he was 16–15 his first year, and usually won a dozen to 15 games in each of the next six seasons, before he was retired.

Meanwhile, in 1966, when he turned 50 years old, Enos Slaughter applied for the pension organized baseball promises its players and which TV supposedly had inflated. He drew his first monthly check—for $400, the same as his first major league salary—in July, 1966; it was not until six months later, just too late, that he learned that the complicated pension rules would have entitled him to $800 a month if he'd waited until 1967 to start taking payments. Years of complaints, to various Commissioners of Baseball and to the Players Association have failed to redress this grievance; in fact, Slaughter says his baseball pension, for some quirky reason, has declined to $379 a month. He had paid into the plan for 20 years.

But there was a final way Slaughter might have been rewarded beyond the fun of the game for his 22 professional seasons of dedicated play, hard running and hard hitting. He had earned little money, been shipped like a chattel among unfeeling teams, found no further place in the game that had been his life, and been shortchanged—at least by his reckoning—on his pension. But the baseball writers, if not baseball's officials, could do something. They had the power to vote him into the Hall of Fame.

That alone, to a man who believed he had given the best of his life to baseball, would have been compensation enough, better than any conceivable perquisite or financial reward, final security within the myth. But the writers have not recognized Enos Slaughter either. In 1978, they chose Eddie Mathews, a home run hitter, with Slaughter coming in second. His last chance was 1979, when the 15 years of his eligibility to be voted in came to an end; after that, he can only hope that the Veterans' Committee might choose him—which is less desirable than selection by the writers.

Why the Hall of Fame has eluded a player of Slaughter's caliber and longevity is a mystery. It's true that writers for the West Coast and Canadian teams, Texas, Houston, Atlanta, never saw him play; it's true also that (to Slaughter's undisguised disgust) home run hitting is the name of the game in Cooperstown—"You hit a few home runs, don't matter you got a lifetime average .270, .280, you go in. . . . I got the pinky on that thing."

One outfielder he played against—a homer-hitter

of brief fame—had an arm so weak, he recalls, "he caught a fly 30 feet behind third base, I'd go home on him." But he's in and Slaughter's not.

Whatever the reason, Slaughter tried to console himself that Red Ruffing and Joe Medwick, "who should have been there earlier," didn't make it until their fifteenth years of eligibility; but an interviewer could sense that he didn't really expect any longer to make it. And he is too honest to act as if he doesn't care.

Exclusion from the Hall of Fame seems to have embittered him far more than the shabby treatment he's had from baseball, which he follows fairly closely. He thinks he could have made more hits in modern ballparks with their symmetrical distances and artificial surfaces, and he thinks that although there are "some great ballplayers today," no team has 25 "top-notch major league players. You hit .275, you're a superstar." He doesn't exactly begrudge today's big salaries but—still the company man who respects the boss—he suggests "they've got out of hand a little bit"; and he sees little of his own hustle and desire in today's players, although he likes to point out that "there's been many a game won by runnin' out a pop fly, 'cause if it falls you're on second base." In 1938, he remembers, he hit a grounder back to Bill Lee, pitching for the Cubs, "and he looked at it a couple of times and when he looked up I was almost on first. He was so surprised he threw it away and I wound up on third. A fly ball got me home and we won the game."

But that's all in the past, however alive that past still seems (Slaughter exemplifies William Faulkner's belief that the past not only isn't dead, "it isn't even past"). Now Enos Slaughter farms six acres of tobacco in Person County, N.C., which, after all, he escaped only temporarily back in 1935. He manages about 2,100 pounds to the acre and bright leaf goes these days for at least $1.50 a pound. There's plenty of time left over for fishing at Kerr Lake, where over the 1978 Fourth of July weekend he and Max Crowder, the Duke trainer, pulled in 53 stripers in four days; and there's good hunting every day in the autumn deer season.

The night Junior Gilliam died ("hell of a ballplayer, I saw him break in with the Dodgers"), just before the 1978 World Series opened, with Helen Slaughter pottering in the kitchen and their daughter Rhonda watching television, Slaughter—aged 62, up to 208 pounds and more than ever fitting the nickname "Country" that Burt Shotton hung on him 40 years ago—summed up his life in baseball:

"I really enjoyed baseball. It was my livelihood. If they wanted me at the ballpark at eight in the morning, I'd be there. I asked no odds and I give none. A guy got in my way, I run over him. If they knocked me down at the plate, I said nothin'. You can't steal first base but if they hit me, I'm on first. And if you don't get on first, you can't score a run."

In the fading light of the myth Enos Slaughter lived—not just the myth of baseball, but the American myth itself—doesn't that get close to a truth? *If you don't get on first, you can't score a run.* So do anything, accept anything, knock down and be knocked down, to get on first, score a run, win the game.

And then what? Don't they let you go when you're gettin' old? And not even the Hall of Fame will bring back a broad-tailed kid who hit .382 at Columbus and ran on his toes everywhere he went.

The plaque that isn't in Cooperstown.

SEVENTH INNING: 1950-1959

I have seen 344 home runs, four triple plays and two no-hit games. Baseball has been one of the greatest pleasures of my life. I have seen 906 speaking plays, 1,050 movies, and I have attended 4,510 church services and read 2,000 books; but I think I have gotten most good out of my 1,134 ball games.

—Frederick S. Tyler, 1948

IN 1950 the Indians won 92 games and the Phillies won 91, but the Phils' 91st victory brought them their first pennant in 35 years and the Indians' 62nd defeat relegated them to being the best fourth-place team in history.

As in 1915, the Phils triumphed by catching the rest of the league napping. While the Dodgers were occupied with watching the Cardinals slump to the second division, and the Giants tried to fuse together a whole new infield, the Phils shot to an enormous lead and entered the final ten days of the season eight games ahead. Injuries to two starting pitchers and the service call-up of Curt Simmons sent them into Ebbets Field on October 1, however, with only a one game lead and no one to summon with the pennant on the line but Robin Roberts, who was forced to start his third game in five days. On the ropes all afternoon in a 1–1 game, Roberts turned the tide in the ninth inning when he retired Carl Furillo and Gil Hodges with the bases loaded after Richie Ashburn had thrown Cal Abrams out at the plate. In the top of the tenth Dick Sisler's three-run homer made the Phils the league champs and Roberts their first 20-game winner since 1917.

The victory climaxed a seven-year rebuilding program undertaken by Robert Carpenter after he purchased the club and vindicated the commitment to youth that Eddie Sawyer had made when he became manager in 1948. First baseman Eddie Waitkus and relief ace Jim Konstanty were the only major contributors over 30, and Ashburn, Roberts, Simmons, Granny Hamner and Willie Jones

Curt Simmons. He signed with the Phillies as an 18-year-old bonus baby in 1947 and matured with 17 wins in 1950. But he was the first player drafted for service in Korea, two weeks before the season ended, and was unable to appear in the Series.

were all still under 25. Jones, Sisler, catcher Andy Seminick, second baseman Mike Goliat and right-fielder Del Ennis also had seasons well above their norms, and Konstanty—never before and never again more than an ordinary pitcher—was so extraordinary in 1950 that he became the only reliever to win an MVP award.

The Yankees seemingly had a much easier time winning their second pennant under Stengel, especially after Whitey Ford, called up from the minors in June, posted a 9–1 record. Yet the real keys were the Tigers' failure to come up with a solid relief pitcher to bolster their aging starters, and the Yankees' success in acquiring Tom Ferrick from the Browns to replace a faltering Joe Page. In third place, displaying the most potent offense of the past 48 years, were the Red Sox. An injury held Williams to only 89 games and undoubtedly cost the Red Sox the pennant. Had they won, their staff ERA of 4.88 would have been even more ludicrous than that of the pennant-winning Cardinals in 1930. With the postwar hitting boom at full throttle, all teams were turning to their bullpens in record fashion, and Early Wynn's 3.20 ERA was the highest ever by a league leader.

The script in the American League for the next three seasons was identical to the one in 1950, the sole exception being that the Indians rather than the Red Sox and Tigers tagged vainly after the Yankees. Possessing the best four starting pitchers

Dick Sisler, Richie Ashburn, Del Ennis (L to R). The big bats of the Whiz Kids had all been recruited by Herb Pennock, the former Yankee pitcher who was general manager from 1944 until his death four years later. In the 35 years since they had last won a pennant, the Phillies finished in the first division only four times.

(Top, L) Jim Konstanty (L) and Robin Roberts; (Bottom, L) Eddie Waitkus; (Bottom, R) Roberts. Konstanty made a record 74 appearances in 1950; Roberts clinched the pennant on the last day of the season, his third start in five days; Waitkus batted .284 and played all 154 games. This was a notable achievement; he had been shot the previous season by a thwarted admirer, Ruth Steinhagen, whose mother said Ruth was "so crazy" about Waitkus that she studied Lithuanian after learning he was of that nationality. (Top, R) Yogi Berra (L) and Whitey Ford, who earned the first of his record ten Series victories against the punchless Phillies. In the four-game Series, they scored only five runs.

of any team in history—Mike Garcia and the three Hall of Famers, Wynn, Feller and Bob Lemon—Cleveland each year tallied the most complete games and had the lowest staff ERA, yet kept missing the pennant by inches. In 1951 the shaky play of Boudreau's replacement at shortstop, Ray Boone, and the inability of rookie Suitcase Simpson to measure up to Yankee rookies Gil McDougald and Mickey Mantle left them five games short of the mark. A year later Feller had a poor season and Boone was again a weak link; yet Cleveland still led much of the summer and finished only two games back. By 1953 it began to seem as if the team had shot its bolt when only Lemon of the Big Four won 20 games and 38-year-old Luke Easter, who had teamed with Al Rosen and Larry Doby to form the most potent central batting order in the league, could not recover from a broken foot.

While Stengel's patchwork trading and platooning tactics kept the Yankees a stride ahead of Cleveland, the Red Sox and Tigers fell farther back into the pack with each passing season, replaced for the moment by the "Go-Go" White Sox. Last in the majors in stolen bases in 1950, the Sox surpassed everyone in steals in 1951 after manager Paul Richards conned Minnie Minoso from the Indians and placed rookie Jim Busby in center field. This pair, along with Ashburn, Jackie Robinson, Giant rookie Willie Mays and Braves speedster Sam Jethroe,

gave the game a dimension that had all but disappeared in 1950, when Dom DiMaggio's 15 steals represented the lowest total ever to lead either league. In 1952 the White Sox began a five-year reign in third place as the Red Sox lost Doerr prematurely to a back ailment and Vern Stephens and Walt Dropo, after accounting for 144 RBIs each two years earlier, couldn't total that many between them.

Wary after having observed the Phils' near collapse the previous summer, the Dodgers did not allow themselves to grow complacent when they took a 13½-game lead over the Giants on August 12, 1951. For the remainder of the month and on through September, they continued to play the same brand of erratically brilliant baseball that had become the club's trademark since the war. But the Giants put on a show that was reminiscent of the Cubs' pennant drive in 1935. Beginning on August 12, Durocher's men reeled off 16 straight victories and went on to win 39 of their last 47 games to end the regular season in a tie with the Dodgers. Bobby Thomson's home run in the third game of the pennant playoff needs no recounting, but many witnesses still insist that Thomson, by all the laws of baseball, should never have come to bat. Working on a 4–1 lead in the bottom of the ninth inning, Don Newcombe gave up a single to lead-off batter Alvin Dark, then another single to Don Mueller that

Nellie Fox, Minnie Minoso, Eddie Robinson (L to R). Paul Richards said of Fox, "Of all the stars now in the game, he's the greatest example to young players and even to players yet unborn." When Minoso joined the Sox, Warren Brown wrote, the team "was off and running, but now, for the first time since 1920, they had a general idea of why and where." Robinson, who hit a club record 29 home runs, was described in a team handout as the "heavy woodman" of the Sox.

could have been a double-play ball if Gil Hodges had been playing off the bag, as would be expected of the first baseman of a team holding a three-run lead in the final inning.

Wasted as a result of the Giant victory was Preacher Roe's .880 winning percentage, the highest ever by a National League 20-game winner. Other leaders in 1951 were Ferris Fain, winner of the first of his two successive batting titles, and his Athletics teammate Gus Zernial, the second in history to lead in homers while dividing the season between two teams and the first ever to lead in RBIs.

After two straight disappointments, the Dodgers left nothing to chance in 1952 by building up such a wide cushion in play against the four second-division teams that none of the other contenders could catch them. That the Giants finished only 4½ games out was perhaps more of a testimony to Durocher's managerial ability than his pennant win a year earlier, for his club lost both Willie Mays and defending RBI king Monte Irvin for nearly the full season and Larry Jansen and Sal Maglie, its two best pitchers, for large portions of it. The arrival of 28-year-old rookie relief sensation Hoyt Wilhelm helped Durocher immensely. Wilhelm finished at 15–3 and led the league in both ERA and winning percentage. Nevertheless, another 28-year-old rookie reliever, Joe Black of the Dodgers, won Rookie of the Year honors and that fall became the

first black pitcher to win a World Series game when he beat the Yankees in the opener.

The Yankees rebounded to triumph in seven games, however, and when they beat the Dodgers again the following year, Stengel had an unprecedented five straight world championships. He used his 1953 team, probably the best of the quintet, in a fashion typical of his mode of operation. Among the pitchers, only Ford worked more than 200 innings, and Billy Martin and McDougald were the only regulars to play more than 140 games. Phil Rizzuto, by now 35, was rested frequently; the other regulars were simply platooned. Gene Woodling, the club's top hitter, did not make enough plate appearances to qualify for the batting championship; sub outfielder Irv Noren got into nearly as many games as the three putative regulars; and first baseman Joe Collins found himself sharing the position with Johnny Mize and Don Bollweg. In direct contrast, every Dodger front-liner except Billy Cox played in over 130 games in 1953, and the third-place Cardinals had five men who played in more than 150 games and no regular who took the field in fewer than 135. The fact that Stengel's methods won must have been absorbed by other managers of the era, but none was blessed with a front office that had the seemingly unlimited resources of the Yankees. Aging players who were of little help to teams that were rebuilding but still

Del Crandall (L) and Sid Gordon, who had just hit his fourth grand slam of the 1950 season. In his first game in the Polo Grounds, in 1941, Gordon was one of four Jewish players with the Giants. The others were Morrie Arnovich, Hank Feldman and Harry Danning.

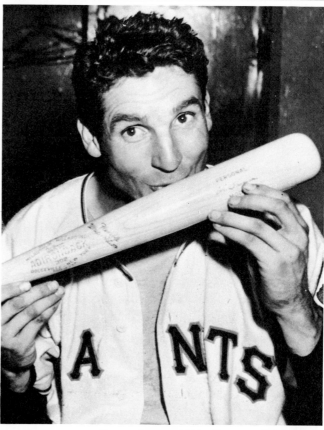

(Top, L) Sal Maglie; (Top, R) Bobby Thomson; (Bottom) Monte Irvin, Willie Mays, Henry Thompson (L to R). One ballplayer told the Boston *Globe,* "Maglie could look a pitch through you. He was so mean he'd get you with sliders. You'd lean forward and think you were safe, and the thing would break right off your neck." When Thomson hit his epic home run in 1951, Carl Hubbell said, "We won't live long enough to see anything like it again." Cool Papa Bell said, "Most of the black ballplayers thought Monte Irvin should have been the first black in the major leagues.... It's not that Jackie Robinson wasn't a good ballplayer, but we wanted Monte because we knew what he could do." Mays said, "When I joined the Giants, Hank Thompson and Monte Irvin were like fathers to me. They took good care of me."

(Top, L) Mickey Mantle, Willie Mays, 1951. In that Series, the two rookies gave no auguries of things to come; they batted a combined .185, scored two runs and batted in one. (Top, R) Casey Stengel and Phil Rizzuto, who had just signed a $50,000 contract for 1951. "If I were a retired gentleman," Stengel said, "I would follow the Yankees around just to see Rizzuto work those miracles every day." For his part, Rizzuto grew to detest Stengel, who would embarrass him by taking him out for a pinch hitter in tight situations. (Bottom) Johnny Mize. He hit 25 home runs in 1950, when he was 37, and Dan Parker wrote: "Your arm is gone; your legs likewise/But not your eyes, Mize, not your eyes."

(Top, R) Billy Martin; (Top, L) Mickey Mantle, Casey Stengel; (Bottom) Hank Bauer, Yogi Berra, Billy Martin, Joe Collins (L to R), 1953. Martin, said Stengel, "is a fresh kid who's always sassing everybody and getting away with it." Ray Robinson added, "In everybody's book, Martin is a pest, a vicious jockey...who is beset with all manner of actual and psychosomatic ailments — including hypertension, anxiety, insomnia and acute melancholia." He might have taken a cue from Hank Bauer, who said, "When you're walking to the bank with that World Series check every November, you don't want to leave. There were no Yankees saying play me or trade me."

had a few good days left were continually being maneuvered into Yankee pinstripes via intricate waiver deals. So in the early fifties fans in the Bronx were treated to the last adagios of such former National League stars as Mize, Konstanty, Sain, Blackwell, Slaughter, Johnny Schmitz, Ralph Branca and Johnny Hopp.

By 1953 the Indians had also caught on that there were ways of circumventing trade restrictions between the two leagues and imported George Strickland from Pittsburgh to fill their shortstop hole. That the Pirates even *had* a player another team coveted was one of the few notes of encouragement for Pittsburgh fans in the early fifties. After edging out the Cubs for seventh place in 1951, the Pirates did not escape the cellar again until 1956. In that interlude Kiner was traded to the Cubs, where he teamed for a while with his 1952 coleader in homers, Hank Sauer, but his period of dominance in National League slugging departments was at an end.

While Kiner was fading in 1953, Al Rosen's star was at its zenith. Rosen missed the triple crown that season by half a step, the distance by which he failed to beat out a ground ball on his last at bat. His lack of foot speed gave the batting title for a second time to Mickey Vernon, who must stand as the most fortunate hitter in the game's history. Just twice in Vernon's long American League career did his name appear among the top seven batters, and both times it came up on top.

Having taken over the moribund St. Louis Brown franchise, Bill Veeck almost immediately began maneuvering to move the team to a more promising territory. With the arrival of television and the increasing popularity of other professional sports, the competition for the entertainment dollar had grown so intense that cities the size of St. Louis could no longer support two major league teams. Annoyed at Veeck's attempts to hype attendance by employing a midget pinch hitter and later hiring as his manager the unrepentant Rogers Hornsby, who proclaimed that the only current player worth paying to see was Jim Rivera—an ex-convict who played in the old Gas House style—American League owners refused the Browns permission to relocate their franchise. The distinction of making the first modern franchise transplant was thus left to Boston Braves owner Lou Perini, who shifted his club to Milwaukee in 1953. When the Braves zoomed from a seventh-place club to an instant contender and set a new league attendance record, American League owners quickly reconsidered their stance on the Browns and allowed them (minus Veeck) to switch to Baltimore for the 1954 season. A year later the Athletics followed suit, moving to Kansas City and leaving Chicago and New York as the only cities with more than one major league team. As all three New York clubs were strong contenders and had distinct identities and rabid followings, the A's desertion of Philadelphia seemed to bring to an end the series of franchise shifts, permitting fans a respite to recover from the game's first geographic upheaval in 50 years.

Unaffected for the moment by the musical-chairs atmosphere were the Indians, who set an American League record for victories in 1954 and brought the Yankees' string of world championships to an end.

The 1953 Yankees, champions for the fifth straight year. In the back row, fifth from right, is a reserve catcher who would get but 43 hits in a nine-year career — 25 of those in his rookie season in 1947. After Ralph Houk became the Yankee manager, then general manager, in the sixties, Jim Bouton wrote, "Houk tried to look comfortable in his new role, but mostly he looked out of place, or as one player said, 'Like a whore in Church.'"

Oddly, the Yankees that season had their best club of all under Stengel and won 103 games in their own right with a pitching staff that included Sain, the league leader in saves, and rookie Bob Grim, the only pitcher ever to win 20 games in less than 200 innings. But under the tutelage of manager Al Lopez, Indian rookie pitchers Don Mossi and Ray Narleski were more than the equal of Grim, and every man on the staff who registered a decision had an ERA under the league average of 3.72. As had the 1906 Cubs, the National League record holders for wins, the Indians entered the Series heavily favored. But again like the Cubs, who were unable to handle the little-regarded George Rohe, Indian pitchers ran into a Giant team blessed by an incredible catch from Mays in the first game and a furious four-game hitting binge from sub outfielder Dusty Rhodes. Whereas the Cubs came back to win the Series in 1907, the Indians have never won a pennant since. The manner in which they lost the 1954 Series and the resultant demoralization that pervaded the franchise is more akin to the 1927 Pirates than the 1906 Cubs. Three years after their record season and only nine years after they had shattered all attendance figures, the Indians were giving serious thought to moving their franchise, and in the two decades since, the club that had the third highest winning percentage in the majors during the first 60 years of the century has only once been a contender, in 1959.

While Cleveland owners were contemplating a franchise shift in 1957, both the team that had been responsible for their demoralization and the team that had set a National League attendance record in 1947 went ahead and moved. Dodger fans who had seen their club win its first championship ever in 1955 and Giant fans who were still aglow from their club's first crown since 1933 a year earlier were staggered when team owners Walter O'Malley and Horace Stoneham, rather lamely complaining that their parks were outmoded and lacked adequate parking facilities, left the Yankees as the sole tenants of New York and laid claim to the rich lode of profits the untapped territory of the West Coast seemed to promise. In their haste to go West, the two clubs did so little to prepare for their move that for their first few years they were forced to play in antiquated Seals Stadium in San Francisco and in the Los Angeles Coliseum, a park so ill-designed for baseball that a screen had to be erected in left field to prevent pop flies from becoming home runs. O'Malley was too shrewd a man not to turn a city the size of Los Angeles, with its many transplanted easterners hungering for a major league team of their own, into one of the game's most successful operations, but the verdict is still out on San Francisco. An ineptly chosen site for its home park, competition from the vast panoply of activities available to Bay Area residents and a series of poor trades that deprived fans of what might have been

Cleveland pitchers, 1955. (L to R) Bob Lemon, Bob Feller, Mike Garcia, Herb Score, manager Al Lopez. Ted Williams said "the Red Sox offered a million for Score, and if he hadn't gotten hurt he would have been worth it." Lemon, Feller and Early Wynn (missing from this picture) all entered the Hall of Fame; Garcia won 79 games over a four-year period. The next year they would be joined by Calvin Coolidge Julius Caesar Tuskahoma McLish, who entered the big leagues billed as a "switch-pitcher."

Willie Mays. "If somebody came up and hit .450, stole 100 bases and performed a miracle in the field every day I'd still look you in the eye and say Willie was better. He could do the five things you have to do to be a superstar: hit, hit with power, run, throw and field. And he had that other magic ingredient that turns a superstar into a super superstar. He lit up the room when he came in. He was a joy to be around." — Leo Durocher

one of the league's strongest teams have made the franchise in recent years far more unstable than the old Giants ever were in the Polo Grounds.

It was as if the record-setting Indians had been only a mild distraction; the Yankees returned to the forefront in 1955 and brooked no further interruption in their control of the American League until 1959. Unlike most seasons when Stengel's men had won while the other clubs had all the individual leaders, the 1955 Yankees had Mantle, the league's homer and slugging king; Ford, the win leader; and the winning percentage leader, Tommy Byrne, back from banishment to the minors where he was able to work on his control. Poor years by Feller and Garcia removed the Indians from the race, but the arrival of yet another Cleveland rookie pitching whiz, Herb Score, made Hal Newhouser say he would trade his past for Score's future in a minute. The bat of the newest Tiger great, Al Kaline, lifted the Bengals above .500 just three years after they had finished last for the first time in their history, and made Kaline the youngest batting leader since Ty Cobb in 1907.

RBI champ Duke Snider was the Dodgers' lone hitting leader in 1955, but their pitching suddenly had become the best in the league. No one could match Roberts who led in wins for the fourth year in a row, but Newcombe was the National League's only other 20-game winner, and Clem Labine and Ed Roebuck were high up on relief pitching charts. In the 1955 Series Labine was the only one of the three to be effective, and when the Yankees took the first two games it appeared that the Dodgers were once more outclassed. On the perverse hunch that a left-hander could contain the predominantly right-handed hitting Yankees, manager Walter Alston started Johnny Podres in game three. Podres had a 9–10 record during the season and the worst ERA among Dodger front-line starters. Surviving a rocky second inning, Podres won 8–3 and was called on again four days later to pitch the seventh game. When he shut the Yankees out, Brooklyn left the Phillies as the sole National League team still without a world championship.

A year later Podres was in the Army, and the Dodgers lost 9–0 in the seventh game of the Series that brought instant immortality to the Yankees' Don Larsen. Larsen's perfect game—the only one ever in the Series and the first in the majors in 34 years—came in game five, only three days after he had been knocked out in the second inning of game two. Newcombe had also failed to last the second inning of that game and was blown out in the fourth inning of the final contest, leaving him with a Series ERA of 21.21 and erasing some of the impact of his splendid 27–7 season. Snider won the homer crown, Musial was the RBI leader and a young Braves star, Hank Aaron, won the batting title, but the team offensive statistics were dominated by the Reds. Traditionally one of the game's weakest hitting clubs, the Reds in 1956 sharply reversed their image. While Frank Robinson was tying Wally Berger's rookie home run mark, the Reds as a unit were tying the major league home run record set by the 1947 Giants. Light-hitting Roy McMillan and second baseman Johnny Temple hit only five homers between them, but the other six regulars

(L to R) Mays at rest; Mays making "The Catch" off Vic Wertz in the 1954 Series; Johnny Antonelli and Dusty Rhodes. Garry Schumacher said Mays "made the hard ones look hard"; Mays himself said "I don't compare them, I just catch them." Arnold Hano called him "the inimitable Mays, most skilled of outfielders, unique for his ability to scent the length and direction of any drive and then turn and move to the final destination of the ball." The brief glory of Dusty Rhodes began when he won the first game of the Series with a classic Polo Grounds "Chinese home run"; his second game blast, he insisted, was "no chop suey." Ten years later, Rhodes was driving a bus at the New York World's Fair.

The 1955 World Series, by Willard Mullin. In the *New York Times*, John Drebinger wrote, "Far into the night rang shouts of revelry in Flatbush. Brooklyn at long last has won a World Series and now let someone suggest moving the Dodgers elsewhere!"

averaged 30 apiece and stirred Cincinnati fans to flood the mails that summer with ballots naming all eight Red front-liners as All-Star starters. Commissioner Ford Frick ultimately disallowed the voting results, but the fans may not have been far wrong; the Reds fell just two games short of the Dodgers with one of the league's poorest pitching staffs. Even closer to the Dodgers were the Braves, who finished a scant game out with the finest pitching in the game. Staff leader Warren Spahn embarked that year on the first of six straight 20-win seasons, and Lew Burdette had the most shutouts and the lowest ERA. The difference between the Braves and the Dodgers came down to one position: second base. Where the Dodgers had the versatile Jim Gilliam, the Braves had the disappointing Danny O'Connell. Early in 1957 Braves manager Fred Haney saw to it that the difference was eliminated. After the All-Star break, the second-base spot in Milwaukee's County Stadium was occupied for the rest of that season and all of the next by the best of his era at the position, Red Schoendienst.

Surprisingly, the Braves' main obstacle to becoming the first team to win a pennant after a franchise shift was neither the Dodgers nor the Reds. With Musial rallying his aging body for one final batting title, the Cardinals led most of the early summer in 1957 and seemed for a time to have found a carbon copy of the Dean brothers in the McDaniels—21-year-old Lindy and 18-year-old Von. When arm trouble finished Von, the Cards were through also and nearly lost second place in the last few days to the Dodgers. One winner, however, was the team's centerfielder, who led all National League outfielders in fielding. Put there out of desperation by Manager Freddie Hutchinson after rookie Charlie Peete was killed in the off season and Bill Virdon was traded, he played only that one season in the outfield, though he was later a frequent All-Star at another position. In 1957, Kenny Boyer ranked ahead of Mays, Ashburn and Snider as the league's surest glove in center field.

The American League's premier centerfielder in 1957, defending triple crown winner Mickey Mantle, hit .365 but achieved only the distinction of having the highest average since 1937 by a batting runner-up as Ted Williams hit .388—the highest average since Williams's own .406 in 1941. By getting good seasons from most of their regulars, the White Sox finally broke out of their third-place rut and claimed second when the Indians crumbled after strikeout leader Herb Score nearly became the Tribe's second on-the-field fatality when he was struck in the face by a line drive. Roy Sievers, now of the Senators, stripped Mantle of the other two legs of his triple crown by taking both the homer and RBI titles but could do little to avert the team's slide into the basement. Although improving a fraction over the previous year when they had recorded only one shutout, Senator pitchers were still the

Mickey Mantle. In 1956, he won not only the triple crown but led the AL in slugging, total bases and runs scored as well. Al Kaline said, "I wish I was half the ballplayer he is."

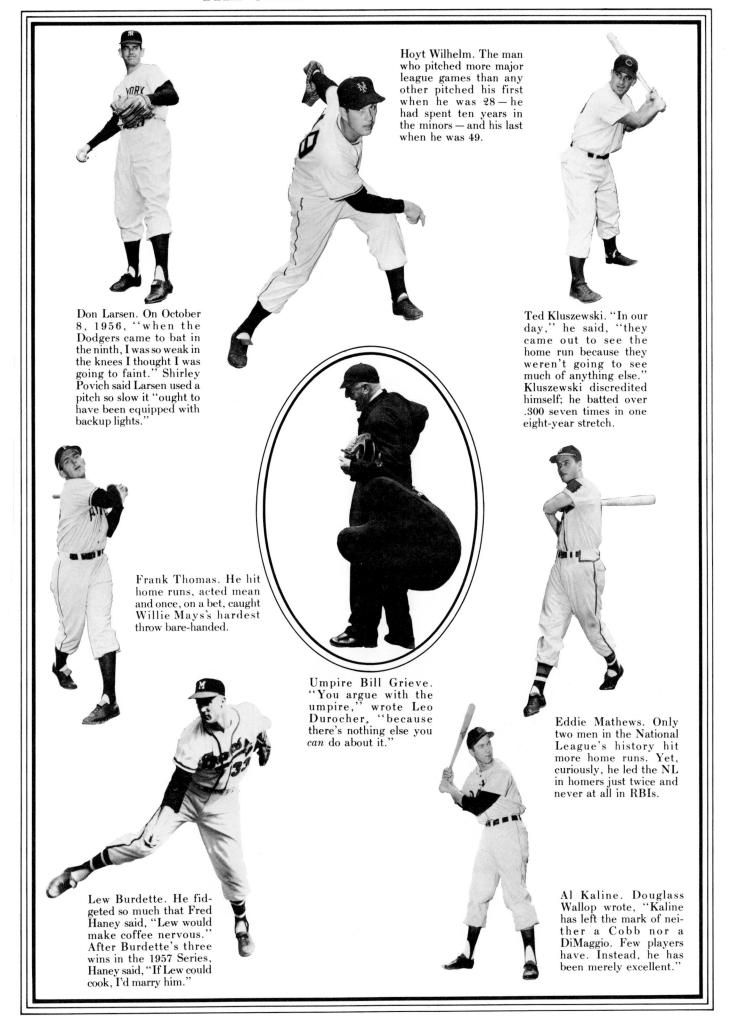

Hoyt Wilhelm. The man who pitched more major league games than any other pitched his first when he was 28 — he had spent ten years in the minors — and his last when he was 49.

Don Larsen. On October 8, 1956, "when the Dodgers came to bat in the ninth, I was so weak in the knees I thought I was going to faint." Shirley Povich said Larsen used a pitch so slow it "ought to have been equipped with backup lights."

Ted Kluszewski. "In our day," he said, "they came out to see the home run because they weren't going to see much of anything else." Kluszewski discredited himself; he batted over .300 seven times in one eight-year stretch.

Frank Thomas. He hit home runs, acted mean and once, on a bet, caught Willie Mays's hardest throw bare-handed.

Umpire Bill Grieve. "You argue with the umpire," wrote Leo Durocher, "because there's nothing else you *can* do about it."

Eddie Mathews. Only two men in the National League's history hit more home runs. Yet, curiously, he led the NL in homers just twice and never at all in RBIs.

Lew Burdette. He fidgeted so much that Fred Haney said, "Lew would make coffee nervous." After Burdette's three wins in the 1957 Series, Haney said, "If Lew could cook, I'd marry him."

Al Kaline. Douglass Wallop wrote, "Kaline has left the mark of neither a Cobb nor a DiMaggio. Few players have. Instead, he has been merely excellent."

worst in either league. The A's pitchers meanwhile kept Kansas City fans on their toes all season trying to learn their names; none of the 20 men whom managers Lou Boudreau and Harry Craft shuttled on and off the mound worked more than 145 innings, making the A's the only team in history without a single ERA championship qualifier.

Burdette's third Series victory in the seventh game not only gave the Yankees their second Series loss in three years, but removed the championship from New York for the first time since 1948. When Spahn shut the Yankees out in game four the following year and gave the Braves a 3-1 lead, it looked as if Milwaukee would house the first National League repeat champion since the 1922 Giants. But Bob Turley, who had been shelled in the first inning of the second game, shut the Braves out in the fifth, saved the sixth and collected a win in the seventh by pitching the last 6⅔ innings in relief. Turley won the Cy Young Award and made the Yankees the first team since the 1925 Pirates to win a Series after trailing three games to one.

The pennant races in both leagues were uneventful in 1958. Once their clubs fell out of contention, observers in most cities followed the struggles of Ashburn and Williams for batting titles, but those in Pittsburgh concentrated solely on the Pirates, who climbed into second place after finishing in the cellar the previous year and no higher than seventh since 1949. An uneven club, Pittsburgh had the league's best keystone pair in Dick Groat and Bill Mazeroski and its worst fielding first baseman in Dick Stuart, who led the league in errors despite playing only 64 games in the field. Stuart, up from the minors after shattering home run records everywhere he played, initially reminded Pirate supporters of other minor league sensations of the early fifties like Ron Necciai, who once struck out 27 batters in a game but was totally out of his element when rushed into a big league uniform, even that of the 1952 Bucs. A more consistent performer was Roberto Clemente. In his fourth season Clemente seemed to be finding his niche as a steady .280 hitter who could be counted on to cut off enemy runs with his strong arm in right field but who would produce few runs himself.

Only six times has a pennant race ended in a tie and required a play-off. Four of the six play-offs have involved the Dodgers, and on three of the occasions they lost. Few have difficulty recalling all three of those defeats, but even longstanding Dodger sympathizers may be hard pressed to come up with the details of the play-off they won. It occurred in 1959, at the conclusion of a season that had been a duplicate, in most respects, of 1915. One major difference was that the Phils, instead of winning, as they had in 1915, finished last. A second was that the Giants probably should have won. With eight games remaining, San Francisco led the Braves and Dodgers by two games and were on the verge of printing World Series tickets. The Braves and Dodgers were still skeptical that the Giants would be the National League representative, but one thing was certain: the decade would end with

Billy Pierce, Roy Sievers, Ernie Banks (L to R). Pierce, said catcher Phil Masi, "throws a 'light' ball. It doesn't crash into your mitt; it just sort of lands there." Sievers labored in vain; in his first ten seasons, his team finished as high as sixth only once. The plight of Banks was similar: "Without him," Jimmy Dykes said, "the Cubs would finish in Albuquerque." He was the only bona fide ballplayer in the double-play combination of "Banks to Baker to Addison Street"; this last was the street that ran behind the first-base seats when Dee Fondy played for the Cubs.

the World Series being played in a city that had not even been in the major leagues at its beginning.

By losing seven of their last eight games, the Giants dropped out of the race, leaving the field open to the Dodgers and Braves. When both won on the final day, attention was removed from Chicago, where the White Sox had just won their first pennant in 40 years, and focused on the second-base problem that existed again in Milwaukee after Schoendienst was sidelined by tuberculosis. Superior in every other respect to the Dodgers, the Braves in 1959 were even poorer at second than they had been in 1956 and were forced to go with either weak-hitting Felix Mantilla or the veteran Bobby Avila, a batting champion in 1954 but of scarcely journeyman caliber thereafter. Although the Braves lost the play-off in two straight games, had Schoendienst been healthy, the club might have been the league's strongest of the entire decade. With Aaron winning his second batting title, Eddie Mathews leading in homers, Burdette and Spahn each winning 21 games and Del Crandall, Joe Adcock, Billy Bruton and Johnny Logan all at the peak of their skills, no other team in either league had a lineup to match the Braves.

The White Sox, for example, won while platooning at three positions for the lack of a solid everyday player at any one of them, and the Indians finished second with an uncharacteristically drab pitching staff and a second-base hole that, after Billy Martin was injured, was as huge as the Braves'. That the two clubs led the league was due more to the grounding of the normally high-flying Yankee batting attack than to their own talents. For the first time since the war-abbreviated 1918 season, the Yankees were without a single hitter who claimed more than 75 RBIs. The White Sox had only one, Sherman Lollar, but one proved enough when Early Wynn won 22 games and Bob Shaw won 18 after being brought into the starting rotation from his seat in the bullpen. Another who spent much of the early season sitting was Tito Francona of the Indians, who didn't get his .363 bat into the regular lineup until mid-June and missed the batting championship by a handful of at bats. Although he was not technically a qualifier for the title, Francona was the closest the Indians have come to having a batting leader in the last 20 years. The radical change in the club's fortunes, which had begun with the Series loss to the Giants, and been heightened by the career-shattering injury to Herb Score, was further amplified by the trade at season's end of slugger Rocky Colavito to the Tigers for batting champion Harvey Kuenn. Colavito's best years were still ahead of him, but Kuenn at 29 was already on the wane. So ever since have been the Indians.

Last in the American League in homers, the White Sox entered the 1959 Series hoping stolen-base king Luis Aparicio and their three swift out-

Warren Spahn. He won the Cy Young Award when he was 36, pitched no-hitters at 39 and 41, and was 23-7 when he was 42. Stan Musial said,"I don't think Spahn will ever get into the Hall of Fame. He'll never stop pitching."

fielders, Jim Landis, Jim Rivera and Al Smith, would be able to exploit the arm of Dodger catcher Johnny Roseboro. But the Dodgers wound up stealing five bases to just two by the White Sox and won in six games. All four Dodger victories bore the mark of reliever Larry Sherry, who won twice and saved the other two for Podres and Don Drysdale. In a Series marked by such oddities as Chuck Essegian's two pinch homers and the White Sox needing three pitchers to post a 1–0 shutout, Ted Kluszewski hit three homers for the White Sox and set the RBI record for a six-game Series. The man who in mid-decade had seemed most likely to be the next threat to Ruth's home run record, Kluszewski apparently had had his career all but ruined in what appeared to have been a clubhouse fight with a Cincinnati teammate. Only 32 when the incident

happened, Kluszewski managed to play five more seasons, but the week of the 1959 Series was the last time he was fully able to mobilize the most remarkable upper torso of his era.

Playing against Kluszewski for much of the season was a third baseman for the Senators who would assume his title of "Mister Torso" for the next decade. But whereas Kluszewski was a complete hitter, Harmon Killebrew was not. In 1959 Killebrew tied for the American League lead in homers on a .242 batting average. The first home run leader in history to hit under .250, he would set many such dubious records in the years ahead. But he would not be alone. The Red Sox had begun the fifties by hitting .302 as a team. In the decade to follow, Boston's Carl Yastrzemski would win a batting title with an average of .301. —David Nemec

"By and large it is the sport that a foreigner is least likely to take to. You have to grow up playing it, you have to accept the lore of the bubble-gum card, and believe that if the answer to the Mays-Snider-Mantle question is found, then the universe will be a simpler and more ordered place." — David Halberstam

FRANCHISE:
Dodgerismus, Brooklyn and L. A.
By John Leonard

GROWING up pimply in Southern California in the late 1940's–early 1950's, just across the San Andreas Fault from right-wing Orange County, meant that we had to borrow our major league baseball from some other state. We had the Saturday "Game of the Week" on radio, and a number of "re-creations"—studio jobs with demented disc-jockeys reading wire-copy and turning up the noise on their crowd machines at every suspenseful moment—on other afternoons, but that was it unless you count the Los Angeles Angels and the Hollywood Stars playing Pacific Coast League Triple A ball in their respective bandboxes. I think Steve Bilko, a gigantic white eggplant, one of those years must have hit a hundred home runs out of the "other" Wrigley Field, our elegant playpen, and

yet he always looked like a stiff whenever the Cubs or anyone else called him up. Besides, the second game of a Pacific Coast League doubleheader went just seven innings and was a cheat.

It was necessary to make a choice, if only to be able to imagine yourself as someone specifically heroic while you dropped a routine pop-up or hit into a double play behind one of the churches, which in my neighborhood were all lined up next to one another on the same two blocks, like filling stations for the soul. I made my choice when I was eight years old. Fans, of course, invent themselves, especially in a vacuum like Southern California, where everybody seemed to come from somewhere else. Our passionate identifications are arbitrary. Because they are arbitrary, they refuse to die.

I was eight years old in 1947, and 1947 was the

(Top, L to R) Tuck Stainback, Buddy Hassett, Kiki Cuyler and Babe Ruth in 1938, when Ruth was a Brooklyn coach. "Fans all over flocked to see him bust the ball in batting practice and then round out the afternoon making gestures in the coaching box," wrote the Brooklyn *Eagle's* Tommy Holmes. (Middle) Charles Ebbets (L), who said "Baseball is in its infancy," when he opened his park in Flatbush; Wilbert Robinson (R), who caught a grapefruit dropped from an airplane and, said Harold Parrott, was "more of a habit than a manager." (Bottom) The 1941 infield of (L to R) Dolf Camilli, Pee Wee Reese, Cookie Lavagetto and Billy Herman, part of the team that ushered in the era of almost-good feeling in Brooklyn.

(Top) Whitlow Wyatt (L), who once said, "You ought to play it mean. They ought to hate you on the field," won 22 games in 1941; so did Kirby Higbe (R). Larry MacPhail (Middle) introduced night baseball in Cincinnati; when he moved to Brooklyn in 1938, attendance increased 67 percent even as the team finished seventh. Early in 1942 he announced his team could not defend its pennant. He quit to join the Army before the year was out; the Dodgers finished second. (Bottom) The 1941 Dodgers.

Hugh Casey (L) and Mickey Owen (R). "The condemned jumped out of the chair and electrocuted the warden" was one description of the consequence of Owen's dropped third strike in the 1941 Series. Years later, Casey admitted he had thrown a spitball; the evening of the game, Yankee Tommy Henrich said of Owen, "That was a tough break. I bet he feels like a nickel's worth of dog meat."

(Middle) Joe Medwick, Cookie Lavagetto, Pete Reiser (L to R). (Bottom) Reiser in a characteristic pose. "Is the *Iliad* true?" David Markson wrote. "Was there an Achilles?" Leo Durocher thought Reiser was the only player he'd ever seen who compared with Willie Mays.

year that Jackie Robinson broke the color line with the Dodgers. He was 28 years old, he was the National League's bowlegged Rookie of the Year, and he played that season, you may be startled to remember, at first base. (Eddie Stanky was on second. Gil Hodges wasn't ready yet for first.) Robinson had a disappointing World Series, hitting only .259, but so did every other Dodger except Carl Furillo (.353) and Pee Wee Reese (.304). Hodges—a harbinger of autumns to come—made one appearance at the plate, as a pinch hitter, and struck out. The Dodgers lost in seven.

That was it for me. I'd never heard of Zack Wheat, the first Great Dodger in the Sky. I'd been two years old at the time of the last Dodger pennant, in pre-war 1941, the time of the team of Cookie Lavagetto, Dolf Camilli, Dixie Walker, Reese, Pete Reiser, Joe Medwick and Mickey (Dropped-Third-Strike) Owen. The Yankees blew that team out in five, but I hadn't noticed. Jackie Robinson, however, was important. So was losing *my* first Series in seven. So was the "moral victory" of breaking up Bill Bevens's no-hitter in the ninth inning of the fourth game. Moral victories are the story of my life.

To explain: My mother, briefly during World War II, was a secretary in Franklin D. Roosevelt's White House. My grandmother, on the non-shanty-Irish side of the family, resigned from the Daughters of the American Revolution when they wouldn't let Marian Anderson sing at Constitution Hall. (That my grandmother had ever belonged to the D.A.R. was a secret kept from me until I went to college and was old enough to forgive her.) I was brought up by women fierce in their liberal sympathies. We may have been, in Murray Kempton's sense, shabby-genteel, down in the money and looking up at a middle class that seemed all Orange County and polyester politics, but they never extinguished this pilot light. We had warm feelings for every dog that was under. That Jackie Robinson was better than the white folks at their own game was a huge help.

Coming close and losing also helped. It was lonely on the Left those days. A beautiful loser has a special grace; "Wait Til Next Year" might have been the slogan of a Revolution that, like Godot, never managed to arrive. My mother didn't go so far as to vote for Henry Wallace in 1948—she never wasted anything, not even a vote—but I was the only kid on my block to root for Truman. When he won, I was as surprised as he was. I was also the only kid on my block to root, at Saturday matinees, for the North against the South in Civil War movies. To be sure, the South was invariably portrayed as a beautiful loser, but it didn't have any Jackie Robinsons playing for its team.

We cherish moral victories for the same reason

Burt Shotton (L), Leo Durocher (R). Before Leo fled to the Giants, he had been suspended for "conduct unbecoming." His replacement was Shotton, an old Rickey retainer whom Dick Young always called KOBS—an acronym for "kindly old Burt Shotton." Durocher had been losing his grip on Brooklyn anyway; when he married the divorced Laraine Day, the borough's CYO withdrew its support of the Knothole Club because "Durocher has undermined the moral training of Brooklyn's Roman Catholic youths."

Jackie Robinson. In a message to the St. Louis Cardinals in May, 1947, Ford Frick said, "If you do this you will be suspended from the league. You will find that the friends that you think you have in the press box will not support you, that you will be outcasts. I do not care if half the league strikes. Those who do it will encounter quick retribution. They will be suspended and I don't care if it wrecks the National League for five years. This is the United States of America, and one citizen has as much right to play as another. The National League will go down the line with Robinson whatever the consequence."

we revere the shin or bone splinter of a saint, the snapshot of an unrequited love: this, at least, has been preserved against the barbarous truth, the deluge of pinstripes. *This* is our honor. Looking back through binoculars of shot-glass at what amounts to no more than nostalgia for myself, the loser's intrepid innocence, I see that I am tired of moral victories and would prefer, on occasion, a rout, a decisive kill for my side. But to deny the past is cowardly.

Nor was it lost on me, then and now, that those of my peers who rooted for the Yankees wore cashmere sweaters and white buck shoes and seemed mostly to be the sons of bankers and dentists. They were accustomed to winning everything from the yo-yo contest at the Towne Theatre in Long Beach to the student body presidency at Wilson High to the drum majorette in the back seat of the Buick. They would graduate to USC and go directly to jail after Watergate. Mine was, from the beginning, a class antagonism.

Besides, my team called itself the *Dodgers*. They had an outlaw quality. They were Felix Krulls, Melville's confidence man. Only the Pirates could compare, by name, with such anarchistic pizzazz. The Dodgers, in fact, were everything as a team that the fifties were not as a decade.

They didn't make it to the Series in 1948. The Braves—then of Boston, subsequently of Milwaukee and Atlanta, eventually, I expect, of Budapest or Singapore or Mars—went instead and lost to the Cleveland Indians in six. It was, perhaps, the only Native American World Series, and the Dodgers, our Apaches, weren't there. I rooted for the Indians because of Larry Doby and Satchel Paige. Paige retired the only two batters he was allowed to face in his only World Series. Black power. Nevertheless, it wasn't the same. It lacked historicity. And the American League was a wimp.

In 1949, the Dodgers went down to the Yankees in five. Rookie Roy Campanella, who in his whole life has never worried about his looks as much as Thurman Munson worries in any given week, was four for fifteen; Robinson was three for sixteen; Hodges was four for seventeen; and Don Newcombe lost two games. The black Newcombe and the white Hodges had already entered into a conspiracy to ruin October for me. Newcombe would become a huge symbol of the intractability of the status quo.

I don't want to think about 1950. In 1950, we went to Korea and the Phillies went to the Series, by virtue of a tenth inning home run by Dick Sisler against my beautiful losers in the last game of the

Gil Hodges (L), Don Newcombe (R). Stan Musial said, "If Hodges had been left-handed, he might have been remembered as the most efficient first baseman ever." Of Newcombe, Ernie Banks said, "Once he got on that mound, he was a monster."

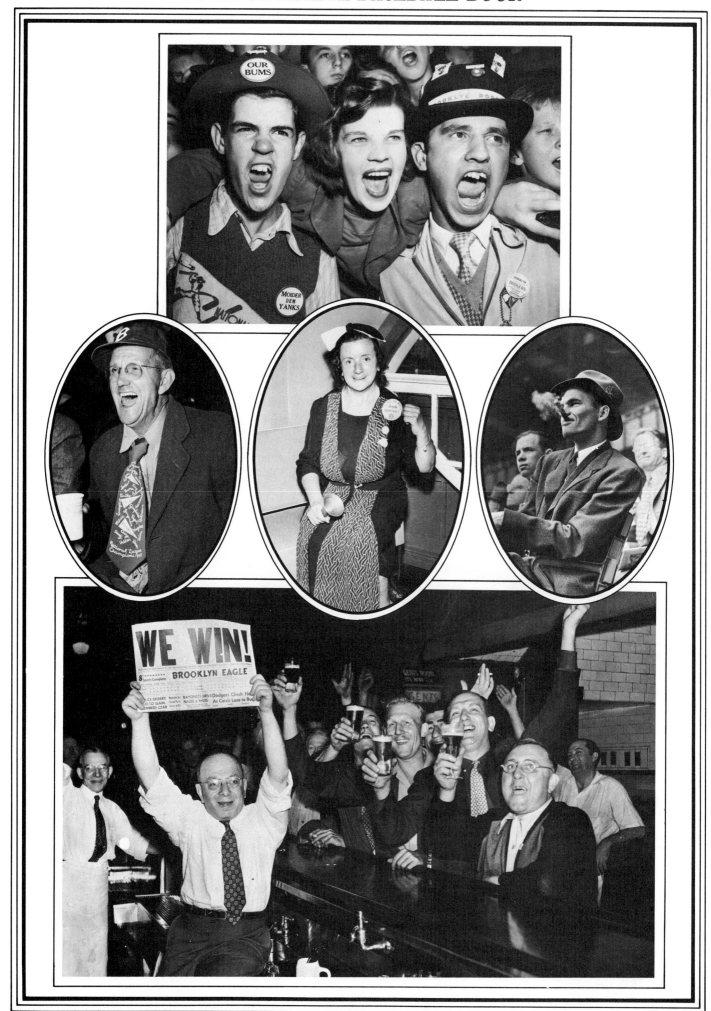

Brooklyn fans, wrote Leo Durocher, "came to root, and they never gave up." The man who exhorted them, Red Barber (at microphone) said, "There were 3,000,000 people in Brooklyn, and if every one of them wasn't rooting for the Dodgers, every one seemed to be." Shorty Laurice (with cigar, playing drum), leader of the Dodger Sym-Phony, died of a Dodger-induced ulcer; Hilda Chester (with bell) was, Tommy Holmes wrote, "the unchallenged dream boat of the cheap seats." Walter O'Malley (opposite Barber), their host, would desert the Brooklyn fans because of a worry about profits. Less than 15 years later, he told Roger Kahn he was worth "about $24,000,000."

National League season, which Phillies dropped four straight to DiMaggio and the rookie Ford Motor Company. Phillies, anyway, is a name for horses, not baseball teams.

In 1951, for reasons that have never been clear to me, I moved to New York, sort of. Sort of, because I lived in surprising Queens. To be more specific, I lived in Jackson Heights, which was then notorious for nothing and is now well-known for cocaine-dealing among various people of the Latin-American persuasion. Jackson Heights was, however, just a subway token away from Ebbets Field, the Fenway Park of the Pleistocene epoch. Preacher Roe! Clem Labine! Carl Erskine! The ineffable Duke! Joe Black relieves, Robinson steals home, Campanella hits a Robin Roberts watermelon into Bed-Stuy, Billy Loes cries because of sunspots! Hard to believe that these sweat-bags are my existential *Other,* by whose exertions I am purified, I am one with the priests and morticians and drunks.

Yes, drunks. I am 12 years old, among bleacher bums, malcontents, losers, who bleed rye whiskey at every nick of fate. My identification with the underclass is perfect. My vocabulary, as a consequence, deteriorates. My mother washes my scatological mouth out with Lin Yutang and *The New Republic.* Among the lumpen losers, I wallow like an Agnew. Norman Mailer would be right, some years later, in proposing the psychic death-wish of the fan who fears so much that he will lose that he causes, with his bad vibrations, the very occasion he fears. His doubt is contagious.

As we invented our doomed fandom, we invoked a Ralph Branca and we fed him to Bobby Thomson, and we blew the play-off, and the Giants lost to the Yankees in six, with a bunt single by the egregious rookie Mickey Mantle and four hits for the rookie nonpareil, Willie Mays. All right: I learned in the stands at Ebbets Field that the underclass is not much more prepossessing than the swamp-monsters of Orange County. I even began to wonder whether "Brooklyn," as a concept, was a cultural fabrication; whether we needed the *idea* of Brooklyn, like the idea of Hollywood and Dubuque, Dallas and Las Vegas, Erie and Cheyenne, in order to achieve a sociological fix on the disordered—indeed, the nihilistic—reality of our American mess. As far as I could see, and I was precocious, Brooklyn had nothing going for it *except* the Dodgers.

Maybe there's a Brooklyn nation, like an Oz.

It is hard to be a radical, although it is even harder to be a Yankee fan. The glory of the Dodgers was to come close and still lose, like most of us. Tomorrow, next year, would surely belong to Harold Stassen or the Viet Cong. My reservations about my fellow fans, like the occasional fevers of my childhood, I would diagnose as internal contradictions. Since the dialectic of history was inevitable, the Dodgers would win a Series. The unprepossessing dispossessed would be permitted a Whitman-esque yawp. The Wobblies would win an election. Suffering anneals.

We made it to the Series in 1952. I made it in person. I saw Joe Black, whose jockstrap the likes of a Sparky Lyle isn't fit to wear, start and beat Allie Reynolds in game one against the all-white Yankees. We lost, again, in seven, to Reynolds in relief of the sinister Lopat. We would lose again—

Preacher Roe. "I got three pitches. My change, my change off my change, and my change off my change off my change." In 1946-47 with the Pirates, Roe was 7-23 with an ERA over 5.00. In 1948 he was traded to Brooklyn and by his own admission learned to throw a fourth pitch, a spitball. He won 93 and lost 37 with the Dodgers, including a 22-3 season in 1951.

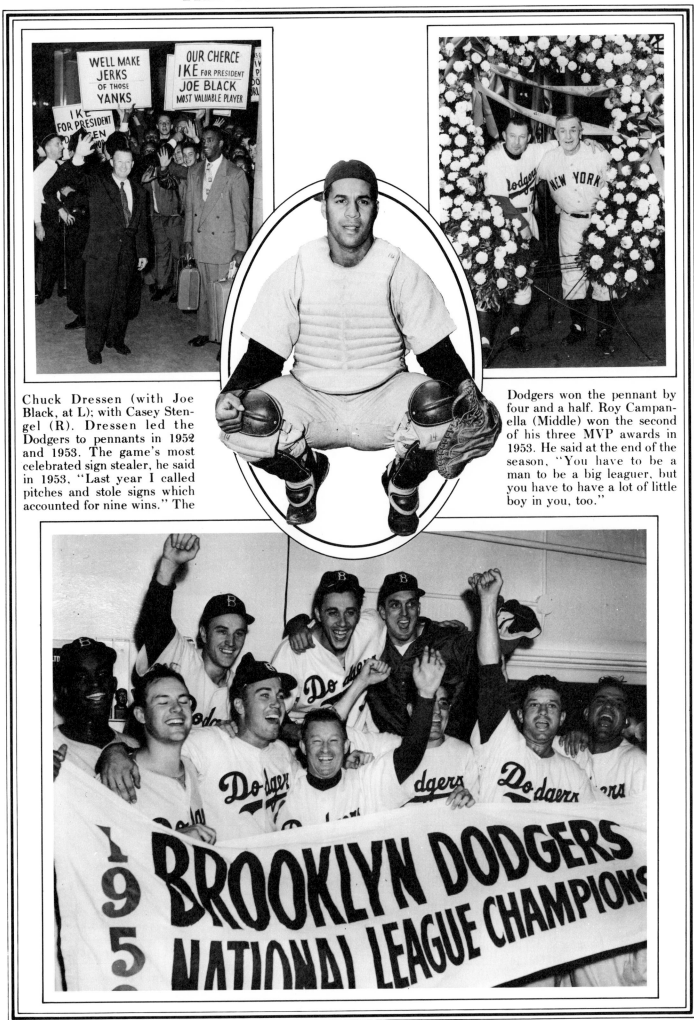

Chuck Dressen (with Joe Black, at L); with Casey Stengel (R). Dressen led the Dodgers to pennants in 1952 and 1953. The game's most celebrated sign stealer, he said in 1953, "Last year I called pitches and stole signs which accounted for nine wins." The

Dodgers won the pennant by four and a half. Roy Campanella (Middle) won the second of his three MVP awards in 1953. He said at the end of the season, "You have to be a man to be a big leaguer, but you have to have a lot of little boy in you, too."

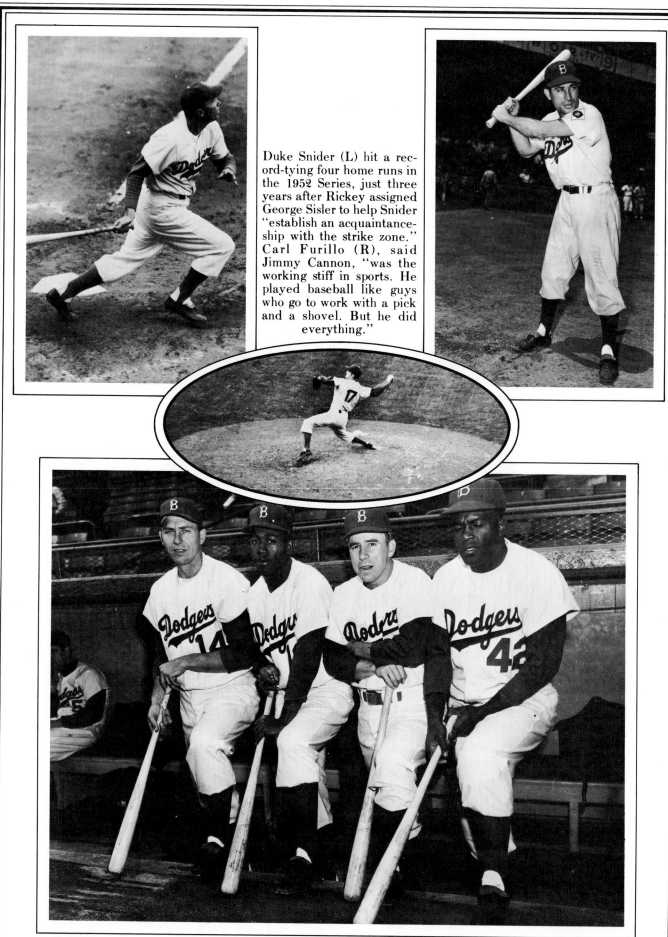

Duke Snider (L) hit a record-tying four home runs in the 1952 Series, just three years after Rickey assigned George Sisler to help Snider "establish an acquaintanceship with the strike zone." Carl Furillo (R), said Jimmy Cannon, "was the working stiff in sports. He played baseball like guys who go to work with a pick and a shovel. But he did everything."

(Middle) Carl Erskine. In 1952, he pitched a no-hit game that would have been perfect save for a walk to the Cubs' pitcher; in 1953, he was 20-6, and set a Series record with 14 strikeouts in the third game. (Bottom) The 1953 infield included (L to R) Hodges, Jim Gilliam, Reese and Robinson. Robinson said of Reese, "No one realizes just what he has meant to the Brooklyn club. No one, that is, but his teammates."

Branch Rickey. When he left St. Louis in 1942 he was earning $80,000 a year; his highest paid player made $15,000. Leaving Brooklyn in 1950, he received $1,050,000 for his share of the club. Dick Young called him "El Cheapo"; Tom Meany dubbed him "Mahatma," citing John Gunther's description of Mahatma Gandhi as "a combination of God, your own father and Tammany Hall."

I am a citizen of the nation of Brooklyn, even though it has never existed—in 1953, with Jim "Junior" Gilliam at second base and Robinson in left field, because Billy Martin got 12 hits for the bad guys. We had our usual moral victory: Carl Erskine struck out 14 in the third game, a new Series record. I am dying of moral victories. I'd settle for an immoral victory. Anyway, I was back, as mysteriously as I had left, in Southern California, where the schools were full of pinko deviationists teaching evolution and Franklin Roosevelt and George Washington Carver with his magic peanut, which caused Orange County to gibber and seethe.

Willie Mays won the 1954 World Series in four straight against a flabby Cleveland for which Bob Lemon, who had done time at the very same high school to which I was at the moment sentenced, lost two games. I kept my lip zipped. The cause of Brooklyn, like that of Montenegro and Estonia, seemed hopeless, which is what made it so attractive: a franchise for losers. In Orange County, behind the patios, inside the hydrangeas, they were shooting socialists and castrating Democrats. I read *The CIO Political Action Weekly* and wondered about Walter Alston, about whom I would wonder for the next 21 years of his one-year contracts as

Johnny Podres. "I'd been 4-F until I won the seventh game of the World Series in 1955," he said eight years later. "They reclassified me 1-A that winter."

(L) Sandy Amoros making the catch off Yogi Berra that saved the 1955 Series for the Dodgers. Asked after the game whether he thought he had a chance for it, Amoros said, "I dunno. I just run like hell." (R) Sal Maglie, at 39, pitched a no-hitter for Brooklyn after being dumped by the Giants in 1956; Roy Campanella congratulates him. (Bottom) Duke Snider's three-run home run in the fourth game of the 1955 Series. When they could not repeat in 1956, the old rallying cry was amended, Roger Kahn wrote, to "Wait till last year."

Snider and Newcombe after 1955 Series victory. Snider was a superb postseason player, with 11 home runs, 26 RBIs and a .594 slugging average in 36 Series games; Newcombe was an October disaster, with an 0-4 record and an 8.59 ERA. He started five Series games in his career and completed only one, lasting a total of 14 innings in the other four.

Dodger manager. Was this Alston Stalin or Trotsky or Captain Kangaroo?

I listened to 1955 on a transistor radio next to a free-form fishpond in the lap of the snot-green petrified lymph of my suspect high school in the morning in between drum majorettes. What can I say? Newcombe, as usual, lost a game; so did Loes; so did the unmemorable Spooner. But Labine and Craig won one each, and the admirable Podres took two, and the immortal Sandy Amoros played Sgt. Friday in left and center, catching everybody, and Robinson, although hitting only .182, stole home on Whitey Ford. The Dodgers, improbably, prevailed. Montenegro had invaded the Soviet Union, burned down Moscow and fried the Fabergé eggs.

A professional loser, a citizen of the state of mind of Brooklyn, doesn't gloat. Just as the Dodgers drank in their local dives, with their fellow bums— unlike the Yankees, known to carouse in the swankest of Manhattan nightclubs—so the Southern California outlaw returns to his tract house to water the marijuana and apply pliers to his younger brother and hum "The Internationale." They never knew, inside their cashmeres and Buicks, my sense

(L) Jackie Robinson rejected a trade to the Giants and retired after the 1956 season. "The game had done much for me," he wrote in 1972, "and I had done much for it." (R) Walter O'Malley (in hat, on ramp) leads his Dodgers to Los Angeles. The editor of that city's *Examiner* immediately decreed that the nickname "Bums" could never be used in his paper.

of transcendence. Had I ever been a Hegelian, I would at last be synthesized. Oh, Podres! His 1.00 ERA over 18 innings was joy-making, especially when one considers the usual Newcombe: a 9.53 ERA in five and two-thirds. For the Yankees, Elston Howard participated, perhaps because we were on the verge of color television.

Any problems I might have had with the ambivalence of being for once a winner were dissipated in October, 1956. I was in college then, in Boston, surrounded by young men, scholarship boys every one of them, from places like South Dakota, Utah and Kentucky. They were to a young man Dodger fans, although they'd never even lived in Queens. It was as if there were an underground nation of social outlaws, the upwardly mobile lower-middle class, and only one baseball team with which to identify.

It was, alas, an old, tired team, lucky to have won the pennant. It lost to the Yankees in seven, giving away a perfect game to Don (Not-That-Good) Larsen. Newcombe outdid himself: an ERA of 21.21 in four and two-thirds innings. Robinson was six for 24 in his last Series.

How were we to know, this underground nation, that something was over? Brooklyn would never win another pennant. Robinson would leave the Dodgers, and the Dodgers would leave Brooklyn: for Los Angeles, of course, my backyard. They had less of an excuse than the Giants, whose attendance at the ramshackle Polo Grounds had dropped 50 percent in three years, while Ebbets Field stayed steady. But Ebbets Field seated just 35,000. The new Dodger Stadium in Chavez Ravine would seat 57,000. And Walter O'Malley dreamt of real estate and pay television, and so they went, exchanging one state of mind for another. And I wrote a flaming editorial for the college newspaper. People in Southern California go to beaches, I said, and racetracks and demolition derbies, not to ballparks. It'll never work; it's a terrible idea. Even if I didn't live in Brooklyn, the Dodgers had to.

As I type this, Dodger attendance for 1978 is over three million, every one of them very polite and many of them celebrities. No bums, no outlaws allowed. The franchise is said to be worth $55 million.

I wish I could say that I gave up, there and then, on the Dodgers; that I went across the street to Fenway Park and never came back. But I was too old to love another team. I was there, in front of my television set in New York City in 1959, when Los Angeles took Chicago in six. We got just one inning of scoreless relief from Clem Labine, although Hodges hit .391 and Snider and Furillo were still around. But who were all those other people: Wills and Roseboro, Fairly and Moon, Drysdale and Koufax? Hell, I'd played basketball against Ron Fairly in high school: what was he doing in a Dodger uniform? The 1960's had begun a little early, and the famous Dodger farm system had struck again, as it would once more in the 1970's

Maury Wills steals his 104th base in 1962; defending third is the Giants' Jim Davenport. Wills, who spent eight years in the minors before reaching Los Angeles, said, "Once I get on first I become a pitcher and catcher as well as a base runner. I am trying to think with them."

Sandy Koufax. "Pitching," he said, "is the art of instilling fear by making a man flinch." Yet his control was such that in 1966, Koufax set a National League record by pitching 323 innings without hitting a single batter. Before he pitched the first game of the 1963 Series (*overleaf*), Koufax recalled, "I felt that I had to show myself and my team, and the Yankees, too, that they were just a team of baseball players, not a pride of supermen." Over his career, he held opposing hitters to a composite average of .204.

with Garvey and Cey and Lopes and Russell.

And I was there in 1962, in Oakland, California, when we didn't make it. Maury Wills broke Ty Cobb's base-stealing record, but the Giants caught the Dodgers on the last day of the season and beat them, of course, in a three game play-off, because Alston wouldn't use Drysdale and Stan Williams couldn't get my grandmother out. I should have been rooting for the Giants. They were, after all, just across the Bay. But I'd been, and froze, at the Cave of Winds called Candlestick, and I'd heard the crowd boo Willie Mays, and any town that boos Willie Mays is a hick town. And so, all summer long at eight o'clock at night, I'd leave my apartment with beer and pretzels and sit in my car at the curb and listen on the powerful car radio to the signal from Los Angeles, and Wills would steal another base and the Dodgers would lose another game off their lead and the neighbors would point me out to their children and shake their heads sadly. This was more like it: I was alone, and I knew in my bones I would lose.

Sixty-three, however, was perfection: it would never again be necessary to take baseball as seriously as life. In 1963 I was in the woods of New Hampshire, writing a novel and listening to the shortwave radio whenever the Dodgers came East. They came East to Yankee Stadium in October,

and kissed the past good-bye. Koufax, Podres, Drysdale, Koufax: four straight. A wipeout. I had been reading too much Mailer and Marx and Freud, and it occurred to me to wonder what a pop-cultural deep-think analyst of the stripe of Leslie Fiedler or Norman O. Brown might have made of the spectacle. I wrote an article rejected by all the best magazines. Here it is:

In October 1963, I turned to a deep study of the World Series, feeling the need to reappraise the nature and destiny of Western man. Stealing from Norman O. Brown and Leslie Fiedler the suspicion that all was not nearly so *mirabile dictu* as everybody pretends, I was dismayed by the scene on my Zenith. When that struggle of contending and incompatible myths concluded so abruptly in Chavez Ravine, I knew, in Antoine Roquentin's revealing phrase, "Something has happened to me, I can't doubt it any more." Indeed, something has happened to all of us—but what?

I submit that we will not find the answer to that question in the sterile chain of mean-minded causalities that oppress the sports pages of our metropolitan newspapers. It lies deeper, festering in the American unconscious. I propose to prove that, in the words of Lionel Trilling, "We are all ill." I address my remarks to those of you intrepid enough

to follow me, with gun and camera as it were, up the anal canal—to find out why, when the Yankees blew four straight, all America cried out with Baudelaire: "Sublime ignominy!"

The truth, the urgent meaning of October 1963, is that 60 million Americans in the spurious safety of their living rooms witnessed nothing less than the Advent of Eros, that Sloucher whose rough hour had come round at last. The victory of Los Angeles over New York was a triumph of Dionysius over Apollo, of hipster (Dodgers) over square (Yankees), of civilian (dour ex-farm boy Alston) over military (pugnacious ex-Marine Houk), of vital self-indulgent nihilistic libido (Hollywood) over Establishmentarian superego (Las Vegas odds)— the symbolic ravishing of Yin by Yang, of Edith Wharton by Jack Kerouac, of . . . and so on.

Let us fix a blank and pitiless gaze on the Bronx that first warm October afternoon. Picture the teams as they disposed at the top of the first inning. Let us ask ourselves: was it an *accident* that the Yankees sent to the mound as their chevalier a man referred to as *Whitey Ford?* Was it an accident that *Whitey* (or *Ford*) sought to thwart the legitimate aspirations of a line-up of nine men (the number of Supreme Court justices), five of whom (a majority) were *black* (Wills, Gilliam, Roseboro and the Davis boys)? And was it an accident that "Whitey" and the "Yankees" were opposed in their campaign of social oppression by . . . a *Brooklyn Jew* (Koufax)?

No! We find in this syzygy of circumstances not accident, but historical design! Not coincidence, but allegory! Not an amusing footnote to von Neumann, but a clash of archetypes in the Play of the Shadow! Now let us cast our cold mind's eye five days forward into time. It is the bottom of the seventh inning of the fourth and final game, in Dodger Stadium. Once again, that old Boer *Whitey* is on the mound for the Yankees, a "money pitcher," as they say. Whitey wheels, deals . . . "Junior" Gilliam (a revealing terminological degradation of a member of the black races) laces a vicious drive down the third-base line . . . Cletis Boyer (a white Southerner) stabs it on one bounce, whirls, and rifles a perfect throw to first. What happens?

Freud has written, "None is too big to be ashamed of being subject to the laws which control the normal and morbid actions"—not even, alas, Joe Pepitone. Let us zoom in by telescopic lens to Pepitone: Yankee first baseman, Bronx-Italian-American *arriviste,* lower middle-class Everyman. Dare we guess at the vague terrors and unacknowledged expectations playing in this man's mind as he waits

with outstretched glove for Boyer's throw? What blind frogs of fantasy stir in the sediment of his subconscious guilt? What antagonistic basilisks of hope and horror raise their snouts? Surely we need not remind ourselves once more of Nelson Algren's "Mammy-freak," a symbol of our time's tortured liberalism. Surely we need not reiterate the dream and the panicked night-sweat of the White American, the psychic exploiter. Let us ask ourselves: if *we* stood in Joe Pepitone's cleated baseball shoes, wouldn't we be torn between contradictory psychopathological desires and needs—on the one hand, the longing for punishment, castration, the come-uppance of death; on the other hand, the longing for chaste Edenic black-white male love? Can you feel the question flex its fingers in your mind as Gilliam hurls himself toward first? Who did Joe Pepitone want "Junior" Gilliam to be? Forgiveness, or Retribution? Love, or Justice? The Raft, or the Rack? *Nigger Jim*—or *Malcolm X?*

He doesn't know! He is paralyzed! The ball eludes his grasp. Gilliam rushes by—achieves second . . . and keeps on going all the way to third. (Repudiation of tokenism: but he is not yet *home.*) That three-base error was more than a simple mistake, or a failure of nerve, or a case of sunspots. It was the confrontation of Hamlet and LeRoi Jones. And while Hamlet was thinking it over, LeRoi Jones scored from third on a fly ball, and Norman Podhoretz—or, perhaps, Koufax is more like the Stern Gang—mopped up with a thousand years of ghetto-cunning. As Irving Howe has written: *"We know that the nightmare is ours."*

Don Drysdale, Tommy Davis and Sandy Koufax (L to R), on the Bob Hope Show after sweeping the Yankees in the 1963 Series. Two years later, when Drysdale was knocked out of the Series opener (Koufax had taken the day off to observe Yom Kippur), Lefty Gomez went to the Dodger clubhouse and said to Walter Alston, "I'll bet you wish Drysdale was Jewish, too."

The Dodgers would be back in 1965, to take Minnesota in seven. And the year after that Baltimore would blow them out in four. And then they would disappear for eight years. But I no longer took it personally. Or so I thought. I was a father, and therefore supposedly an adult, and no longer permitted to be an outlaw, and had other bridges to burn.

In the course of being a father, however, I took my son a couple of years ago to Shea Stadium for a Mets-Dodgers game. His loyalties are uncomplicated. He grew up on the Red Sox and the Mets. Such is his basic decency that he disdains the Yankees, that gang of mercenary gunslingers. Like me, he wouldn't be caught dead in George Steinbrenner's box with the Roy Cohns of this world.

So there we were in the top of the eighth, two Dodgers on, two Dodgers out, and Lopes hit one over the wall, and I was on my feet screaming, and I was alone. My son looked up at me, stricken. I was rooting for the enemy. I had betrayed him.

Well, I wasn't rooting for Los Angeles. I think Los Angeles is a bad idea. And I wasn't rooting for Brooklyn. Brooklyn no longer exists. And I wasn't rooting for the greater glory or the fatter wallet of Walter O'Malley. Walter O'Malley has too much money already. If, in standing and screaming, I betrayed my son, at least I didn't betray myself. I was rooting for my youth, for the idea of the Dodgers that informed that youth, for the beautiful losers and 28-year-old rookies and Don Newcombe and Marian Anderson and my grandmother and my own class origins.

And now: now these new, square Dodgers, keen of eye and firm of jaw and weak in the hands, these Dodgers have managed to lose three World Series in the last five years. That's more like my franchise, the franchise that invented me. I abide in my fandom.

Duke Snider. "A whole country was stirred by [their] high deeds and thwarted longings.... The team was awesomely good and yet defeated. Their skills lifted everyman's spirit and their defeat joined them with everyman's existence." — Roger Kahn

EIGHTH INNING:
1960-1969

Gentlemen of baseball—practical men, as you think yourselves: Not in the name of sentiment, but in the name of absolute, hard-nosed, hard-headed pragmatism, the man you need may be Henry David Thoreau, and what you need may be, not expansion but contraction, not speed but the nourishment of old roots, not closer fences or lowered scoreboards but a renewed connection between the game and its essential followers, not the eye of the camera but the vision of Time Past and Time to Come.

—Mark Harris, 1969

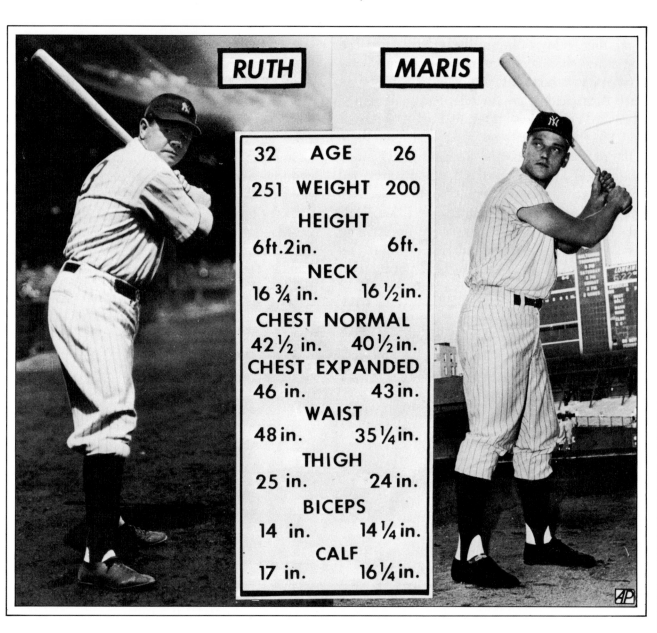

RUTH		MARIS
32	AGE	26
251	WEIGHT	200
	HEIGHT	
6ft.2in.		6ft.
	NECK	
16 ¾ in.		16 ½in.
	CHEST NORMAL	
42 ½ in.		40 ½in.
	CHEST EXPANDED	
46 in.		43 in.
	WAIST	
48 in.		35 ¼in.
	THIGH	
25 in.		24 in.
	BICEPS	
14 in.		14 ¼ in.
	CALF	
17 in.		16 ¼in.

SINCE moving to Baltimore and becoming the Orioles in 1954, the old St. Louis Browns franchise had shown slow but steady improvement. Narrowly escaping the cellar in their first two seasons in Baltimore, the Orioles by 1960 were ready to nose out the defending champion White Sox for second place and exert mild pressure on the Yankees. With an infield built around Brooks Robinson, already the game's best third baseman in only his third full season, manager Paul Richards needed only to find a leader among his multitude of talented young pitchers to go over the top. For the Yankees were clearly ripe for the taking. The 1960 club had only one .300 hitter and came the closest of any pennant winner in history to being without a pitcher who worked in 200 innings. Salvation had come temporarily in the person of Roger Maris, George Weiss's latest prize from the Athletics. A Yankee Triple A farm team before obtaining a major league franchise, Kansas City—so the feeling ran in the other American League cities—had somehow not yet grasped that it was no longer a farm club but an entity of its own.

Pirate farm teams, meanwhile, had contributed Bob Friend, Vern Law and Roy Face—the heart of a pitching staff that was just good enough to bring the parent club its first pennant in 33 years. Although solid at every position, the Pirates had only one offensive leader, Dick Groat, whose .325 average earned him the batting title and the MVP Award. In a season when there were no striking batting achievements—no one in either league had 200 hits—record-minded fans missed noting that Ernie Banks became the only shortstop ever to lead his league in both homers and fielding. Losing by scores of 16–3, 10–0 and 12–0, Pirate pitchers added to their 7.11 Series ERA by giving up nine runs in the seventh game yet came out on the winning end when Bill Mazeroski, who had only 11 homers during the regular season, hit his second game-winning Series homer to give Pittsburgh a 10–9 win and the championship. In a losing cause, the Yankees had the eerie distinction of setting Series records for the most runs, the most hits and the highest team batting average. So perturbed was the Yankee front office by the nightmarish quality of the defeat that a statement was sent to the press

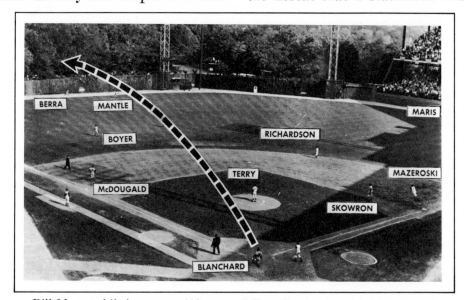

Bill Mazeroski's home run (Above and Top, R) that beat the Yankees in 1960. "I was too excited and too thrilled to think," he said. "It was the greatest moment of my life." Jim Coates, who had been replaced by Ralph Terry, told the losing pitcher, "I sure hate to see it happen to you, but you sure took me off the hook."

Bob Friend, Bill Mazeroski, Roy Face (L to R). Friend
had the sort of record that came from being a good pitcher on a generally bad
team: he is the only man in major league history to lose 200 games in his career
without winning 200. Mazeroski's glove was generally more distinguished than
his bat; he holds seven National League and four major league fielding records.
Face's 1959 record of 18-1 is the best single-season record in history. It also
included the lion's share of 22 straight relief victories over two years.

informing them that Casey Stengel's advanced age now made his retirement imperative.

Scarcely able to contain their glee when Branch Rickey's Pirates languished at the bottom of the National League in the early fifties, the O'Malleys and Stonehams were made to realize by the end of the decade that the Mahatma had one last ace up his sleeve: his proposed Continental League so whetted the appetites of cities without major league franchises that the game could no longer put off expansion. In 1961 the American League installed teams in Los Angeles and Washington—the latter to placate Senator fans when their club moved to Minnesota—and the National League followed a year later by giving Houston its first look at major

Roger Maris in the Yankee Stadium outfield, 1961. "It would have been a
helluva lot more fun," Maris later told Joe Reichler, "if I had never hit
those 61 home runs. . . . All it brought me was headaches."

(Top, L to R) Norman Cash, whose 41 home runs, 132 RBIs and .361 average were overshadowed by the feats of Roger Maris; the Maris swing; Jim Bouton. (Middle, L to R) The Mickey Mantle swing, left-handed; a chronological map of Mantle's injuries; the Mantle swing, right-handed. (Bottom) The 1961 Yankees. "The community of baseball feels Mantle is a great player," wrote Jimmy Cannon. "They consider Maris a thrilling freak who batted .269." Early Wynn, who watched Mantle dress for an All-Star game, said, "I watched him bandage that knee — that whole leg — and I saw what he had to go through every day to play. Seeing those legs, his power becomes unbelievable." Mantle said, "I always loved the game, but when my legs weren't hurting, it was a lot easier to love." Bouton said, "I always felt the same way that the other guys felt about Mantle. I loved him." Asked about Bouton after *Ball Four* was published, Mantle asked, "Jim who?"
  Yankee coach Jim Turner was more loquacious: "That book would go over great in Russia."

Casey of the Mets. Warren Spahn, who pitched for the Mets in his last season and also had played for Stengel with the Braves in 1942, said, "I'm probably the only guy who worked for Stengel before and after he became a genius." Bill Veeck wrote, "The Mets...achieved total incompetence in a single year, while the Browns [which Veeck had owned] worked industriously for almost a decade to gain equal proficiency." Billy Loes said, "The Mets is a very good thing. They give everybody a job. Just like the WPA."

NEW YORK NATIONAL LEAGUE BASEBALL CLUB

Mets

OFFICIAL YEAR BOOK 1962

50¢

league baseball, and New York its first look at minor league baseball played in major league uniforms. From the outset it was obvious that the National League had moved more wisely in its initial expansion. The same was true again in 1969, when the NL put new teams in Montreal and San Diego while the American League went into Seattle by choice, and into Kansas City to avoid a suit by Missourians over commitments the A's had left unhonored when they decamped to Oakland. In each instance one of the American League's expansion franchises had to be shifted precipitously to another city, resulting in further lawsuits and forcing yet a third expansion in 1977 that made the league a clumsy 14-team operation and left city officials in Washington—which had been abandoned by the second edition of the Senators in 1971—still engaged in legal efforts to regain a major league franchise.

The National League's more astute executive acumen began to reflect itself on the playing field as well as in the front office. In All Star play, the best measure of the talent in each league, the National League has won all but two of the 22 games played since 1960. A large part of the reason is the greater efficiency with which its teams have scouted, signed and developed black and Latin talent. In the last 17 years only four National League batting titles, one slugging championship and five home run championships have been won by white players.

By 1961 the disparity between the two leagues in

Gary Peters (L) and Pete Rose, 1963 Rookies of the Year. "The only way I can't hit .300 is if there is something physically wrong with me," Rose said a few years later. He had done it 14 times through 1978.

their recruitment of black and Latin players was evident. Whereas the three top sluggers and three of the five leading hitters in the National League were either black or Latin, the American League's top five hitters and sluggers were all white. The dilution of pitching depth created by expansion served to conceal for that one season a second phenomenon present in the American League: a sharp

Harmon Killebrew (L) had two career distinctions: only Babe Ruth had more seasons with more than 40 home runs—and, in his entire career, Killebrew in 8,147 at bats never once made a successful bunt. It is not recorded whether he ever tried. Juan Marichal (R) pitched a one-hitter in his first major league game, then won 242 more games over the next 16 years.

Tommy Davis. In 1962, wrote Sandy Koufax, "every time there was a man on base he'd knock him in, and every time there were two men on base, he'd hit a double and knock them both in."

Ron Santo. He was loved in Chicago, but not by Leo Durocher. "Five runs ahead, and he'd knock in all the runs I could ask for. One run behind and he was going to kill me."

Sam McDowell. He said, "Almost every batter guesses a few times a game. This is an advantage for me....Hell, most of the time I don't know what I'm going to throw."

(Top, L to R) Bo Belinsky, who split up with actress Mamie Van Doren and said, "I need her like Custer needed Indians"; Willie McCovey, who was asked how he felt pitchers should pitch to him and said, "I'd walk me"; Don Drysdale, who said, "I've got one way to pitch to righties — tight." (Bottom, L to R) Ken Boyer, said *Sports Illustrated*, was "a big, strong guy who can play third base flawlessly, run like a deer and kill you with his bat." Curt Flood set a record for errorless chances accepted, hit .293, sued for his freedom and moved to Europe; Tony Oliva led the AL in batting and in hits his first two big league seasons.

drop in hitting. When Norm Cash won the batting title with a .361 average and Maris broke Ruth's home run record, it obscured for several years the fact that batting titles were being won with the lowest averages since the dead ball era. Cash, in fact, was the sole American Leaguer during the first nine years of the decade to hit over .330. His unexpectedly fine season in 1961 spirited the Tigers to their best record since 1934; that their 101 victories left them eight games short of the Yankees was due not only to Ford's 25–4 season and the slugging of Maris and Mantle but also to the torrid late-season hitting of catcher Elston Howard, and the 29 saves and 15 wins chipped in by reliever Luis Arroyo.

After winning easily over the Reds in the 1961 Series, the Yankees were extended to the full seven games by the Giants the following year, before Bobby Richardson speared Willie McCovey's liner with two on and two out in the ninth inning to preserve Ralph Terry's 1–0 shutout. A 23-game winner, Terry saw the Cy Young Award (until 1967, pitchers in both leagues competed for one award) go to Don Drysdale, who posted 25 wins but missed the one that would have brought the Dodgers the pennant. Headed by Tommy Davis, who won the batting title and knocked home the most runs by any hitter in the last 29 years, and Maury Wills's record-breaking 104 stolen bases, the Dodgers overcame the mid-season loss of Sandy

Koufax and began the final two weeks of the season with a four-game lead over the Giants. But in an ending that evoked memories of 1951, the Giants caught the Dodgers on the season's last day, then won the play-off by erasing a 4–2 Dodger lead in the final game with a four-run ninth inning.

Because Wills's stolen-base record and Maris's 61 homers had come on the new 162-game schedule, there was considerable support for commissioner Ford Frick's notion of placing an asterisk beside their names in the record books. The critical factor for both, however, was not the increased schedule but the fact that they timed their big seasons to correspond with expansion years in their respective leagues. The edge Maris received batting against thinned pitching staffs was readily perceptible. Wills's extra edge was less apparent, but there can be little doubt that he benefited considerably from being able to run against the many pitchers and catchers who were new to the league and to each other—and especially those of the New York Mets, losers in their inaugural season of a twentieth-century record 120 games. In their ineptness the Mets drew attention away from their fellow expansion team, the Houston Colt .45s, who somehow pieced together a decent pitching staff out of the culls thrown their way by the rest of the league and finished ahead of the Cubs. The performances of the Colt .45s and the Los Angeles Angels—winners of 70 games in

Yogi Berra (L) took the Yankees to the seventh game of the 1964 World Series and was fired; his replacement, Johnny Keane (R), took them to last place in little more than one year. In August, 1964, wrote Bill Veeck, Ralph Houk decided that "the Yankees were going to lose; that it was all Yogi Berra's fault; and that Yogi would therefore have to go. When they fooled him and won, he went ahead with his plan just as if they hadn't."

their first season and, remarkably, a third-place team in 1962—deceived some into believing that the expansion teams could quickly become competitive; but it was not until 1969 that any of the four new franchises made a serious pennant bid, and the Mets remain the only one of the first generation of expansion teams to win even a division title.

In 1963 it looked for a time as if it were the Cardinals' turn to make a successful stretch run at the Dodgers' expense, but Koufax's 25–5 record and the ability to come up with his best efforts in big games were too much for St. Louis to match. The Yankees also found Koufax more than they could handle and stunned everyone by losing the Series in four straight games. Being the victims of a Series sweep was only one of the club's firsts that season. A second, and one which had much broader implications, was their winning without a single regular who hit above .287. Hitting in the American League as a whole had sunk so low that Harmon Killebrew won the slugging crown in 1962 on a .242 batting average. Maris's record and the acclaim he received had removed the final hinge on the door that restrained batters from ignoring everything they had learned about hitting in order to aim for home runs. By 1963 even the White Sox had hopped on the bandwagon. In their search to end their record as the only franchise that had never had a home run leader, they employed such wild swingers as Dave Nicholson, who struck out 175 times in only 449 at bats. Other young players like Pete Ward of the White Sox and the Yankees' Tom Tresh started off their careers as solid hitters but soon found their

averages in the low .200's when they lost their timing trying to emulate Maris.

The sixties were replete with players who had outstanding rookie seasons but then were snared by the home run craze and disappeared prematurely from the majors. Most, like Tresh and Ward, played in the American League, but hitters everywhere were swinging so carelessly that pitchers in both circuits began registering vastly increased strikeout totals. In the course of the decade Koufax and Sam McDowell of the Indians became the first pitchers since 1946 to strike out over 300 batters in a season, but it can be argued that these two were so overpowering that they would have stood out in any era. A better measure of the change that pervaded the game was provided by Bob Gibson. Over a career that began in 1959 and ended in 1975, Gibson was considered very difficult to hit but hardly on a par with a Feller or a Koufax. Just once, in fact, did he lead the National League in strikeouts. Yet, by pitching in the era of the free-swinger, Gibson managed to total more strikeouts than any other pitcher in history except Walter Johnson.

In the middle sixties, Tony Oliva and Roberto Clemente stood out in sharp relief. While others were going for the long ball, they never lost sight of a good batter's first objective: making solid contact on each swing. As Latins and repeat batting title winners in 1964 and 1965, they had much in common, but there was an important difference between them. Oliva was already a polished hitter when he came to the majors; Clemente was not. It was not until 1963, his ninth season, that Clemente

The Brothers Alou. (L to R) Jesus, Matty and Felipe. They were together in San Francisco only in 1963, but would eventually register 13 seasons of .300 hitting among them. In 1966, Matty and Felipe finished one-two in batting in the National League.

(Top L, Top C, Middle) Brooks Robinson. "I could field as long as I can remember," he said. "But hitting has been a struggle all my life." In 1966, his 100 RBIs put him fourth in the league. First was teammate Frank Robinson, (Top, R), the triple crown winner, to whom Brooks was runner-up in the MVP voting; said Brooks, "Frank was not out to make friends, but to knock someone on his tail." Boog Powell (Bottom, L) was third in the MVP race. (Bottom, R) Wally Bunker (L) had won 19 games as a 19-year-old in 1964; Jim Palmer (R) won 15 at age 20 in 1966, not including a four-hit Series shutout of the Dodgers. Baltimore pitchers held Los Angeles scoreless for 33 straight innings in the four-game sweep; the Dodgers had but two runs and 17 hits in the entire Series.

lifted his career average over .300 for the first time. In the nine seasons remaining to him before his death he would average over .330 and become the first right-handed hitter since Rogers Hornsby to win four batting titles.

In 1964, the Phillies made their first pennant run since 1950. Taking a six-and-a-half-game lead into the final weeks of the season, the Phils suddenly lost ten in a row and wound up having to play a spoiler's role by beating the Reds in their last game and giving the pennant to the Cardinals. Managers had an unusually large hand in the denouement. The Reds lost the pennant after Freddie Hutchinson, suffering from a fatal cancer, left the club in September, and Johnny Keane's dismissal was imminent before the Cards came on to win. Rookie manager Yogi Berra had dissension problems, but he seemed to save his job when he rallied the Yankees for a 22–6 finish that left the White Sox a game back at the curtain. The Yankees' second Series loss in a row, however, caused general manager Ralph Houk to fire Berra and name as his surprise replacement Keane, who had resigned his post with the Cardinals after the Series.

The year 1964 marked the only time in history that both MVP winners were third basemen. Ken Boyer earned his title by leading in RBIs and playing on the world champs, and Brooks Robinson won by also being an RBI leader and inspiring the Orioles to a third-place finish, just two games off the pace. Outstanding third basemen, usually in short supply, were suddenly abundant. Ron Santo of the Cubs hit .313 and knocked in 114 runs, and the Phils had Dick Allen, the Rookie of the Year. Another Dick—Radatz—didn't play third base, but the Red Sox desperately wished they could get him into the lineup every day. Pitching for a club that won only 72 games, he tallied 16 victories and a record-tying 29 saves.

In 1965 the Reds solved the third-base problem that had been their bane a year earlier by giving the job to Deron Johnson and watching him lead the league in RBIs. But pitcher Jim Maloney exemplified the Reds' luck that season when he pitched two no-hitters, yet nearly wound up the losing pitcher in both; and the pennant went instead to the Dodgers, who had to call Jim Gilliam off the coaching lines after an ill-conceived third-base experiment with John Kennedy and Dick Tracewski failed.

Third base was about the only position that held up for the Yankees in their first year under Johnny Keane. Injuries landed the club in sixth place, its worst finish in 40 years. Given their chance to take command, neither the White Sox nor the Orioles could get their pitching untracked, and the Twins

Roberto Clemente, Carl Yastrzemski, Orlando Cepeda (L to R). Clemente was originally signed by the Dodgers; later, Al Campanis said, "He was the most complete ballplayer I ever saw." Ted Williams said, "I remember the first time I saw Carl Yastrzemski, a youngster in the batting cage...; he positively quivered waiting for the next pitch." Cepeda, said *Sports Illustrated*, "will swing at anything that looks like a baseball."

had the honor of being the first transplanted franchise in the American League to win a pennant. The 1965 Twins were one of the more interesting clubs of the era. Two years earlier the team had led the majors with 225 homers—the most by a club in a nonexpansion year—but the pennant winner received below-average seasons from all its sluggers, was last in fielding and still won rather easily. True, Oliva and Mudcat Grant were the league's top hitter and pitcher, but the real impetus was shortstop Zoilo Versalles, the American League MVP. Versalles led the Twins to victory in the first two games of the Series, but after that, Koufax took over and pitched two shutouts to bring the Dodgers their third world championship in seven years.

The Dodgers stood to make it a fourth championship in 1966 as Koufax won 27 games in his final season and Phil Regan logged 21 saves and a 14–1 record in relief. Opposing them were the Orioles with Boog Powell, the two Robinsons—Brooks and triple crown winner Frank, acquired from the Reds —and a patchwork pitching staff that had set a record for the fewest complete games by a pennant winner. Expecting a feast of Dodger runs in the Series, spectators instead found themselves incredulous as Oriole pitchers conceded a run to the Dodgers in the third inning of the first game and then held them scoreless for the remaining 33 innings of the Series. To add insult, the three pitchers who shut the Dodgers out in the final three games had *among* them totaled but one shutout all season.

It had been over 20 years since New Yorkers had gone two seasons in a row without seeing at least one of their teams in a Series, but after the events in 1966, no one in New York was thinking much about that. The Mets were occupied in celebrating their first season out of the cellar, while the Yankees were mourning a trio of rainouts that had caused them to finish in last place, a half game behind the Red Sox. In this moment—the first such for Yankee fans since 1912—no one had the remotest notion that it was less significant in the long view that the Yankees finished last, than that the Red Sox did not.

Never in modern major league history has a team climbed from last place to the pennant in the space of a single season. When the Red Sox won in 1967 after finishing next to last the year before, historians had to dig back into old American Association archives to find a parallel in the 1889–90 Louisville club. Nowhere was there a parallel to the 1967 American League pennant race itself, however, in which the Red Sox, Tigers, Twins and White Sox entered the last week of the season in a virtual tie for the lead. While the White Sox were being eliminated by Kansas City, the Twins and Red Sox squared off for a two-game series on the final weekend of the season with the Twins a game in front. Boston fans, remembering the numbing losses that

(L to R) Bob Gibson, Mickey Lolich, Denny McLain. When Gibson was in trouble in the seventh game of the 1964 Series, Johnny Keane left him in: "I had a commitment," Keane said later, "to his heart." After Lolich's third victory in the 1968 Series, he said, "All my life somebody else has been the big star and Lolich was number two. I figured my day would come." Number One had been McLain, who won 31 games that year; he would be suspended for erratic behavior three times and, in 1970, would be declared by Bowie Kuhn "not mentally ill." Wrote Roger Angell, "McLain's sole immediate consolation may be the thought that he is the only right-hander in the American League who is officially sane."

had ended the 1948 and 1949 seasons, and having had nothing much to remember since, saw Carl Yastrzemski put on perhaps the greatest display of clutch hitting in history as the Red Sox swept both games. But the season was still not over. With the league now spread out over four different time zones, everyone in Boston had to wait until the Tigers, who had a chance to tie for the pennant, dropped the second game of a doubleheader to the Angels in California.

Yastrzemski's heroics brought him the triple crown and hid events in Chicago where the White Sox came within an ace of winning the pennant without a single regular who hit above .241. Batting marks in the National League were slightly better —thanks mostly to the Pirates, who had Clemente's .357 average and the magic bat of Matty Alou, the last National Leaguer to hit .330 or better four years in a row. The Giants still finished second to the Cardinals despite having a double-play pair who hit .209 and .213, and the Dodgers extended to absurdity their dearth of runs when Jim Lefebvre led the club in RBIs with 55.

The World Series promised to be a slugging contest between the two MVPs, Yastrzemski and the Cardinals' Orlando Cepeda. Yastrzemski did his part, but Cepeda's bat came up lame, and it was left to teammate Lou Brock to take up the slack by hitting .414 and stealing a record seven bases. After being down three games to one, the Red Sox won

twice in a row, and the final game came down to an unprecedented duel between two pitchers, both shooting for their third Series wins. Bob Gibson, injured much of the regular season, won out over Jim Lonborg, but Lonborg still received a Cy Young Award and Red Sox skipper Dick Williams was named Manager of the Year, giving the Sox a clean sweep of the major awards in a season that had begun with their being rated 100-to-1 shots for the pennant.

Yastrzemski concluded the 1968 season with another furious hitting binge. This one did not bring the Red Sox another pennant, but it did lift his average to .301 and spared the American League the embarrassment of a season without a single .300 hitter. When the game's policymakers removed their heads from the sand at the end of the summer, they saw the following: Bob Gibson's 1.12 ERA was the best since 1914; Don Drysdale had pitched a record six straight shutouts and 58⅔ scoreless innings; the Tigers had won the pennant with an infield that had a composite .210 batting average; both leagues had ERAs under 3.00; the Yankees finished in the first division with a team batting average of .214; only two teams scored over four runs a game; the Dodger home run leader was Len Gabrielson, with 10; Bert Campaneris was the lone American Leaguer to make more than 170 hits. Something obviously had to be done to restore a semblance of balance between pitchers and hitters. Moving the

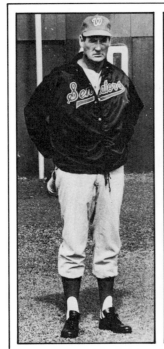

Ted Williams (L), Bowie Kuhn. Williams managed for four seasons, then returned to fishing. Upon his retirement as a player, curiously, he did not hold a single major league batting record. Kuhn became commissioner in 1969; in the ensuing years he presided over the end of the reserve clause, the elevation of a journeyman pitcher's baseball exposé to best-seller status, the beginning of different playing rules for the two leagues, and the institution of World Series games after dark, in New England, in October.

Tom Seaver, Jerry Koosman, Gary Gentry, Nolan Ryan; Tommie Agee (L to R). The Mets' starters in 1969 did not give up a home run for a period of more than one month — and the oldest and most experienced among them was Koosman, who was 25 and had appeared in only 44 big league games before the 1969 season. Agee led the World Champions with an astonishingly low RBI total of 76; there were 24 players in the league who did better.

mound back had worked once, but was certainly too extreme to consider again. Livening the ball had also been tried successfully numerous times, but the problem now wasn't the composition of the ball—it was that contact between ball and bat was occurring all too seldom.

While committees were being drafted to consider solutions to the pitching explosion, the Cardinals tried to become the first National League team in 46 years to win back-to-back world championships. After bombing the Tigers 10–1 in game four, Red Schoendienst's club held a 3–1 lead—then ran into the same problem that befell the Braves in 1958: a red-hot pitcher, in this instance Mickey Lolich. Instead of the Cardinals becoming the first National League repeat champions in 46 years, Lolich became the first left-hander in Series history to win three complete games. Cy Young honors went to Lolich's teammate, Denny McLain, whose 31 victories that season were the most since 1931. With everyone else bemoaning the absence of hitting, fans in Cincinnati were lamenting a pitching collapse that had relegated the game's best offense to a fourth-place finish. Over the past decade the Reds had been assembling a lineup of hitters that seemed unaffected by the batting decline. One of them, Pete Rose, became the first switch-hitter in the century to win a National League batting championship, and another—catcher Johnny Bench—was voted Rookie of the Year, the only nonpitcher to win an award in 1968.

To bring the game out of its slump, club owners rectified in part their earlier, inexplicable appointment of commissioner William Eckert and fired him, naming Bowie Kuhn, a Wall Street attorney, in his place. On the field, the pitching mound was lowered and the strike zone reduced. But these moves were slight compared to the decision to expand teams for the 1969 season to 24 and institute divisional play, with the two winners to meet in a three-out-of-five play-off in October to determine the league pennant winners. The second expansion assured that even if tinkering with the pitching mechanism failed, there would be an increase in hitting.

The Chicago Cubs, perhaps the game's best team during the first two decades of the century, had gone 24 years without a pennant by 1969. In recent seasons the club and its owner, P. K. Wrigley, had become laughingstocks of a sort. Wrigley's refusal to install lights in his home park, once considered an act of admirable individualism, now made his franchise seem anachronistic, and his experiment with rotating managers or "coaches" in the early sixties had given a carnival atmosphere to the Cubs' dugout, where a different ringmaster appeared every few days or so to put the team through its paces. Even Leo Durocher, named manager in 1966, seemed overwhelmed by the task of reviving the Cubs when he brought them home last in his first season. But the following year the team had shot up to third place, and by 1969—with the Dodgers, Reds and Giants conveniently out of the way in the Western Division of the league—Durocher seemed ready to challenge the Cardinals for the top spot in the East.

The division title and ultimately the pennant went instead to the New York Mets, resulting from a chain of circumstances seemingly even more improbable than those present in the American League two years earlier when the Red Sox won. But the only circumstance that mattered was that the expansion draft to stock the new teams had left all

★★★★
FINAL

DAILY ● NEWS

NEW YORK'S PICTURE NEWSPAPER ®

8¢

10¢ OUTSIDE L I AND SUBURBS

Vol. 51. No. 79   New York, N.Y. 10017, Thursday, September 25, 1969★   WEATHER: Partly cloudy, breezy, mild.

WE WIN IT!

It was seven years after Jimmy Breslin had written, "They lost an awful lot of games by one run, which is the mark of a bad team. They also lost innumerable games by 14 runs. This is the mark of a terrible team.... They lost at home and they lost away, they lost at night and they lost in the daytime. And they lost with maneuvers that shake the imagination." It was seven years after Richie Ashburn had said, "I don't know what's going on, but I know I've never seen it before."

The 1969 Mets. Gil Hodges (Above, L) had, as a player, been called by Bill Roeder "the Dodger they don't boo"; as a manager, said Ed Kranepool, "You played his way or you didn't play. He molded young players. He was the turning point." Joseph Durso said, "He led by sheer moral force." (L) In the second row, third from left, is Al Weis, who retired after 1971 with a career .219 batting average; in 1969, he had hit four points below that. Such was the Year of the Mets that Weis batted .455 in a Series that had begun with Baltimore's Brooks Robinson saying, "We are here to prove there is no Santa Claus."

other contenders with at least one glaring weakness, while leaving the Mets relatively untouched. A ninth-place club in 1968, the Mets nevertheless already had the makings of the league's best pitching staff. Operating the following summer with an extra year's experience under their belts, young Met pitchers grew stronger as the season wore on while older pitching staffs in the league were tiring. Even so, the deciding issue was not pitching but center-field play. A rejuvenated Tommie Agee—once the American League's Rookie of the Year but a disappointment ever since—gave the Mets their first quality player at the position; the Cubs entered the final weeks of the season with no one better than Don Young, a .239 hitter whose uncertain fielding cost them a game against the Mets that Durocher insisted was the one that turned the season around.

The Braves team that met the Mets for the league championship had only Hank Aaron left from the club that had ended the last decade with a play-off loss to the Dodgers. Mediocre since abandoning Milwaukee for Atlanta in 1966, the Braves won the National League's first Western Division title by squeezing one last good season out of several veterans, like Cepeda and Tony Gonzalez, after acquiring them in trades. Aaron, Cepeda and Gonzalez all ripped Met pitchers as if it were batting practice, but the Braves got so little pitching of their own that the Mets scored 27 runs in a three-game sweep.

When the Met balloon flew over the Orioles' nest in the World Series, it was expected to be punctured quickly. The Orioles had just finished winning more games than any team since the 1954 Indians and had held the Twins to just five runs in sweeping the pennant series. Against Met pitchers, however, the Orioles hit a meager .146 and won only one game. By triumphing, the Mets became the seventh team to win a world championship during the decade and, more importantly, the first expansion club to rise to the top.

The play of the Kansas City Royals—who gave promise of being the Mets of the future by finishing fourth in their division in their maiden season and showcasing the league's top rookie, Lou Piniella—and the hitting of Twin second baseman Rod Carew, the first American League batter since 1961 to average one hit in every three at bats, consoled some American Leaguers after the Orioles' defeat. But followers of the White Sox and Indians were for the moment beyond solace. The league's top team at the end of the fifties, the White Sox ended the sixties in an all-out struggle with the Seattle Pilots for last place in their division, and the Indians, second best ten years before, had the poorest record in the league. —David Nemec

Marianne Moore at Yankee Stadium; she was also a frequent visitor to Shea Stadium. "Our team," said M. Donald Grant in October, 1969, "finally caught up with our fans."

EXPANSION:
Up from the Minors in Montreal
By Mordecai Richler

PRONOUNCING on Montreal, my Montreal, Casey Stengel once said, "Well, you see they have these polar bears up there and lots of fellows trip over them trying to run the bases and they're never much good anymore except for hockey or hunting deer."

Alas, we have no polar bears up here, but kids can usually heave snowballs at the outfielders at the opening game of the season, and should the World Series ever dare venture this far north, it is conceivable that a game could be called because of a blizzard. Something else. In April, the loudest cheers in the ball park tend to come when nothing of any consequence seems to have happened on the field, understandably baffling the players on visiting teams. These cheers spring from fans who sit huddled with transistor radios clapped to their ears and signify that something of importance has happened, albeit out of town, where either Guy Lafleur or

Pierre Mondou has just scored in a Stanley Cup play-off game.

Baseball remains a popular game here, in spite of the Expos, but hockey is the way of life.

Montreal, it must be understood, is a city unlike any other in Canada. Or, come to think of it, the National League. On the average, eight feet of snow is dumped on us each winter and, whatever the weather, we can usually count on three bank robberies a day here.

This is the city of wonders that gave you Expo in 1967, the baseball Expos a couple of years later and, in 1976, the Olympic Games, its legacy, among other amazing artifacts, a stadium that can seat or intern, as some have it, 60,000 baseball fans. I speak of the monstrous Big O, where our inept Expos disport themselves in summer, their endearing idea of loading the bases being to have two of their runners on second. Hello, hello. Their notion of striking fear into the heart of the opposition being to confront them with muscle, namely one of their pinch-hitting behemoths coming off the bench: group average, .135.

Major league baseball, like the Olympics and the Big O itself, was brought to this long suffering city through the machinations of our very own Artful Dodger, Mayor Jean Drapeau.

Bringing us the Games, he assured Montrealers that it would be as difficult for the Olympics to cost us money as it would be for a man to have a baby. He estimated the total cost of all facilities at $62.2 million but, what with inflation and unfavorable winds, his calculations fell somewhat short of the mark. Counting stationery and long distance calls, the final cost was $1.2 billion. Never mind. To this day our ebullient mayor doesn't allow that the Games were run at a loss. Rather, as he has put it to the rest of us, there has been a gap between costs and revenue. And, considering the spiffy facilities we have been left with, it would be churlish of us to complain.

Ah, the Big O. The largest, coldest slab of poured concrete in Canada. In a city where we endure seven punishing months of winter and spring comes and goes in an afternoon, it is Drapeau's triumph to have provided us with a partially roofed-over $520 million stadium, where the sun never shines on the fans. Tim Burke, one of the liveliest sportswriters in town, once said to me, "You know, there are lots of summer afternoons when I feel like taking in a ball game, but I think, hell, who wants to sit out there in the dark."

"Shivering in the dark" might be more accurate, watching the boys lose line drives in the seams of the artificial turf.

"The outfield," another wag remarked, "looks just like the kind of thing my aunt used to wear."

Furthermore, come cap day or bat night ours is the only park in the National League that fills a social office, letting the poor know where to get off, which is to say, the scruffy kids in the bleachers are beyond the pale. They don't qualify.

It's a shame, because the Expos, admittedly major league in name only, came to a town rich in baseball history and, to begin with, we were all charged with hope. In their opening game, on April 9, 1969, the Expos took the Mets 11–10 at Shea Stadium, collecting three homers and five doubles. Five days later, the 29,184 fans who turned up for the home opener were electrified by an announcement over the public address system. "When the

Newark Bears managers Tris Speaker (L), Walter Johnson. "A man could spend an entire career in the minor leagues," Robert Creamer wrote, "and major league veterans who had seen their best days would come back down and play another half dozen seasons in the high minors." Neither of these men was a playing manager, although Johnson did pitch one game for the Bears.

(Top) The 1913 Newark Club, International League champions. Dick Rudolph, who would lead the 1914 "Miracle Braves" to a World Series victory, is in top row, second from left. (Bottom) The 1929 Rochester Red Wings' infield. Specs Toporcer (third from L) was on his way down from the Cardinals; Rip Collins (R) was on his way up. Although Collins enjoyed nine big league seasons, he spent 16 years in the minors; in 1930 he led the International League with 180 RBIs and a .376 average.

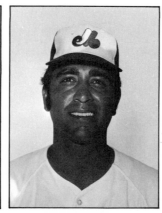

Early Expos. (L to R) Ken Singleton, Rusty Staub, Mike Torrez, Mack Jones. Singleton, who had the distinction of living in the same Mt. Vernon, N.Y., house that Ralph Branca had been born in, was a bona fide star, but suffered from an allergy to the material of which Expos uniforms were made. Staub, *le Grand Orange*, went so far as to take French lessons. Torrez, like Singleton, married a local woman, and also like Singleton continued to live in Montreal long after being traded away. Jones was not much of a player — .252 career batting average, 133 home runs in ten years — but he and Staub were all the 1969 Expos had.

Expos play a doubleheader," we were informed, "the second game will go the full nine innings, not seven."

Those of us old enough to remember baseball's glory here, the Montreal Royals of the old International League, nodded our heads, impressed. This was the big time. "Montreal," said Warren Giles, president of the National League, "is a growing and vibrant city." Yessirree. And we hollered and stamped our feet as our champions took to the field under the grim gaze of manager Gene Mauch, who had the look of a Marine drill sergeant.

I still have that incomparably bubbly opening day program. *Votre première équipe des ligues ma-jeures. Vol. 1, No. 1. Publié par Club de Baseball Montreal Ltée.* "The Expos believe they landed a real prize when they snatched Gary Sutherland from the Philadelphia Phillies. Big things are expected from John Bateman, the former Houston Astros' fine receiver. Bob Bailey impressed everybody with his tremendous hustle. Ty Cline is a two-way player. 'In the field,' said Larry Shepard, manager of the Pittsburgh Pirates, 'Don Bosch can be compared with none other than Willie Mays.' Larry Jaster has youth on his side. This may be the year Don Shaw comes into his own. Angel Hermoso is one of the fine young Expo prospects the scouts have hung a 'can't miss' label on. On a given

The Original Expos. Staub is in front, third from right; Jones is in front, fourth from left. Third row, second from left, is Claude Raymond, the first native-born French Canadian to play for the Expos. Until he arrived in Montreal he had been called "Frenchy" everywhere he played.

Parc Jarry. The right field bleachers were, rather hopefully, called "Jonesville," at least until Mack Jones was dropped from the club in

1971. Claude Raymond said it was "for the people of Montreal what Ebbets Field is for the people of Brooklyn."

day, Mike Wegener, only 22, can throw with the best. Don Hahn was a standout performer during spring training. Bob Reynolds' main forte is a blistering fastball. Expansion could be 'just what the doctor ordered' for Coco Laboy."

To be fair, the original Expos included Rusty Staub, sweet Mack Jones and Bill Stoneman, a surprisingly effective player who pitched two no-hitters before his arm gave out. Manny Mota, another original draft choice, was one of the first to be sent packing by a management that was to become celebrated for its lame-headed dealings, its most spectacular blunder being a trade that sent Ken Singleton and Mike Torrez to Baltimore for a sorearmed Dave McNally and a totally ineffective Rich Coggins. It should also be noted that the Expos did take their home opener, defeating the Cardinals 8–7, and that tiny parc Jarry, where they were to play, futile in their fashion, for another eight years, was a charming, intimate stadium with the potential to become another Fenway Park.

Opening day, I recognized many of the plump faces in the box seats on the first-base line. Among them were some of the nervy kids who used to skip school with me on weekday afternoons to sit in the left-field bleachers of Delormier Downs, cheering on the Royals and earning nickels fetching hot dogs for strangers. Gone were the AZA windbreakers, the bubble gum, the scuffed running shoes, the pale wintry faces. These men came bronzed to the ball park from their Florida condominiums. Now they wore foulards and navy blue blazers with brass buttons; they carried Hudson's Bay blankets in plastic cases for their bejeweled wives; and they sucked on Monte Cristos, mindful not to spill ashes on their Gucci sandals. Above all, they radiated pleasure in their own accomplishments and the occasion. And why not? This was an event and there they were, inside, looking out at last, right on the firstbase line. Look at me. "Give it some soul, Mack," one of them shouted.

An article in that memorable opening day program noted that while the province of Quebec had never been known as a hotbed of major league talent, we had nevertheless produced a few ballplay-

Olympic Stadium, 1976. The city had obtained a major league franchise by promising that a stadium seating 55,000 would be open by 1971; it took six years longer than that. When the franchise was granted to

Montreal, Judge Robert Cannon of Milwaukee — representing that city's attempt to return to the majors — said, "It's unthinkable that baseball would do this to cities in the United States, which made baseball what it is."

ers, among them pitchers Claude Raymond and Ron Piché, and that three more native sons, Roland Gladu, Jean-Pierre Roy and Stan Bréard had once played for another ball club here, the Montreal Royals.

O, I remember the Royals, yes indeed, and if they played in a Montreal that was not yet growing and vibrant, it was certainly a place to be cherished.

Betta Dodd, "The Girl in Cellophane," was stripping at the Gayety, supported by 23 Kuddling Kuties. Cantor Moishe Oysher, The Master Singer of his People, was appearing at His Majesty's. The Johnny Holmes Band, playing at Victoria Hall, featured Oscar Peterson; and a sign in the corner cigar-and-soda warned Ziggy Halprin, Yossel Hoffman and me that

LOOSE TALK COSTS LIVES!
Keep It Under
Your
STETSON

I first became aware of the Royals in 1943. Our country was already 76 years old, I was merely 12, and we were both at war.

MAY U BOAT SINKINGS EXCEED REPLACEMENTS; KING DECORATES 625 CANADIANS ON BIRTHDAY

Many of our older brothers and cousins were serving overseas. Others on the street were delighted to discover they suffered from flat feet or, failing that, arranged to have an eardrum punctured by a specialist in such matters.

R.A.F. HITS HARD AT COLOGNE AND HAMBURG
2,000 Tons of Bombs
Rain on Rhine City

On the home front, sacrifices were called for. On St. Urbain Street, where we served, collecting salvage, we had to give up American comic books for the duration. Good-bye, Superman, so long, Captain Marvel. Instead, we were obliged to make do with shoddy Canadian imitations printed in black and white. And such was the shortage of ballplayers that the one-armed outfielder, Pete Gray, got to play for the Three Rivers club on his way to the Browns and French Canadians, torn from the local sandlots, actually took to the field for our very own Royals: Bréard, Gladu, Roy.

Even in fabled Westmount, where the very rich were rooted, things weren't the same anymore. H.R., emporium to the privileged, enjoined Westmount to "take another step in further aid of the Government's all out effort to defeat aggression!"

Ollie Carnegie (L), Pete Gray. Carnegie, who began his *minor* league career at 31, was a classic International League star. He played 13 seasons for Buffalo, hitting .310 with 258 home runs (still an IL record), but never spent so much as a day in the majors. Gray — shown here as Southern Association MVP with the Memphis Chicks — played his first professional ball in Three Rivers, Quebec, in the Canadian-American League, in 1942.

(Top, L) Managers Burt Shotton (L) of the Columbus Red Birds and Ossie Vitt of the Newark Bears, at the 1937 Little World Series. (Top, R) Managers Del Bissonette (L) of the Toronto Maple Leafs and Buddy Hassett of the Newark Bears, 1949. (Bottom) Warren Sandell, Bruno Betzel, Clay Hopper, Barney DeForge (L to R), Opening Day, Jersey City, 1946. Betzel had been manager of the Royals before Hopper, who on this day became Robinson's first manager in Organized Baseball. A Mississipian, Hopper, who had early in the season asked Rickey, "Do you really think a nigger's a human being?", gave this farewell to Robinson when the season ended: "You're a great ballplayer and a fine gentleman. It's been wonderful having you on the team."

(L to R) Dan Bankhead; Jim Gilliam and Joe Black; Sam Jethroe. Bankhead would be the first black pitcher in the major leagues and, in 1951, the first black manager in the minors, at Farnham, Quebec, in the Provincial League. Gilliam and Black followed the same underground railway track as Robinson, from the black leagues to Montreal to Rookie of the Year awards in Brooklyn. Jethroe took the same path through Montreal to the Boston Braves.

HOLT RENFREW ANNOUNCE THAT BEGINNING JUNE FIRST <u>NO DELIVERIES</u> OF MERCHANDISE WILL BE MADE ON <u>WEDNESDAYS</u>

This forethought will help H.R. to save many gallons of gasoline...and many a tire...for use by the government. Moreover, will it not thrill you to think that the non-delivery of your dress on Wednesday will aid in the delivery of a 'block-buster' over the Ruhr...Naples...Berlin...and many other places of enemy entrenchment?

Our parents feared Hitler and his Panzers, but Ziggy, Yossel and I were in terror of Branch Rickey and his scouts.

Nineteen thirty-nine was not only the date we had gone to war, it was also the year the management of the Royals signed a contract with Mr. Rickey, making them the number one farm club of the Brooklyn Dodgers. This dealt us young players of tremendous promise, but again and again, come the Dodgers' late-summer pennant drive, the best of the bunch were harvested by the parent team. Before we had even reached the age of puberty, Ziggy, Yossel and I had learned to love with caution. If after the first death there is no other, an arguable notion, I do remember that each time one of our heroes abandoned us for Ebbets Field, it stung us badly. We hated Mr. Rickey for his voracious appetite. "There has been no mention officially that the Dodgers will be taking Flowers," Lloyd MacGowan wrote in the *Star* on a typical day, "but Rickey was in Buffalo to watch the team yesterday. The Dodgers can't take Flowers without sending down a flinger, but chances are the replacement for the burly lefty will hardly be adequate."

The International League, as we knew it in the forties, its halcyon years, was Triple A and comprised of eight teams: Montreal, Toronto, Syracuse, Jersey City, Newark, Rochester, Baltimore and Buffalo. Newark was the number one farm team of the Yankees and Jersey City filled the same office for the Giants. But organized baseball had actually come to Montreal in 1898, the Royals then fielding a team in the old Eastern League, taking the pennant in their inaugural year. In those days the Royals played in Atwater Park, which could seat 12,000, and from all accounts was a fine and intimate stadium, much like parc Jarry. During the 21 years the Royals played there they offered Montreal, as sportswriter Marc Thibault recently wrote, "*du baseball parfois excitant, plus souvent qu'autrement, assez détestable,*" the problem being the troubled management's need to sell off their most accomplished players for ready cash. Be that as it may, in 1914, long before we were to endure major league baseball in name only here, George Herman Ruth came to Atwater Park to pitch for the Baltimore Orioles. Two years later, the team folded, a casualty of World War I, and another 11 years passed before the Royals were resuscitated.

It was 1928 when George Tweedy "Miracle Man" Stallings bought the then-defunct Syracuse franchise and built Delormier Downs, a stadium with a 22,000 capacity, at the corner of Ontario and Delormier streets. An overflow crowd of 22,500, including Judge Kenesaw Mountain Landis, was at the opening game, which the Royals won, defeating the fearsome Reading Keystones, 7–4. Twelve

International League champions. (Top) 1950 Montreal Royals. On the way up on this team were Sam Jethroe (front, extreme L) and Don Newcombe (rear, second from R); going down was Al Gionfriddo (front, fifth from L); going nowhere, but eventually to a Hollywood career that paralleled his baseball one in mediocrity, was Chuck Connors (rear, fifth from L). (Bottom) Rochester Red Wings, 1951. Steve Bilko (middle row, third from L) fit Howard Senzel's statement on his hometown team: "Players who played for the Red Wings would, by definition, always be minor." He hit nothing but homers in the minors, and nothing at all in several tries in the majors. The Red Wings' manager was Johnny Keane (front, fifth from L).

months later Stallings died. In 1929, not a vintage year for the stock market, the Royals finished fourth. Two years later, Delormier Stadium, like just about everybody, was in deep trouble. There were tax arrears and a heavy bank debt to be settled. The original sponsors resigned.

In the autumn of 1931 a new company was formed by a triumvirate which included a man who had made millions in gas stations, the rambunctious, poker-playing J. Charles-Emile Trudeau, father of our present prime minister. Another associate of the newly-formed club, Frank "Shag" Shaughnessy, cunningly introduced the play-off system in 1933, and two years later became the club's general manager. In 1935, fielding a team that included Fresco Thompson, Jimmy Ripple and Del Bissonette, the Royals won their first pennant since 1898. However, they finished poorly in '37 and '38 and, the following year, Mr. Rickey surfaced, sending in Burleigh Grimes to look after his interests.

Redemption was at hand.

Bruno Betzel came in to manage the team in 1944, the year the nefarious Branch Rickey bought the Royals outright, building it into the most profitable club in all of minor league baseball, its fans loyal but understandably resentful of the head office's appetite, praying that this summer the Dodgers wouldn't falter in the stretch, sending down for fresh bats, strong arms, just when we needed them most.

The Royals finished first in 1945, and in '46 and '48 they won both the pennant and the Little World Series. They were to win the pennant again in '51 and '52, under Clay Hopper, and the Little World Series in '53, when they were managed by Walter Alston. The Royals fielded their greatest team in 1948, the summer young Duke Snider played here, appearing in 77 games before he was snatched by Mr. Rickey. Others on that memorable team included Don Newcombe, Al Gionfriddo, Jimmy Bloodworth, Bobby Morgan and Chuck Connors. The legendary Jackie Robinson and Roy Campanella had already come and gone.

Sam Jethroe was here in 1949 and two years later Junior Gilliam was at third and George Shuba hit 20 home runs. In 1952, our star pitcher was southpaw Tommy Lasorda, the self-styled Bob Feller of the International League. Lasorda pitched his last game for the Royals on July 4, 1960, against Rochester, which seemed to be hitting him at will. Reminiscing recently, Lasorda recalled, "I knew I was in trouble when I saw our manager's foot on the top of the dugout step. If the next guy gets on base, I'm going to be out of there. I turned my back to the hitter and looked up toward the sky. Lord, I said, this is my last game. Get me out of this jam. I make the next pitch and the guy at the plate hits the damnedest line drive you ever saw. Our third baseman, George Risley, gets the tips of his fingers on it but can't hang on. The ball bloops over his

Jackie Robinson (L, in Kansas City Monarchs uniform), signing his Montreal contract, flanked by (L to R) Royals president Hector Racine, Branch Rickey Jr. and J. Romeo Gauvreau, Royals vice president. Jimmy Powers wrote in the New York *Daily News*, "We don't believe Jackie Robinson, colored college star signed by the Dodgers for one of their farm teams, will ever play in the big leagues. We question Branch Rickey's pompous statements that he is another Abraham Lincoln and that he has a heart as big as a watermelon and he loves all mankind."

Tommy Lasorda and Ron Hunt (inset). Lasorda played nine years with the Royals and won more games than any other pitcher in the team's history. He wrapped this experience around 26 major league innings, in one of which he tied the record for most wild pitches in one inning. Hunt, with the Expos, set the season record for most times hit by pitch (50, in 1971). "Everything worthwhile in life is worth a price," he said. "Some people give their bodies to science; I give mine to baseball."

hand and our shortstop, Jerry Snyder, grabs it. He fires it to Harry Shewman at second base, who relays it to Jimmy Korada at first. Triple play."

A year later the Royals were dissolved and in 1971 the Delormier Stadium was razed to make way for the Pierre Dupuy School.

On weekday afternoons kids were admitted free into the left-field bleachers and by the third inning the more intrepid had worked their way down as far as the first-base line. Ziggy, Yossel and I would sit out there in the sun, cracking peanuts, nudging each other if a ball struck the Miss Sweet Caporal sign, hitting the young lady you-know-where. Another diversion was a porthole in the outfield wall. If a batter hit a ball through it, he was entitled to a two-year supply of Pal Blades. Heaven.

Sunday afternoons the Royals usually played to capacity crowds, but come the Little World Series fans lined up on the roof of the adjoining Grover Knit-To-Fit Building and temporary stands were set up and roped off in center field. Consequently, as my cousin Seymour who used to sit there liked to boast, "If I get hit on the head, it's a ground rule home run." After the game, we would spill out of the stadium to find streetcars lined up for a half mile, waiting to take us home.

In 1945, the Royals acquired one of ours, their first Jewish player, Kermit Kitman, a William and Mary scholarship boy. Our loyalty to the team was redoubled. Kitman was a centerfielder and an opening day story in *La Presse* declared, *"Trois des meilleurs porte-couleurs du Montréal depuis l'ouverture de la saison ont été ses joueurs de champ: Gladu, Kitman et Yeager. Kitman a exécuté un catch sensationnel encore hier après-midi sur le long coup de Torres à la 8e manche. On les verra tous trois à l'oeuvre cet après-midi contre le Jersey-City lors du programme double de la 'Victoire' au stade de la rue Delormier."*

In his very first time at bat in that opening game against the Skeeters, Kitman belted a homer, something he would not manage again until August. Alas, in the later innings he also got doubled off second. After the game, when he ventured into a barbershop at the corner of St. Catherine and St. Urbain, a man in another chair studied him intently. "Aren't you Kermit Kitman?" he asked.

"Yeah," he allowed, grinning, remembering his homer.

"You son-of-a-bitch, you got doubled off second, it cost me five hundred bucks."

Lead-off hitter for the Royals, Kitman was entitled to lower berth one on all their road trips.

Only 22 years old, but a college boy, he was paid somewhat better than most: $650 monthly for six months of the year. And if the Royals went all the way, winning the Little World Series, he could earn another $1,800. On the road, his hotel bill was paid and he and the other players were each allowed three bucks a day meal money.

There was yet another sea change in the summer of 1946. After scouting what were then called the Negro Leagues for more than a year, Mr. Rickey brought the first black player into organized baseball. So that spring the Royals could not train in the regular park in Daytona, which was segregated, but had to train in Kelly Field instead.

Actually, Jackie Robinson had been signed on October 23, 1945, in the offices of the Royals at Delormier Stadium, club president Hector Racine saying, "Robinson is a good ball player and comes highly recommended by the Brooklyn Dodgers. We paid him a good bonus to sign with our club."

The bonus was $3,500 and Robinson's salary was $600 monthly.

"One afternoon in Daytona," Kermit Kitman told me, "I was lead-off hitter and quickly singled. Robinson came up next, laying down a sacrifice bunt and running to first. Stanky, covering the sack, tagged him hard and jock-high. Robinson went down, taking a fist in the balls. He was mad as hell, you could see that, but Rickey had warned him, no fights. He got up, dusted himself off and said nothing. After the game, when he was resting, Stanky came over to apologize. He had been testing his temper, under orders from Rickey."

Kitman, a good glove man, was an inadequate hitter. Brooklyn born, he never got to play there. Following the 1946 season he was offered a place on the roster of another team in the Dodger farm system, but elected to quit the game instead.

The 1946 season opened for the Royals on April 18, with a game in Jersey City. The AP dispatch for that day, printed in the Montreal *Gazette,* ran: "The first man of his race to play in modern organized baseball smashed a three-run homer that carried 333 feet and added three singles to the Royals' winning 14–1 margin over Jersey City. Just to make it a full day's work, Robinson stole two bases, scored four times and batted in three runs. He was also charged with an error."

Robinson led the International League in hitting that year with a .349 average. He hit three home runs, batted in 66 runs, stole 40 bases, scored 113 runs and fielded .985 at his second-base position. And, furthermore, Montreal adored him, as no other ballplayer who has been here before or since.

Jackie Robinson. The next year, he would be in Brooklyn, where, wrote Roger Kahn, "He charged at ball games....His bunts, his steals, and his fake bunts and fake steals humiliated a legion of visiting players. He bore the burden of a pioneer and the weight made him more strong. If one can be certain of anything in baseball, it is that we shall not look upon his like again."

No sooner did Robinson reach first base, on a hit or a walk, than the fans roared with joy and hope, our hearts going out to him as he danced up and down the base path, taunting the opposing pitcher with his astonishing speed.

We won the pennant that year and met the Louisville Colonels, another Dodger farm club, in the Little World Series. The series opened in Louisville, where Robinson endured a constant run of racial insults from the Colonels' dugout and was held to a mere single in two games. Montreal evened the series at home and returned to Delormier Downs for the seventh and deciding game. "When they won it," Dick Bacon recently wrote, recalling that game in the 200th anniversary issue of the *Gazette,* "Jackie was accorded an emotional send-off unseen before or since in this city.

"First they serenaded him in true French Canadien spirit with, '*Il a gagné ses Epaulettes,*' and then clamored for his reappearance on the field.

"When he finally came out for a curtain call, the fans mobbed him. They hugged him, kissed him, cried, cheered and pulled and tore at his uniform while parading him around the infield on their shoulders.

"With tears streaming down his face, Robinson finally begged off in order to shower, dress and catch a plane to the States. But the riot of joy wasn't over yet.

"When he emerged from the clubhouse, he had to bull his way through the waiting crowd outside the stadium. The thousands of fans chased him down Ontario Street for several blocks before he was rescued by a passing motorist and driven to his hotel.

"As one southern reporter from Louisville, Kentucky, was to write afterward:

"'It's probably the first time a white mob of rioters ever chased a Negro down the streets in love rather than hate'."

That was a long time ago.

I don't know whatever became of Red Durrett. Marvin Rackley, of whom Mr. Rickey once said, "I can see him in a World Series, running and hitting," has also disappeared. Roland Gladu, who got to play 21 games with the old Boston Braves, failed to sign the major league skies with his ability. Robinson died in 1972 and in 1977 a plaque to his memory was installed in the chilly Big O. Jean-Pierre Roy now does the French-language broadcasts for the Expos and a graying but still impressive Duke Snider is also back, doing the color commentary for Expo games on CBC-TV, trying his best to be kind to an uninspired bunch without compromising himself.

The Expos have yet to play .500 ball or, since Mack Jones's brief sojourn here, come up with a player that the fans can warm to. But there is hope. Next year, or maybe five years from now, the Big O will be completed. The retractable roof will be set in place. And, in this city of endless winter and short hot summers, it will be possible to watch baseball played under a roof, on artificial grass, in an air-conditioned, possibly even centrally-heated, concrete tomb.

Progress.

Jackie Robinson signs his Brooklyn contract, April 11, 1947. "One of the reasons for the reception we received in Montreal," he said, "was that people there were proud of the team that bore their city's name."

NINTH INNING:
1970-1980

Baseball's status in the life of the nation is so pervasive that it would not strain credulity to say the Court can take judicial notice that baseball is everybody's business. To put it mildly and with restraint, it would be unfortunate indeed if a fine sport and profession, which brings surcease from daily travail and an escape from the ordinary to most inhabitants of this land, were to suffer in the least because of undue concentration by any one or any group on commercial and profit considerations. The game is on higher ground; it behooves everyone to keep it there.

—Judge I. B. Cooper, Flood v. Kuhn, 1970

DECADE after decade, they had followed, most of them, the same path. Signed off the sandlots by major league scouts, they had then spent several years honing their skills in the minor leagues before being summoned to the parent club where, barring trades or waiver deals, they were indentured to spend the remainder of their careers. Some, seemingly blessed with extraordinary talent, received large bonuses when they initially committed their signatures to major league contracts. Most received nothing and considered themselves fortunate merely to get the chance. All, however, had one thing in common: given the choice, they put baseball ahead of everything else.

By 1980 this was no longer true. Prospective major league players were not randomly signed off the sandlots but selected in a draft carefully devised to equalize the amateur talent as much as possible among the 26 teams. Few spent any appreciable time in the minor leagues, and none thought of themselves as irrevocably bound to the team with which they began their careers. The notion that they were fortunate to be in a major league uniform was considered naïve by most. Many had gravitated to baseball by default rather than by choice, after being unable to succeed in other professional sports that oftentimes paid better and offered more opportunities for developing outside business interests. In consequence, where once almost all the country's top athletes had grown up wanting nothing more

Earl Weaver. His motto was "bad ballplayers make good managers." He never played a game in the major leagues, and said the best part of his game was "the base on balls." His record over 12 years demonstrated that only Joe McCarthy — if anyone — was better.

than to be baseball players, a goodly portion of the modern generation of major leaguers had grown up without baseball much on their minds.

Denny McLain, Hawk Harrelson and Curt Flood were three outstanding examples of the new breed. Twice a Cy Young winner, McLain realized there was big money to be made from his reputation as a ballplayer and tried a number of business ventures. One, unfortunately for McLain, was as a

Jim Palmer, Dave McNally, Pat Dobson, Mike Cuellar (L to R). Each man won at least 20 games in 1971; with such pitching, it was easy for Earl Weaver to devise strategy: "My best game plan," he said, "is to sit on the bench and call out specific instructions like, 'C'mon, Boog,' 'Get hold of one, Frank' or 'Let's go, Brooks.'"

Roberto Clemente. Roger Angell wrote that, in the 1971 Series, he played "a kind of baseball that none of us had ever seen before — throwing and running and hitting at something close to the level of absolute perfection, playing to win but also playing the game almost as if it were a form of punishment for everyone else on the field." (Insets) Steve Blass (T), Nelson Briles (B). Blass was the Pirates' best pitcher through 1972 — then, inexplicably, without warning, his control was gone. In Series play, Briles won a game in '67, lost one in '68, pitched a shutout in '71 — and sang the National Anthem *a cappella* in 1973.

Joe Torre, Dick Allen, Ferguson Jenkins (L to R). Torre broke in with the Braves two years after their last pennant, was traded to the Cards the year after that team's last, then to the Mets two years after theirs. He batted .297 in an 18-year career. Allen's troublous disposition may have resulted from the fact that he broke in with the Phillies in 1964. He had 138 RBIs, was Rookie of the Year and lived through the greatest choke in modern baseball history. In 1980, Jenkins became one of the few men with 100 wins in each major league.

bookmaker, and resulted in his suspension for half of the 1970 season. Returning to uniform out of shape, he couldn't regain his fastball and was never again more than an average pitcher. Harrelson also missed most of the 1970 season, but unlike McLain his absence was by choice. Annoyed when the Red Sox traded him to the Indians, he decided baseball wasn't the only game in town and elected to try the professional golf circuit in the belief that it would bring him more autonomy and money. He may have found the former, but certainly not the latter. Flood's dispute with the game was also the result of a trade. Sent by the Cardinals to the Phillies in 1970, he refused to report and filed an antitrust suit against baseball's reserve clause, claiming the right to sign with any team of his choice. Flood ultimately lost his case, but he set in motion a series of similar suits by others like Andy Messersmith and Dave McNally that resulted in players earning the legal right to perform one season without a signed contract, then to become free agents at liberty to sell their services to the highest bidder.

While many of the other clubs were manned by players who had their minds elsewhere, the Reds began the decade by demonstrating that they still thought about nothing but baseball. Winning their division by 14½ games, they had no difficulty in the pennant series with a Pirate team that had won in the East with a .549 percentage after Met pitchers stumbled and the Cubs still could not fill their void in center field. With an attack built around Pete Rose, Tony Perez and Johnny Bench, who that season became the first catcher ever to be a league leader in homers and RBIs, the Reds also had the best pitching in their division but were overmatched against the Orioles' three 20-game winners —Jim Palmer, Dave McNally and Mike Cuellar.

For the second year in a row this trio had dispensed with the Twins in three straight games in the pennant series, yet curiously that season's Cy Young Award went to Twin right-hander Jim Perry. National League awards were dispatched without exception to the most obviously deserving, but the season's most extraordinary performance was turned in by a nonaward winner, Giant outfielder Bobby Bonds, who struck out a record 189 times and yet still registered 200 hits and a .302 average.

Just about all the achievement awards in the National League in 1971 went to Joe Torre of the Cardinals, who hit .363. A catcher during his early career, Torre later played both first and third base. He just missed becoming one of the few players in history who saw action in over 1,000 games at each of two different positions, but Ernie Banks, one of his contemporaries, made it. Playing his last innings in 1971, Banks ended 19 years of emptiness with the Cubs that were made yet more frustrating by the club's disappointing pennant misses during his final seasons. In spite of having the league's top winner, Ferguson Jenkins, the Cubs dropped another notch in their division as the Pirates used Dave Giusti's 30 saves to support tottering starting pitchers all season and then got three more saves from him in their pennant series win over the Giants.

After sweeping the Oakland A's in the American League pennant series, the Orioles had won three straight pennants and nine straight pennant series games. Heavily favored over the Pirates in the 1971 World Series, Baltimore manager Earl Weaver had four 20-game winners—the three of the year before plus Pat Dobson—and three relief pitchers, Eddie Watt, Dick Hall and Pete Richert, who were among the best in the game. All pitched decently in the Series, but none was exceptional. The

(L to R) Yogi Berra as Mets manager; Mrs. Joan Payson and Willie Mays; M. Donald Grant. Berra was first hired by the Mets, wrote Bill Veeck, as "the easiest possible way of bringing the Yankee fans into Shea Stadium." "Willie is with the Mets," wrote Charles McCabe, "because a rich Long Island lady had a crush on him." Grant, who presided over the destruction of what he had built when he traded Tom Seaver, in 1957 had a different sort of distinction: he was the only member of the board of the Giants to vote against moving to San Francisco. "It just tears my heart to see them go," he said at the time.

Pirates had a trio of pitchers who were. Giusti was one; the other two were Nelson Briles and Steve Blass, both of whom had relied on Giusti's relief work during the season but between them pitched three complete games in the Series and gave up only two runs. When Roberto Clemente provided the offense by hitting .414, Pirate manager Danny Murtaugh, after a wait of 11 years, found himself again the leader of a world champion.

The decision to divide each league into two divisions to promote closer races had paid dividends for the first time in 1971 when the Giants, in a near reversal of the script that had been enacted 20 years earlier, led the Dodgers by 8½ games on September 5, then had to scramble all month to hold on to the one-game margin by which they eventually won. Below-average seasons by Giant pitching aces Juan Marichal and Gaylord Perry had prevented the club from being a runaway winner, but the other Bay Area team, the A's, utilized a superb season by Vida Blue to give the franchise its first taste of postseason play in 40 years. Last in 1967, their final year in Kansas City, the A's had borne out owner Charlie Finley's contention that a change of scene was essential, if they were ever to improve, by finishing above .500 their very first season in Oakland and showing a gain in every year since.

A second club in the American League's Western Division was making progress of a different kind. After suffering the label "Hitless Wonders" for 70 years, in 1971 the White Sox saw Bill Melton become their first player to lead the league in homers, then astounded their followers again a year later by having their second in Dick Allen, who was making Chicago his fourth stop in a career that was

beginning to resemble that of early-day gypsy Bill Keister. Allen, probably the most talented hitter of the era, had played for several years now with a damaged hand that would have finished a lesser player. In addition, he carried a reputation for being unmanageable that was partly of his own making and partly a result of the inability of the managers he played under to adapt to the changing attitudes of the times. Players were no longer content to put in their nine innings and then blend quietly into the decor of their hotel rooms and wait for the next day's game. Most saw baseball not as a raison d'être but rather as just one facet of their lives and not necessarily the most vital or the most interesting. Two such players were the batting title winners in 1970, Rico Carty and Alex Johnson. Injuries and clashes with managers had reduced both of them to part-time players by 1972. Carty would again star when the American League began using Designated Hitters a year later, but Johnson, nearly as talented as Allen, ended his career with most of his vast potential still unrealized.

Contrasted to Johnson were Billy Williams of the Cubs, Joe Rudi of the A's, Wilbur Wood of the White Sox and practically every member of the 1972 Reds and Tigers. Williams, after ten seasons of solid but unspectacular play, won the National League batting title in 1972 at the age of 34. Wood, nearing 31, led the American League in wins just a year after being converted from a relief pitcher to a starter. A weak hitter at the beginning of his career, Rudi led the American League in hits and gave Dick Williams's club the final dimension it needed to win a pennant in 1972.

The Reds and Tigers both began spring training without the ingredients of which pennant winners

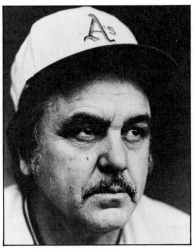

Catfish Hunter, Dick Williams, Vida Blue (L to R). "Nothing mysterious about Hunter," Earl Weaver said. "He just throws strikes." In 1973, Williams said of Charles Finley, "He has been wonderful to me. I have nothing but the highest regard for him." In 1974, Williams said, "A man can take just so much of Finley." He was released from his Oakland managerial contract after the 1973 season only on the proviso that he not sign with the Yankees, the team that had offered him a job. Blue once paid an Oakland fine of $250 totally in coins. "I wanted to make it all pennies, but they're hard to come by," he said.

are made. While their managers, Billy Martin and Sparky Anderson, were struggling to straighten out disorganized pitching staffs, the veteran players in both leagues went on strike to protest several issues, the largest being the conditions of their pension plan. Because of the strike, 13 days and 86 games were lopped off the regular season, and a ruling was made that if games affecting division races were among those lost, they would not be made up. The Tigers were thus able to win the American League East title by half a game over the Red Sox but missed becoming the second Tiger team to gain a pennant because of postponements when they lost the fifth game of the pennant series to the A's, 2–1. In the National League, neither the Reds nor the Pirates would have been in danger from also-rans if the schedule had been lengthened to 200 games. Pirate pitchers were expected to bring Pittsburgh its second pennant in a row, but instead they handed it to the Reds when Dave Giusti allowed Johnny Bench to tie the fifth game of the pennant series with a ninth inning homer, gave up two singles and was relieved by Bob Moose, whose wild pitch brought home the winning run.

For the first time in recent years the World Series did not have a clear-cut favorite. The A's had superior pitching—as did almost every contender the Reds played that season—but balancing that advantage was the loss of Reggie Jackson to a hamstring injury. Instead, Red pitchers (Jack Billingham in particular) showed up better, but none of them could control Gene Tenace, the A's catcher. A .225 hitter during the regular season, Tenace had four homers over the seven games, drove in nine runs and broke Joe Harris's record for the highest slugging average in a seven-game Series.

The year 1972 was a season for unlikely heroes. Milt Pappas of the Cubs became the first pitcher to win 200 games without having a single 20-win season. Giant right-hander Jim Barr pitched only two shutouts all season, but he put them back-to-back and retired 41 batters in a row, breaking a record set by Harvey Haddix in his 12-inning perfect game back in 1959. Steve Carlton, a 20-game winner for the Cardinals the year before, entered the 20-game circle again. Nothing unlikely about that, for the Cards were a strong team in 1972. The kicker was that Carlton had been traded over the winter to the Phils, who were not a strong team. In fact, they had the poorest record in the National League, and when Carlton won not a mere 20 for them but an unreal 27, he set a modern record for the most wins by a pitcher with a last-place team.

While experts at the end of the 1973 season were analyzing the effects of the American League's new Designated Hitter rule, two more significant statistics eluded them. For the first time since the introduction of the lively ball in 1920, runners in the two leagues combined to steal over 2,000 bases. Also, no less than seven of the game's 24 first-string shortstops went through the entire season without hitting a home run. The increase in stolen bases had been documented to some extent, but the mushrooming number of "banjo hitters" had not. When Rod Carew went homerless while winning the batting title in 1972, it marked the first such occurrence since Zack Wheat's championship in the war-shortened 1918 season. What this phenomenon suggested, when linked with the sudden influx of adroit base stealers and no appreciable dropoff in slugging, was that the major league game, approaching its cen-

Rod Carew. Through 1980 he had hit over .300 for 12 straight years. In 1977, he had at least one hit in all but 24 games he played, an American League record. His average that year was the highest for any player with 600 at bats since 1930. He shares the major league record for stealing home in one season (seven), and accomplished it in a season when he missed more than 30 games because of injury. (Insets) (L) Tom Seaver. Dock Ellis said in 1975, "He's one of the best pitchers to come around, but he's with the wrong team." (R) Johnny Bench. He attributed his hitting success to "inner conceit. It's knowing within yourself you can meet any situation." His defense was noteworthy too: Harry Dalton said, "Every time Bench throws, everybody in baseball drools."

Henry Aaron. He didn't have the flash of Mays or the charm of Mantle. "I came to the Braves on business," he said, "and I intended to see that business was good as long as I could." Stan Musial said, "He thinks there's nothing he can't hit." (Inset) Gaylord Perry. Luis Aparicio said, "Once in my life I'd like to play shortstop behind Gaylord, to watch him work. It'd be an honor." When Perry's agent approached the makers of Vaseline, the product Perry reputedly used for his spitball, for a possible endorsement contract, a company representative replied, "We soothe babies' asses, not baseballs."

tennial, was more diverse now than at any previous time in its history.

A further look at statistics after the 1973 season reflected that all seven of the teams that played .540 ball or better achieved an almost perfect balance between stolen bases and home runs and totaled over 100 of each. Because of the manner in which the league divisions were arranged, however, only three of those seven teams found themselves in postseason play. The National League East entrants in the pennant series were the Mets, a club that collected just 27 stolen bases, had no .300 hitters, was 11th in the league in runs scored and had a .509 winning percentage. So uneven were the two divisions in the National League that season that the Mets lost only one less game than the fourth-place Astros in the Western sector, and were the lone Eastern team to finish above .500. Pitted against the Reds for the pennant, the Mets got outstanding work from each of their three front-line starters and won in five games. The A's also took five games to beat the Orioles. And when the A's needed to go the full seven games to win the World Series, all three postseason series for the second year in a row had gone the limit.

The most mediocre team in history to win a pennant, the Mets nevertheless succeeded in making Yogi Berra only the second manager to win pennants in both leagues; a man with far more opportunities, Joe McCarthy, had been the other. Met pitcher Tom Seaver, a 19-game winner, was given the Cy Young Award over Ron Bryant of the Giants, who had won 24 games—an act that incensed National League fans everywhere but in New York. Catfish Hunter, the A's ace, won the American League Cy Young Award in competition with nine other 20-game winners, including Nolan Ryan of the Angels, who struck out a record 383 batters, and Wilbur Wood, the first pitcher in 57 years to be a 20-game winner and 20-game loser in the same season. The Designated Hitter rule had not only increased hitting in the American League but had also inflated the statistics of starting pitchers to the highest point since the dead ball era, as managers no longer had to remove their starters for pinch hitters in close games. In spite of the increase in complete games, Tiger reliever John Hiller tallied a record 38 saves.

The respectability of batting averages as a whole and the slugging of Hank Aaron, who ended the season just one home run shy of Babe Ruth's all-time record of 714, kept from scrutiny the fact that for the first time in history the lineup of neither World Series entry had a .300 hitter. The Mets,

furthermore, had been the first club to win a pennant without *either* a .300 hitter or a 20-game winner. In 1974 the A's once again arrived in the World Series without a .300 hitter. The Dodgers had two, however, plus Mike Marshall, the first pitcher to appear in over 100 games in a season. A kinesiologist, Marshall believed that with proper conditioning a pitching arm could be put to work every day and complained when he appeared only twice in the pennant series against the Pirates. The A's saw Marshall in all five games of the World Series and scored only one run off him. But it came in the seventh inning of the final game, and it made losers of both Marshall and the Dodgers.

By winning their third championship in a row, the A's had accomplished what seemed impossible a few years earlier, when the yearly draft of amateur players had been implemented to prevent a repetition of the Yankee dynasties of the past. The A's originally had seemed a product of the managerial genius of Dick Williams, but the 1974 club won without Williams, who had resigned after a bitter dispute with owner Charlie Finley. After Finley blocked Williams's attempt to accept an offer to become the Yankee manager, he appointed Alvin Dark as his replacement. Fired by Finley in 1967 and conspicuously unsuccessful in inspiring modern-day players ever since his triumph with the 1962 Giants, Dark had little difficulty obtaining the same results with the Oakland cast as had Williams, and he followed Berra by a year in becoming the third manager to win pennants in both leagues.

The 1974 season marked the first time that all four division races were closely contested. The Orioles overtook the Yankees by winning 28 of their last 34 games; the A's had to hold off the surprising Texas Rangers; the Pirates edged the Cardinals by only a game and a half; and the Reds missed overhauling the Dodgers by just four games. The races for individual honors were not nearly as competitive, but even if they had been, the focus would have mostly been on Hank Aaron and Lou Brock. On April 8, some two months short of his 40th birthday, Aaron climaxed his pursuit of Ruth's home run record by hitting his 715th homer off Al Downing of the Dodgers. Aaron's feat represented the pinnacle of a career that was matched in longevity and productivity by only Ty Cobb and Cap Anson. Although he never hit more than 47 homers in a season and compiled over 200 hits on only three occasions, Aaron retired with a lifetime home run total that will probably never be equalled and a hit total second only to Cobb's. At 35, an age when most National League batters were looking longingly toward the American League in the hope of latching on for a final fling as a Designated Hitter, Brock stole a record 118 bases and placed himself in a position to shatter Cobb's lifetime mark of 892 in 1977.

A decade before, the records of Cobb and Ruth had seemed unassailable. That both would topple was remarkable enough, but the truly astonishing thing was that they would fall only three years apart, for each had been set in a vastly disparate era. The bulk of Cobb's stolen bases had come during the dead ball period when base-running skills were highly valued. Ruth's slugging had blossomed after the lively ball was introduced, and the home run proceeded to replace the stolen base as the main offensive weapon. The work of Aaron and Brock stood as final proof that the game in the seventies encompassed a broader spectrum of playing styles and skills than at any previous time in history.

For years the honor given the Reds of playing the opening game of each National League season had seemed a sop to tradition. The fact that the Reds had been the game's first outstanding professional team was lost on most fans, who saw instead a club that won only one pennant in the National League's first 63 years and was generally one of the more colorless teams in the majors. In recent years, however, it has become increasingly clear that just as the Reds were the team most responsible for major league baseball getting its start, they may one day be acknowledged as the team most responsible for its survival. While the other franchises either ceded supremacy to the Yankees and their win-at-any-cost owner George Steinbrenner or else attempted to compete with Steinbrenner in the astronomical bidding wars that have resulted from the present-day free-agent rule, the Reds managed to stay at or near the top by the old-fashioned method of developing young players in their farm system and trading wisely for established veterans.

When the Reds and Red Sox each won their divisions in 1975 and then beat the Pirates and A's in the pennant series, it meant the two would meet in a World Series for the first time and assured that the championship would go to a team that had not won since World War II. Since the Red Sox had been the best hitting team in the majors and the Reds the highest scoring, some relief seemed likely from the emphasis on pitching that had keynoted the last few World Series. Moreover, the Red Sox had Fred Lynn, the first rookie to win an MVP Award, while the Reds had the highest winning percentage of any National League team since 1944.

By winning the fifth game in Cincinnati, the Reds traveled to Boston with a 3–2 lead in games and seemed headed for their first championship since 1940, when they took a 6–3 lead into the bottom of the eighth inning of game six. But a three-run pinch homer by Bernie Carbo sent the game into extra innings and set the stage for Carlton Fisk to homer in the bottom of the twelfth to tie the Series. The following night it was the Red Sox' turn to lose a three-run lead in the late innings. With the score tied in the ninth, Pete Rose singled, then moments later broke up a double play, enabling Joe Morgan to single in the run that won the Series and left an estimated 71 million TV viewers aware that they had witnessed perhaps the most exciting 24 hours in all of sports history. The sixth Series game, in fact, was voted the following year during baseball's Centennial celebration to be the greatest major league game ever.

For his superlative seasons, Joe Morgan won the MVP Award in 1975 and again in 1976. When George Foster won the award in 1977, he became the fourth Red during the decade to be selected. (The two men joined Rose and Bench.) All were still front-line performers in 1978, making the Reds the only team in history to have more than three MVPs in their lineup and creating the strong possibility that whereas the last Red repeat pennant winners in 1939–40 had no Hall of Famers, the 1975–76 edition may one day have at least four.

Among the other National League winners in 1975 were five fairly recent arrivals in the majors: Bill Madlock, the top hitter; Mike Schmidt, home run leader; Greg Luzinski, RBI champ; Dave Parker, best slugging average; and Dave Cash, most hits. Three of the five—Cash, Schmidt and Luzinski—were members of the Phillies. A year later this trio teamed with Garry Maddox, Larry Bowa and Steve Carlton to lift the Phils to the National League East title. Although they lost the pennant series to the Reds, the Phils for the first time in their history looked as if they had the makings of a team that would linger a while on top. Another team giving intimations that it would have to be reckoned with in the immediate future was San Diego. After escaping the cellar for the first time in 1975, the Padres had their first major award winner in 1976, when Randy Jones received the Cy Young trophy for his 22 wins. Replacing the Padres for the moment at the rear of the National League West were the Braves and Astros. In 1972 the Astros had finished second in the division when their young outfielder Cesar Cedeno hit .320 and stole 55 bases. Only 25 in 1976, Cedeno already had

(L to R) Don Gullett; Pete Rose; Joe Morgan. Gullet, at the end of 1978, was not far off Spud Chandler's career percentage record. Rose summed up his attitude toward baseball during the sixth game of the 1975 Series, when he turned to Carlton Fisk in the tenth inning and said, "This is some kind of game, isn't it?" Morgan, wrote Roger Angell, "has the conviction that he should affect the outcome of every game he plays in every time he comes up to bat and every time he gets on base."

over 1,000 hits, but many in Houston were afraid that injuries, legal problems and a lack of concentration on baseball would prevent him from ever reaching 2,000. Cedeno was only one part of the Astros' problem. Over the course of the decade the team had allowed Joe Morgan, Jack Billingham, Cesar Geronimo, Lee May and Jim Wynn to pass through its hands without receiving much of anything in exchange.

Executives of the Kansas City Royals have been both incredibly lucky and incredibly astute. Placed fortuitously in the weakest of the four major league divisions in 1969, the Royals are the only expansion team never to finish in last place. By a combination of shrewd trades and a skillful use of their selections in the amateur draft, the club was ready to replace Oakland at the head of the American League West in 1976. Opposing them in the pennant series were the Yankees, who had traded with equal dexterity, obtaining Graig Nettles, Mickey Rivers, Willie Randolph, Chris Chambliss, Dock Ellis, Sparky Lyle, Dick Tidrow and Ed Figueroa at a total cost of only two players who were playing regularly elsewhere in 1976. Former Oakland stars Catfish Hunter and Ken Holtzman gave the Yankees a pitching staff that was superior to Kansas City's, but the pennant series still came down to the final pitch of the final game—a home run ball delivered by Royal reliever Mark Littell to Chambliss.

Still exhilarated by their last-minute victory when they opened the World Series, the Yankees were brought quickly down to earth by the Reds. Winning in four straight games, the Reds succeeded in doing what so many other National League clubs in the last half century could not: putting together

back-to-back world championships. Bill Madlock also became a repeat champion when he wrested the National League batting title away from the Reds' Ken Griffey on the season's final day. But Madlock's win seemed mundane compared to the finale of the American League batting race. In an ending that jogged historians to rehash the events of 1910, when the Browns tried to hand Nap Lajoie the batting crown, George Brett of the Royals beat out teammate Hal McRae by a single point when Steve Brye of the Twins allowed Brett's fly ball to drop safely on his final at bat.

Two points behind Brett was Rod Carew. His string of batting titles broken at four, Carew began the 1977 season as if he were going to hit .400. Finishing at .388, he won the championship by 52 points, the greatest margin by a leader since 1941. Carew's performance has been called by some the best in history, in view of his having to hit against the slider and play the majority of his games under artificial light, but it cannot be forgotten that he did it during an expansion year. One statistic on the caliber of pitching in the American League in 1977 will suffice. Despite the Designated Hitter rule still being in effect, the 14-team American League had three fewer 20-game winners than the 12-team National League, and for the first time in league history the Cy Young Award went to a reliever, Sparky Lyle.

Another statistic suggesting the game is presently more conducive to hitters than pitchers lies in the number of men who have reached the 3,000-hit plateau in recent years. When Pete Rose joined the list early in the 1978 season, he became the fifth during the decade to hit the mark. The comparable

Pete Rose hits safely in his 44th consecutive game, 1978. "Probably only one man in all the land thought Rose had any chance of breaking Joe DiMaggio's record of hitting in 56

straight games," wrote Curry Kirkpatrick. "Simply because that man wore Cincinnati uniform No. 14, the hunt became vastly more invigorating."

figure for pitchers has always been 300 wins. At present only the ageless Gaylord Perry, Cy Young winner at 40 in 1978, rates more than an outside shot to score that high. The reason seems to be that the demands of today's game take a greater toll of pitchers than hitters. For the most part, those with greatest longevity are knuckleballers like Phil Niekro or control specialists like Jim Kaat and Gaylord Perry. It is highly improbable that the game will ever again know a Walter Johnson or even a Warren Spahn, whose career becomes all the more remarkable when it is considered that, despite losing three years to the service during World War II, he is the only pitcher in the last 50 years to win more than 300 games.

Ironically, the team that has suffered most from pitching fragility of late is the Yankees. Were it not for the arm ailments contracted by so many key pitchers, Steinbrenner's checkbook would have made the Yankees unstoppable in 1977. As it was, they had to wait until the last weekend of the season to clinch their division and then had to rally again in the late innings of the final pennant series game against the Royals to win the pennant. The Dodgers got to the World Series by a much smoother route. After building a wide lead over the Reds early in the season, they coasted to an easy division win, then came back to beat the Phillies three straight games in the pennant series after losing the opener. Reggie Jackson's three home runs in three swings in the sixth game of the World Series ended a 15-year wait between world championships for Yankee supporters.

Other teams that had had to wait a bit longer than 15 years between world championships watched helplessly while Steinbrenner spent the winter after

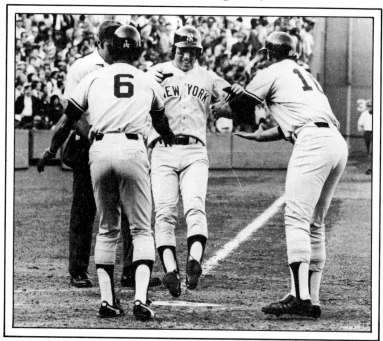

Bucky Dent's home run in the 1978 American League East playoff. In that game, and the ensu-

ing World Series, he had ten RBIs; it was fully one-fourth his total for the regular season.

(Top, L to R) Ron Guidry, Billy Martin, Reggie Jackson. Guidry in 1978 had the best season for a pitcher since Lefty Grove's dominance in 1929-1930-1931; Jackson said that in clutch situations, "I have a feeling of relaxedness." Martin never had that feeling. Described by John Schulian as "a mouse studying to be a rat," he was fired from every managing job he had held, just as he succeeded enormously in each of them. Lee Allen's words on Rogers Hornsby might have applied to Martin, who said his employer was "convicted" and his star player "a liar": "He was frank to the point of being cruel, and subtle as a belch." (Middle) Graig Nettles. His performance in the 1978 Series compared to Brooks Robinson's in 1970, when Robinson won the sports car given the Series MVP. "If we'd known he wanted a car so bad," Johnny Bench said, "we'd have given it to him." (Bottom) Tommy Lasorda. His players in the 1978 Series had earned an average salary of $198,000.

the 1977 season snagging two more high-priced free-agent pitchers, Rich Gossage and Rawly Eastwick. The White Sox by 1978 had been 19 years without a pennant, and the crosstown Cubs had not won in 33 years. Unbelievably, neither Chicago entry had won a world championship since 1917. The Indians began 1978 without a World Series win in 30 seasons; the Braves franchise hadn't won a Series since 1957; and the Phils had never won one.

Fortunately for the game, among the teams able to keep pace financially with the Yankees were the main competition within their division, the Red Sox. Without a world champion in six decades, the Sox exploited Steinbrenner's greatest weakness by signing Yankee pitcher Mike Torrez before the 1978 season. Steinbrenner's habit of quickly losing interest in players once he had wooed them into Yankee uniforms had created considerable dissension within the 1977 club. One of the league's better pitchers, Torrez refused to sign a Yankee contract unless his salary figures matched those of the many free agents Steinbrenner had brought to the Bronx. By moving to Boston, Torrez and an off-season acquisition from the Indians, Dennis Eckersley, gave the Red Sox in 1978 the nucleus of their best pitching staff since the days of Babe Ruth and Carl Mays. Nonetheless, it was a staff that could not hold a 14½-game lead over the Yankees, and the Red Sox lost the pennant not on the final weekend, but on the final day: a postseason play-off that preceded yet another Yankee triumph over the Royals, yet another Yankee championship over the Dodgers (who had, again, beaten the Phillies). Winning the play-off game was Ron Guidry—scouted, drafted, signed and nurtured by the Yankees, and a 25–3 pitcher who established a welter of major league records. The play-off loser: the much-traveled free agent, Mike Torrez, wearing his fifth uniform in as many seasons.

The seventies moved to their close with a few surprises: Gene Autry's California Angels, long a laughing-stock, emerged on top of the American League West, and Willie Stargell, at 38, became the oldest winner of a Most Valuable Player Award. Although Stargell shared his regular-season honor with Keith Hernandez of St. Louis, he swept the play-off and World Series MVP prizes as the Pirates beat Cincinnati and then Baltimore. In the ten post-season games, Stargell hit .414, slugged .927, and knocked in 13 runs.

The aging Stargell ceded baseball's center stage in 1980 to the youthful George Brett. Only 26 when the season began, Brett was nonetheless a fixture in the game, a star from the time he was 21. When he hit .390—after reaching as high as .407 as late as August—he confirmed the judgment of those who ranked him among the game's greatest third basemen ever. Yet even though the remarkable Brett was able to lead Kansas City—the glittering jewel among baseball's ten expansion clubs—into its first World Series, final glory was conferred on an aging team with a long, if agonizing, history. Paced by Pete Rose, 39, Steve Carlton, 35, and Tug McGraw, 36, the Philadelphia Phillies won their first World Championship in the club's 97 years. When the Phillies opened up for business in 1883, there were teams in Providence, Buffalo, Louisville and Columbus; players earned as little as $1,000 per year; a foul ball was not a strike; uniforms were flannel, gloves were minuscule, the pitching mound was 50 feet from home, and the entire Phillies squad hit only four home runs. But in 1980, watching Rose, McGraw, Carlton, Brett and so many others play with utter intensity and devotion to their craft, one could argue that the game hadn't changed at all. —David Nemec

Reggie Jackson (L) and Jim Rice. "The whole history of baseball has the quality of mythology." — Bernard Malamud

BALLPARK:
Fenway, with Tears
By George V. Higgins

FENWAY Park was old when it was new. It is unsightly from the outside, looking rather like an old brick warehouse rambling around a misshapen plot of land. It is able to accommodate less than 36,000 spectators, most of whom are ill-humored by the time they reach it, having been forced to park their cars outside of Worcester, some 40 miles away. They guzzle beer and are given to hooting and jeering when displeased, while bellowing extravagant praises when their savage instincts are delighted.

Fenway Park has its faults. As do the adult men who play their boys' games in it, and the noisy crowds who take them seriously. Left field, cramped in by the Green Monster to a depth widely suspected to be considerably less than its advertised distance of 315 feet to home plate, has tempted many a right-handed pull-hitter to tinker fatally with his stance. It has driven more resolute batsmen to the brink of despair by turning line shots on the rise into long singles, rebounded viciously back close to the edge of the grass at shortstop.

The park is too small: it is maddening, in March, to order tickets for a Baltimore series scheduled for September, and to receive in April tickets for seats situated in right field.

The hot dogs, which for years were actual delicacies, are now abominable, and the liquid refreshment issue has been greatly complicated by the actions of those who consume much stuff stronger than beer before entering the park with additional supplies stashed in their clothing—this is still Boston, and we still have wowsers in our midst, cheerfully at the ready to make political hay by banning beer sales in the stands. And then there is the team, which would try the patience of anyone,

The Huntington Avenue Grounds, Fenway's predecessor, on October 3, 1903, during the first World Series.
It sat on land owned by the New York and New Haven Railroad, and the first lease on it was signed by the
ubiquitous Connie Mack — acting as an advance agent for Ban Johnson.

drunk, stoned or sober, and has been doing so for years.

But each of these flaws is in its way redemptive, meshing with reassuring fitness with the certitudes of life that large numbers of New Englanders acquire between birth and adulthood. (You will note that I have said nothing about maturity, it having been reliably suggested that my behavior at Fenway Park, and that of adjacent celebrants, does not constitute mature behavior; I dispute this, but I remain uneasy that the charge may be true. Not that it would matter, of course.)

There were two men in their twenties shouldering their way through the crowds of people bunched up at the gates to the grandstand. They both wore windbreakers and painter's hats. The hats were red, and carried white lettering: "Rooster. Dewey. Yaz. Pudge. Boomer. Fred. Jim. Rico." The *Rico* was for Rico Petrocelli, who was playing third base in 1975 when the hats were sold. For flimsy hats, they had proven very sturdy.

The young man with the sandy hair was talking as he shoved. "Didn't have a ticket, he tells me. Tells his wife he's gotta be away overnight on business, and grabs a plane to Cincinnati. You beat that? Cincinnati? He was gone for four days. Had a credit card and about three hundred bucks and he just took off. Now he gets out to Riverfront. He's

sleeping in this joint that was all he could get without no reservation, and it's over the river in Newport, Kentucky, and he thinks it was probably a cathouse. People coming and going all hours the night. Goes over the stadium, sees this kid and he's selling programs. Buys all the scorecards off the kid for a hundred bucks and gets the jacket and the badge thrown in. Got into all three games. You beat that? 'Third game,' he said to me, 'I was practically killing people, wanted get my last programs before I got inside. Sold them all, too. Cost me about fifty bucks, see three games, I kept the jacket and the badge, too. Hadda sleep onna couch a few days when I got home, but it was worth it. Jesus was she mad.' "

We are born into a harsh climate, which is forever teasing us with brief intervals of sunshine and crisp air, in order to make more telling the taunts of raw winds, fog and drizzle. Billy Herman, Red Sox manager from 1964 to 1966, had much to grieve, but his most memorable complaint was about the weather: "Boston has two seasons," he said, "August and winter."

In August in Boston we divert ourselves from the coming winter by following the Red Sox. In this context, "Boston" is bounded on the south by Long Island Sound and the New York-Connecticut border, on the west by the Buffalo city limits, and

(Top) Crowds at the 1912 World Series, the year Fenway opened. (Middle) "Because of the contour of the plot of ground purchased," Fred Lieb wrote, "the field is shaped something like a piece out of a jigsaw puzzle, with 17 facets and walls and barriers breaking off at odd angles. There was a ten-foot embankment in left field . . . , and Duffy Lewis would scamper up it like a Rocky Mountain goat to make some of his best catches." (Bottom) In 1903, the team that would win the first World Series trained at Macon, Georgia.

to the north by Canada. One can take a two-hour ramble among the catwalks of the Nantucket Boat Basin, stopping to inspect yacht after yacht, without missing a single inning of the Red Sox game. When your car radio loses the signal from the station in Hartford (WTIC), you have a choice of several more stations. One of them will be playing on the radio in the general store and gas station which you make your pit stop in eastern Vermont. In Rome for the election of Pope John Paul I, Boston's Humberto Cardinal Medeiros sidled up to a Boston newsman and inquired how the Red Sox were doing (this was before the Great Nose-dive of '78); informed that they remained in first place, the Cardinal said *"Deo Gratias,"* and returned to matters more felicitously supervised by the Holy Spirit. In the winter we keep August green by talking of the Red Sox; in April, which is usually still winter in Boston, we declare that spring has come the day that the Red Sox open at Fenway.

Such stimuli are lacking to baseball partisans in Los Angeles, Oakland and San Francisco. If they set their minds to it, the Dodgers could play all year round, establishing a December competition with the Padres, a January uproar with the Giants, a February skirmish with Oakland, and a Pacific Series with the two best in March, concluding just in time for the opening of spring training.

They like baseball in LA, but for them it lacks the pastoral symbolism it enjoys in New England; cooped up all winter, with slush seeping in over the tops of our galoshes and memorial services being held for middle-aged friends who shoveled snow despite the strictures of family physicians, we throng to freeze our asses off in Fenway Park in April. To Dodgers customers, their games are entertainment; to us, Red Sox games are certificates of survival, renewal and rebirth.

That pagan atavism of ours is what makes us care so passionately about the Red Sox. Reinforced by the dominant theologies of the area, it is recapitulated by the behavior of the team, which annually re-enacts the parable of temptation and surrender in the Garden of Eden located next to Lansdowne Street.

While I do not for one minute doubt that an occasional practitioner of the Bahai faith, or some

Smead Jolley (L), Bob Fothergill. Jolley could not negotiate Duffy's Cliff, the slope in Fenway's left field that was named after Duffy Lewis, who had handled it so well. "They taught me how to run up the cliff," Jolley said, "but they never taught me how to run down it." Jolley's fielding abilities were such that he could barely handle any kind of outfield: even a .305 career average could not keep him in the big leagues for more than four years. "Fat" Fothergill carried 230 pounds onto Duffy's Cliff; he once tripped, and all 230 pounds rolled down it. The Cliff was removed in 1934.

(Clockwise from Top, L) Tex Hughson, Boo Ferriss, Willard Nixon, Mel Parnell. The aristocracy of Fenway pitching from the early 1940s through the middle fifties, these men endured, despite the unforgiving confines of the field. Only Parnell was able to deploy his talent consistently against top competition — and only Parnell was a lefty, regularly facing batters seduced by the enticing proximity of the Monster. (C) The Wall, 1916.

other religion of reasonable optimism, has bought a ticket to a game at Fenway Park, I think it beyond dispute that most in attendance were brought up to profess a creed positing a stern and retributive God.

There are Catholics of Italian, Polish, German and Chinese origin in Boston, but their first teachers, in all likelihood, were Irish Catholics, priests and laymen. Whether it was to the student's taste or not, he got a generous portion of the bogtrotter's pessimism, that nagging assurance that when things are going good, somebody is about to trick you into a disaster.

Protestants in Boston, on the other hand, subscribe in numbers of considerable size to a Calvinistic view fully compatible with Jansenist Catholicism, a *Weltanschauung* heavily imbued with *Weltschmerz*, if you will. About the only difference between the Catholics and the Wasps is that the Catholics expect the worst, and the Protestants suspect the best. Those of the Jewish faith are even more biliously suspicious of the best than the Protestants. The blacks of the African Methodist Episcopal Church are reminded each Sunday that whatever it is they are up to, God is unlikely to let them get away with it much longer, particularly if they seem to be enjoying it.

Thus in August, knowing that the winter is coming, convinced that a vengeful Deity is only setting us up in order to knock us down, we proceed in a ragtag ecumenical procession to the place of secular festival, our mental baggage crammed to the bursting with a lifetime of pessimistic impedimenta.

The man and four young boys had seats behind the Red Sox dugout, right behind first base, and all the kids wore plastic imitation protective batting helmets. Red, with the blue *B* logo. They ate popcorn and they talked about Jim Rice. They ate ice cream and they talked about Jim Rice. They were impatient for the vendor to bring the Fenway Franks around, because Jim Rice advertises Fenway Franks. One of the boys—they were all about the same size—was noisy in his criticism of Yaz. He did not like Yaz because as long as Yaz persisted in playing, Jim Rice could not play left field.

The man wore a three-piece glen plaid suit and a challis tie. He listened to the boys without showing any of the amusement that he felt, calculating that this was easily the best birthday party his son had ever requested. If the kid was nine, the man had only nine years to wait before the kid would be old enough to be as interested in the whereabouts of the beer stand as the man was. The man draped his left arm over as much of the two empty seats to his left as he could manage, in order to demonstrate a proprietary interest in them and discourage the cruisers from the upper rows of the grandstand.

After a while the man's wife appeared with the little girl, who had a slice of pizza in her hand and some pizza sauce on her white sweater. She was carrying an inflated Red Sox doll, and she had been crying. The woman and the little girl waited while the man got up and let them past him to the two vacant seats. The woman wore a tan and white plaid blazer and white slacks. "These are very good

Carl Yastrzemski could always handle left field in Fenway. What he couldn't handle, early in his career, was himself. Billy Herman, who managed the Sox in the Dark Ages of the middle sixties, said to Donald Honig, "How did I get along with Yastrzemski? Like everybody else. By that I mean nobody ever got along with Yastrzemski."

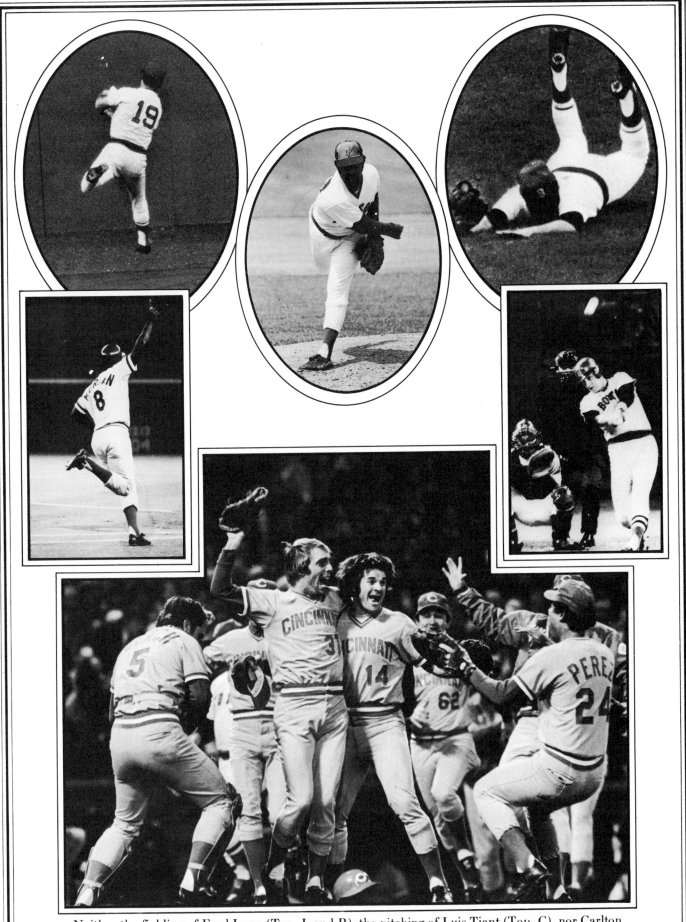

Neither the fielding of Fred Lynn (Top, L and R), the pitching of Luis Tiant (Top, C), nor Carlton Fisk's dramatic sixth-game home run (Middle, R) could win the 1975 Series from Joe Morgan (Middle, L) and his Cincinnati teammates (Bottom). But, wrote Roger Angell, describing the fans leaving Fenway when it was all over, "They did not look bitter, and perhaps they felt, as I did, that no team in our time had more distinguished itself in the World Series than the Red Sox — no team, that is, but the Cincinnati Reds."

seats," she said. She did not sound happy about it.

"Yeah," he said. "McGinnis does good work."

"I can imagine what they cost," she said.

"That's about what I have to do, too," he said. "He didn't send me the bill yet."

"He will," she said, with a certain grimness.

"That was a really great idea," he said, nodding toward the little girl. "Pizza goes well with that outfit. What'd that sweater set me back with Mister Lord and Mister Taylor? About thirty bucks? Before it was ruined, I mean."

"About that," the woman said with satisfaction. "I'm surprised you haven't got a beer in your hand."

"I will," he said. "I will." He got up and left. When he got back, the Red Sox were taking infield under the lights. His son said: "Dad, how much does George Scott weigh?"

"A lot," the man said. "Way too much. He's too fat. That's why it takes three tugs to dock him."

"Why don't they make him lose some weight?" one of the other boys said.

The man sat down. "Because the only way they can think of is boiling him," the man said, "and that's against the law or something, I guess." He drank his beer.

The Red Sox finished infield and went back into the dugout. Sherm Feller began to announce the starting lineups on the PA system. The woman said: "It's too bad you can't even let yourself enjoy the baseball game." The man did not answer for a while. Then he said: "It certainly is."

Like Heaven, Fenway Park is very difficult to get into. This of course is as it should be. In Cincinnati, stolid and sensible loyalists of the Reds enjoy a commodious new stadium, with sundry color-coded entrances, ample nearby parking, comfortable seats, excellent beer, fine sausages and reasonable protection from the elements. In 1975, more than 55,000 of the good burghers saw each of the three Cincinnati-Boston games played at Riverfront; at Fenway, each of the four games was sold out: 35,205. It is fair to say that there were at least 20,000 more New Englanders denied a salvation which they greatly craved. That is 20,000 people per game, so that some 80,000 souls were again admonished that they not only could not take it with them, but couldn't even get their hands on it in the first place.

On October 21, 1975, the sixth game left the fortunate few in a state of high exaltation as Bernie Carbo tied it up with a pinch-hit home run into the center-field bleachers. And Carlton Fisk, our peerless receiver, won it with that shot in the twelfth that he kept just fair with body English. All excluded from the spectacle felt suitably punished, which left God with the task of unbending the stiff-necked faithful who had tickets to the seventh game.

God brought it off. He had Darrell Johnson pull Jim Willoughby in the ninth inning, replacing him with Jim Burton, who gave up a bloop single at the end to Cincinnati's premier second base-

Harry Frazee (L) in 1923, with Frank Chance, who managed the Red Sox for one year. Frazee sold the Yankees 15 players in five years. In 1934, when Tom Yawkey acquired Hank Johnson from the Yankees, the Boston *Record* headlined, "Man Bites Dog."

(Top, L and R) Babe Ruth. "I believe the sale of Babe Ruth will ultimately strengthen the team," Frazee said. (C) Carl Mays. He jumped Frazee's club before landing in New York. He was a man of cantankerous disposition, probably the least-liked player in the league, even before he killed Ray Chapman with a pitched ball. In 1971 he said, "I think I belong in the Hall of Fame. I know I earned it. What's wrong with me?" (Bottom) The Golden Outfield. Tris Speaker (L), the first Boston star to be auctioned off, was sent to Cleveland before the era of Frazee; Duffy Lewis (R), after whom the incline in Fenway's left field was named "Duffy's Cliff," was unloaded to the Yankees; Harry Hooper (C) was traded to Chicago. He said of Frazee, "He sold the whole team down the river to keep his dirty nose above water. What a way to ruin a ball club!" From 1922 on, the Sox finished last in all but one of the next nine years.

man, Joe Morgan. Final: Cincinnati 4, Boston 3. Salt was thus rubbed in the wounds of those who had gained admission in apparently-predestined superiority to their fellows, rebuking them for their sins of pride and maintaining the venerable and reciprocal tradition of the August-winter cycle. This, in times of woe, is expressed: "I knew it." And in times of joy: "Wait and see—they'll blow it." The summer will end and the Red Sox if trailing will fade; if leading, will fold.

It is of course easy to scoff at such dour predictions. Their makers display no faith in human resourcefulness, in Red Sox dedication, in the luck of our pitchers or the fearsomeness of our batters. In fact there is but one circumstance that makes the scoffing difficult: 60 years of history.

The federal government authorized the Red Sox to win their last World Series. That was in 1918, when there was a war on and the Cubbies from Chicago carried the flag of the National League. Special permission was required for an event then considered frivolous, when in fact a two-week holiday should have been declared so that all might properly contemplate the occasion: the Red Sox had the pitching to win the Series. They had Babe Ruth, who pitched 20 consecutive scoreless innings and won two games, and Carl Mays, who had some trouble later on (he killed a man with a pitch), also winner of two games.

Then came the famine. Red Sox owner Harry Frazee, busily engaged in financing his Broadway production of *No, No, Nanette,* sold off Ruth to the Yankees in time for the 1920 season, and Mays in time for 1921 followed Ruth down old Route One, the Post Road. Then there began the era of maximum frustration in the Fenway, every triumph carrying with it the certitude of incipient tragedy, every ecstasy of victory the assurance of the redoubled agony of defeat. Because, you see, the Red Sox never win the Last One. They win the Next To Last One. They never win the Last One.

In the 1946 World Series, Enos Slaughter's manic dash took the seventh game for the St. Louis Cardinals. In 1948, Gene Bearden pitched the Cleveland Indians to a play-off victory over the Red Sox—who chose undistinguished Denny Galehouse for the mound, and omitted to advise Ted Williams that he had damned right well better hit to left against the Williams Shift, or lose his blasted job. They lost and they lost and they lost, the club getting worse and worse and worse, until at last they started up the hill again, all in one season, and put the Cardinals through six games of hair on the walls and blood on the floor until an exhausted Jim Lonborg, pitching with too little rest, went up against Bob Gibson in the seventh game. And lost.

In 1975, Carl Yastrzemski, again playing like a man possessed, saw to the elimination of the Oakland A's in the American League play-offs, and brought the Red Sox back to Fenway, there to confront the Cincinnati Reds in the World Series. In the twelfth inning of what remains the greatest baseball

Opening Day, 1947. American League President Will Harridge, Red Sox manager Joe Cronin and Washington manager Ossie Bluege (L to R). Cronin managed at Fenway for 13 years; only Pinky Higgins, of other Sox managers, lasted half so long. Cronin was originally sold to Yawkey by Clark Griffith of Washington — and Cronin was Griffith's son-in-law. One contemporary columnist wrote, "Maybe Griffith has something. I wish I could sell my son-in-law for $250,000."

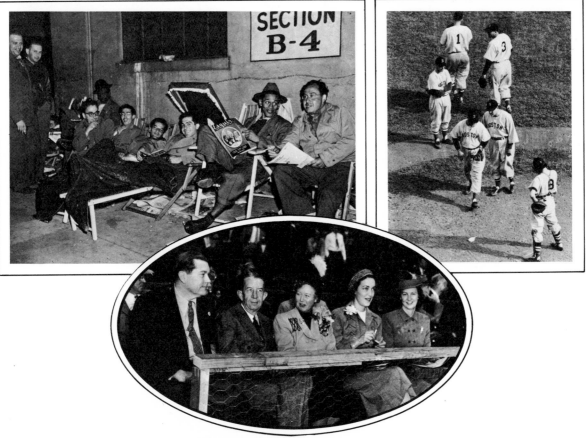

The 1946 pennant was Boston's first since 1918. Outfielders that season were (L to R) Ted Williams, Leon Culberson, Dom DiMaggio, Catfish Metkovich (who earned his nickname not by catching one, but by stepping on it and injuring his foot), Johnny Lazor, Wally Moses. In the 1946 Series (Middle, L, the faithful wait for tickets) Joe Cronin (Middle, R, at R, facing camera) brought in Joe Dobson (next to Cronin) to replace Boo Ferriss in the seventh game. In this picture, Johnny Pesky's arms are folded; they were similarly immobile when Enos Slaughter scored the run that beat the Red Sox. The Boston *Record* the next day ran a banner headline: "CASHMAN EXONERATES PESKY." Joe Cashman was not a Sox executive but a baseball writer for the *Record*; such was the self-image of the Boston press at the time. (Bottom, L to R) Tom Yawkey, Eddie Collins, Mrs. Yawkey, Mrs. Collins, Mrs. Joe Cronin. Collins, Yawkey's general manager, signed Williams for a $1,000 bonus.

Ted Williams, 1941. As a rookie two years earlier, he said, "All I want out of life is that when I walk down the street folks will say, 'There goes the greatest hitter who ever lived.'"

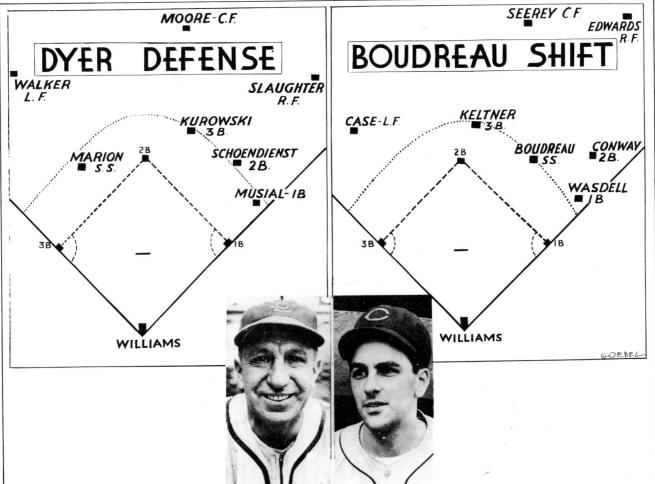

(Top, L) Ted Williams in 1955. (Top, R) A Willard Mullin cartoon that ran two painful days too early in 1949. It was the second straight year the Sox would lose the pennant on the last day of the season. Said Williams, after that season was over "I just wanted to go and hide somewhere." (Bottom) Defenses devised for Williams by Eddie Dyer and Lou Boudreau. Boudreau's was first, Dyer's was more effective. Williams had only five hits in the 1946 Series; one caused a Boston newspaper to headline its lead story that day not with the score but with "WILLIAMS BUNTS."

game that I have ever seen in my life—and not so secretly believed to be the greatest ballgame that anyone has ever seen—the magnificent Carlton Fisk, who takes these matters personally, it seems, got the damned ball into the screen, just fair. Next day, Sox lost.

In 1977 the Sox collapsed in the stretch, not having done all that well out of the blocks. In 1978 they won 99 games out of 162, but lost 64 out of 163, dropping the divisional play-off to the Yankees. We have two headlines in Boston, and we use them every year that the Red Sox have a good team. When it's still warm we use **PENNANT FEVER GRIPS HUB**; and when it gets chilly we use **SOX LOSE**. Usually by one run. In the end: **SOX LOSE**. In 1978, to assure the fitness of things unchanged in the eternal order, Don Zimmer left Mike Torrez in too long, so that banjo-hitter Bucky Dent could get up off his butt where he had fallen swinging wildly at a Torrez pitch, and golf one into the left-field screen to score three runs. So it was that with the Sox one down, two out in the ninth, Captain Carl came to the plate with Rick Burleson 90 feet away, the tying run on third, and popped out foul to Graig Nettles, just as he had done in similar circumstances to make the last out in the '75 Series.

The guy in the twenty-third row of Section 17 was not pleased. "Pisses me off," he said, as Torrez lobbed a few before facing the Yankees in the fifth, in the 1978 playoff. "Fuckin' thing, you know? Zimmer's leaving him in. Zimmer shouldn't be leaving him in. Lee's right—guy looks like a gerbil. Which would be all right if he didn't think like fuckin' Darrell Johnson. There was only one time in his life that Johnson was too early pullin' a pitcher, and that was when he takes Willoughby out in the seventh game, inna goddamned *ninth,* and puts in that asshole Burton, and we lose. We'll blow this one, too. Wait and see if we don't blow this one, just like we did all the others."

No one sane in Fenway (if there were any such on that October day) could hold a grudge against Yastrzemski. In his seventeenth season, turning 39 in August, he played his bloody guts out. The first Boston run in that play-off was his homer into the right-field seats, and his play in left field should have been the envy of his teammates in their twenties all season long. The man is a total pro, but he, Fisk, Remy, Burleson and Hobson could not beat the Yankees by themselves—they needed four other guys who want it just as badly.

That is what has plagued the Red Sox ever since

Jim Lonborg (L), Bob Gibson (R). Lonborg won nine more games than Gibson in 1967 but had also pitched 98 more innings. It showed when they met in the final Series game; Lonborg gave up seven runs in six innings, while Gibson pitched a three-hitter. It was Lonborg's fourth critical start in 11 days.

(Top, L to R) Ellis Kinder, Pumpsie Green, Jim Piersall. Kinder won 102 games for the Red Sox but, Henry Berry wrote, "His liquor consumption went unrecorded." Green, the first black Red Sox player, resisted teammate Gene Conley's attempt to persuade him to jump the team and join him on a trip to Israel; Green declined because, he said, he didn't speak Hebrew. In the summer of 1952, Warren Brown wrote: "Young Jim Piersall, the Red Sox eccentric, continues to make his pitch as the game's most distinctive crowd-pleaser." Two months later, Piersall was in the violent room at Westborough State Hospital. (Middle) Thomas Austin Yawkey. In 1946, asked about adding a second deck to the Fenway grandstand, he said, "I like my ballpark as it is." (Bottom) Carl Yastrzemski in 1967. In the last two weeks of that season he went 23 for 44, including five home runs; in the last two games, when Boston needed both to win the pennant, he was 7 for 8.

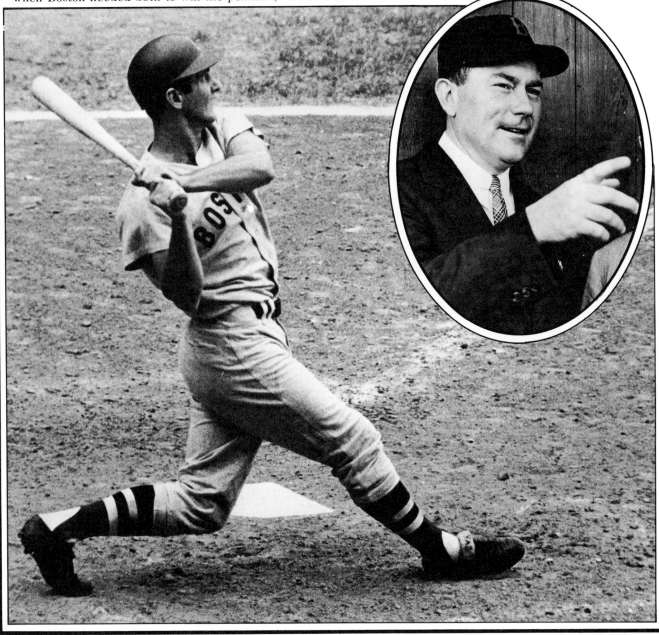

The 1938 infield of (L to R) Bobby Doerr, Joe Cronin, Mike Higgins, Jimmie Foxx. Theirs was a classic Fenway team; team batting average, .299; team ERA, 4.46. They finished second to the Yankees.

In 1952, Lou Boudreau (C) was flanked (L to R) by Jimmy Piersall, Ted Lepcio, Faye Throneberry and Sammy White. Lepcio was Piersall's "keeper"; in one tense moment, he persuaded his irate teammates not to beat up the troubled Piersall. White's greatest moment occurred on June 18, 1953, when he scored three runs in Boston's extraordinary 17-run seventh inning against the Tigers.

I can remember. For some reason or another, we are always about four guys short of nine guys who breakfast on fish hooks and broken glass before afternoon games, and snack on barbed wire before the ones at night. We get a Billy Goodman or a George Kell who dines on carpet tacks and washes them down with piss from his own horse, and team him up with some rump-sprung relic going through the motions. After a while, the natives get restless, and then in Fenway Park, too small for a ballgame, too big for a bridge tournament, too old for a shopping mall and too young for a shrine, from the outside downright ugly; a jagged structure wandering all over the place in Back Bay; from the inside, under the grandstand, sterile concrete, confusing to the outlander, ill-equipped with rest rooms, full of concrete ramps that don't seem to go anywhere —in Fenway Park, the roar of disapproval ascends.

Those concrete ramps do go somewhere. One leads to your seats on a warm May night. You grab the red metal rail and dodge the kids who run up and down, until you emerge into the softness of the evening, the everlasting green of The Wall and the field and the grandstand itself, and hear the sounds of a springtime night in Boston.

You will notice that I said "hear." It is customary to say that Fenway Park is the best park in baseball in which to watch a game. This may very well be so, although I am inclined to think that

Riverfront in Cincinnati, and Dodger Stadium in LA, are certainly in contention. So, for that matter, are Tiger Stadium, which I liked better when it was Briggs Stadium, and Municipal Stadium in Cleveland. Of course nobody knows about Municipal Stadium in Cleveland, any more than they do about Memorial Stadium in Baltimore, because nobody in either city ever goes to the ball park. They do not have the religion. Seeing the game is not the issue. Hearing the game is the issue.

At Fenway you can hear the game. People come out of their seats at the crack of the bat, when the ball is mashed and headed for the arc lights of the summer night. Long before the rising liner clears the pitcher's mound on its way to the center-field bleachers, the onlookers are screaming: "Yes, yes, *yes*." In the bleachers you can hear the pitchers grousing in the bullpen. When you attend a game at Fenway Park, you are on your feet much of the time, because the people in front of you get up quite rapidly when they hear a solid hit, to track it into the New England night, or the serene blue sky of a New England Sabbath.

It's the park that does it. Once you are out of the runways, the park assaults your senses. The Red Sox have gone to doubleknits, but they have shown the good sense to order white doubleknits. The Red Sox have improved their field, but they have done so by evicting football teams and cultivating grass.

Fenway. The Green Monster may be more monstrous than Boston has been willing to admit. In the past 40 years, the AL batting championship has been won 12 times by four different Red Sox — all of them left-handers.

The Red Sox have erected an electronic scoreboard but they did so in center field, where the Buck Printing sign used to loom above the action (long ago, a drunk seated behind me and my father urged Walt Dropo to hit it over the Buick Painting sign. He didn't). It doesn't make any difference.

It does not matter because, as you might imagine after 60 years of tinkering, Fenway Park is now very nearly perfect for disappointments. Did Ted Williams bottle up rampaging emotion when SOX LOST, or shrug it off because he'd won the batting title once again? Did Ellis Kinder bottle down strong spirits in the bullpen, leading astray an entire generation of young pitchers while leaving the empties under the bench? Was Dominic DiMaggio, as the song claimed, better than his brother Joe, but disinclined to prove it? Should Jimmy Piersall have been traded; Jim Gosger allowed to play in center field; Jackie Jensen made to fly? Should Vern Stephens, slower than a disabled half-track on Normandy Beach, have been permitted to play short; or should Don Buddin have been summarily executed before Mike Higgins took it into his head to install him in the lineup at the same place, that Buddin might for eternity earn the name of "Bootsie"? Doesn't anybody know anything?

No. Nobody in Boston knows anything. Not about baseball. In Boston we believe, and we are never disappointed, because what we believe is this: the world will break your heart some day, and we are luckier than most—we get ours broken every year, at Fenway Park.

Ted Williams, 1952. He was leaving for Korea, and Dave Egan of the *Record* wrote, "Why are we having a day for *this* guy?" On his retirement, eight years later, Williams said, "Despite some of the terrible things written about me by the knights of the keyboard...my stay in Boston has been the most wonderful part of my life."

BOX SCORE: Baseball Up To Now

The standings on this page are designed to measure the relative strength of the various franchises since the beginning of the modern era in 1901. The first four columns reduce 87 years of competition to a one-season composite. The last two columns indicate the number of seasons each team had its league's best record (BR), and its worst record (WR). Note that, for the years since the plague of divisional play was introduced, the team with the best record is not necessarily the pennant-winner.

The standings include all regular-season games played by the teams indicated, and by their predecessor teams. Thus are the Orioles' statistics, for instance, held earthbound by more than 50 years of play as the Browns.

Since the 1984 edition of this book was published, the glacier of history has moved ever so slightly—the Red Sox have overtaken the Indians, Toronto has pulled ahead of Texas, and the Mets have passed the Phillies. And on the strength of their 1987 performance, the Twins have edged the Orioles: over nearly nine decades, the Minnesota (formerly Washington) franchise has won 6,386 games, the Baltimore (formerly St. Louis) team 6,382. The Yankees? They've won 350 more games than their closest competitor, the Giants.

AMERICAN LEAGUE

TEAM	W	L	PCT.	GB	BR	WR
Yankees	87	66	.569	—	32	4
Royals	83	76	.522	7	1	0
Tigers	80	74	.519	7½	10	2
Red Sox	78	75	.5098	9	9	10
Indians	79	76	.5097	9	3	5
White Sox	77	77	.500	10½	6	6
Angels	77	82	.484	13	0	1
Brewers	76	83	.478	14	1	1
Twins	73	81	.474	14½	4	11
Orioles	73	81	.474	14½	8	11
Athletics	73	81	.474	14½	12	24
Blue Jays	73	83	.468	15½	1	3
Rangers	71	88	.447	19	0	6
Mariners	65	92	.414	24	0	4

NATIONAL LEAGUE

TEAM	W	L	PCT.	GB	BR	WR
Giants	83	71	.539	—	16	5
Dodgers	81	74	.523	2½	16	1
Pirates	80	74	.519	3	10	10
Cardinals	80	74	.519	3	15	6
Cubs	78	76	.506	5	11	9
Reds	77	77	.500	6	9	9
Astros	77	83	.4813	9	1	2
Expos	76	82	.4810	9	0	2
Braves	72	82	.468	11	4	10
Mets	73	87	.456	13	2	8
Phillies	70	84	.455	13	3	23
Padres	69	90	.434	16½	0	6

INDEX

INDEX

INDEX

PHOTO CREDITS

P. 1, Harris Lewine (8). P. 2, Culver. P. 11, Culver. P. 12 (Top) Brown Brothers; (Bottom) Harris Lewine. P. 13 (L to R) Harris Lewine; Brown Brothers (2). P. 14, Harris Lewine (2). P. 15 (L to R) Bettmann; Brown Brothers. P. 16 (L to R) Harris Lewine (2); National Baseball Hall of Fame. P. 17, Culver. P. 18, NBHF. P. 19 (Top, L to R) Harris Lewine (2); (Bottom, L to R) NBHF (2). P. 20 (Top, L to R) NBHF; Brown Brothers; NBHF; (Bottom) NBHF. P. 21, Brown Brothers. P. 22, NBHF (2). P. 23 (Top) Bettmann; (Bottom) NBHF. P. 24, Culver. (3). P. 25, Culver. P. 26, NBHF. P. 27, Boston Public Library. P. 28 (Top) NBHF; (Bottom) Culver. P. 29, NBHF (2). P. 30, NBHF. P. 31, Brown Brothers. P. 32 (L to R) NBHF; Richard Merkin; Culver. P. 34, Brown Brothers. P. 35 (Top) Harris Lewine; (Middle, L to R) NBHF (3); (Bottom, L to R) NBHF (2); Culver. P. 37, NBHF. P. 38 (L to R) NBHF; Brown Brothers. P. 39, Culver. P. 41, NBHF. P. 42, NBHF (2). P. 43 (Top) Culver; (Middle, L to R) Culver; NBHF; (Bottom) Brown Brothers. P. 44, Harris Lewine. P. 45, Culver. (2). P. 46 (Top) NBHF; (Bottom) Culver. P. 48, Culver. P. 49, Brown Brothers. P. 51, Harris Lewine. (2). P. 52 (L to R) Culver; United Press International. P. 53, Boston Public Library (2). P. 54, Bettmann. P. 55 (L to R) Culver; NBHF; Culver. P. 56 (Top) Boston Public Library; (Bottom, L to R) NBHF; Culver; NBHF. P. 57 (Top, L to R) Brown Brothers; Culver; (Bottom) Bettmann. P. 58 (Top, L to R) Bettmann; NBHF; Culver; (Bottom) NBHF. P. 59 (Top) NBHF, Courtesy of Bill Drake; (Bottom) NBHF, Courtesy of Robert W. Peterson. P. 60, Brown Brothers (2). P. 61 (Top) NBHF; (Bottom) Harris Lewine. P. 62, Bettmann. P. 64, Harris Lewine. P. 65, Brown Brothers. P. 66, Culver. P. 67 (Center) Culver; NBHF (6). P. 68 (Top, L to R) Ring Lardner, Jr.; Harris Lewine. (Middle, L to R) Brown Brothers; Culver; (Bottom) Brown Brothers. P. 69, Culver. P. 71, Culver. P. 72, NBHF (2). P. 73, Brown Brothers (2). P. 74 (Top, L to R) Brown Brothers (2); (Middle, L to R) Bettmann; Culver; Brown Brothers; (Bottom, L to R) Brown Brothers (2). P. 75 (Top) NBHF; (Bottom) Culver. P. 76, Culver. P. 77, Brown Brothers. P. 78 (Top, L to R) Culver. (2); Boston Public Library; (Bottom) Brown Brothers. P. 79 (Top, L to R) Culver; Bettmann (2); (Bottom) Bettmann. P. 80, NBHF. P. 81, Brown Brothers. P. 82 (Top) Brown Brothers; (Bottom) Culver. P. 83 (Top) Culver (2); (Middle, L to R) Culver; Brown Brothers; (Bottom) Brown Brothers. P. 84 (Top) Culver; (Bottom) NBHF. P. 85 (Top, L to R) NBHF; (Bottom) Frank Driggs. P. 86 (Top, L to R) Culver; Harris Lewine; (Bottom) Culver. P. 87, Brown Brothers. P. 88 (Top, L to R) Brown Brothers; Culver; (Bottom) Culver. P. 89 (Top, L to R) Robert Gallagher (2); Bettmann; (Bottom) UPI. P. 90 (Top) Culver; (Middle, L to R) Robert Gallagher; Richard Merkin (2); (Bottom) Bettmann. P. 91 (Top, L to R) Culver; Brown Brothers; (Bottom) UPI. P. 92 (Top) Harris Lewine (2); (Bottom) Culver. P. 93 (Top, L to R) Harris Lewine; Culver; Harris Lewine; (Bottom, L to R) Harris Lewine; Bettmann. P. 94 (Top) Harris Lewine; (Bottom) UPI. P. 95, Culver. P. 96, UPI. P. 97 (Top, L to R) UPI; Culver; (Middle) UPI; (Bottom) UPI. P. 98 (L to R) Culver; Bettmann. P. 99, NBHF (3). P. 100 (Top, L to R) UPI; Brown Brothers; (Bottom, L to R) Culver; Bettmann; UPI. P. 101 (L to R) UPI; Harris Lewine; Culver. P. 102, Bettmann. P. 104, Culver. P. 105, UPI. P. 106 (L to R) Brown Brothers; Harris Lewine. P. 107, UPI. P. 108, Culver. P. 109 (L to R) Culver; Brown Brothers; (Middle) Culver; Brown Brothers (2). P. 110 (Top and Middle) Culver; (Bottom) Brown Brothers. P. 111 (Top) Brown Brothers; (Bottom) Culver. P. 112, NBHF. P. 113, NBHF (2). P. 114 (L to R) UPI; Bettmann. P. 115 (Top, L to R) Bettmann (3); (Middle) UPI; (Bottom) Bettmann; UPI; Bettmann. P. 116, UPI. P. 117, Bettmann. P. 118, UPI (2). P. 119 (Top, L to R) UPI; Wide World; (Middle) UPI; (Bottom) UPI (2). P. 120, NBHF. P. 121, Culver. P. 122, Bettmann. P. 123, UPI (3). P. 124, Bettmann (2). P. 125, Bettmann (2). P. 126, UPI. P. 127 (Top, L to R) Wide World; Culver; (Middle, L to R) UPI; Bettmann; (Bottom) UPI. P. 128, Bettmann. P. 129, Bettmann; (Inset) UPI. P. 130 (Top, L to R) Bettmann (2); NBHF; (Bottom) Culver. P. 131, Courtesy of Matthew J. Bruccoli. P. 132 (Top, L to R) Bettmann; Culver; Bettmann; (Middle, L to R) Wide World; Culver; UPI; (Bottom) Bettmann. P. 133, Bettmann (2). P. 134 (L to R) Bettmann; UPI. P. 135, Bettmann. P. 136 (Top, L to R) Bettmann; UPI; (Bottom) Bettmann. P. 137, UPI. P. 138, Bettmann. P. 139 (Top) UPI; (Bottom) Bettmann. P. 140, UPI (3). P. 141, Culver. P. 142 (Top, L to R) Bettmann; Culver; (Middle, L to R) UPI; Culver; (2) (Bottom) Bettmann (2). P. 143 (Top) Bettmann (2); (Bottom, L to R) UPI; Bettmann; Culver. P. 144, Bettmann. P. 145, Bettmann (3). P. 146 (Top) UPI; (Bottom) Wide World. P. 147, Bettmann (2). P. 149 (Top, L to R) Bettmann (2); Harris Lewine; (Bottom) Bettmann. P. 150 (L to R) NBHF; Frank Driggs. P. 151, Bettmann (3). P. 152, Bettmann. P. 153, Wide World. P. 154, Wide World. P. 155, Bettmann. P. 156 (Top, L to R) Bettmann; UPI; (Bottom) Bettmann. P. 157, UPI. P. 158, Culver. P. 159 (Top) Wide World; (Bottom) UPI. P. 160 (L to R) Bettmann; UPI. P. 161 (Top, L to R) UPI; Bettmann; (Middle) Bettmann; (Bottom, L to R) UPI; Wide World. P. 162 (L to R) UPI; Bettmann. P. 163, NBHF. P. 164 (L to R) UPI; Harris Lewine; Bettmann. P. 165, Bettmann. P. 166 (Top, L to R) Bettmann; UPI; (Middle) UPI; (Bottom, L to R) UPI; Wide World. P. 167, UPI (4). P. 168, Bettmann. P. 169, Wide World. (2). P. 170, Bettmann. P. 171, Wide World. P. 172 (Top) Wide World; (Bottom, L to R) Bettmann; UPI. P. 173, Wide World. P. 174 (Top, L to R) Harris Lewine; Wide World; Bettmann; (Bottom) Richard Merkin. P. 175 (Top) UPI; (Bottom, L to R) UPI; Brown Brothers. P. 176 (L to R) Culver; Bettmann. P. 177 UPI; (Bottom) Frank Driggs. P. 178, NBHF (5). P. 179, NBHF (2). P. 180, Wide World. P. 181, UPI (2). P. 182, Harris Lewine. P. 183, Photo by Nelson, Courtesy of Condé Nast Publications, Inc. P. 184 (Top) Wide World; (Bottom) Bettmann. P. 185, Bettmann. P. 186 (Top) Harris Lewine (2); (Bottom) UPI. P. 187 (Top) Wide World. (Bottom) Richard Merkin. P. 188 (Top, L to R) Wide World; UPI; (Bottom) UPI (2). P. 189 (Top) Bettmann; (Bottom, L to R) Wide World; Bettmann; UPI. P. 190 (Top, L to R) UPI; Bettmann; (Bottom, L to R) Harris Lewine; Bettmann. P. 191, Harris Lewine. P. 192, UPI. P. 193, Wide World. P. 194 (L to R) H.T. Webster © 1951 by The New York Herald Tribune, Inc.; Frank Driggs. P. 195, Bettmann. P. 196 (Top) UPI; (Middle, L to R) Brown Brothers; Wide World, (2); (Bottom) Richard Merkin. P. 197, UPI (2). P. 198, Wide World. P. 199 (Top, L to R) Bettmann; UPI; (Middle) Wide World; (Bottom, L to R) Wide World; UPI. P. 200, UPI. P. 201, Wide World. P. 202 (Top) UPI (2); (Bottom) Wide World. P. 203, UPI; (Inset) Wide World. P. 204 (L to R) UPI; Wide World. P. 205 (Top) UPI (2); (Bottom, L to R) Wide World; Bettmann. P. 206 (Top) UPI; (Bottom) Bettmann. P. 207 (L to R) UPI; Wide World. P. 209 (Top) UPI (2); (Bottom) Harris Lewine. P. 210, Wide World. P. 211, Wide World. P. 212 (Top) Wide World; (Bottom) UPI. P. 213, UPI. P. 214 (Top) UPI; (Bottom) Harris Lewine. P. 215 (Top) Bettmann (3); (Middle, L to R) Harris Lewine (2); UPI; (Bottom) Richard Merkin (3). P. 216 (Top, L to R) UPI; Wide World; (Bottom) Harris Lewine. P. 217, UPI (3). P. 218 (L to R) Wide World; UPI; Wide World. P. 219, UPI (2). P. 220, UPI (4). P. 221, UPI. P. 222, UPI. P. 223, UPI. P. 224 (Top and Middle) UPI; (Bottom) NBHF. P. 225 (Top) Harris Lewine (2); (Middle, L to R) UPI; Wide World; UPI; (Bottom) Frank Driggs (2). P. 226 (Top, L to R) Wide World; Harris Lewine (2); (Middle, L to R) UPI; Harris Lewine (2); Wide World; (Bottom, L to R) UPI; N.Y. Daily News. P. 228, UPI (3). P. 229, UPI. P. 230, UPI. P. 231, Wide World. P. 232 (L to R) UPI; Wide World. P. 233, Wide World. P. 234, UPI (2). P. 235, UPI (5). P. 236 (L to R) Wide World; UPI (2). P. 237, UPI (2). P. 238, UPI. P. 239 (Top, L to R) Wide World; Richard Merkin; Wide World; (Bottom) Wide World. (2). P. 243 (Top, L to R) UPI; Wide World; (Middle, L to R) Wide World; UPI; (Bottom) Wide World. P. 244 (L to R) Wide World. (2); UPI. P. 246, UPI. P. 247, UPI. P. 248 (Top) UPI; (Bottom) Wide World. P. 249 (Top, L to R) Wide World; UPI; (Bottom, L to R) UPI; Robert Lifson. P. 250, UPI. P. 251, Wide World. P. 252, UPI (3). P. 253 (Top, L to R) UPI; Wide World; (Bottom) Wide World. P. 254, UPI (3). P. 255, UPI. P. 256, UPI. P. 257, Robert Lifson; (Inset) UPI. P. 258 (L to R) Wide World; UPI (2). P. 259, Williard Mullin, Syracuse University Library. P. 260, Wide World. P. 261 (Top, L to R) N.Y. Daily News; UPI (2); (Middle, L to R) UPI (3); (Bottom, L to R) Wide World; UPI. P. 262 (L to R) UPI; Wide World; UPI. P. 263, UPI. P. 264, UPI. P. 265, UPI. P. 266 (Top) Richard Merkin; (Middle, L to R) Culver; Brown Brothers; (Bottom) Wide World. P. 267 (Top) Richard Merkin (2); (Middle) Wide World; (Bottom) UPI. P. 268 (Top) Richard Merkin (2); (Middle, L to R) Richard Merkin; Bettmann; Frank Driggs; (Bottom) UPI. P. 269, N.Y. Daily News. P. 270, Culver. P. 271, UPI (2). P. 272 (Top) UPI; (Middle, L to R) Culver; (Bottom) Culver. P. 273 (Top) Culver; (Middle, L to R) UPI; Wide World; (Bottom) UPI. P. 274, UPI. P. 275, UPI (4). P. 276 (Top, L to R) UPI; Wide World; (Middle) UPI; (Bottom) Wide World. P. 277, UPI (2). P. 278, UPI (3). P. 279 (Top) Wide World; (Bottom) UPI (2). P. 280, UPI. P. 281, UPI. P. 282, UPI. P. 283, UPI. P. 284, UPI. P. 285, Wide World. P. 286 (Top) UPI; (Bottom) Wide World. P. 287 (Top) Wide World; (Bottom) UPI. P. 288 (Top, L to R) UPI (2); Wide World; (Middle, L to R) Wide World; UPI (2); (Bottom) UPI. P. 289, Courtesy of Bruce Stark; (Inset) Harris Lewine. P. 290 (Top) UPI; (Bottom, L to R) UPI; Wide World. P. 291 (Top, L to R) Frank Driggs (3); (Middle, L to R) UPI; Wide World. (2); (Bottom, L to R) Wide World; UPI; N.Y. Daily News. P. 292 (L to R) UPI; Wide World. P. 293, Wide World. P. 294 (Top, L to R) Wide World; UPI (2); (Middle) UPI; (Bottom) Wide World. (2). P. 295 (L to R) UPI; Wide World. (2). P. 296 (L to R) Wide World. (2); UPI. P. 297, Wide World. (2). P. 298, N.Y. Daily News (2). P. 299, N.Y. Daily News; (Inset) UPI. P. 300, UPI. P. 301, NBHF. P. 302 (L to R) Wide World; Bettmann. P. 303, NBHF (2). P. 304 (Top) Harris Lewine (4); (Bottom) NBHF. P. 305 (Top) Wide World, (Bottom) UPI. P. 306, Wide World. P. 307, Wide World. (3). P. 308 (L to R) NBHF; Wide World. (2). P. 309, NBHF (2). P. 310 (L to R) Wide World; UPI. P. 311, NBHF; (Inset) UPI. P. 313, Wide World. P. 314, UPI. P. 315, Wide World. P. 316, UPI (2). P. 317, UPI (3). P. 318, UPI (3). P. 319, UPI (3). P. 320 (L to R) UPI; Wide World; UPI. P. 321, John Iacono © Sports Illustrated; (Inset, L) UPI; (Inset, R) UPI. P. 322, UPI (2). P. 325, UPI (3). P. 326, UPI (2). P. 327 (L to R) UPI; Susan Meiselas © Magnum Photos, Inc.; UPI; (Middle) UPI; (Bottom) UPI. P. 328, Wide World. P. 329, Culver. P. 330, Boston Public Library. P. 331 (Top) Bettmann; (Middle) Culver. (2); (Bottom) Boston Public Library. P. 332 (L to R) UPI; Wide World. P. 333 (Top) UPI (2); (Middle) Brown Brothers; (Bottom) UPI (2). P. 334, UPI. P. 335 (Top, L to R) UPI; Wide World. (2); (Middle) UPI (2); (Bottom) UPI. P. 336, Wide World. P. 337 (Top) Bettman (3); (Bottom, L to R) Paul Gallagher; Brown Brothers; Bettmann. P. 338, Wide World. P. 339 (Top) UPI; (Middle, L to R) Culver; UPI; (Bottom) Wide World. P. 340, Wide World. P. 341 (Top, L to R) UPI; Williard Mullin, Courtesy of Syracuse University Library; (Bottom) UPI. P. 342, Wide World. (2). P. 343 (Top, L to R) Wide World; UPI; Wide World; (Bottom) UPI; (Inset) Wide World. P. 344 (Top) Wide World; (Bottom) UPI. P. 345, UPI. P. 346, Brown Brothers.